INJUSTICE 2

VOLUME 2

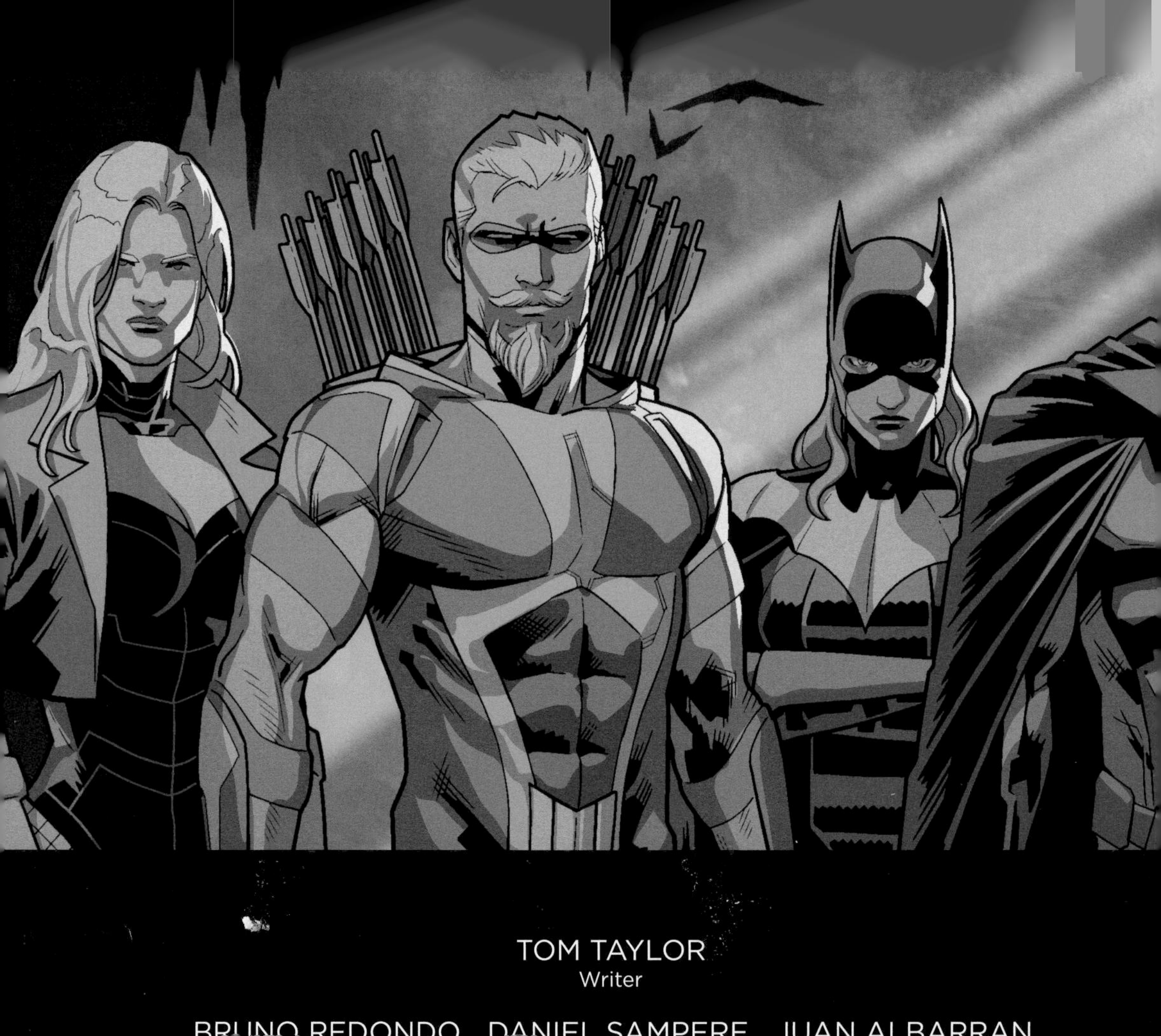

TOM TAYLOR
Writer

BRUNO REDONDO DANIEL SAMPERE JUAN ALBARRAN

TICE™ 2

VOLUME 2

SUPERMAN created by JERRY SIEGEL & JOE SHUSTER
SUPERGIRL based on the characters created by JERRY SIEGEL & JOE SHUSTER

JIM CHADWICK Editor – Original Series
ROB LEVIN Associate Editor – Original Series
LIZ ERICKSON Assistant Editor – Original Series
JEB WOODARD Group Editor – Collected Editions
ALEX GALER Editor – Collected Edition
STEVE COOK Design Director – Books
LOUIS PRANDI Publication Design

BOB HARRAS Senior VP – Editor-in-Chief, DC Comics
PAT McCALLUM Executive Editor, DC Comics

DIANE NELSON President
DAN DiDIO Publisher
JIM LEE Publisher
GEOFF JOHNS President & Chief Creative Officer
AMIT DESAI Executive VP – Business & Marketing Strategy,
    Direct to Consumer & Global Franchise Management
SAM ADES Senior VP & General Manager, Digital Services
BOBBIE CHASE VP & Executive Editor, Young Reader & Talent Development
MARK CHIARELLO Senior VP – Art, Design & Collected Editions
JOHN CUNNINGHAM Senior VP – Sales & Trade Marketing
ANNE DePIES Senior VP – Business Strategy, Finance & Administration
DON FALLETTI VP – Manufacturing Operations
LAWRENCE GANEM VP – Editorial Administration & Talent Relations
ALISON GILL Senior VP – Manufacturing & Operations

INJUSTICE 2 VOLUME 2

DC Comics, 2900 West Alameda Ave., Burbank, CA 91505
Printed by LSC Communications, Kendallville, IN, USA.
3/23/18. First Printing.
ISBN: 978-1-4012-7841-0

Library of Congress Cataloging-in-Publication Data is available.

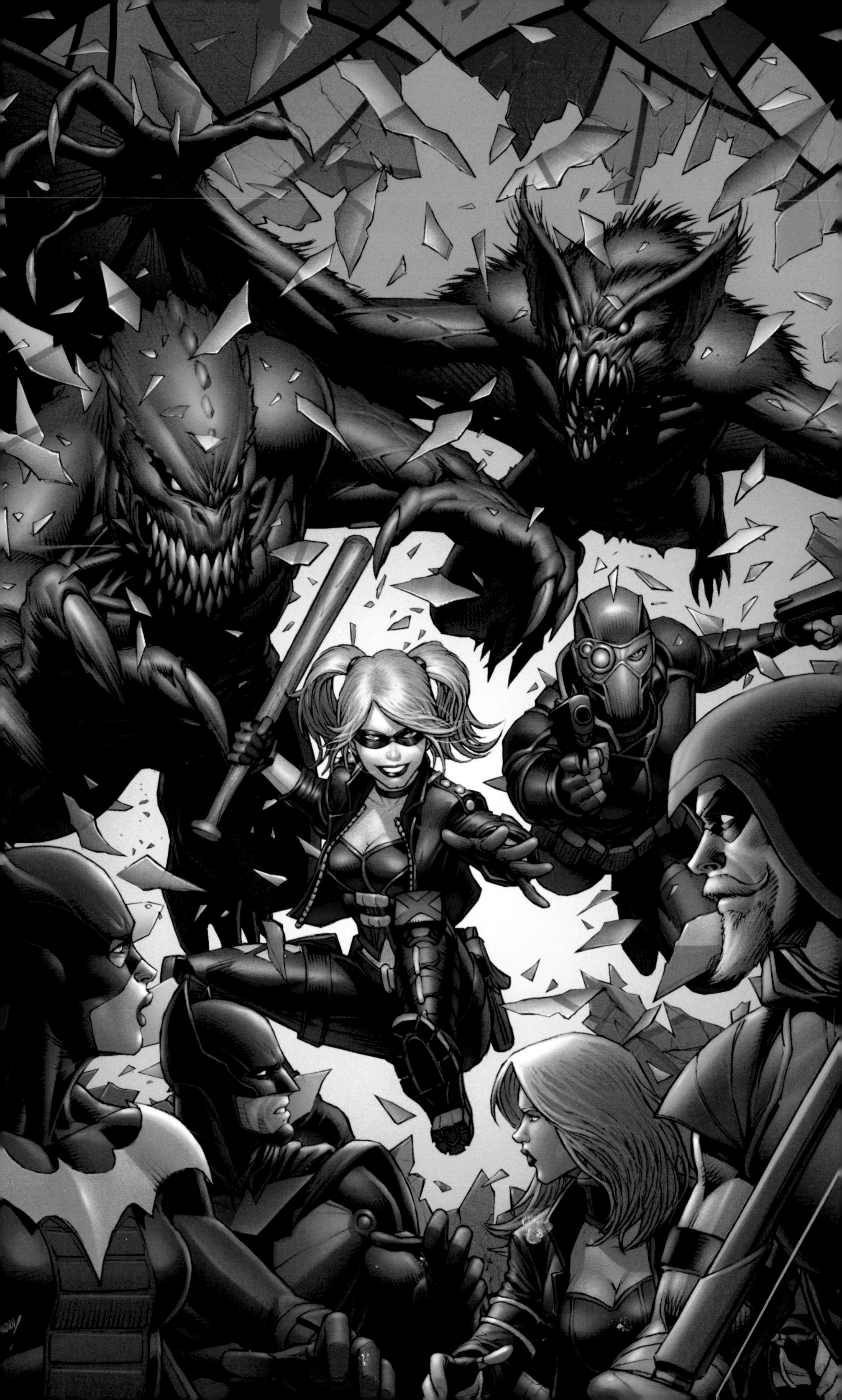

"Green Wedding"

Tom Taylor Writer **Bruno Redondo** Penciller **Juan Albarran** Inker
Rex Lokus Colorist Cover art by **Dale Keown**

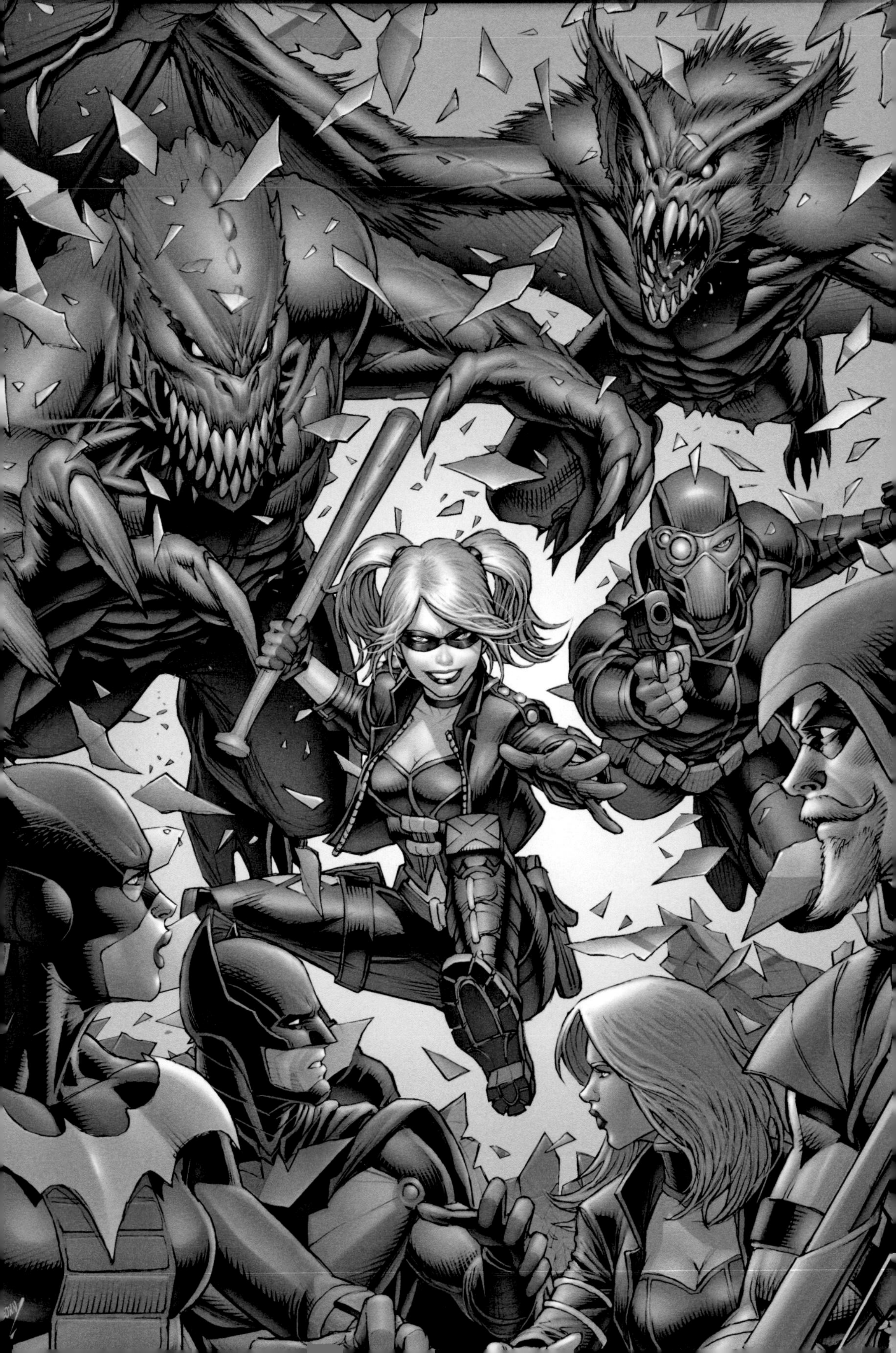

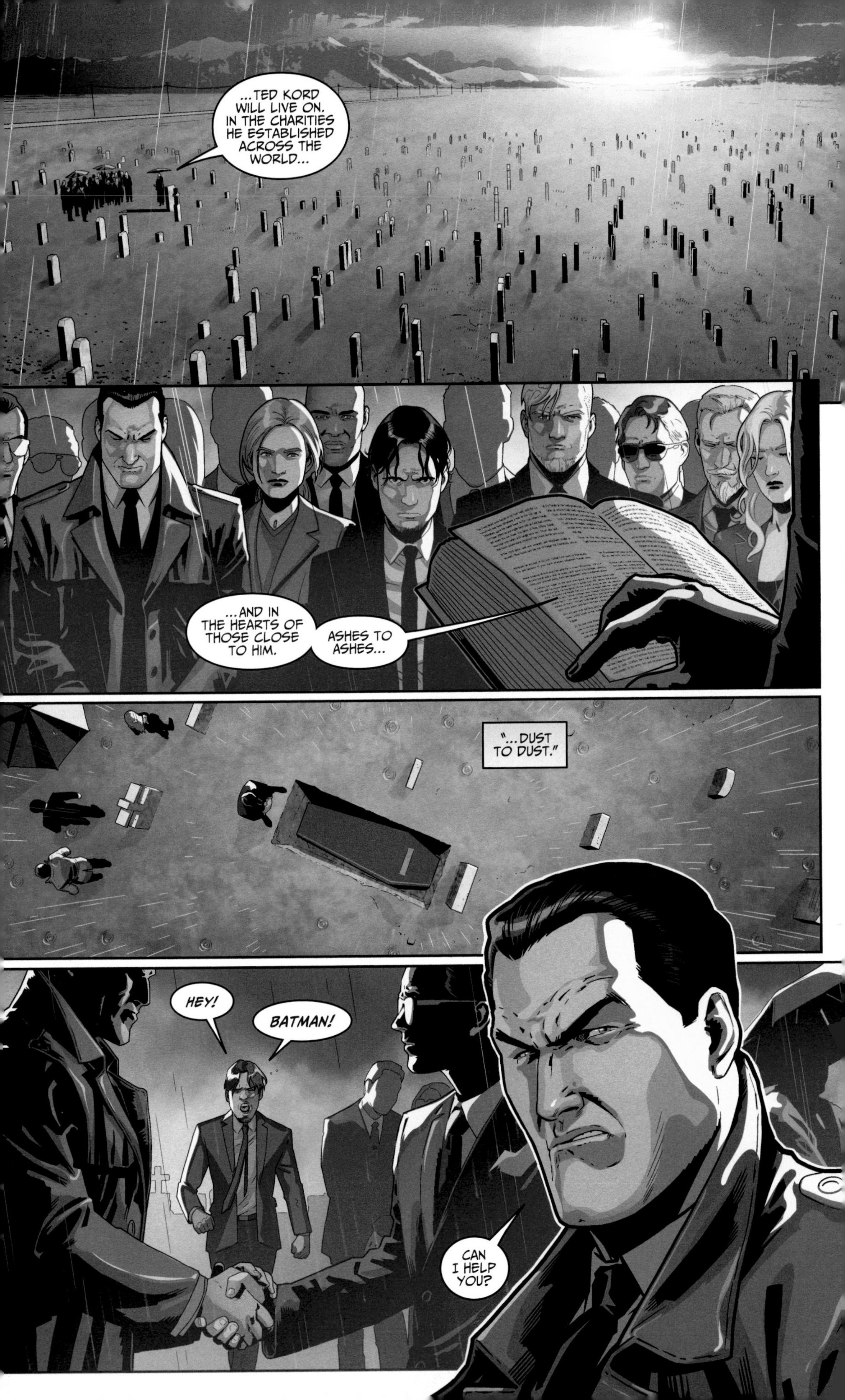
...TED KORD WILL LIVE ON. IN THE CHARITIES HE ESTABLISHED ACROSS THE WORLD...
...AND IN THE HEARTS OF THOSE CLOSE TO HIM.
ASHES TO ASHES...
"...DUST TO DUST."
HEY!
BATMAN!
CAN I HELP YOU?

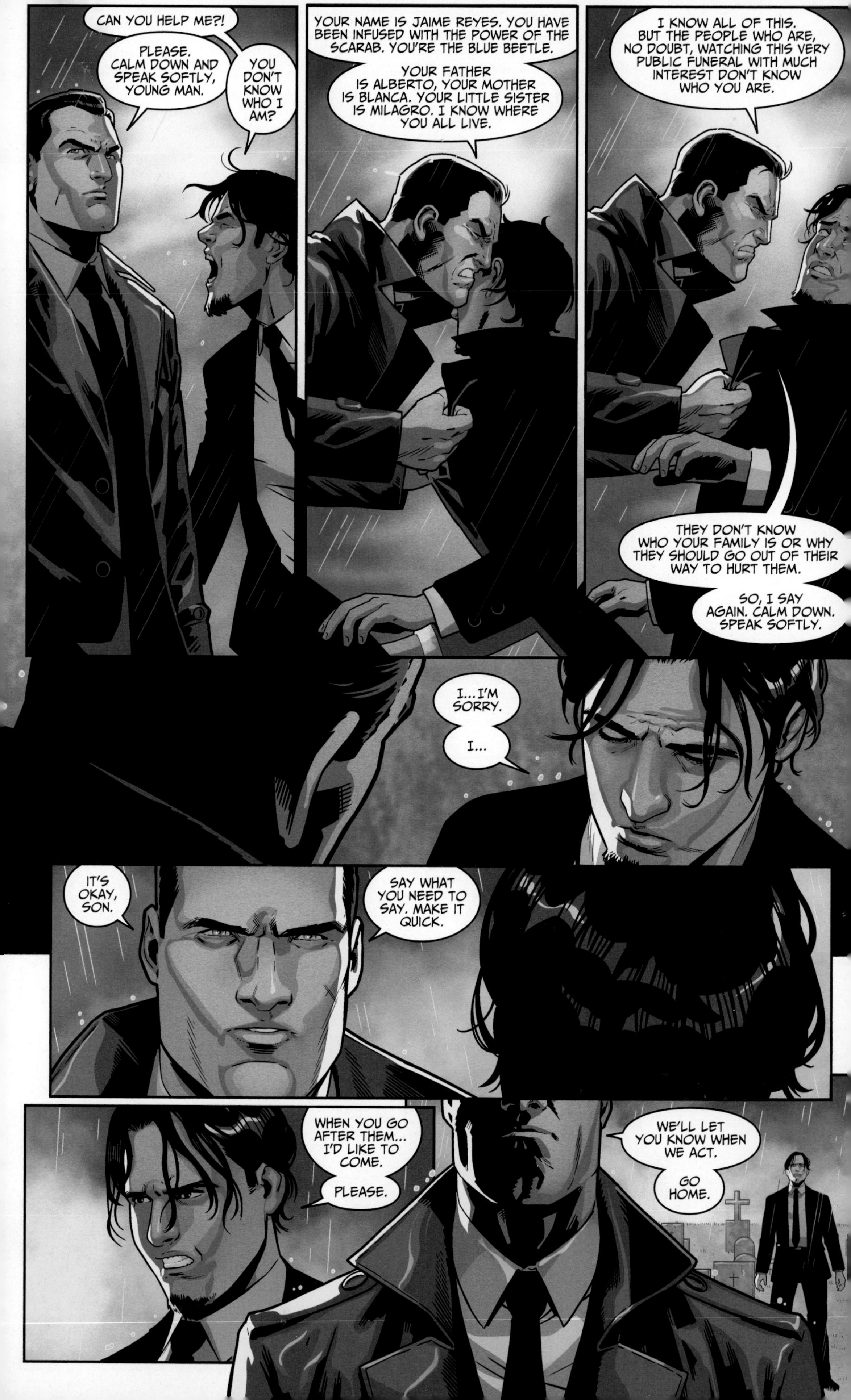

CAN YOU HELP ME?!
PLEASE. CALM DOWN AND SPEAK SOFTLY, YOUNG MAN.
YOU DON'T KNOW WHO I AM?
YOUR NAME IS JAIME REYES. YOU HAVE BEEN INFUSED WITH THE POWER OF THE SCARAB. YOU'RE THE BLUE BEETLE.
YOUR FATHER IS ALBERTO, YOUR MOTHER IS BLANCA. YOUR LITTLE SISTER IS MILAGRO. I KNOW WHERE YOU ALL LIVE.
I KNOW ALL OF THIS. BUT THE PEOPLE WHO ARE, NO DOUBT, WATCHING THIS VERY PUBLIC FUNERAL WITH MUCH INTEREST DON'T KNOW WHO YOU ARE.
THEY DON'T KNOW WHO YOUR FAMILY IS OR WHY THEY SHOULD GO OUT OF THEIR WAY TO HURT THEM.
SO, I SAY AGAIN. CALM DOWN. SPEAK SOFTLY.
I...I'M SORRY.
I...
IT'S OKAY, SON.
SAY WHAT YOU NEED TO SAY. MAKE IT QUICK.
WHEN YOU GO AFTER THEM... I'D LIKE TO COME.
PLEASE.
WE'LL LET YOU KNOW WHEN WE ACT.
GO HOME.

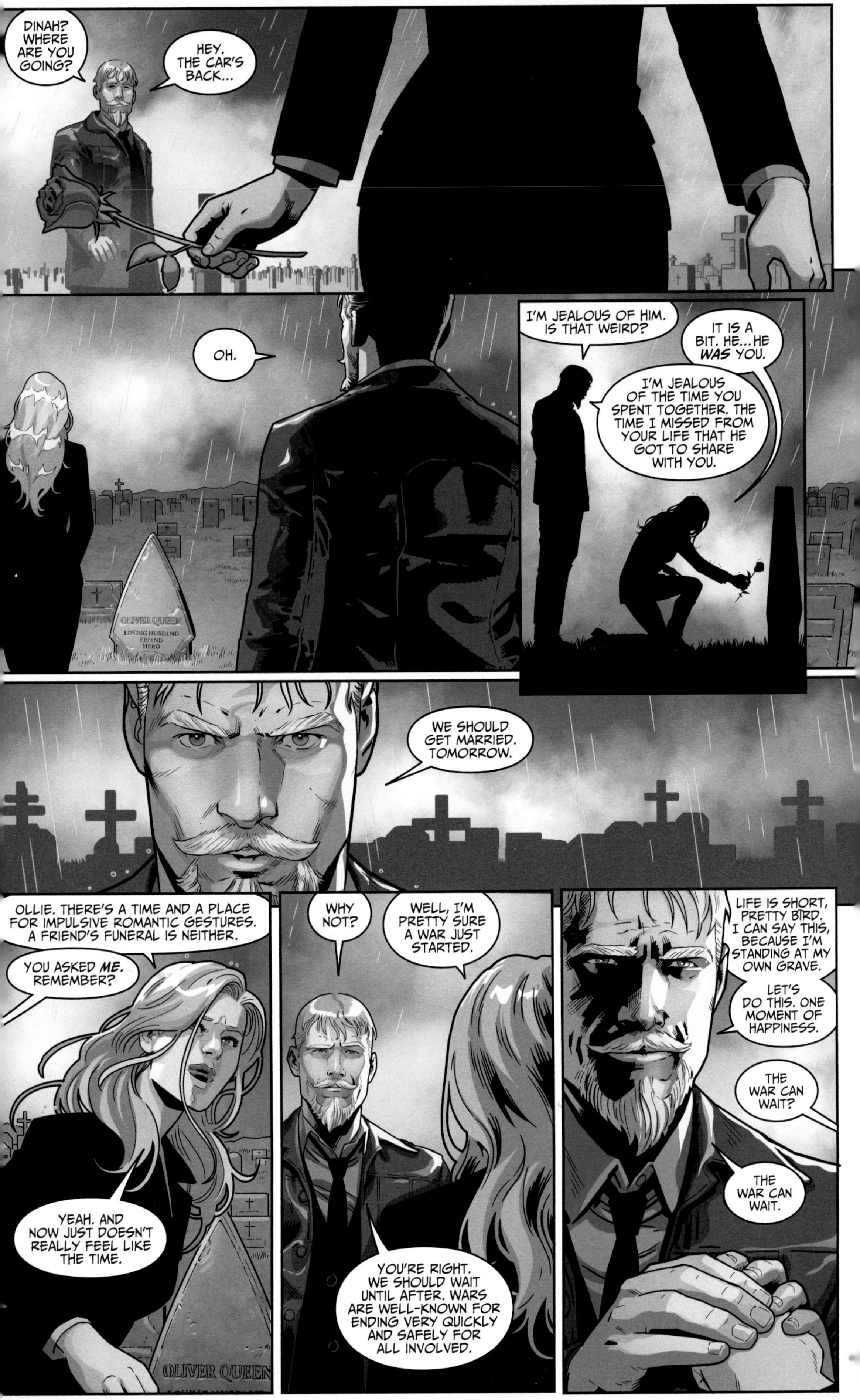
DINAH? WHERE ARE YOU GOING?
HEY. THE CAR'S BACK...
OH.
OLIVER QUEEN
LOVING HUSBAND
FRIEND
HERO
I'M JEALOUS OF HIM. IS THAT WEIRD?
IT IS A BIT. HE...HE *WAS* YOU.
I'M JEALOUS OF THE TIME YOU SPENT TOGETHER. THE TIME I MISSED FROM YOUR LIFE THAT HE GOT TO SHARE WITH YOU.
WE SHOULD GET MARRIED. TOMORROW.
OLLIE. THERE'S A TIME AND A PLACE FOR IMPULSIVE ROMANTIC GESTURES. A FRIEND'S FUNERAL IS NEITHER.
YOU ASKED *ME*. REMEMBER?
YEAH. AND NOW JUST DOESN'T REALLY FEEL LIKE THE TIME.
OLIVER QUEEN
WHY NOT?
WELL, I'M PRETTY SURE A WAR JUST STARTED.
YOU'RE RIGHT. WE SHOULD WAIT UNTIL AFTER. WARS ARE WELL-KNOWN FOR ENDING VERY QUICKLY AND SAFELY FOR ALL INVOLVED.
LIFE IS SHORT, PRETTY BIRD. I CAN SAY THIS, BECAUSE I'M STANDING AT MY OWN GRAVE.
LET'S DO THIS. ONE MOMENT OF HAPPINESS.
THE WAR CAN WAIT?
THE WAR CAN WAIT.

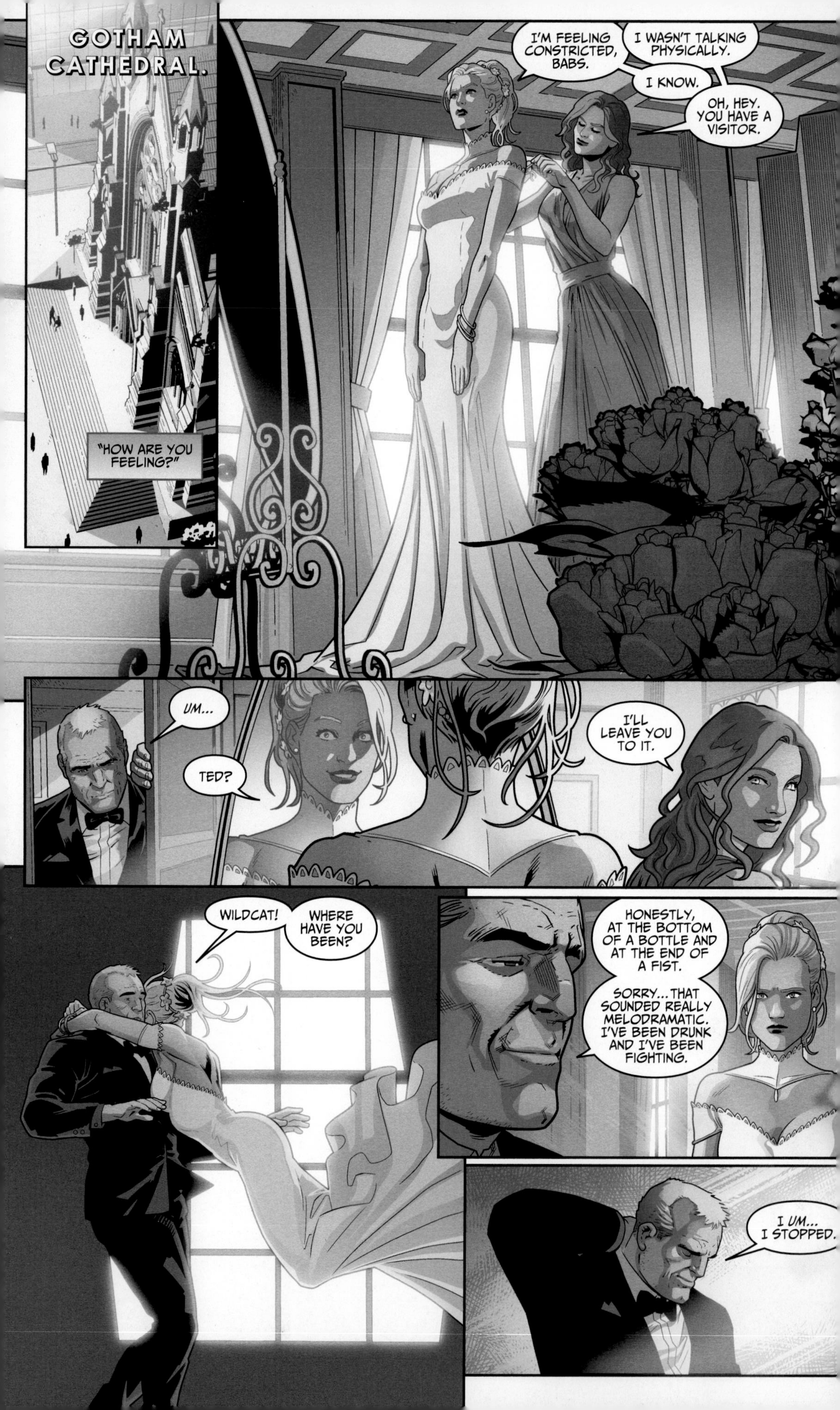
GOTHAM CATHEDRAL.
"HOW ARE YOU FEELING?"
I'M FEELING CONSTRICTED, BABS.
I WASN'T TALKING PHYSICALLY.
I KNOW.
OH, HEY. YOU HAVE A VISITOR.
UM...
TED?
I'LL LEAVE YOU TO IT.
WILDCAT!
WHERE HAVE YOU BEEN?
HONESTLY, AT THE BOTTOM OF A BOTTLE AND AT THE END OF A FIST.
SORRY... THAT SOUNDED REALLY MELODRAMATIC. I'VE BEEN DRUNK AND I'VE BEEN FIGHTING.
I UM... I STOPPED.

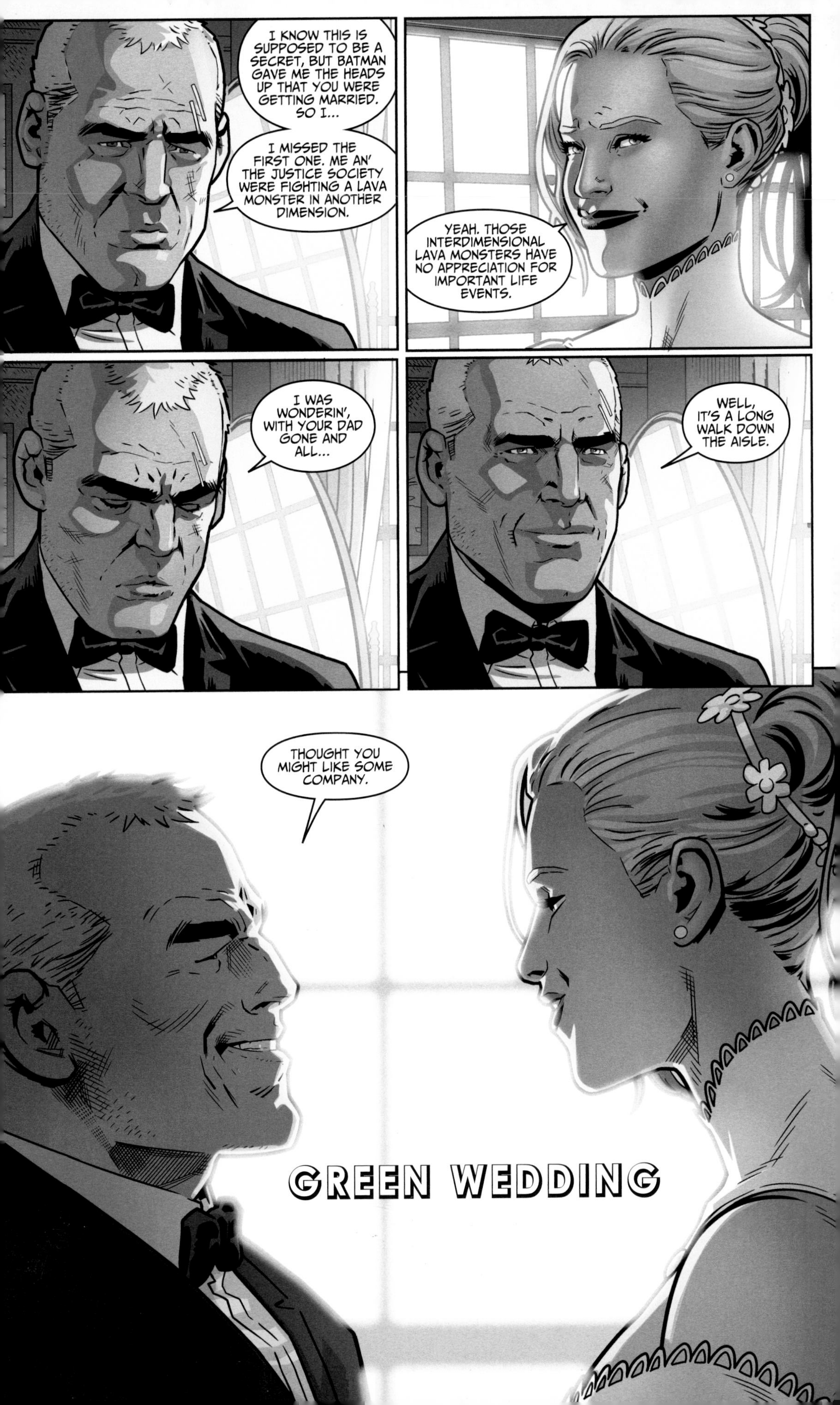
I KNOW THIS IS SUPPOSED TO BE A SECRET, BUT BATMAN GAVE ME THE HEADS UP THAT YOU WERE GETTING MARRIED. SO I...
I MISSED THE FIRST ONE. ME AN' THE JUSTICE SOCIETY WERE FIGHTING A LAVA MONSTER IN ANOTHER DIMENSION.
YEAH. THOSE INTERDIMENSIONAL LAVA MONSTERS HAVE NO APPRECIATION FOR IMPORTANT LIFE EVENTS.
I WAS WONDERIN', WITH YOUR DAD GONE AND ALL...
WELL, IT'S A LONG WALK DOWN THE AISLE.
THOUGHT YOU MIGHT LIKE SOME COMPANY.
GREEN WEDDING

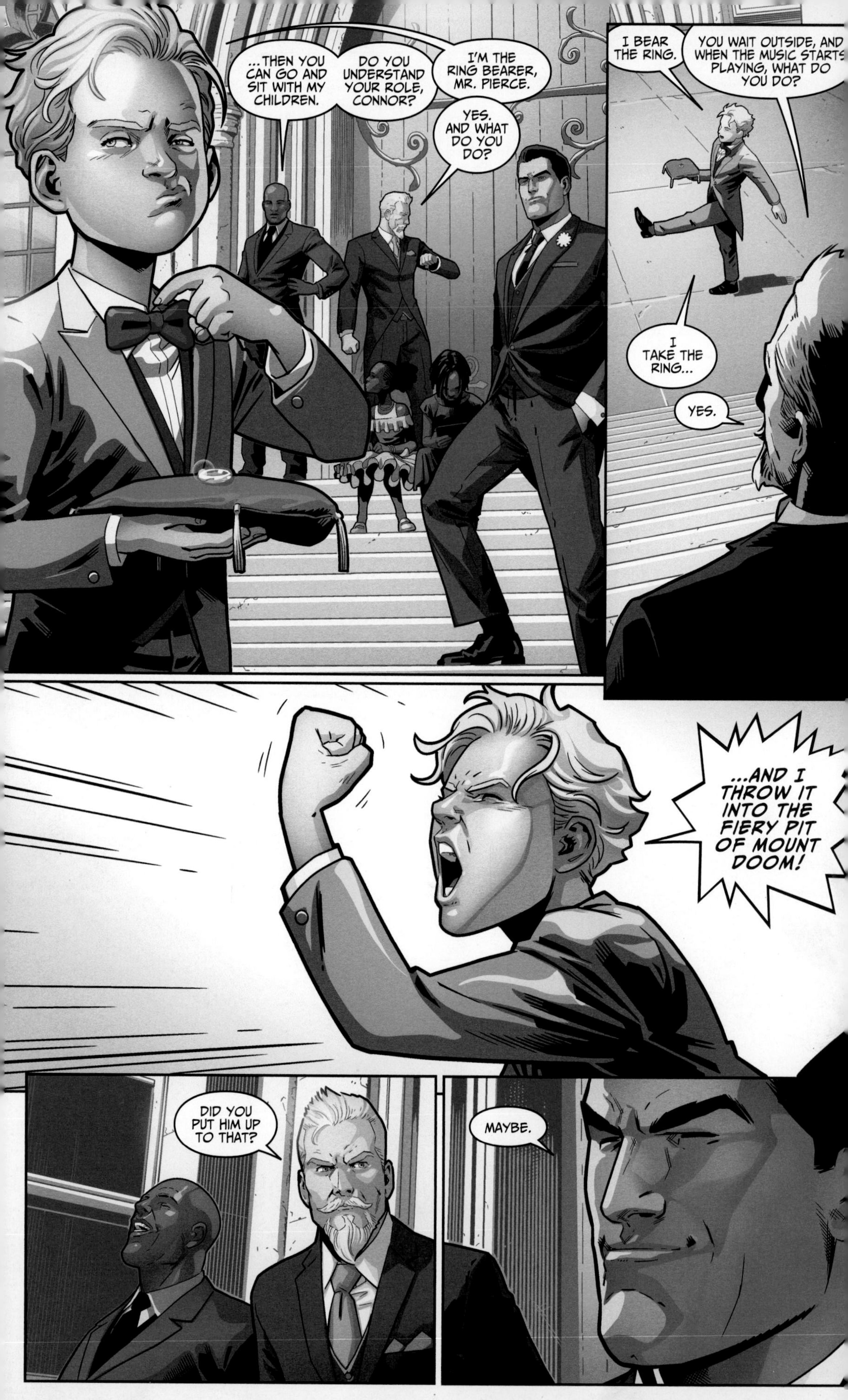
...THEN YOU CAN GO AND SIT WITH MY CHILDREN.
DO YOU UNDERSTAND YOUR ROLE, CONNOR?
I'M THE RING BEARER, MR. PIERCE.
YES. AND WHAT DO YOU DO?
I BEAR THE RING.
YOU WAIT OUTSIDE, AND WHEN THE MUSIC STARTS PLAYING, WHAT DO YOU DO?
I TAKE THE RING...
YES.
...AND I THROW IT INTO THE FIERY PIT OF MOUNT DOOM!
DID YOU PUT HIM UP TO THAT?
MAYBE.

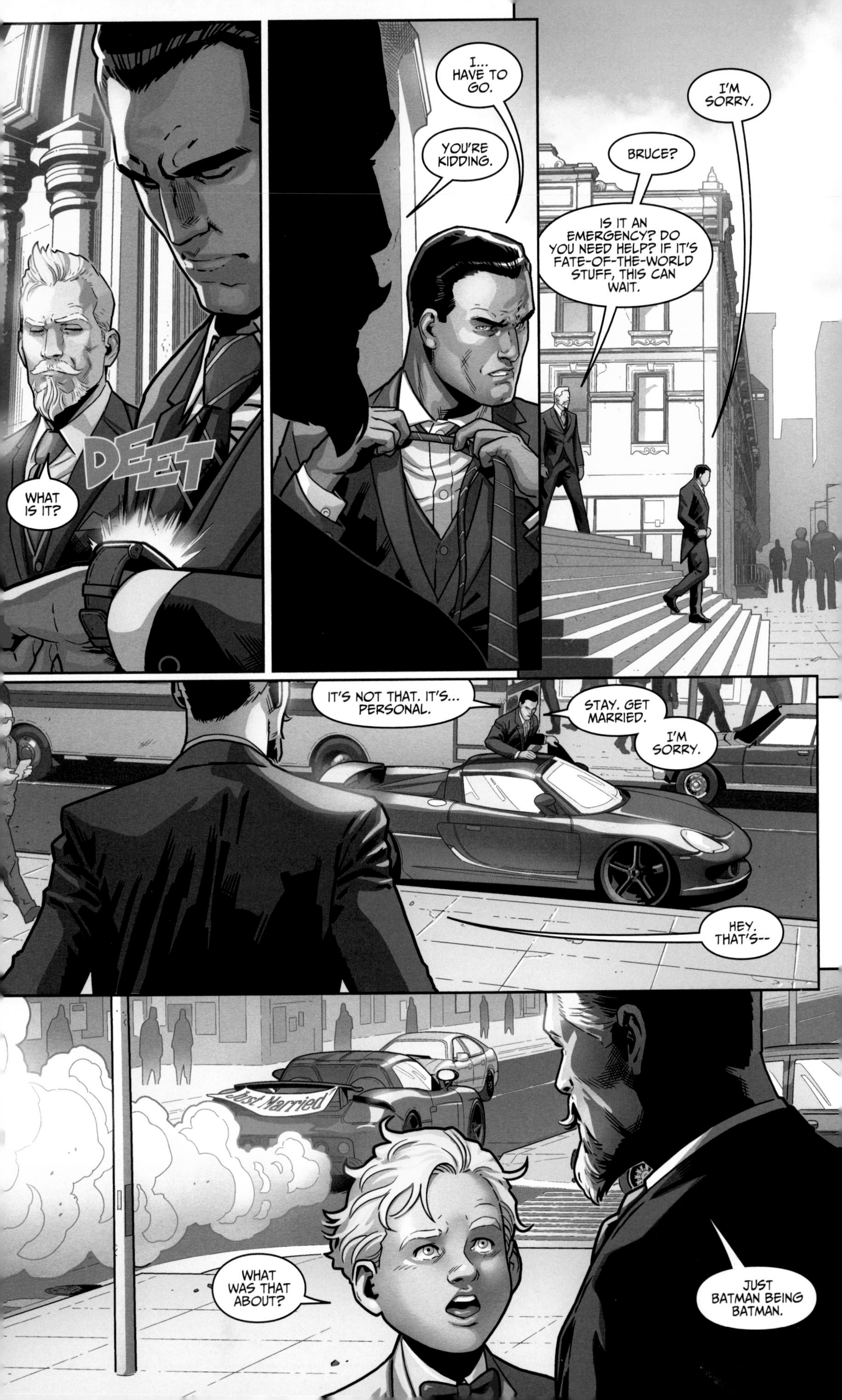

DEEET
WHAT IS IT?
I... HAVE TO GO.
YOU'RE KIDDING.
BRUCE?
IS IT AN EMERGENCY? DO YOU NEED HELP? IF IT'S FATE-OF-THE-WORLD STUFF, THIS CAN WAIT.
I'M SORRY.
IT'S NOT THAT. IT'S... PERSONAL.
STAY. GET MARRIED.
I'M SORRY.
HEY. THAT'S--
Just Married
WHAT WAS THAT ABOUT?
JUST BATMAN BEING BATMAN.

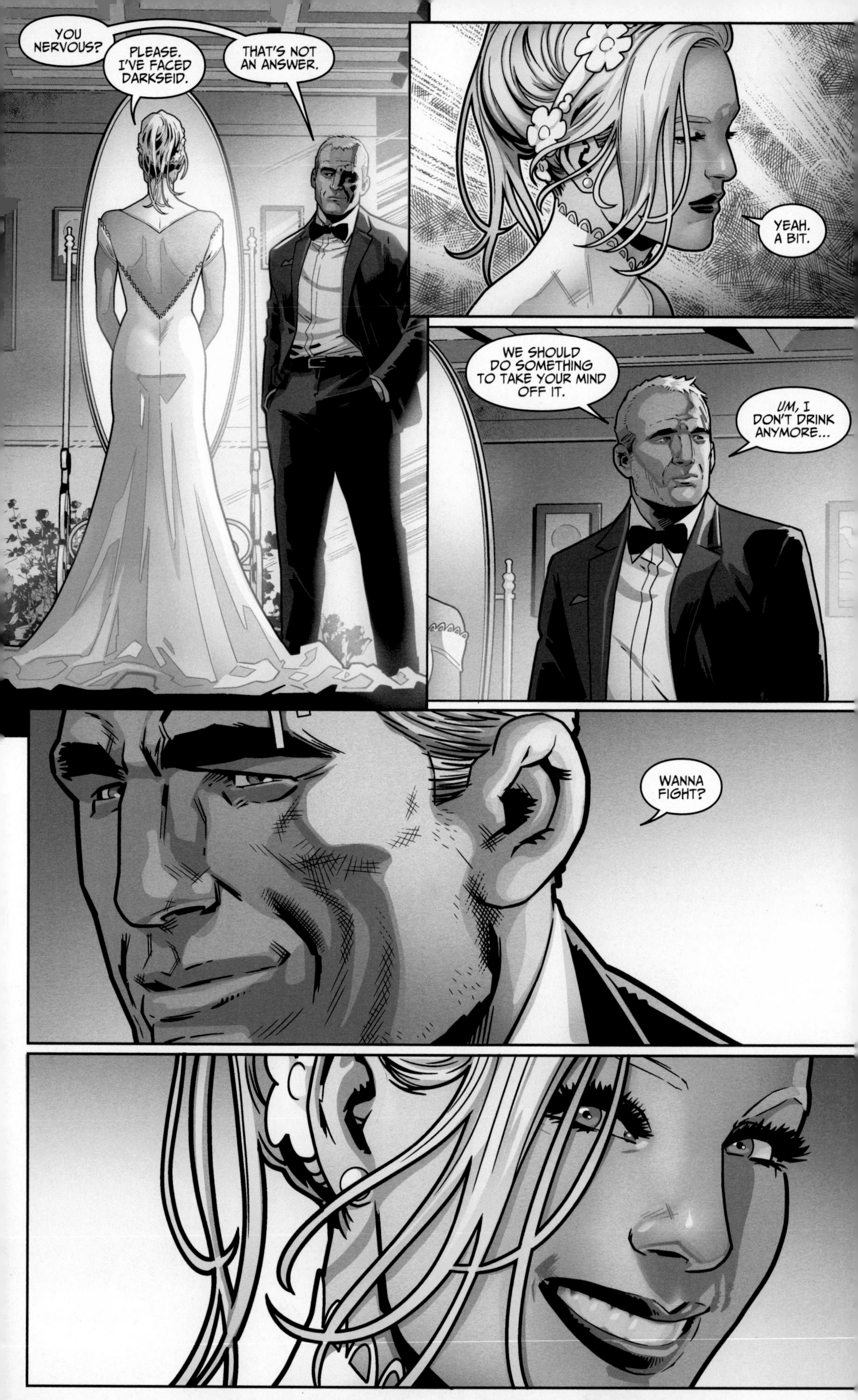
YOU NERVOUS?
PLEASE. I'VE FACED DARKSEID.
THAT'S NOT AN ANSWER.
YEAH. A BIT.
WE SHOULD DO SOMETHING TO TAKE YOUR MIND OFF IT.
UM, I DON'T DRINK ANYMORE...
WANNA FIGHT?

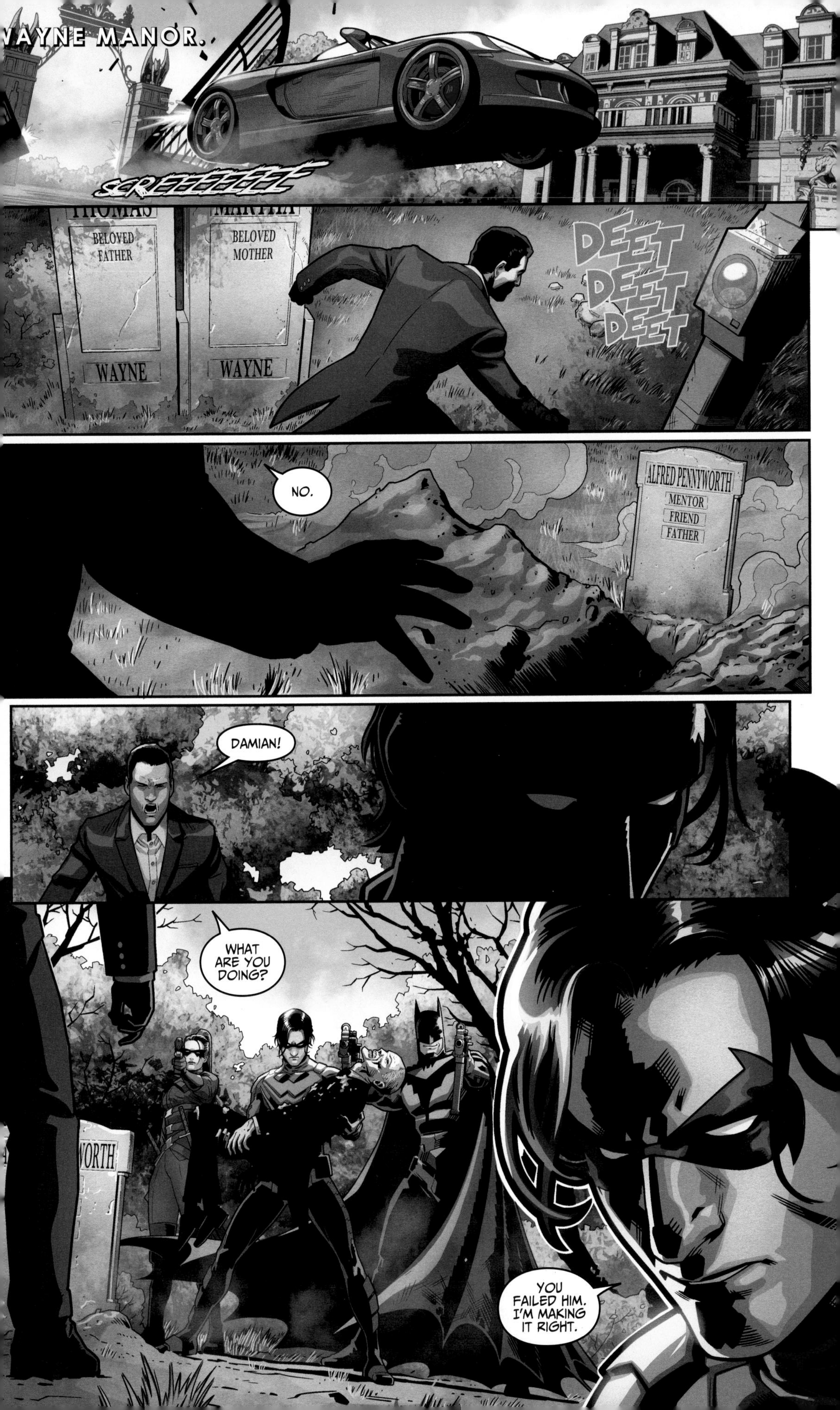
WAYNE MANOR.
SCREEEEEEEE
BELOVED FATHER
WAYNE
BELOVED MOTHER
WAYNE
DEET DEET DEET
NO.
ALFRED PENNYWORTH
MENTOR
FRIEND
FATHER
DAMIAN!
WHAT ARE YOU DOING?
WORTH
YOU FAILED HIM. I'M MAKING IT RIGHT.

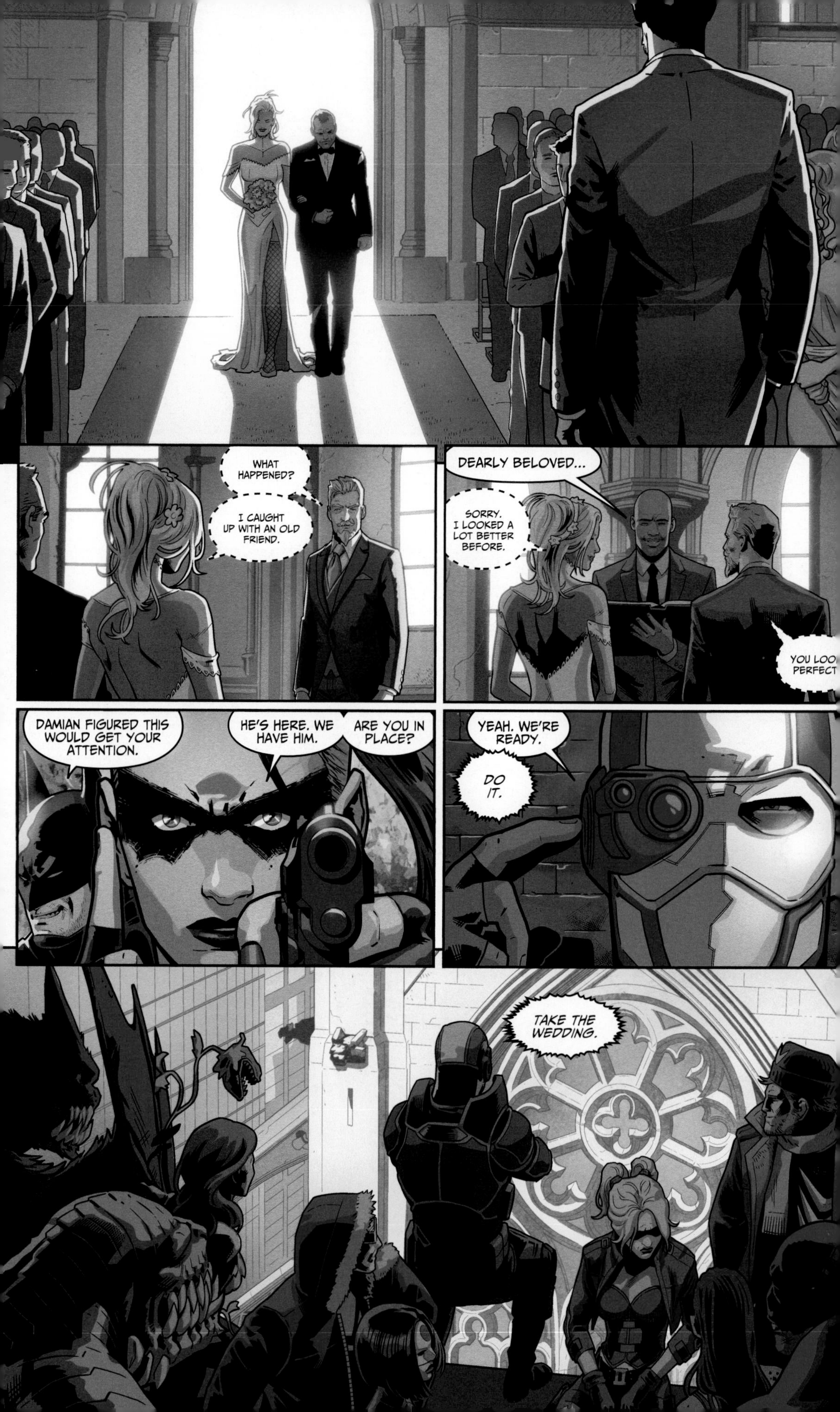
WHAT HAPPENED?
I CAUGHT UP WITH AN OLD FRIEND.
DEARLY BELOVED...
SORRY. I LOOKED A LOT BETTER BEFORE.
YOU LOO PERFECT
DAMIAN FIGURED THIS WOULD GET YOUR ATTENTION.
HE'S HERE. WE HAVE HIM.
ARE YOU IN PLACE?
YEAH. WE'RE READY.
DO IT.
TAKE THE WEDDING.

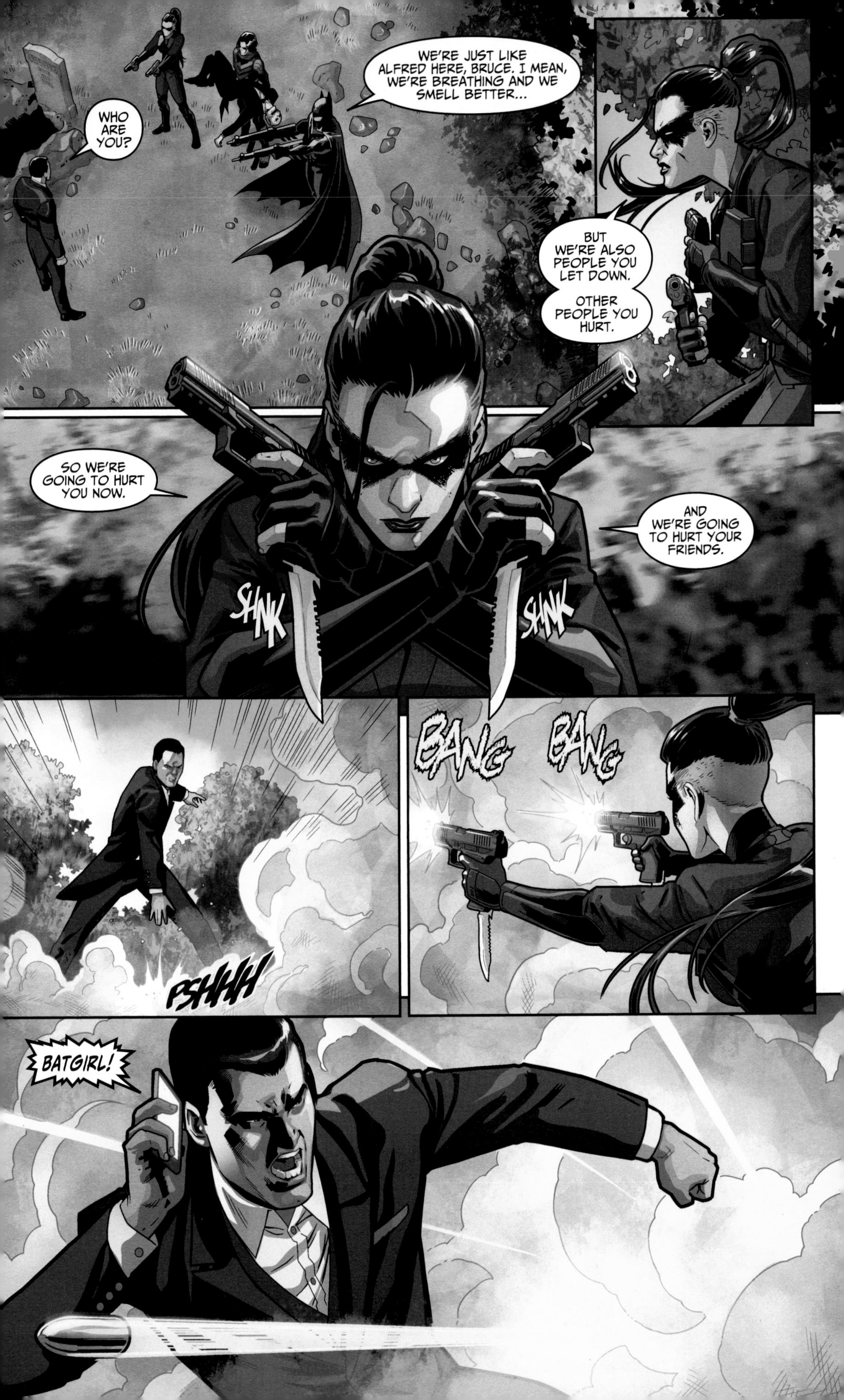
WHO ARE YOU?
WE'RE JUST LIKE ALFRED HERE, BRUCE. I MEAN, WE'RE BREATHING AND WE SMELL BETTER...
BUT WE'RE ALSO PEOPLE YOU LET DOWN.
OTHER PEOPLE YOU HURT.
SO WE'RE GOING TO HURT YOU NOW.
AND WE'RE GOING TO HURT YOUR FRIENDS.
SHNK
SHNK
PSHHH
BANG
BANG
BATGIRL!

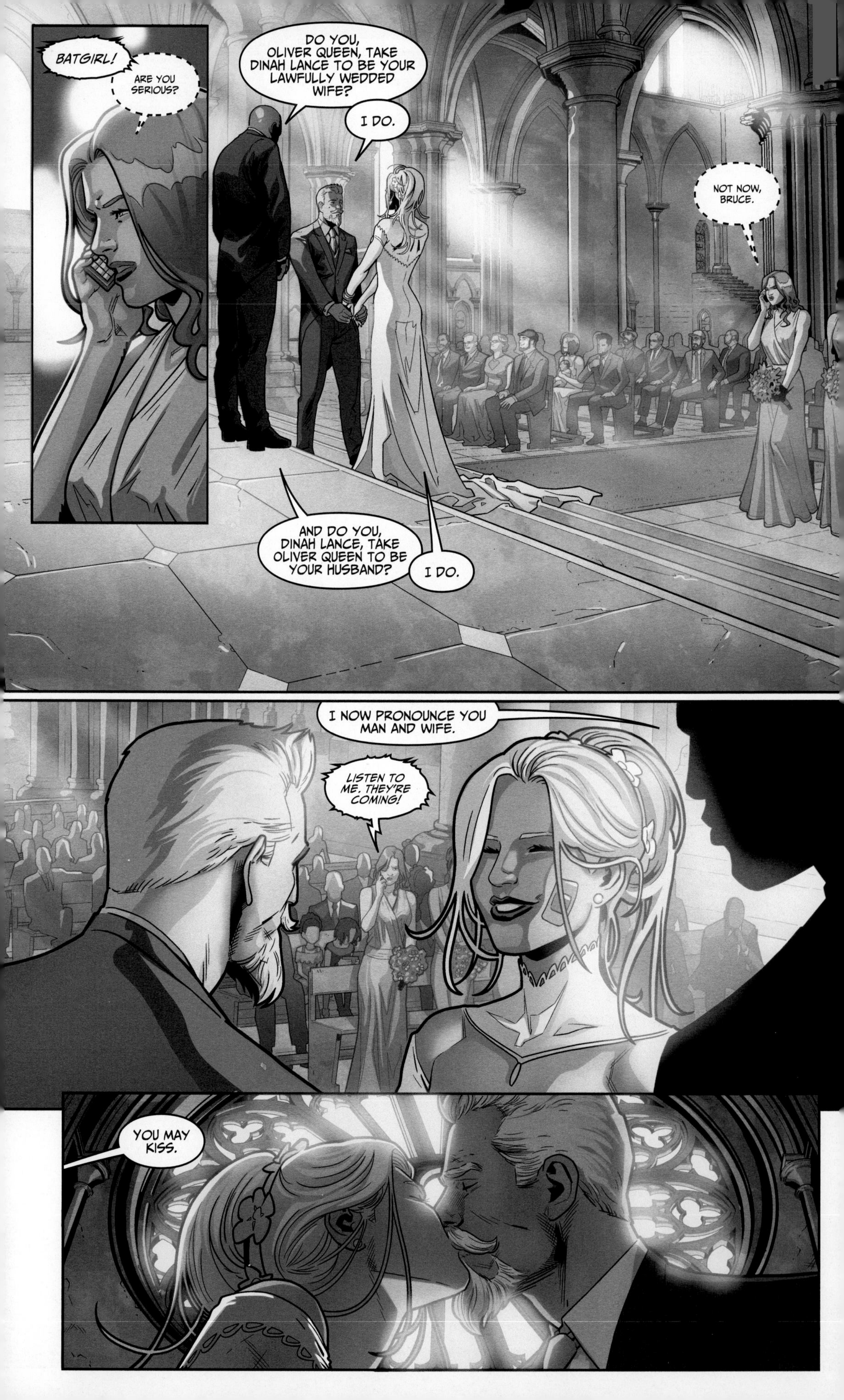
BATGIRL!
ARE YOU SERIOUS?
DO YOU, OLIVER QUEEN, TAKE DINAH LANCE TO BE YOUR LAWFULLY WEDDED WIFE?
I DO.
NOT NOW, BRUCE.
AND DO YOU, DINAH LANCE, TAKE OLIVER QUEEN TO BE YOUR HUSBAND?
I DO.
I NOW PRONOUNCE YOU MAN AND WIFE.
LISTEN TO ME. THEY'RE COMING!
YOU MAY KISS.

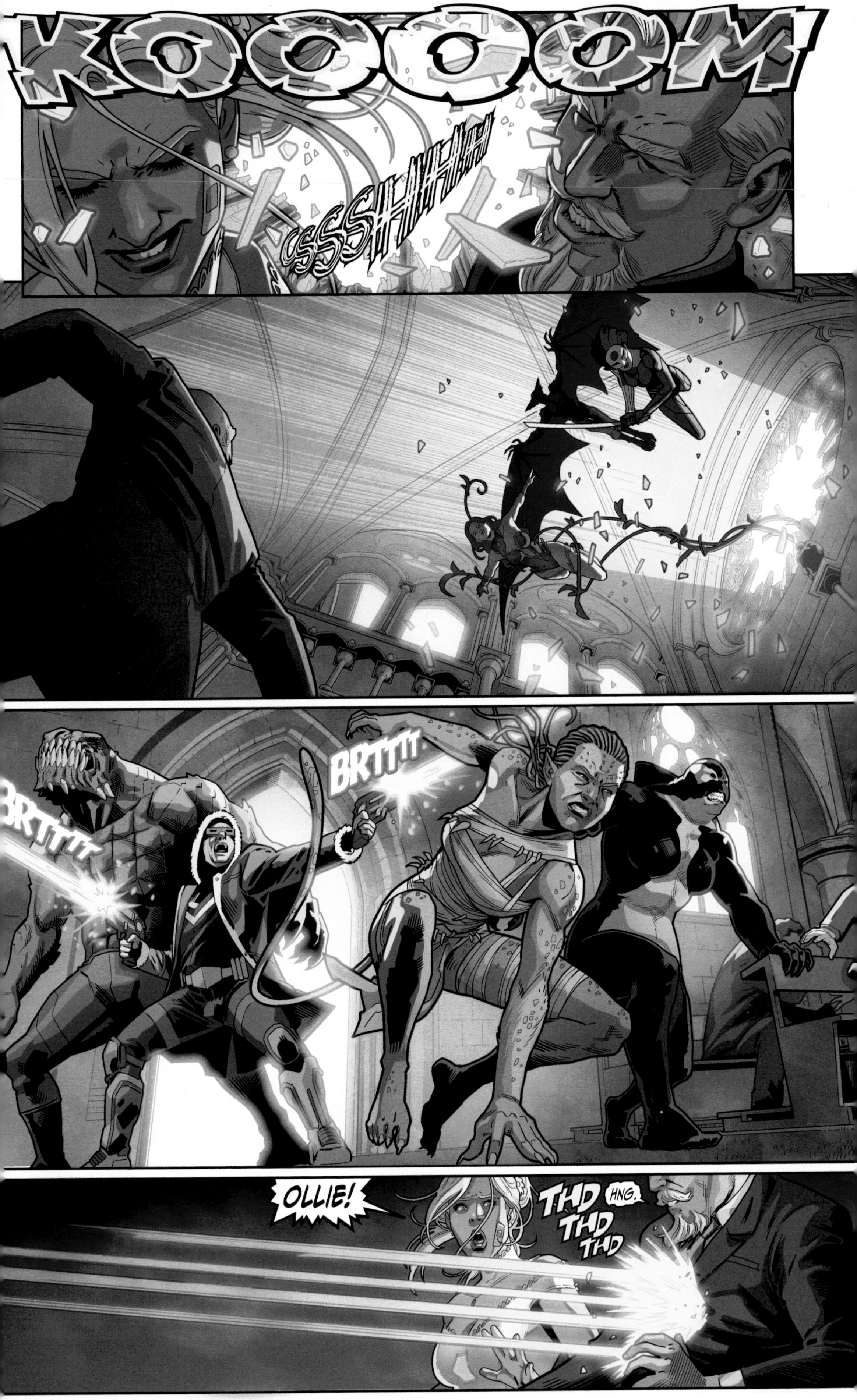
KOOOOOM
SSSHHHHH
BRTTTT
BRTTTT
OLLIE!
THD THD THD
HNG.

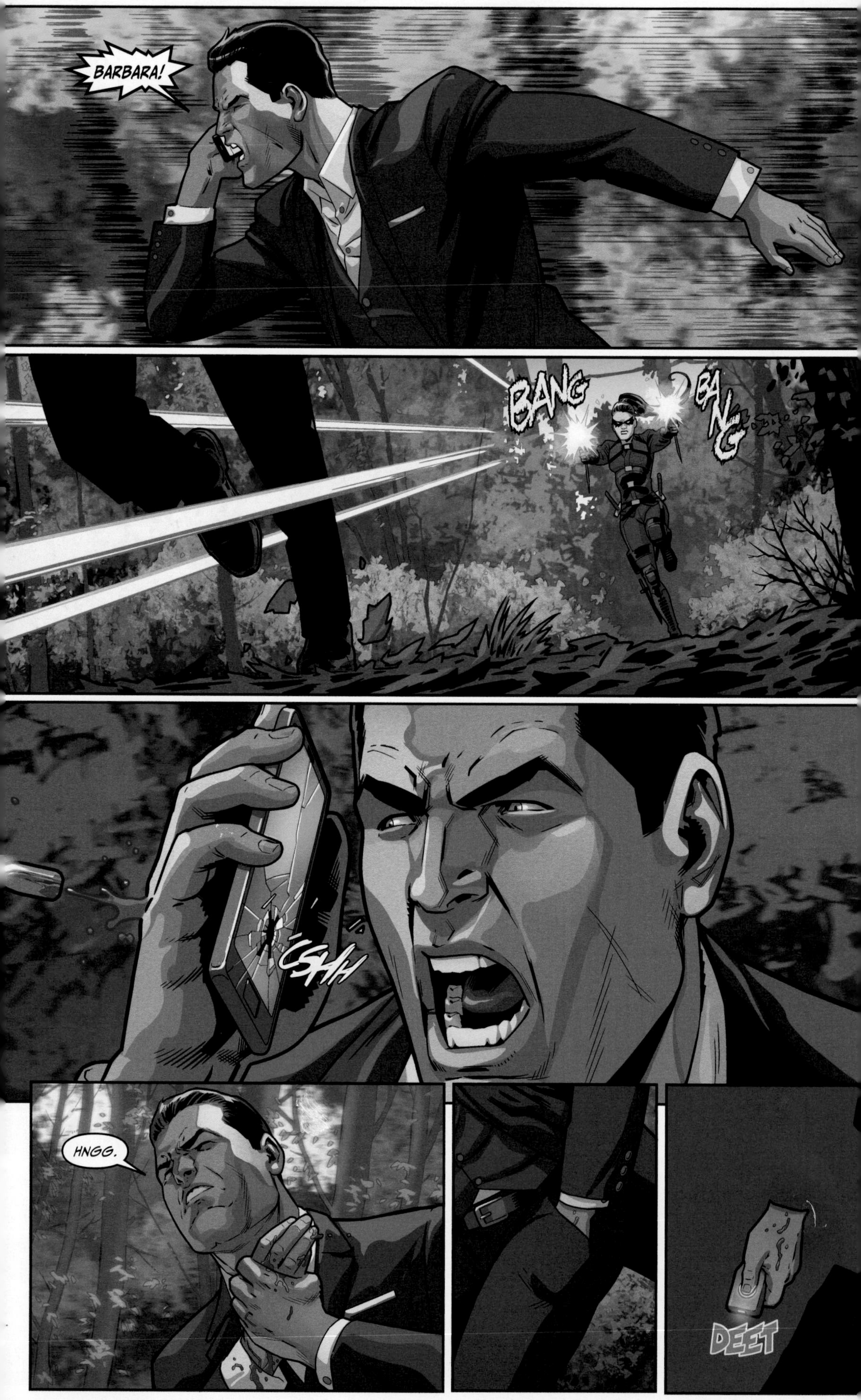
BARBARA!
BANG
BANG
CSHH
HNGG.
DEET

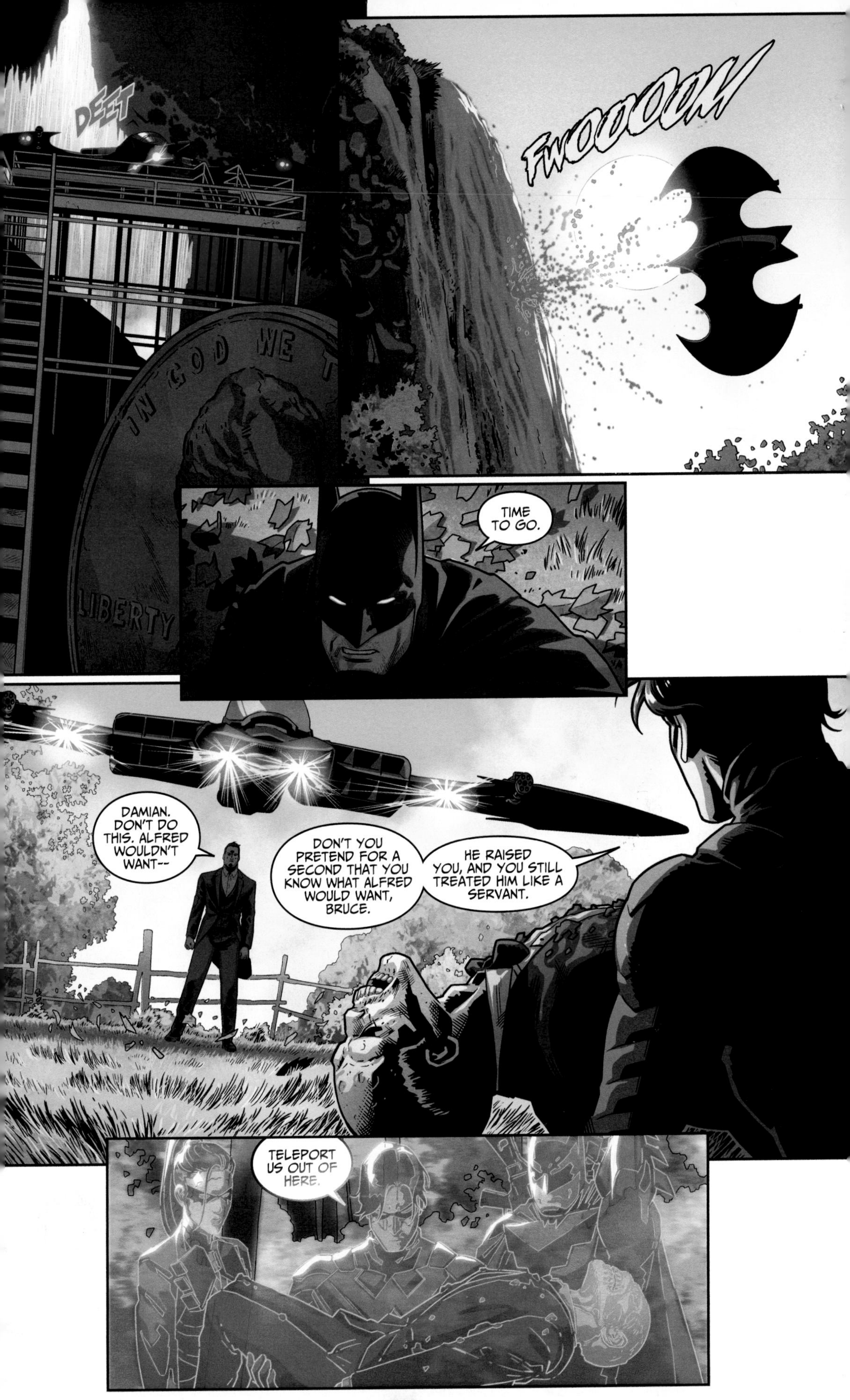

DEET
FWOOOOM!
IN GOD WE T
LIBERTY
TIME TO GO.
DAMIAN. DON'T DO THIS. ALFRED WOULDN'T WANT--
DON'T YOU PRETEND FOR A SECOND THAT YOU KNOW WHAT ALFRED WOULD WANT, BRUCE.
HE RAISED YOU, AND YOU STILL TREATED HIM LIKE A SERVANT.
TELEPORT US OUT OF HERE.

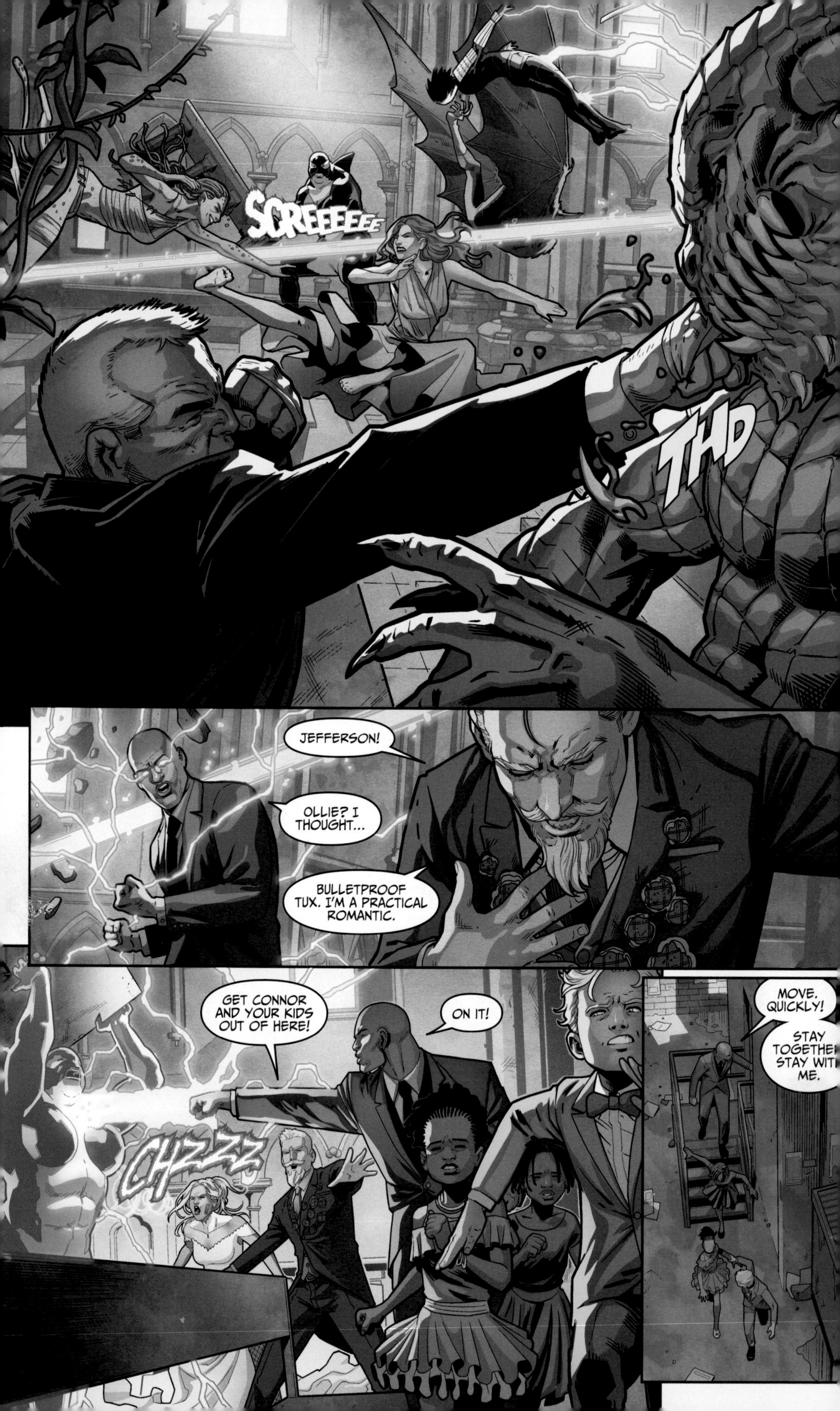

SCREEEEEEE
THD
JEFFERSON!
OLLIE? I THOUGHT...
BULLETPROOF TUX. I'M A PRACTICAL ROMANTIC.
GET CONNOR AND YOUR KIDS OUT OF HERE!
ON IT!
CHZZZ
MOVE. QUICKLY!
STAY TOGETHE STAY WIT ME.

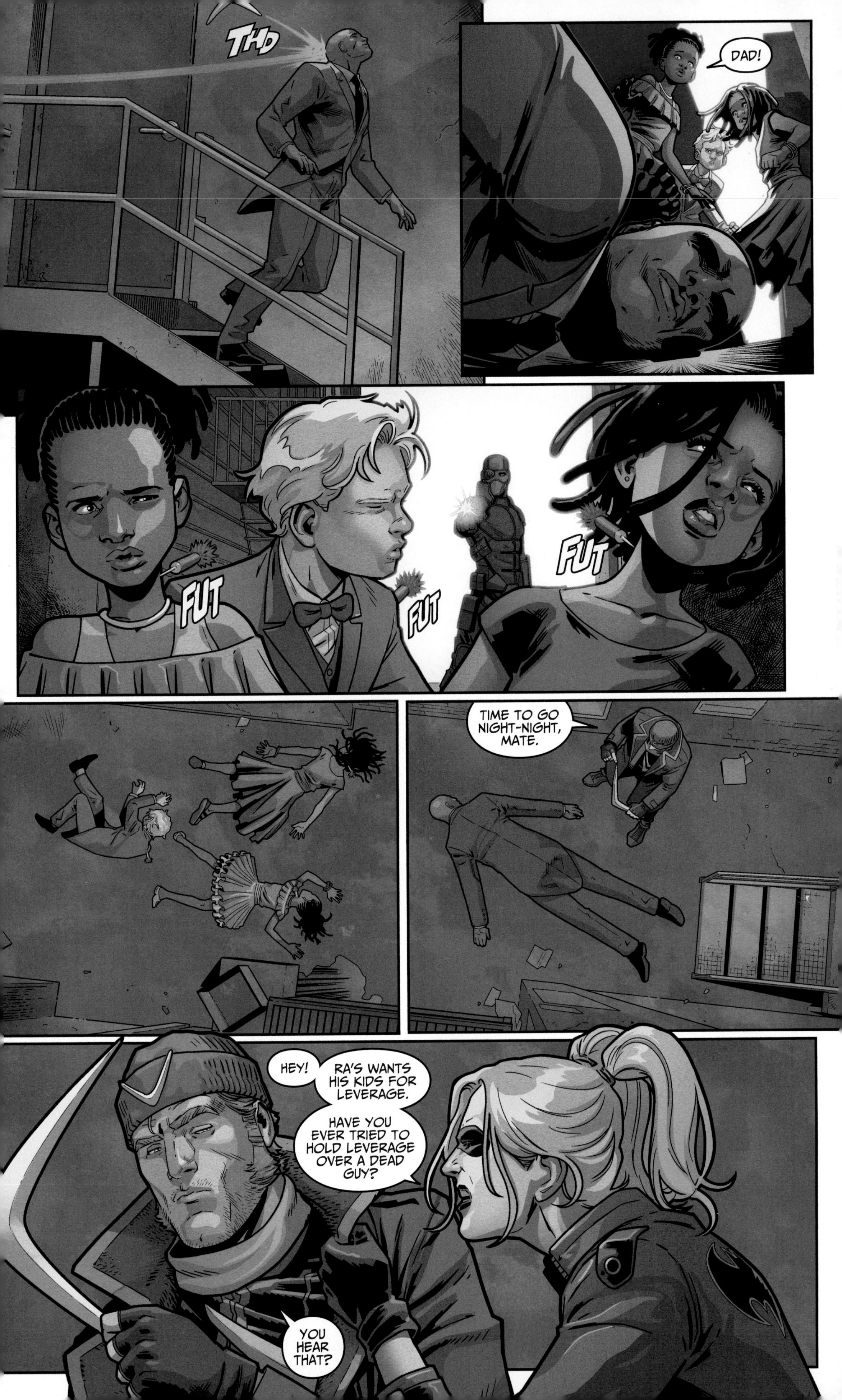
THD
DAD!
FUT
FUT
FUT
TIME TO GO NIGHT-NIGHT, MATE.
HEY!
RA'S WANTS HIS KIDS FOR LEVERAGE.
HAVE YOU EVER TRIED TO HOLD LEVERAGE OVER A DEAD GUY?
YOU HEAR THAT?

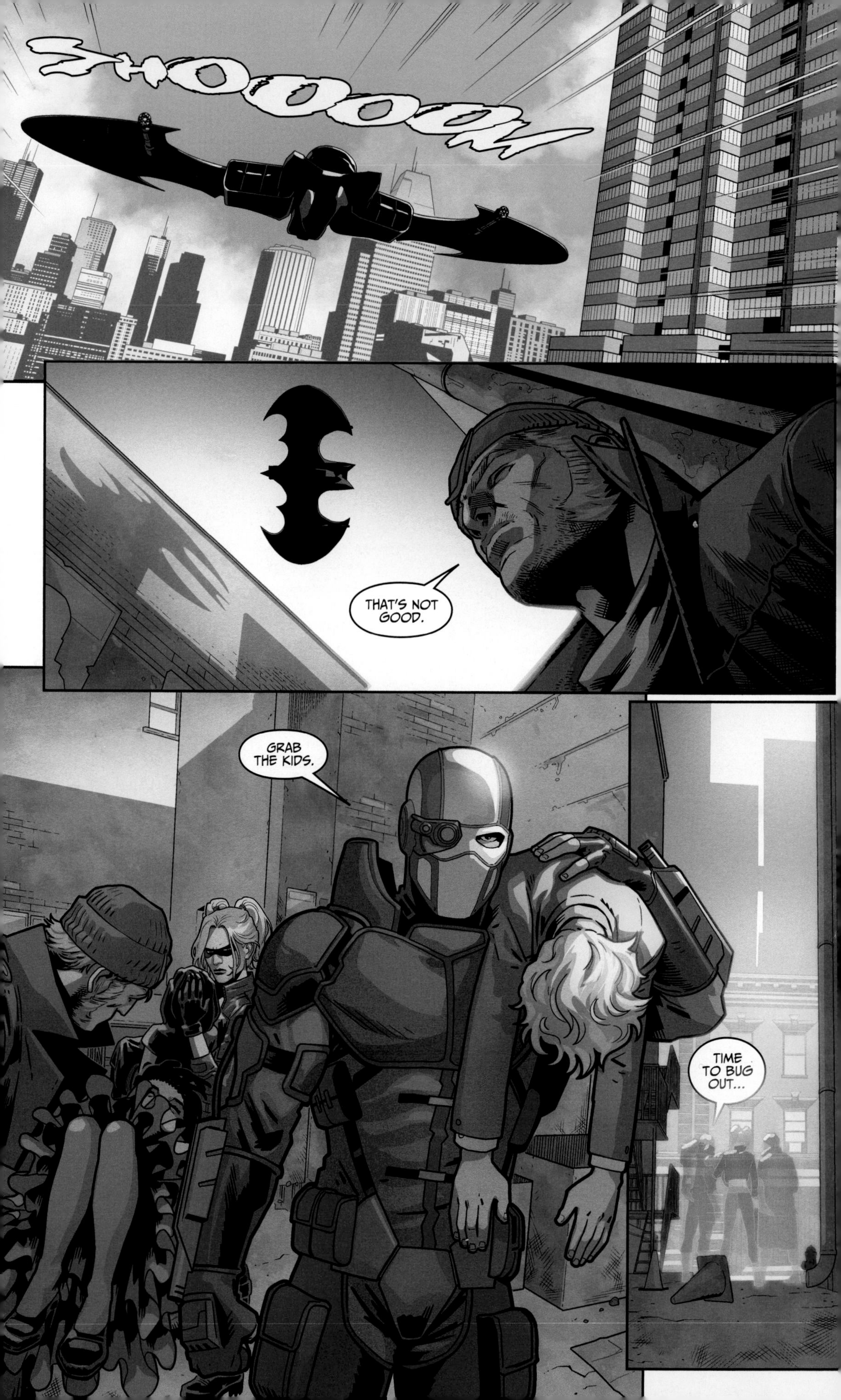
THOOOOOM
THAT'S NOT GOOD.
GRAB THE KIDS.
TIME TO BUG OUT...

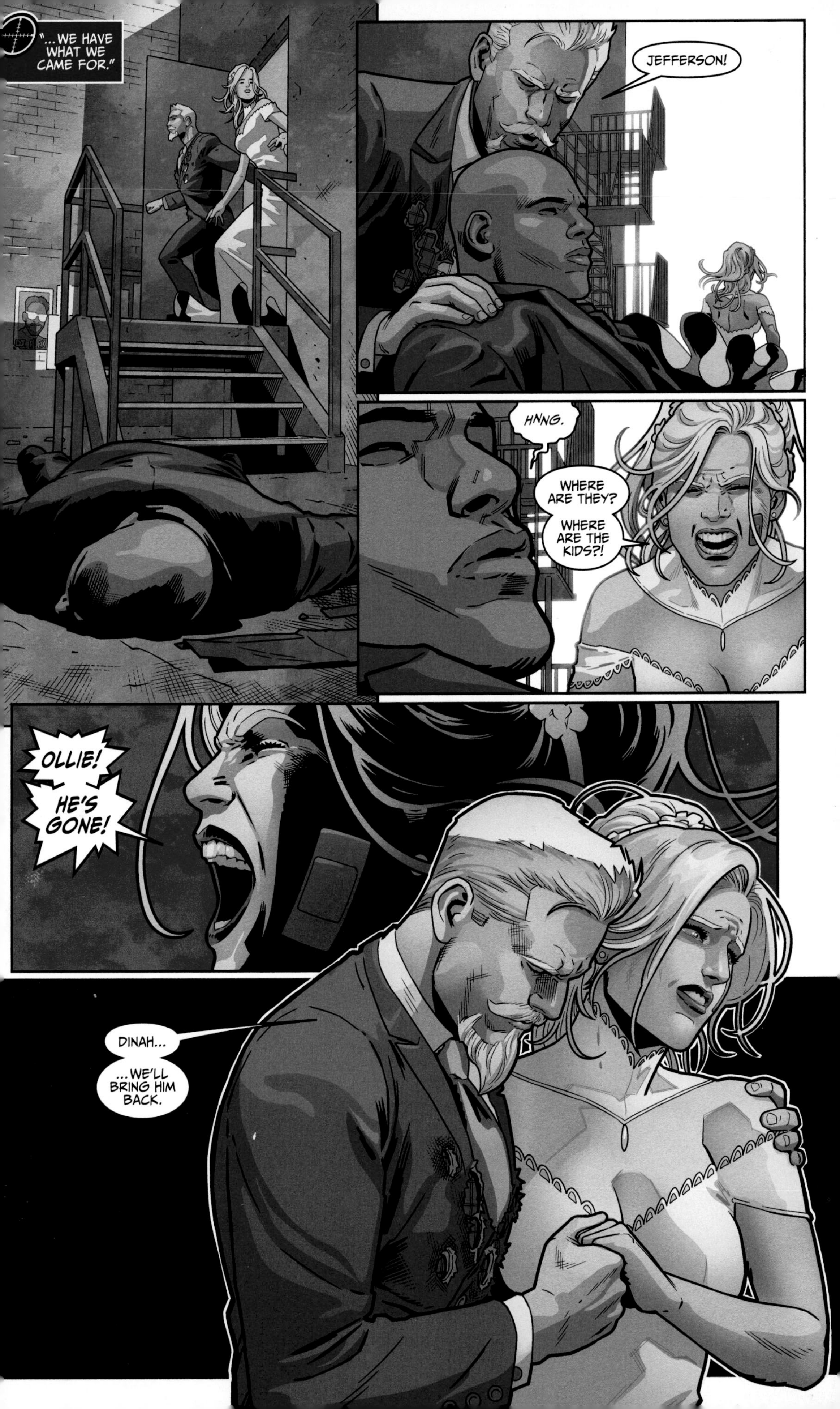
"...WE HAVE WHAT WE CAME FOR."
JEFFERSON!
HNNG.
WHERE ARE THEY?
WHERE ARE THE KIDS?!
OLLIE!
HE'S GONE!
DINAH...
...WE'LL BRING HIM BACK.

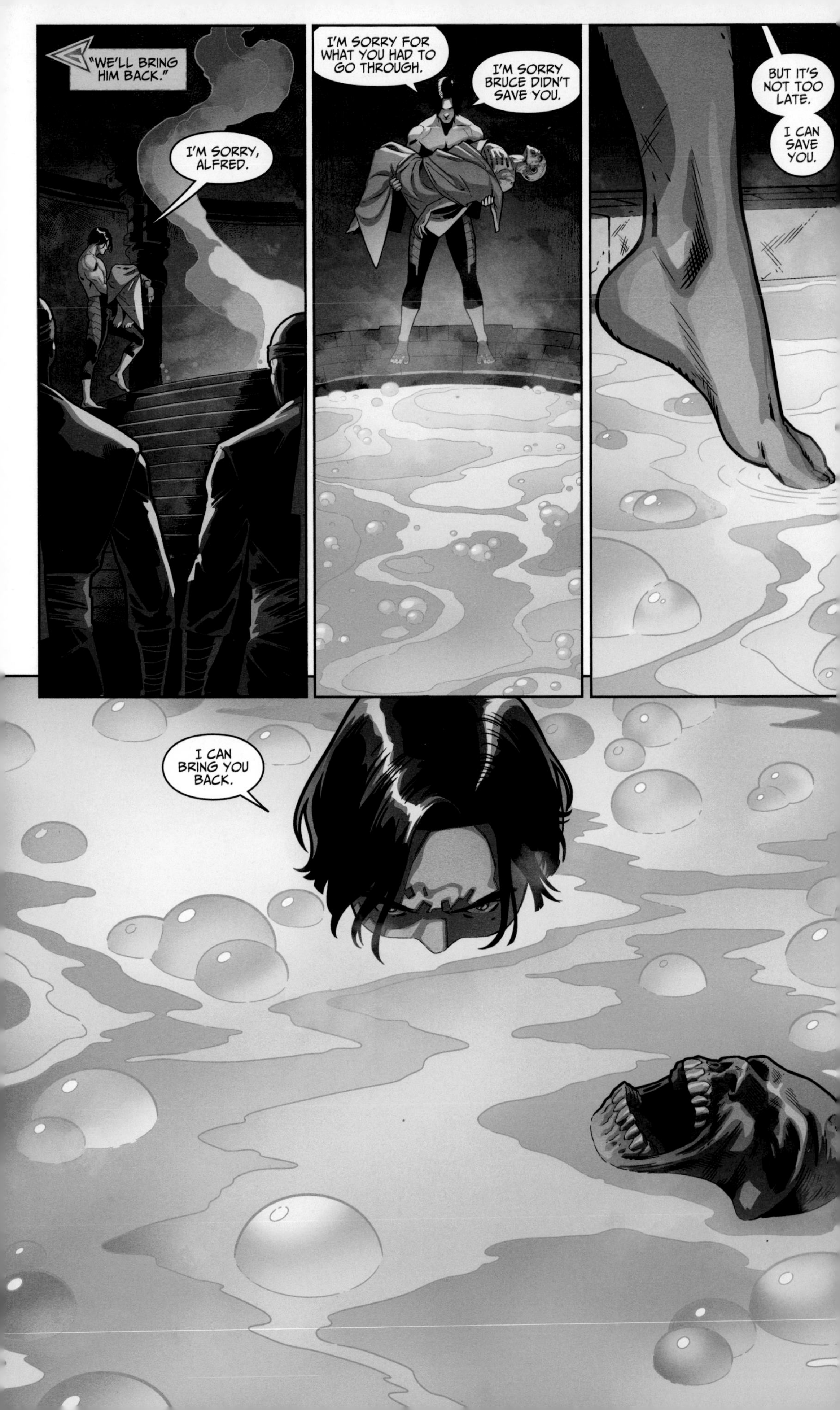
"WE'LL BRING HIM BACK."
I'M SORRY, ALFRED.
I'M SORRY FOR WHAT YOU HAD TO GO THROUGH.
I'M SORRY BRUCE DIDN'T SAVE YOU.
BUT IT'S NOT TOO LATE.
I CAN SAVE YOU.
I CAN BRING YOU BACK.

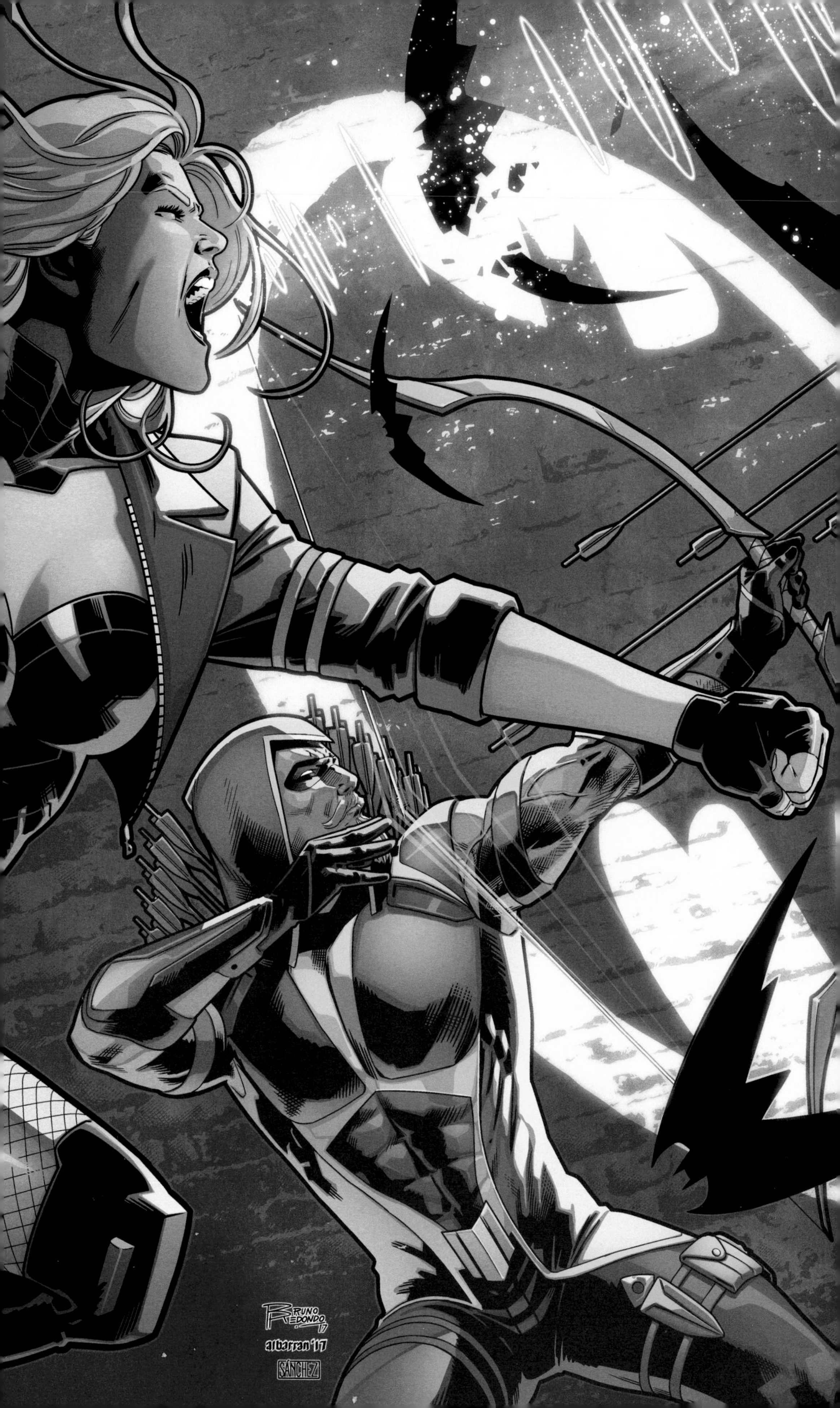

BRUNO REDONDO '17
albarran '17
SÁNCHEZ

"The Search"

Tom Taylor Writer **Bruno Redondo** Penciller **Juan Albarran** Inker **Rex Lokus** Colorist
Wes Abbott Letterer Cover art by **Bruno Redondo**, **Juan Albarran** and **Alejandro Sanchez**

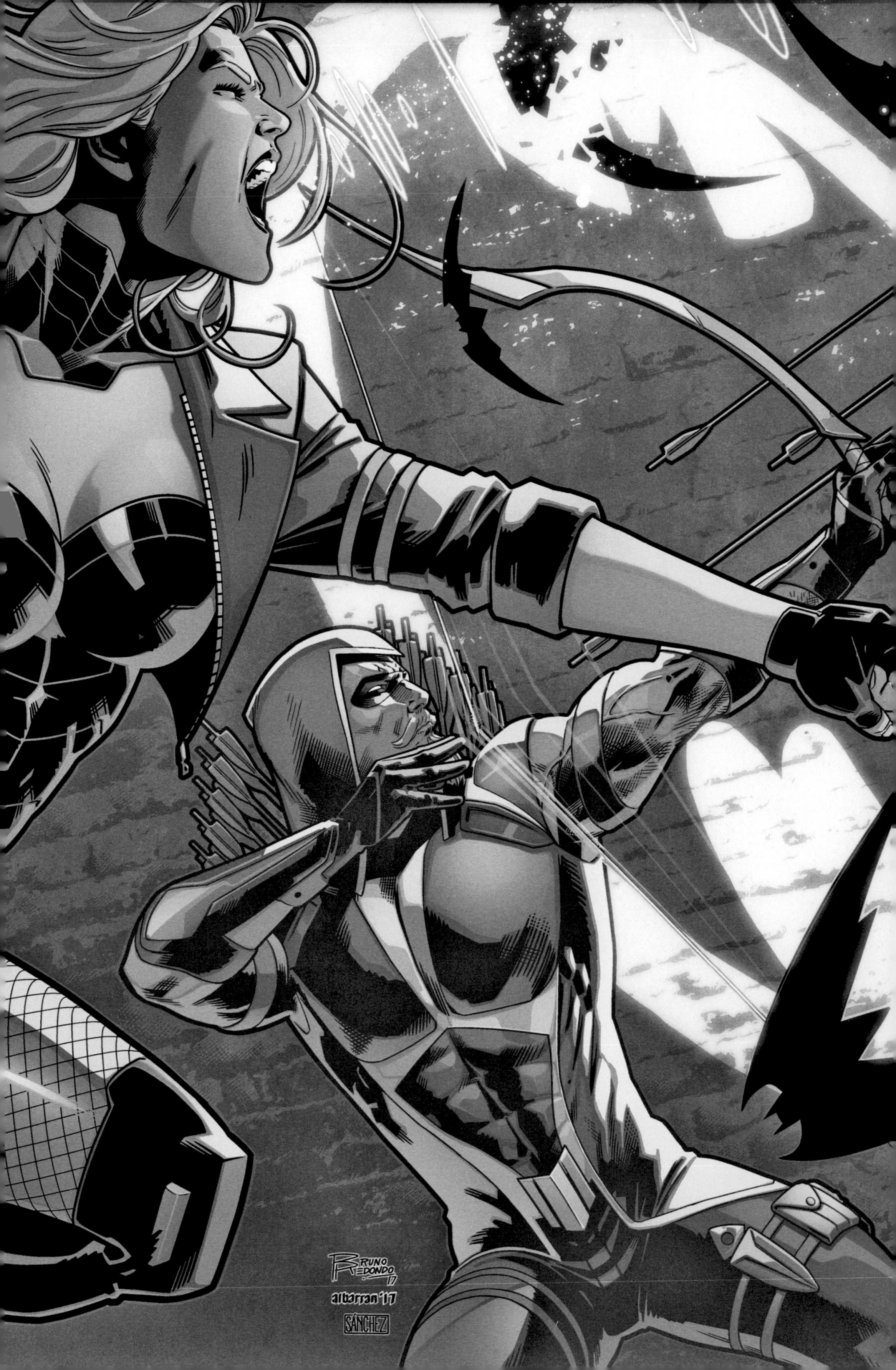
BRUNO REDONDO '17
albarran '17
SÁNCHEZ

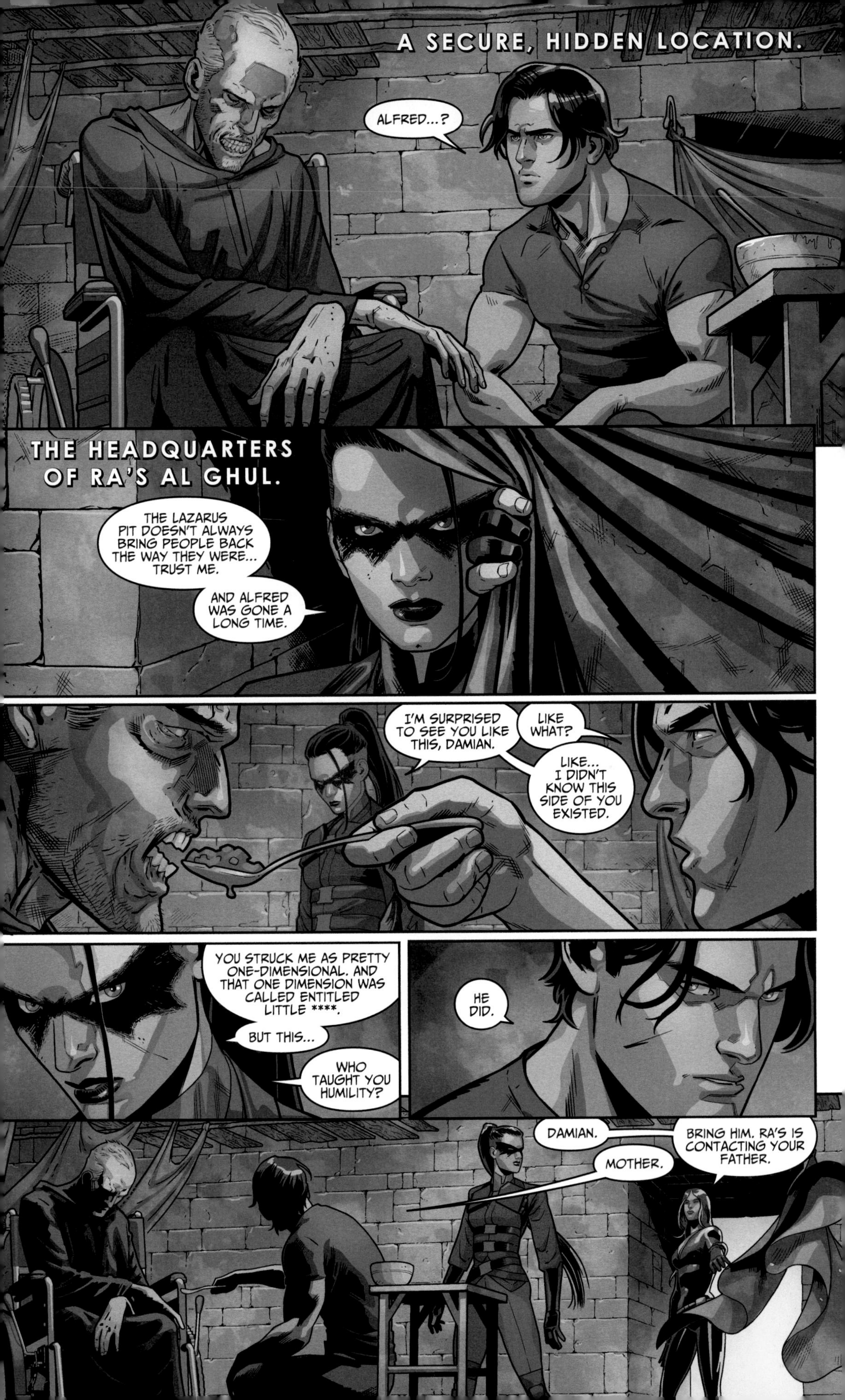
A SECURE, HIDDEN LOCATION.
ALFRED...?
THE HEADQUARTERS OF RA'S AL GHUL.
THE LAZARUS PIT DOESN'T ALWAYS BRING PEOPLE BACK THE WAY THEY WERE... TRUST ME.
AND ALFRED WAS GONE A LONG TIME.
I'M SURPRISED TO SEE YOU LIKE THIS, DAMIAN.
LIKE WHAT?
LIKE... I DIDN'T KNOW THIS SIDE OF YOU EXISTED.
YOU STRUCK ME AS PRETTY ONE-DIMENSIONAL. AND THAT ONE DIMENSION WAS CALLED ENTITLED LITTLE ****.
BUT THIS...
WHO TAUGHT YOU HUMILITY?
HE DID.
DAMIAN.
MOTHER.
BRING HIM. RA'S IS CONTACTING YOUR FATHER.

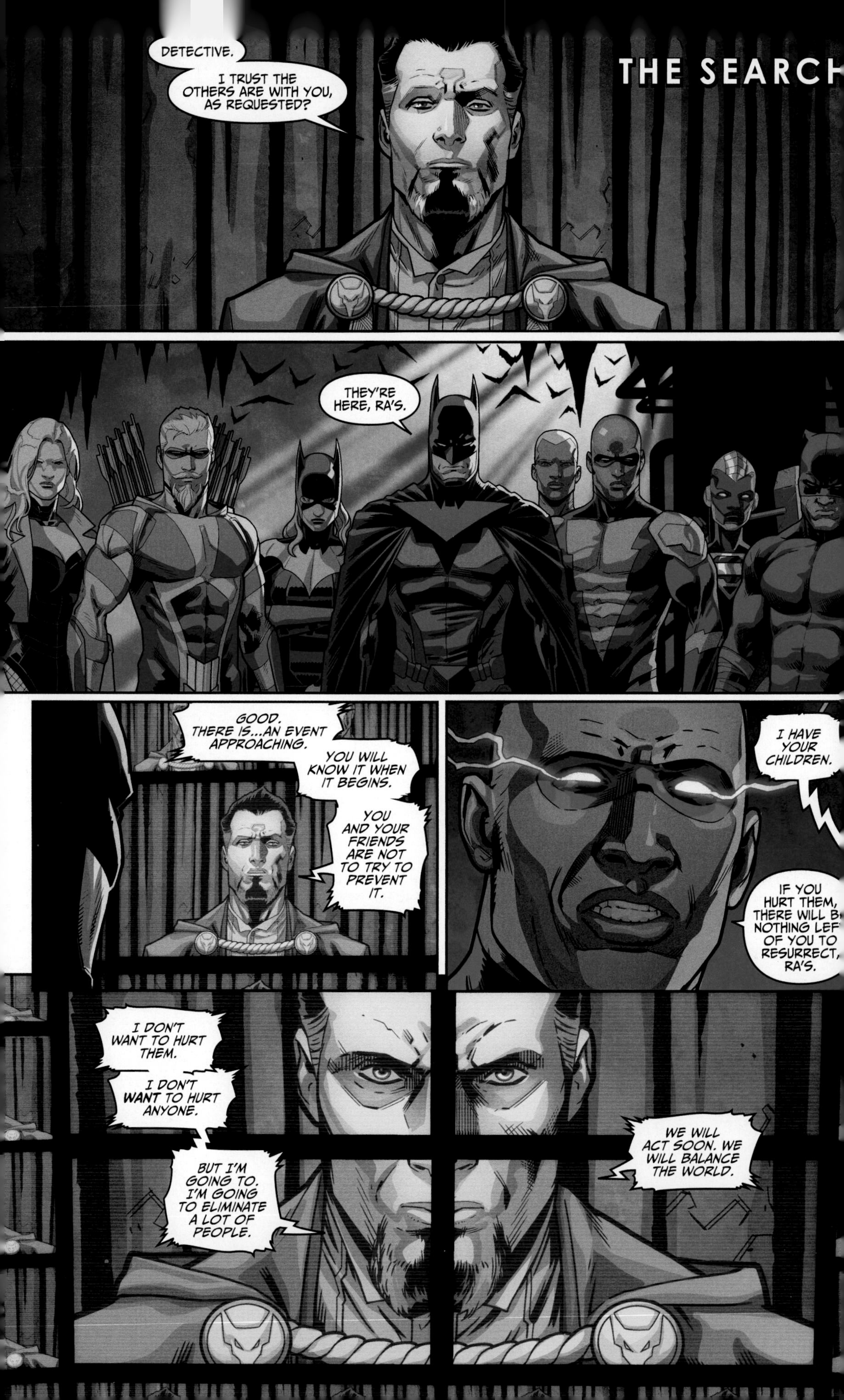
DETECTIVE.
I TRUST THE OTHERS ARE WITH YOU, AS REQUESTED?
THE SEARCH
THEY'RE HERE, RA'S.
GOOD. THERE IS...AN EVENT APPROACHING.
YOU WILL KNOW IT WHEN IT BEGINS.
YOU AND YOUR FRIENDS ARE NOT TO TRY TO PREVENT IT.
I HAVE YOUR CHILDREN.
IF YOU HURT THEM, THERE WILL B NOTHING LEF OF YOU TO RESURRECT, RA'S.
I DON'T WANT TO HURT THEM.
I DON'T *WANT* TO HURT ANYONE.
BUT I'M GOING TO. I'M GOING TO ELIMINATE A LOT OF PEOPLE.
WE WILL ACT SOON. WE WILL BALANCE THE WORLD.

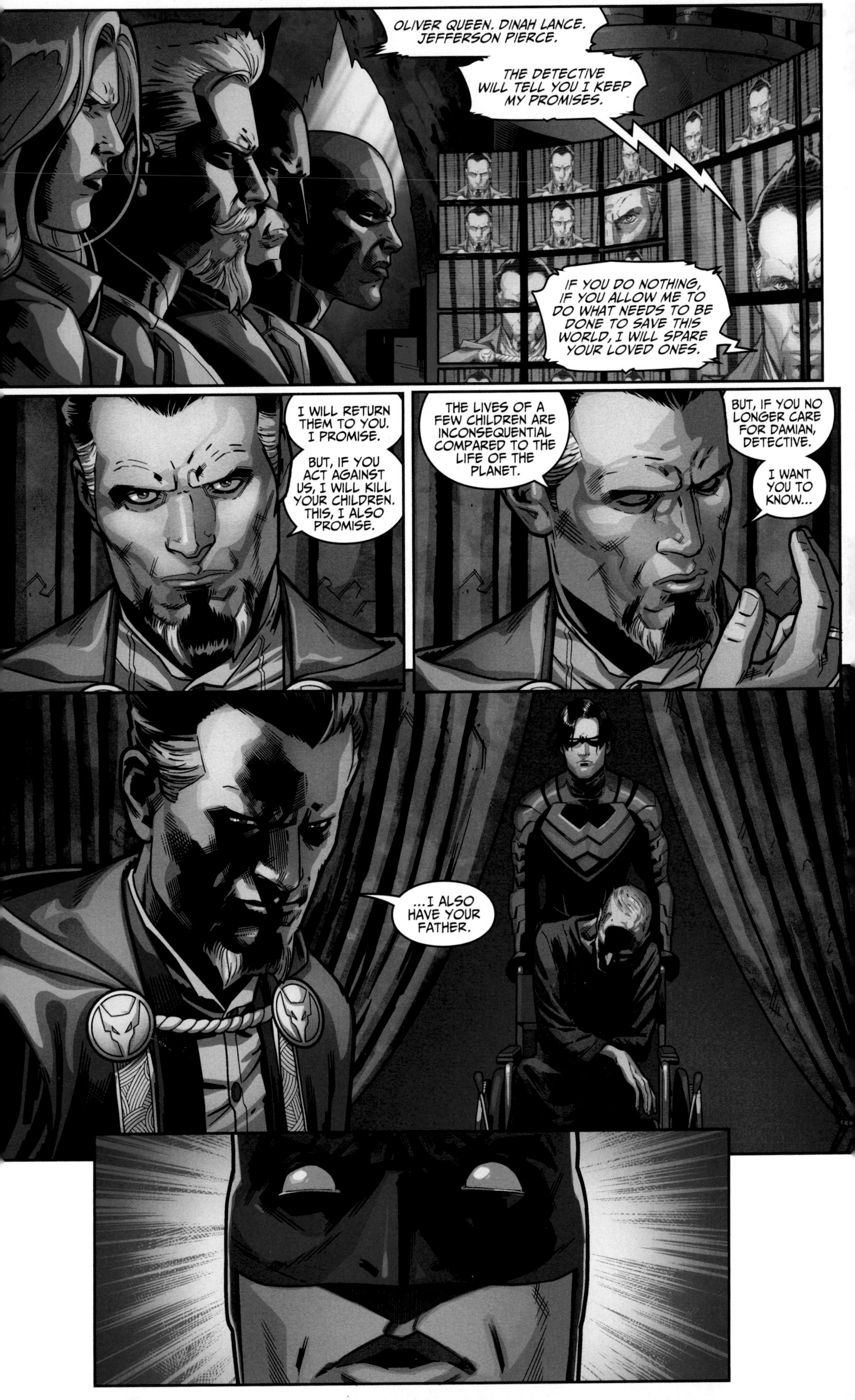

OLIVER QUEEN. DINAH LANCE. JEFFERSON PIERCE.
THE DETECTIVE WILL TELL YOU I KEEP MY PROMISES.
IF YOU DO NOTHING, IF YOU ALLOW ME TO DO WHAT NEEDS TO BE DONE TO SAVE THIS WORLD, I WILL SPARE YOUR LOVED ONES.
I WILL RETURN THEM TO YOU. I PROMISE.
BUT, IF YOU ACT AGAINST US, I WILL KILL YOUR CHILDREN. THIS, I ALSO PROMISE.
THE LIVES OF A FEW CHILDREN ARE INCONSEQUENTIAL COMPARED TO THE LIFE OF THE PLANET.
BUT, IF YOU NO LONGER CARE FOR DAMIAN, DETECTIVE.
I WANT YOU TO KNOW...
...I ALSO HAVE YOUR FATHER.

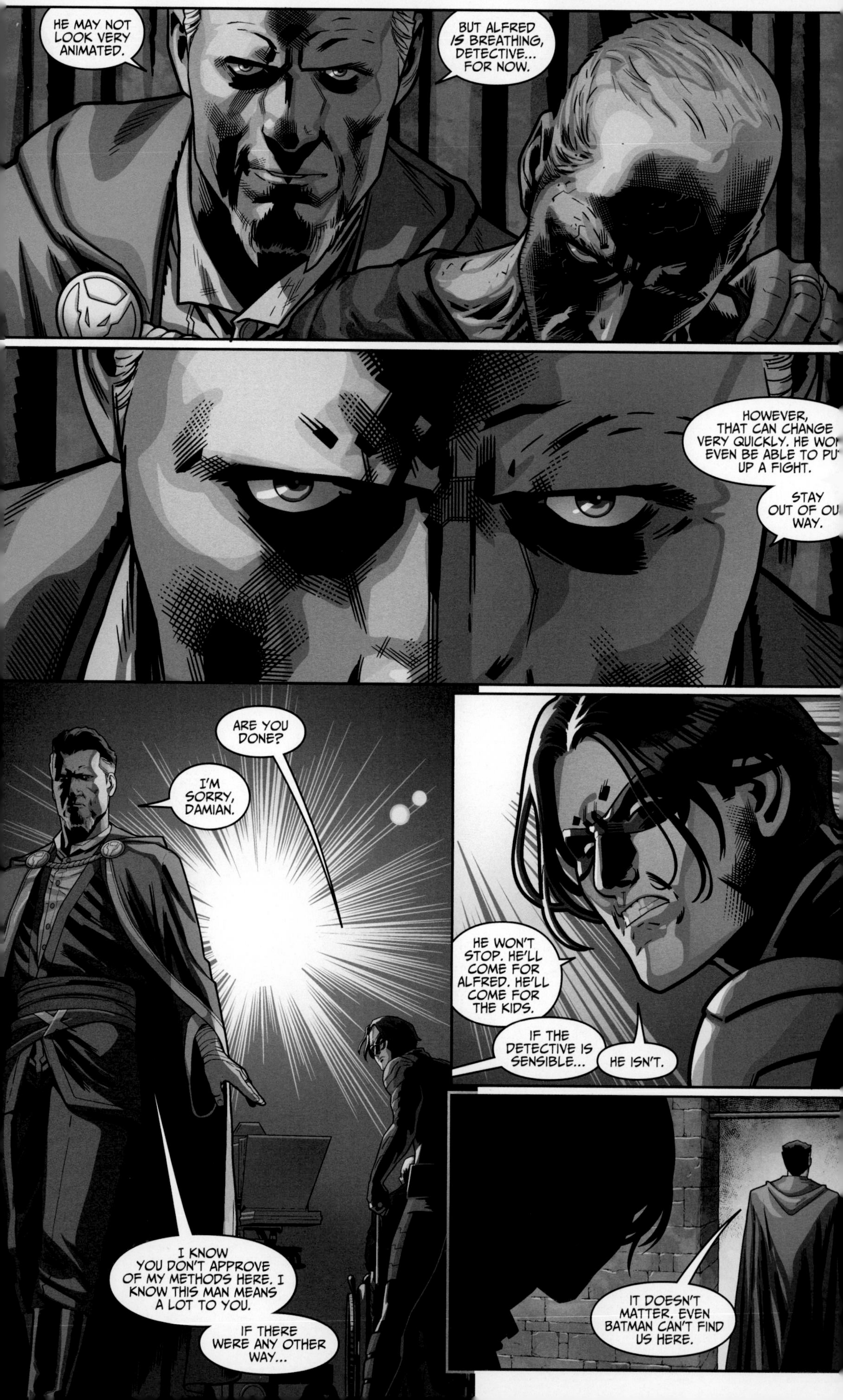
HE MAY NOT LOOK VERY ANIMATED.
BUT ALFRED *IS* BREATHING, DETECTIVE... FOR NOW.
HOWEVER, THAT CAN CHANGE VERY QUICKLY. HE WON EVEN BE ABLE TO PU UP A FIGHT.
STAY OUT OF OU WAY.
ARE YOU DONE?
I'M SORRY, DAMIAN.
I KNOW YOU DON'T APPROVE OF MY METHODS HERE. I KNOW THIS MAN MEANS A LOT TO YOU.
IF THERE WERE ANY OTHER WAY...
HE WON'T STOP. HE'LL COME FOR ALFRED. HE'LL COME FOR THE KIDS.
IF THE DETECTIVE IS SENSIBLE...
HE ISN'T.
IT DOESN'T MATTER. EVEN BATMAN CAN'T FIND US HERE.

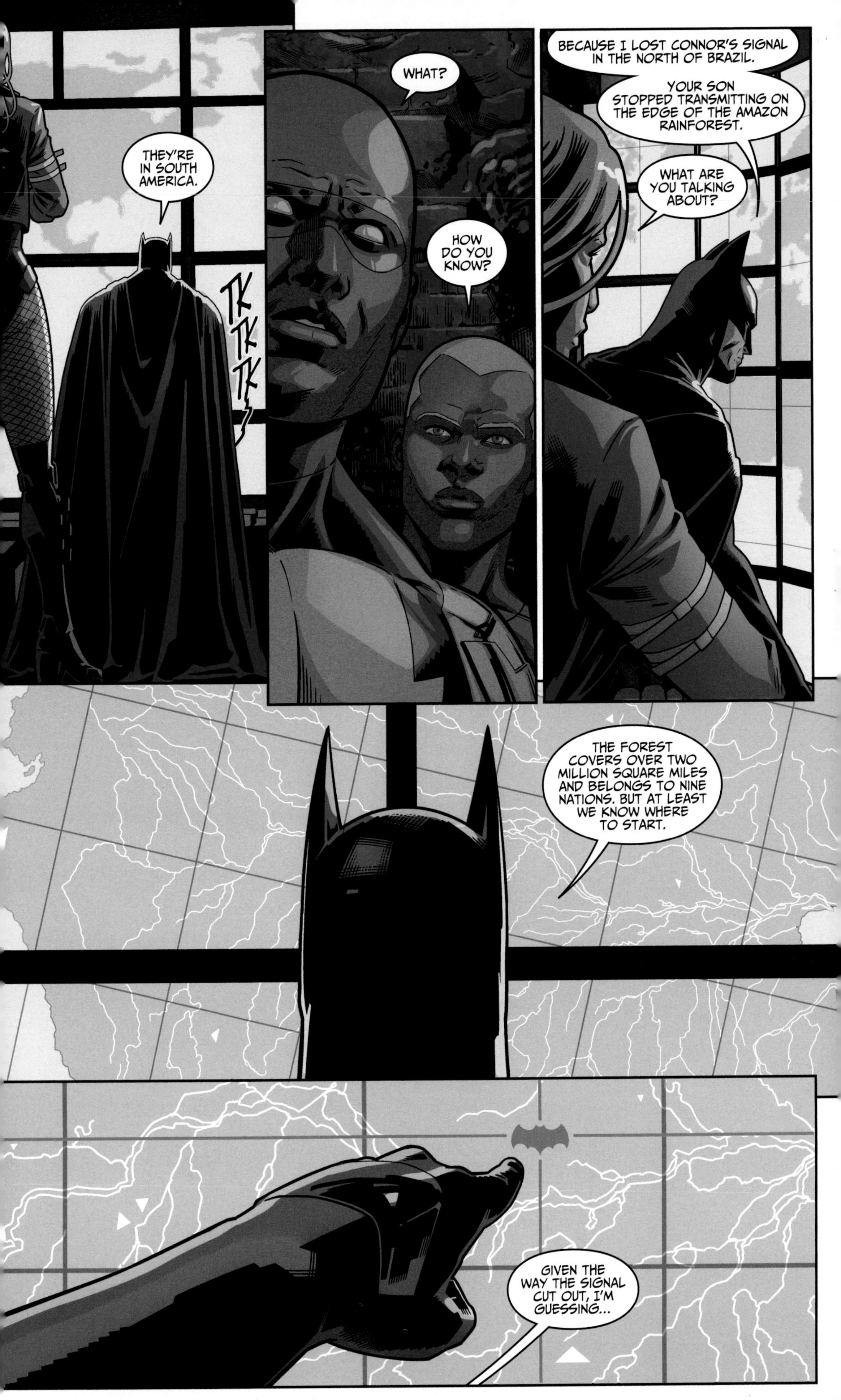
THEY'RE IN SOUTH AMERICA.
TK TK TK
WHAT?
HOW DO YOU KNOW?
BECAUSE I LOST CONNOR'S SIGNAL IN THE NORTH OF BRAZIL.
YOUR SON STOPPED TRANSMITTING ON THE EDGE OF THE AMAZON RAINFOREST.
WHAT ARE YOU TALKING ABOUT?
THE FOREST COVERS OVER TWO MILLION SQUARE MILES AND BELONGS TO NINE NATIONS. BUT AT LEAST WE KNOW WHERE TO START.
GIVEN THE WAY THE SIGNAL CUT OUT, I'M GUESSING...

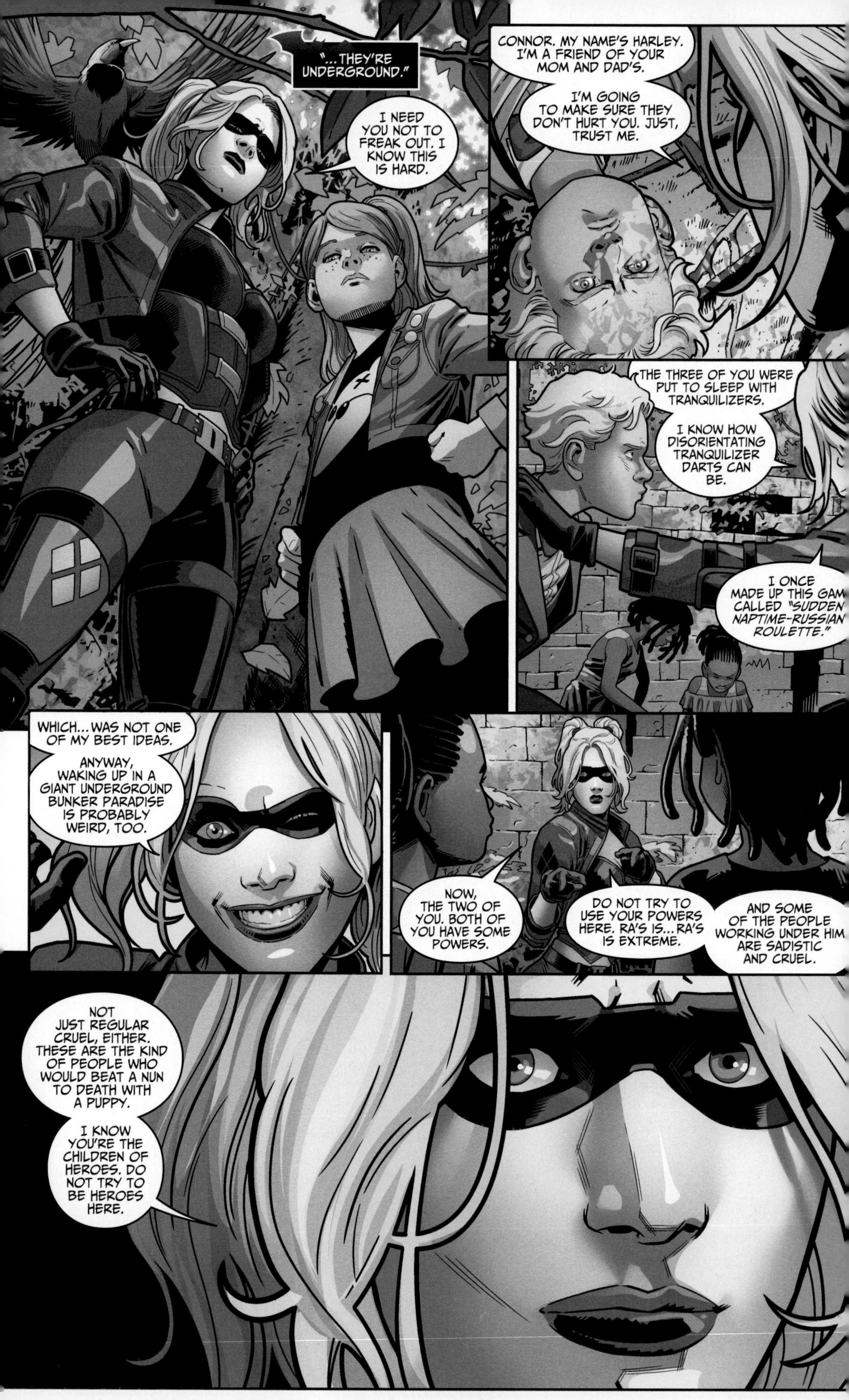
"...THEY'RE UNDERGROUND."
I NEED YOU NOT TO FREAK OUT. I KNOW THIS IS HARD.
CONNOR. MY NAME'S HARLEY. I'M A FRIEND OF YOUR MOM AND DAD'S.
I'M GOING TO MAKE SURE THEY DON'T HURT YOU. JUST, TRUST ME.
THE THREE OF YOU WERE PUT TO SLEEP WITH TRANQUILIZERS.
I KNOW HOW DISORIENTATING TRANQUILIZER DARTS CAN BE.
I ONCE MADE UP THIS GAM CALLED "SUDDEN NAPTIME-RUSSIAN ROULETTE."
WHICH...WAS NOT ONE OF MY BEST IDEAS.
ANYWAY, WAKING UP IN A GIANT UNDERGROUND BUNKER PARADISE IS PROBABLY WEIRD, TOO.
NOW, THE TWO OF YOU. BOTH OF YOU HAVE SOME POWERS.
DO NOT TRY TO USE YOUR POWERS HERE. RA'S IS...RA'S IS EXTREME.
AND SOME OF THE PEOPLE WORKING UNDER HIM ARE SADISTIC AND CRUEL.
NOT JUST REGULAR CRUEL, EITHER. THESE ARE THE KIND OF PEOPLE WHO WOULD BEAT A NUN TO DEATH WITH A PUPPY.
I KNOW YOU'RE THE CHILDREN OF HEROES. DO NOT TRY TO BE HEROES HERE.

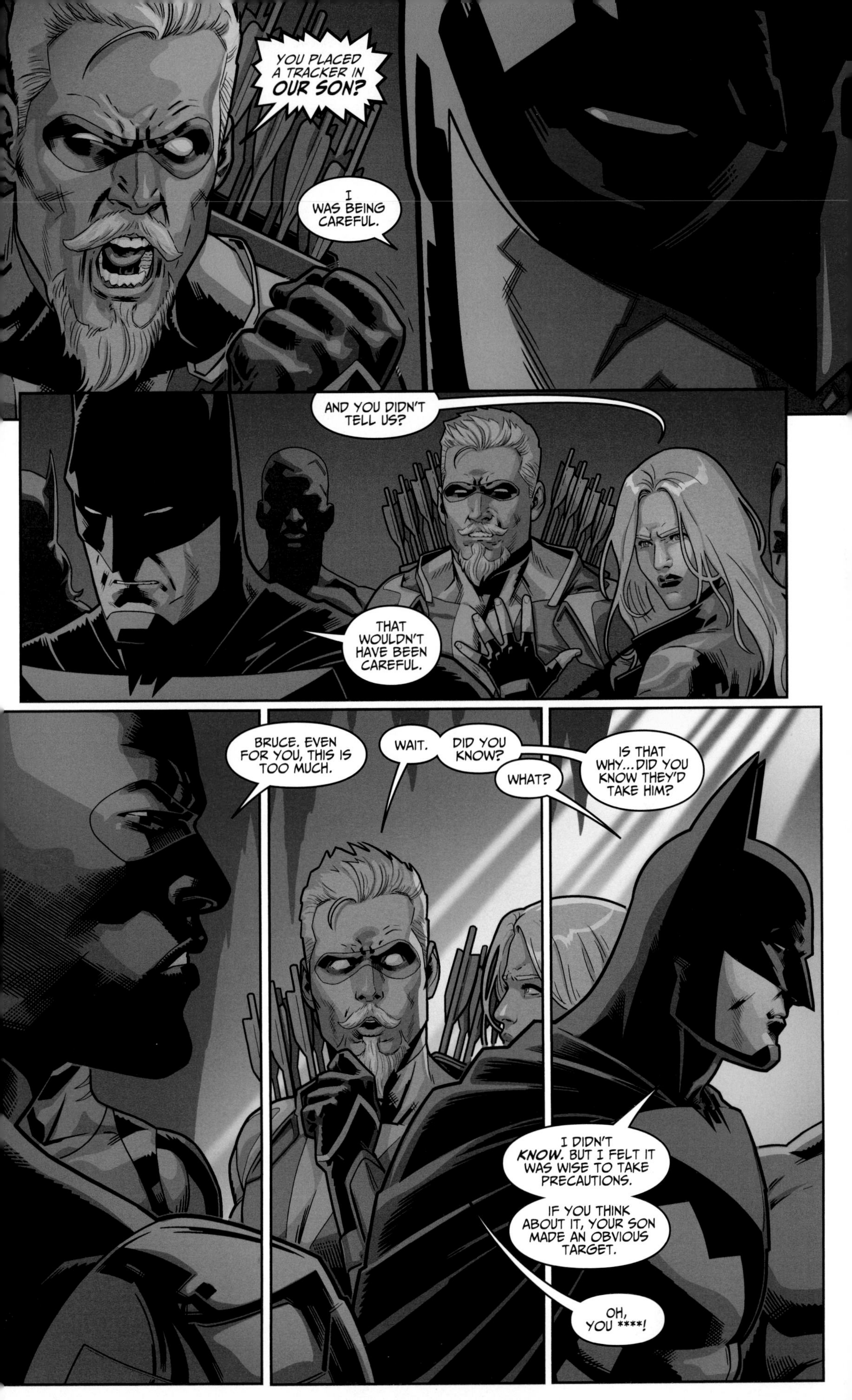
YOU PLACED A TRACKER IN OUR SON?
I WAS BEING CAREFUL.
AND YOU DIDN'T TELL US?
THAT WOULDN'T HAVE BEEN CAREFUL.
BRUCE. EVEN FOR YOU, THIS IS TOO MUCH.
WAIT.
DID YOU KNOW?
WHAT?
IS THAT WHY...DID YOU KNOW THEY'D TAKE HIM?
I DIDN'T KNOW. BUT I FELT IT WAS WISE TO TAKE PRECAUTIONS.
IF YOU THINK ABOUT IT, YOUR SON MADE AN OBVIOUS TARGET.
OH, YOU ****!

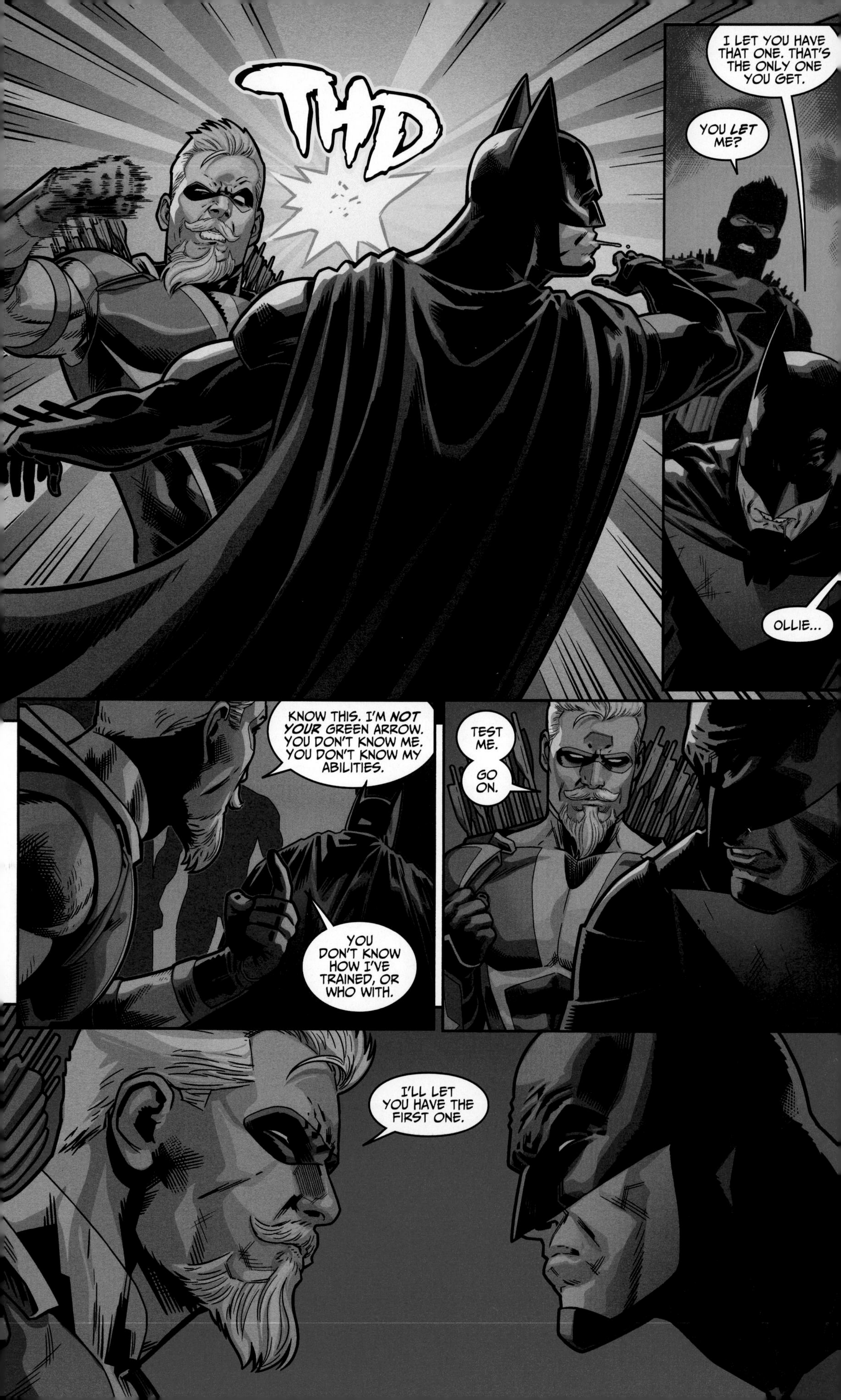
THD
I LET YOU HAVE THAT ONE. THAT'S THE ONLY ONE YOU GET.
YOU LET ME?
OLLIE...
KNOW THIS. I'M NOT YOUR GREEN ARROW. YOU DON'T KNOW ME. YOU DON'T KNOW MY ABILITIES.
YOU DON'T KNOW HOW I'VE TRAINED, OR WHO WITH.
TEST ME.
GO ON.
I'LL LET YOU HAVE THE FIRST ONE.

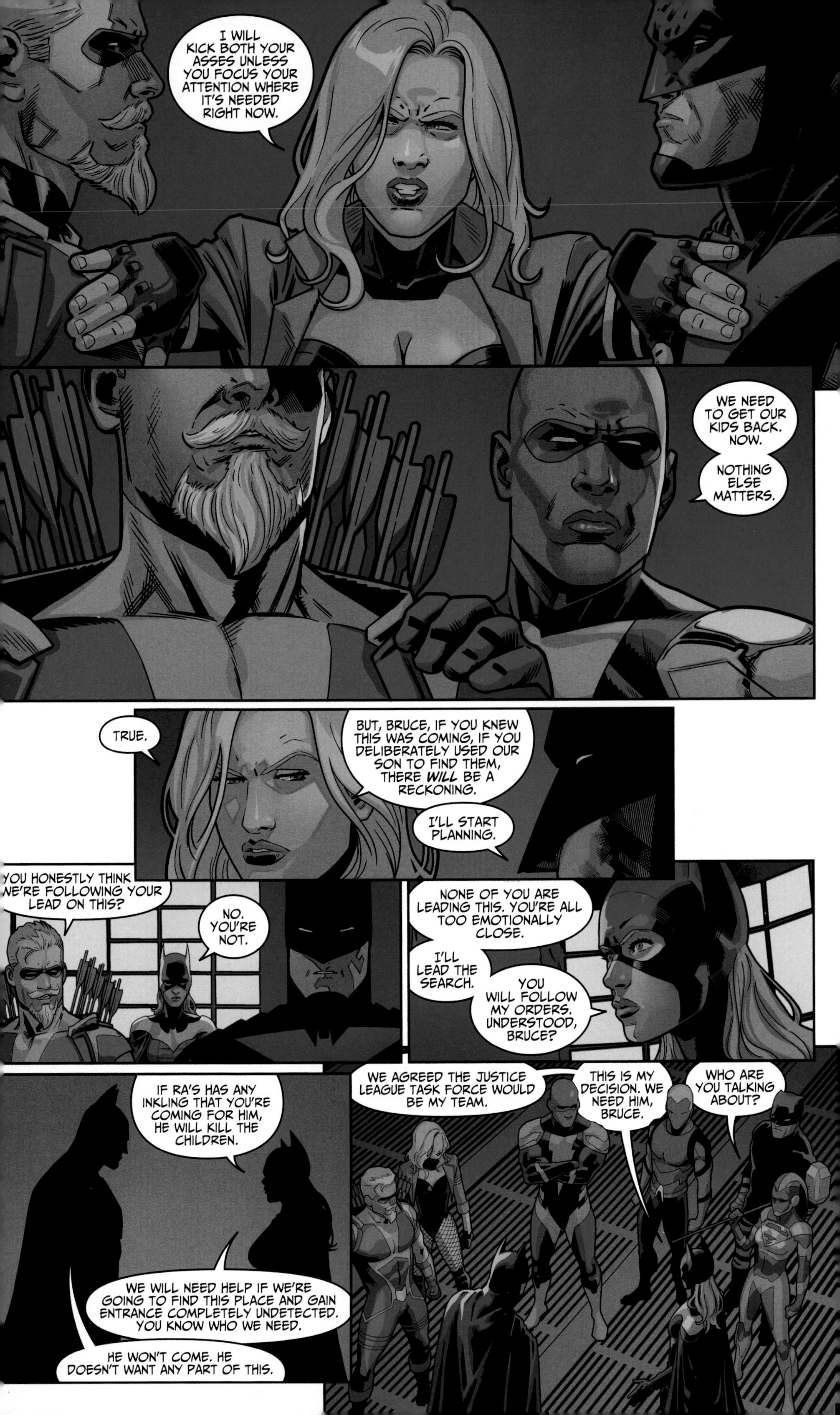
I WILL KICK BOTH YOUR ASSES UNLESS YOU FOCUS YOUR ATTENTION WHERE IT'S NEEDED RIGHT NOW.
WE NEED TO GET OUR KIDS BACK. NOW.
NOTHING ELSE MATTERS.
TRUE.
BUT, BRUCE, IF YOU KNEW THIS WAS COMING, IF YOU DELIBERATELY USED OUR SON TO FIND THEM, THERE *WILL* BE A RECKONING.
I'LL START PLANNING.
YOU HONESTLY THINK WE'RE FOLLOWING YOUR LEAD ON THIS?
NO. YOU'RE NOT.
NONE OF YOU ARE LEADING THIS. YOU'RE ALL TOO EMOTIONALLY CLOSE.
I'LL LEAD THE SEARCH.
YOU WILL FOLLOW MY ORDERS. UNDERSTOOD, BRUCE?
IF RA'S HAS ANY INKLING THAT YOU'RE COMING FOR HIM, HE WILL KILL THE CHILDREN.
WE WILL NEED HELP IF WE'RE GOING TO FIND THIS PLACE AND GAIN ENTRANCE COMPLETELY UNDETECTED. YOU KNOW WHO WE NEED.
HE WON'T COME. HE DOESN'T WANT ANY PART OF THIS.
WE AGREED THE JUSTICE LEAGUE TASK FORCE WOULD BE MY TEAM.
THIS IS MY DECISION. WE NEED HIM, BRUCE.
WHO ARE YOU TALKING ABOUT?

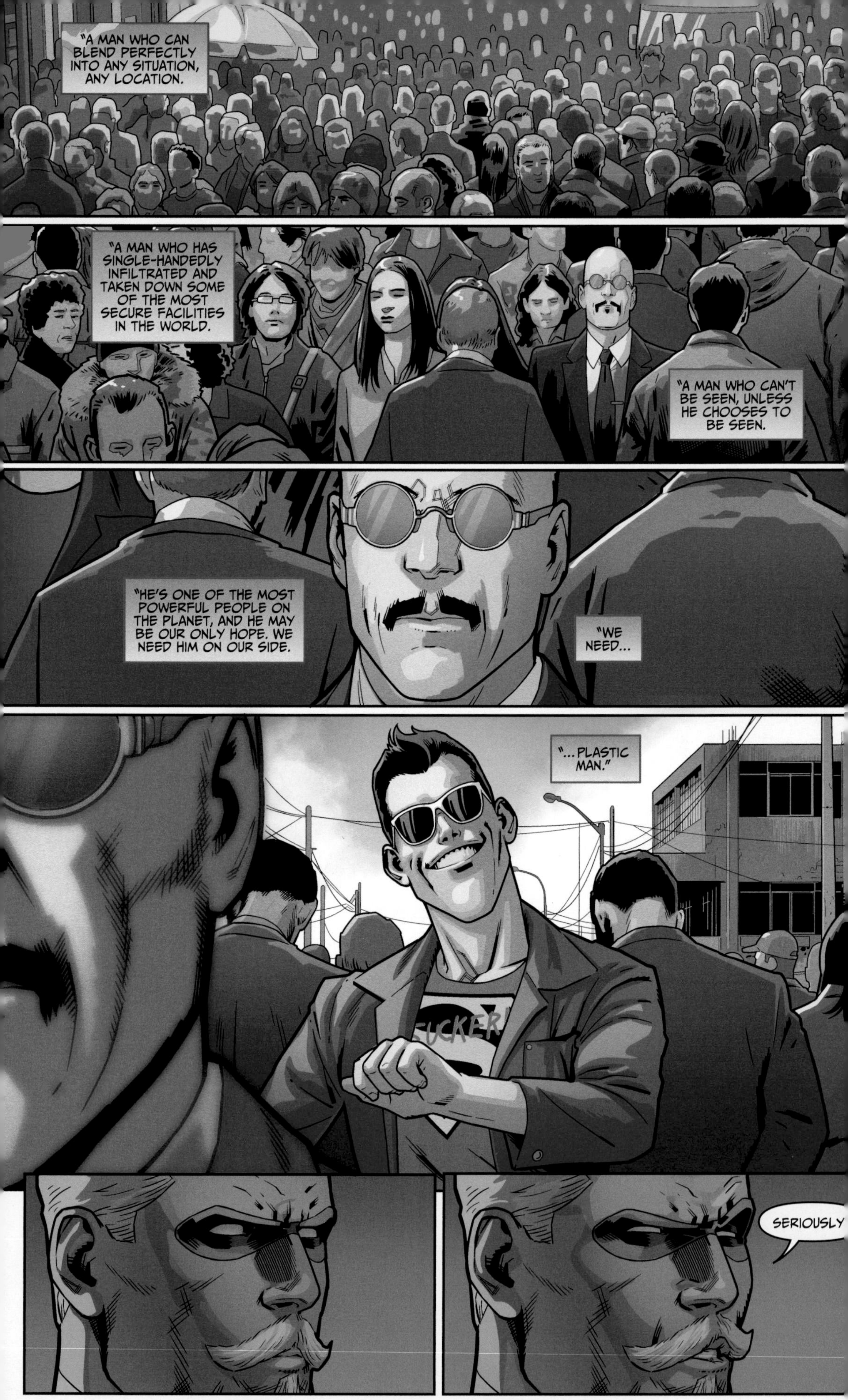
"A MAN WHO CAN BLEND PERFECTLY INTO ANY SITUATION, ANY LOCATION.
"A MAN WHO HAS SINGLE-HANDEDLY INFILTRATED AND TAKEN DOWN SOME OF THE MOST SECURE FACILITIES IN THE WORLD.
"A MAN WHO CAN'T BE SEEN, UNLESS HE CHOOSES TO BE SEEN.
"HE'S ONE OF THE MOST POWERFUL PEOPLE ON THE PLANET, AND HE MAY BE OUR ONLY HOPE. WE NEED HIM ON OUR SIDE.
"WE NEED...
"...PLASTIC MAN."
SERIOUSLY

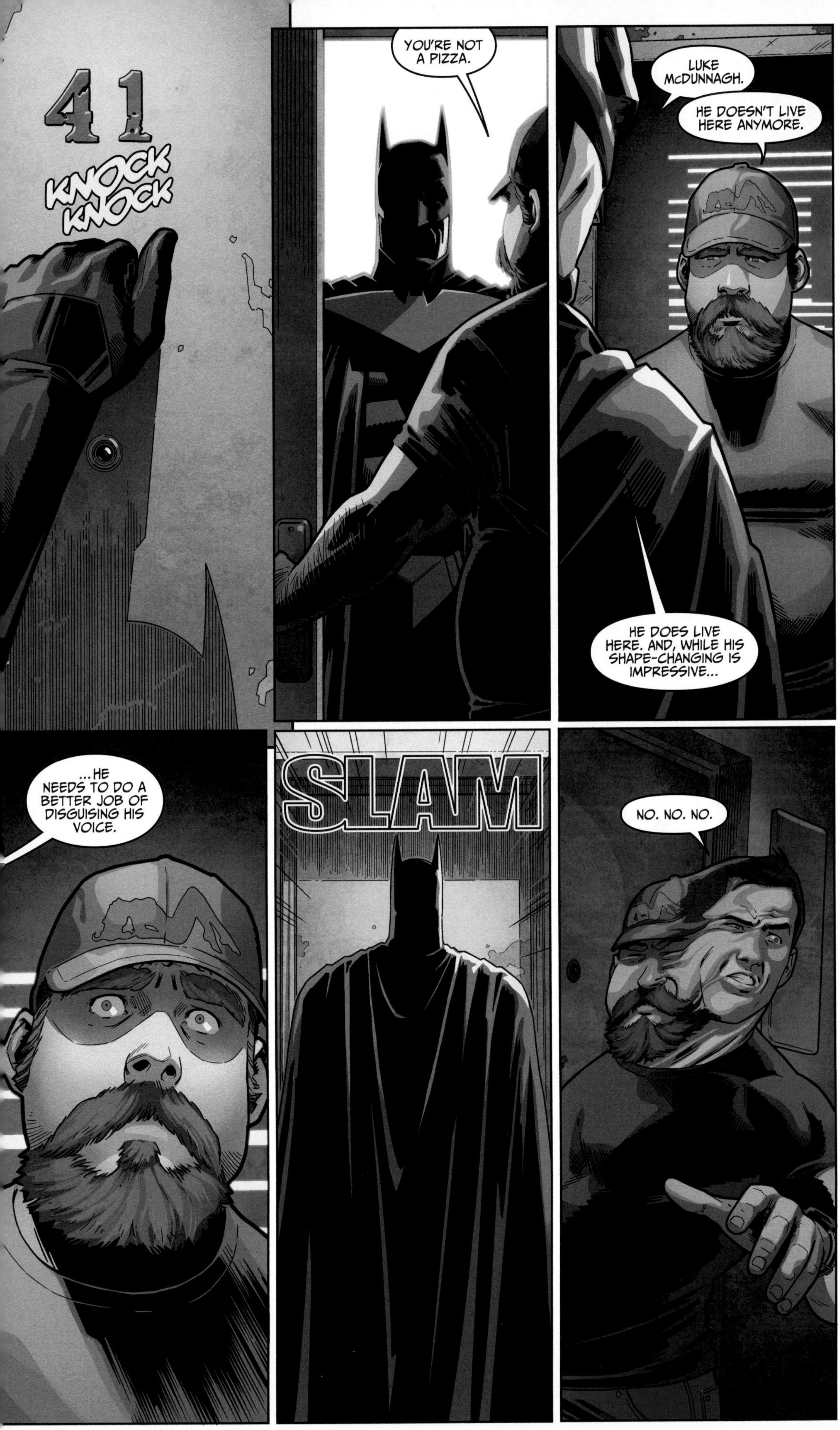
41
KNOCK KNOCK
YOU'RE NOT A PIZZA.
LUKE McDUNNAGH.
HE DOESN'T LIVE HERE ANYMORE.
HE DOES LIVE HERE. AND, WHILE HIS SHAPE-CHANGING IS IMPRESSIVE...
...HE NEEDS TO DO A BETTER JOB OF DISGUISING HIS VOICE.
SLAM
NO. NO. NO.

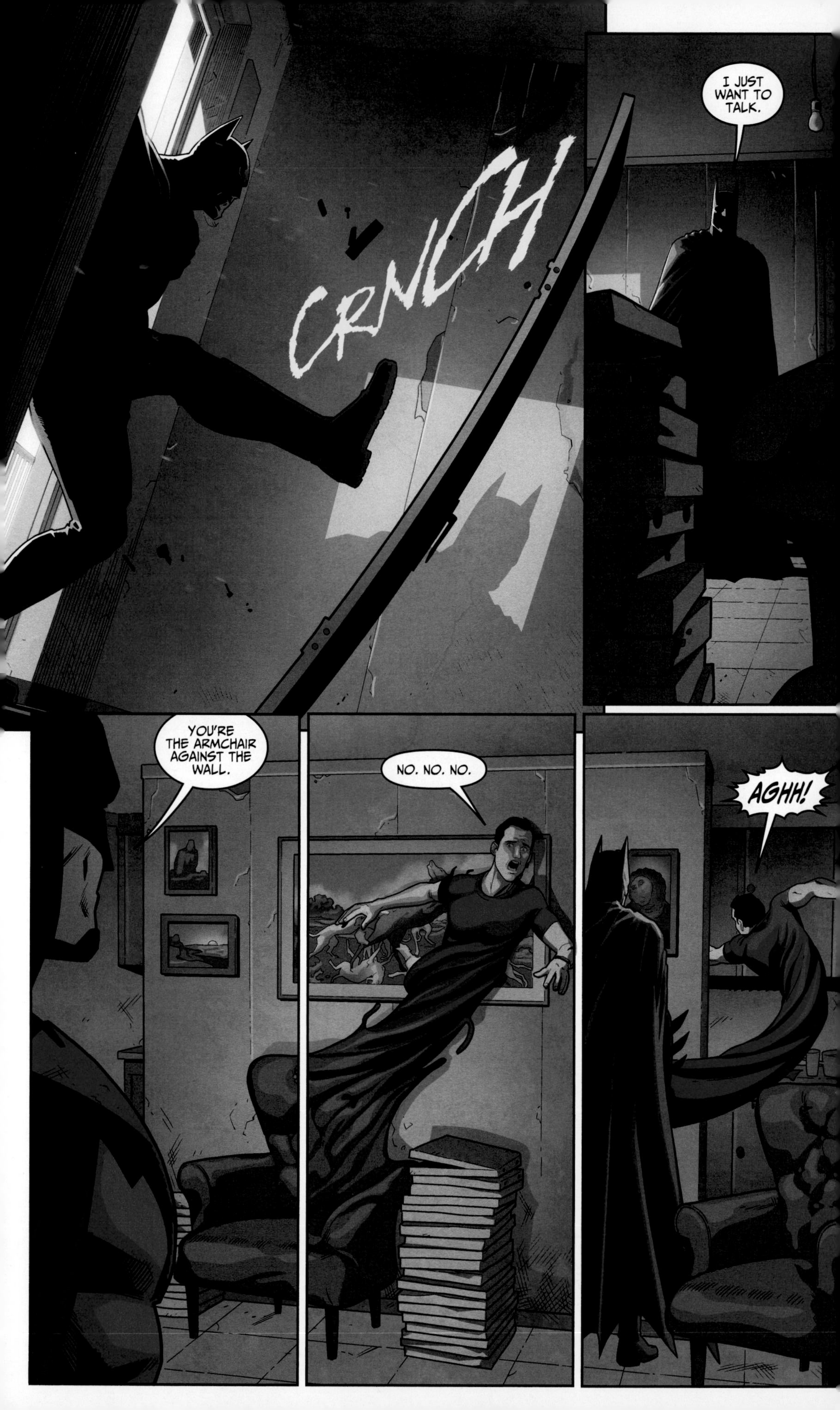
CRNCH
I JUST WANT TO TALK.
YOU'RE THE ARMCHAIR AGAINST THE WALL.
NO. NO. NO.
AGHH!

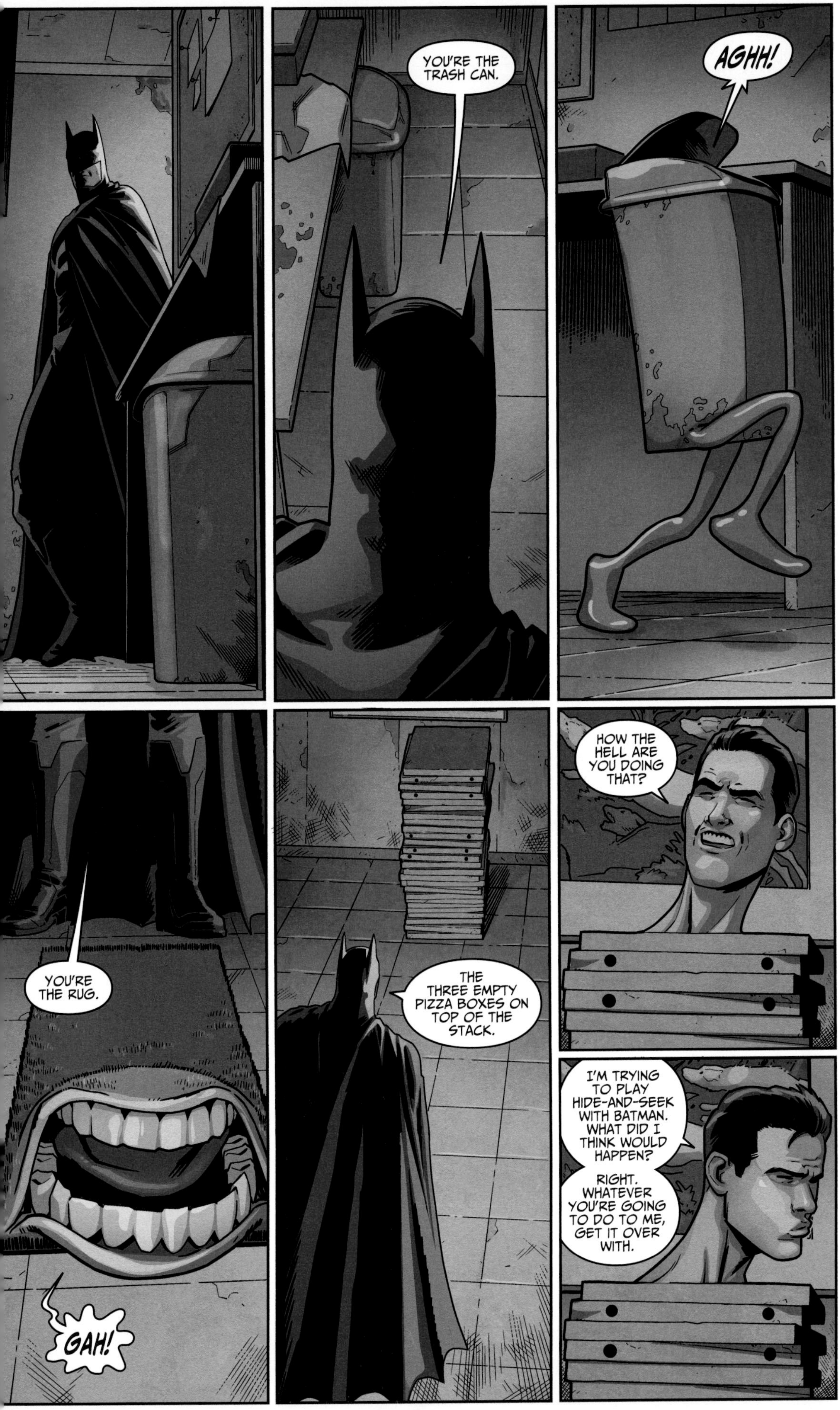
YOU'RE THE TRASH CAN.
AGHH!
YOU'RE THE RUG.
GAH!
THE THREE EMPTY PIZZA BOXES ON TOP OF THE STACK.
HOW THE HELL ARE YOU DOING THAT?
I'M TRYING TO PLAY HIDE-AND-SEEK WITH BATMAN. WHAT DID I THINK WOULD HAPPEN?
RIGHT. WHATEVER YOU'RE GOING TO DO TO ME, GET IT OVER WITH.

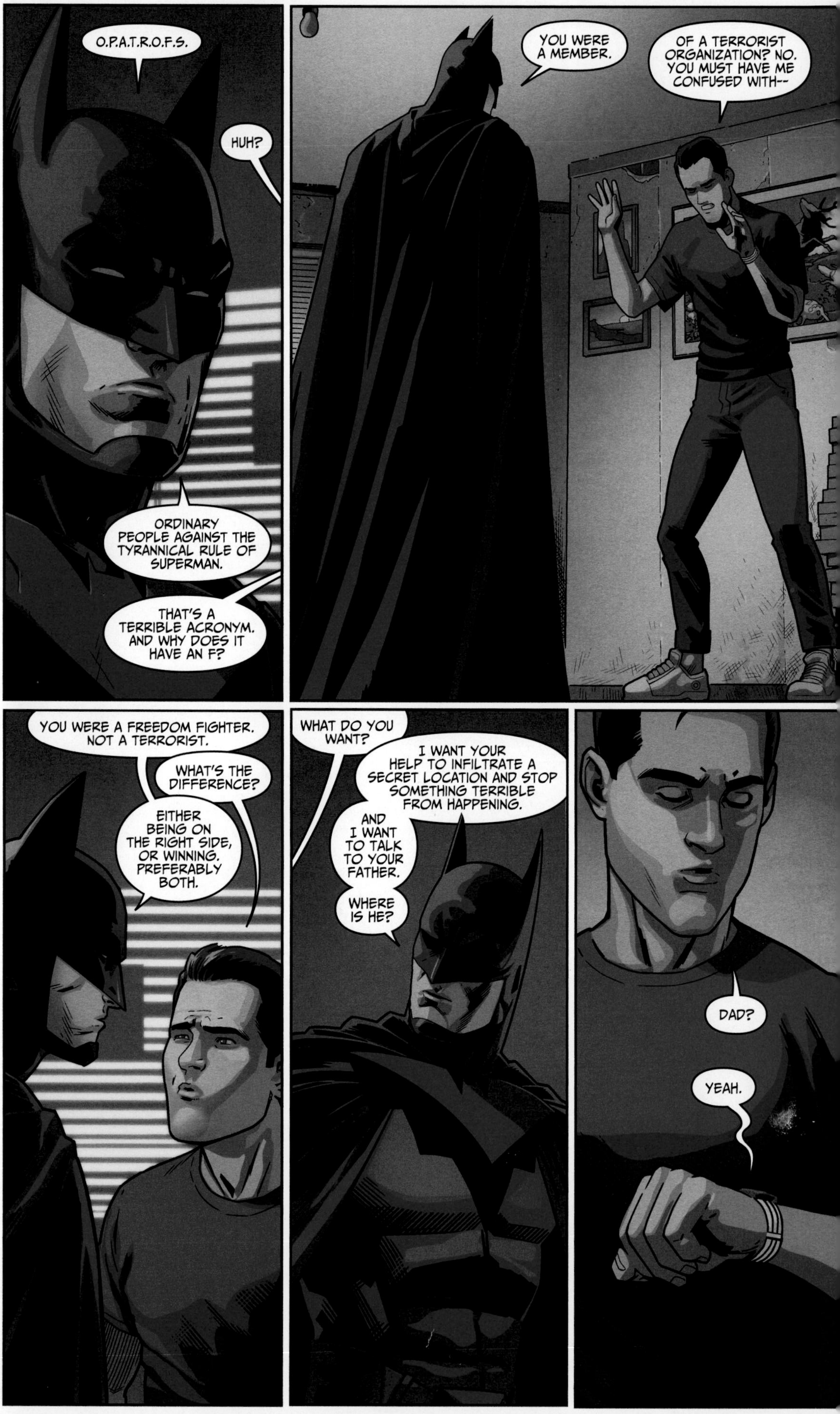
O.P.A.T.R.O.F.S.
HUH?
ORDINARY PEOPLE AGAINST THE TYRANNICAL RULE OF SUPERMAN.
THAT'S A TERRIBLE ACRONYM. AND WHY DOES IT HAVE AN F?
YOU WERE A MEMBER.
OF A TERRORIST ORGANIZATION? NO. YOU MUST HAVE ME CONFUSED WITH--
YOU WERE A FREEDOM FIGHTER. NOT A TERRORIST.
WHAT'S THE DIFFERENCE?
EITHER BEING ON THE RIGHT SIDE, OR WINNING. PREFERABLY BOTH.
WHAT DO YOU WANT?
I WANT YOUR HELP TO INFILTRATE A SECRET LOCATION AND STOP SOMETHING TERRIBLE FROM HAPPENING.
AND I WANT TO TALK TO YOUR FATHER.
WHERE IS HE?
DAD?
YEAH.

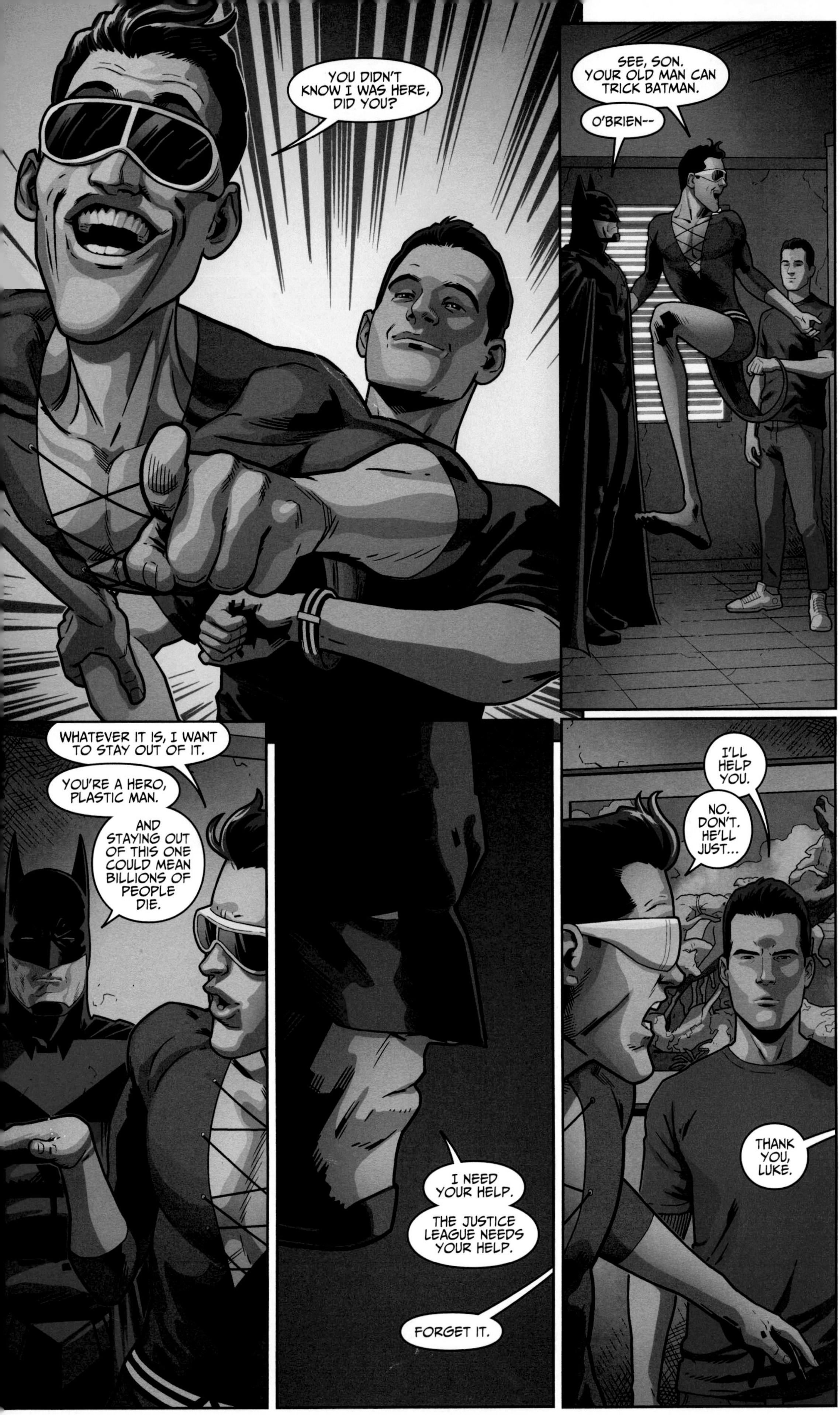
YOU DIDN'T KNOW I WAS HERE, DID YOU?
SEE, SON. YOUR OLD MAN CAN TRICK BATMAN.
O'BRIEN--
WHATEVER IT IS, I WANT TO STAY OUT OF IT.
YOU'RE A HERO, PLASTIC MAN.
AND STAYING OUT OF THIS ONE COULD MEAN BILLIONS OF PEOPLE DIE.
I NEED YOUR HELP.
THE JUSTICE LEAGUE NEEDS YOUR HELP.
FORGET IT.
I'LL HELP YOU.
NO. DON'T. HE'LL JUST...
THANK YOU, LUKE.

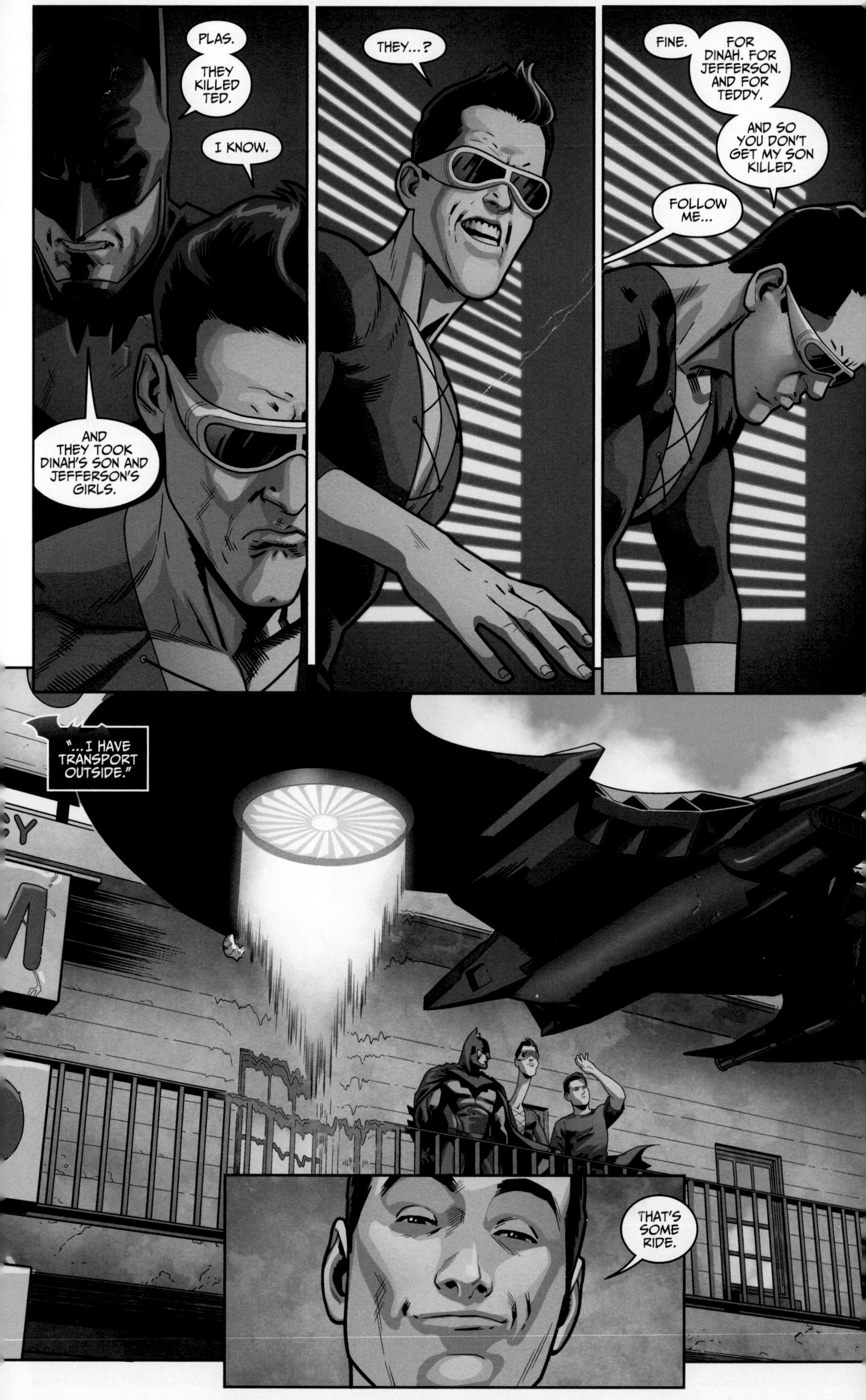
PLAS.
THEY KILLED TED.
I KNOW.
AND THEY TOOK DINAH'S SON AND JEFFERSON'S GIRLS.
THEY...?
FINE.
FOR DINAH. FOR JEFFERSON. AND FOR TEDDY.
AND SO YOU DON'T GET MY SON KILLED.
FOLLOW ME...
"...I HAVE TRANSPORT OUTSIDE."
THAT'S SOME RIDE.

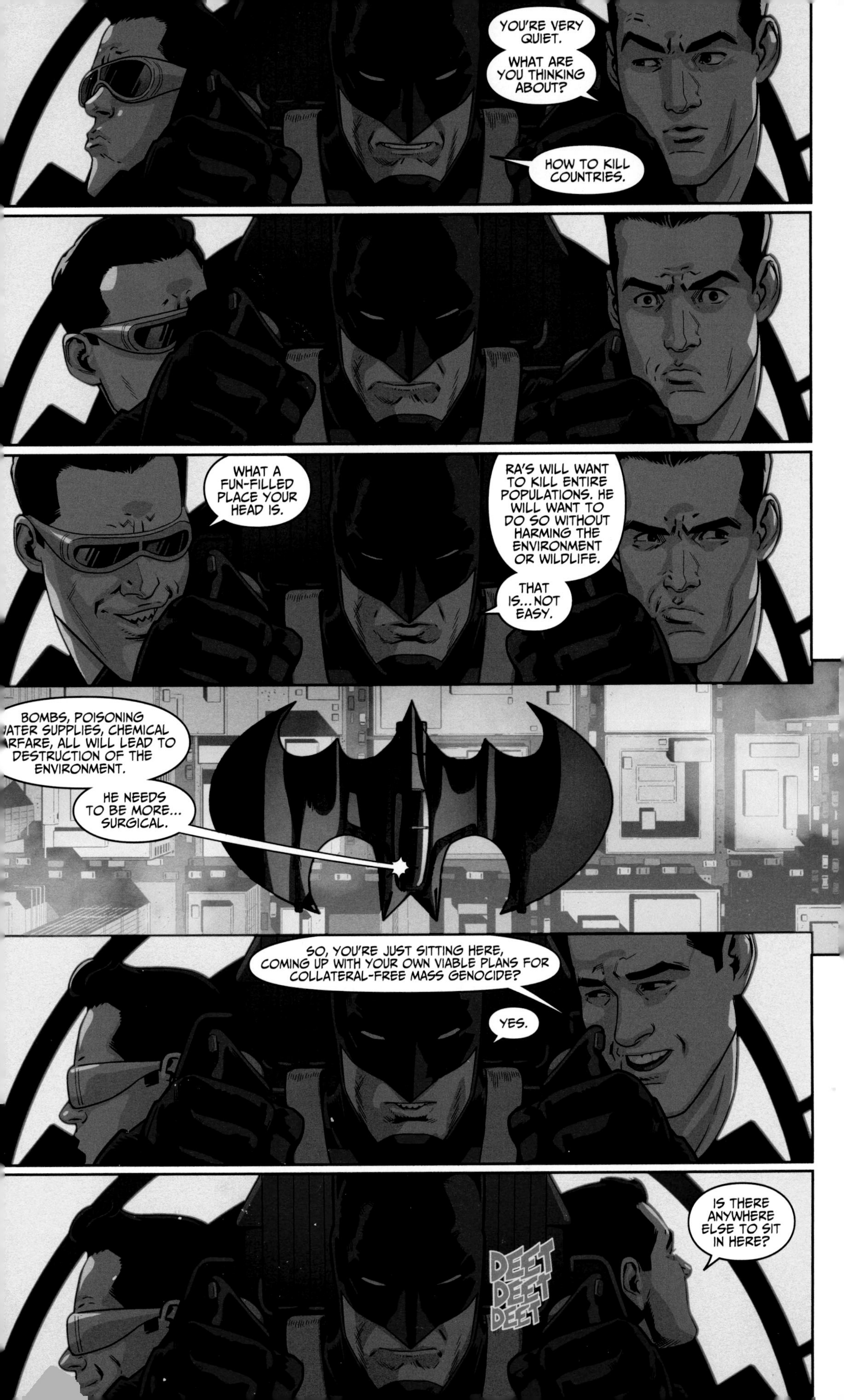
YOU'RE VERY QUIET.
WHAT ARE YOU THINKING ABOUT?
HOW TO KILL COUNTRIES.
WHAT A FUN-FILLED PLACE YOUR HEAD IS.
RA'S WILL WANT TO KILL ENTIRE POPULATIONS. HE WILL WANT TO DO SO WITHOUT HARMING THE ENVIRONMENT OR WILDLIFE.
THAT IS...NOT EASY.
BOMBS, POISONING WATER SUPPLIES, CHEMICAL WARFARE, ALL WILL LEAD TO DESTRUCTION OF THE ENVIRONMENT.
HE NEEDS TO BE MORE... SURGICAL.
SO, YOU'RE JUST SITTING HERE, COMING UP WITH YOUR OWN VIABLE PLANS FOR COLLATERAL-FREE MASS GENOCIDE?
YES.
IS THERE ANYWHERE ELSE TO SIT IN HERE?
DEET DEET DEET

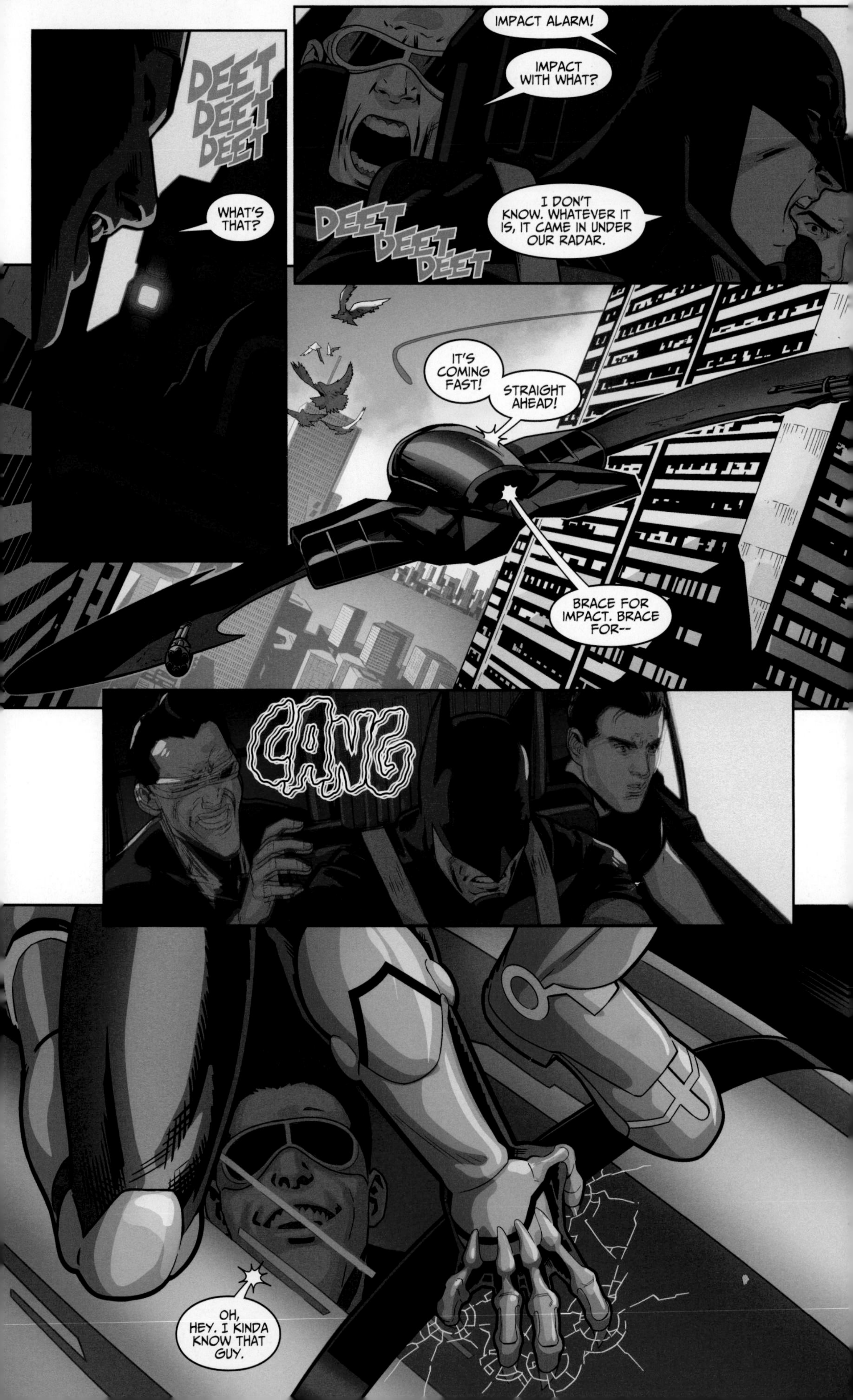
DEET DEET DEET
WHAT'S THAT?
IMPACT ALARM!
IMPACT WITH WHAT?
DEET DEET DEET
I DON'T KNOW. WHATEVER IT IS, IT CAME IN UNDER OUR RADAR.
IT'S COMING FAST!
STRAIGHT AHEAD!
BRACE FOR IMPACT. BRACE FOR--
CANG
OH, HEY. I KINDA KNOW THAT GUY.

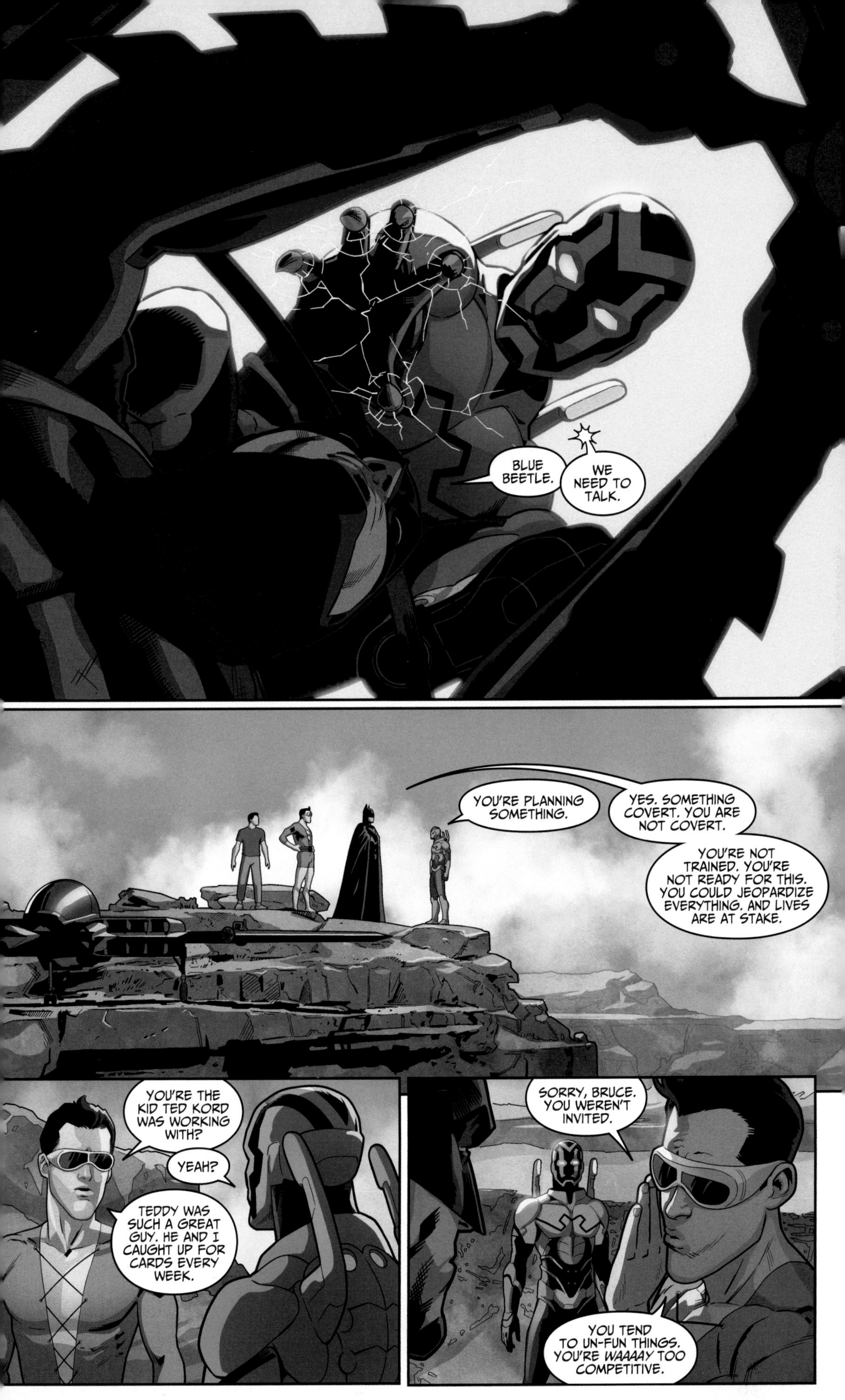

BLUE BEETLE.
WE NEED TO TALK.
YOU'RE PLANNING SOMETHING.
YES. SOMETHING COVERT. YOU ARE NOT COVERT.
YOU'RE NOT TRAINED. YOU'RE NOT READY FOR THIS. YOU COULD JEOPARDIZE EVERYTHING. AND LIVES ARE AT STAKE.
YOU'RE THE KID TED KORD WAS WORKING WITH?
YEAH?
TEDDY WAS SUCH A GREAT GUY. HE AND I CAUGHT UP FOR CARDS EVERY WEEK.
SORRY, BRUCE. YOU WEREN'T INVITED.
YOU TEND TO UN-FUN THINGS. YOU'RE *WAAAAY* TOO COMPETITIVE.

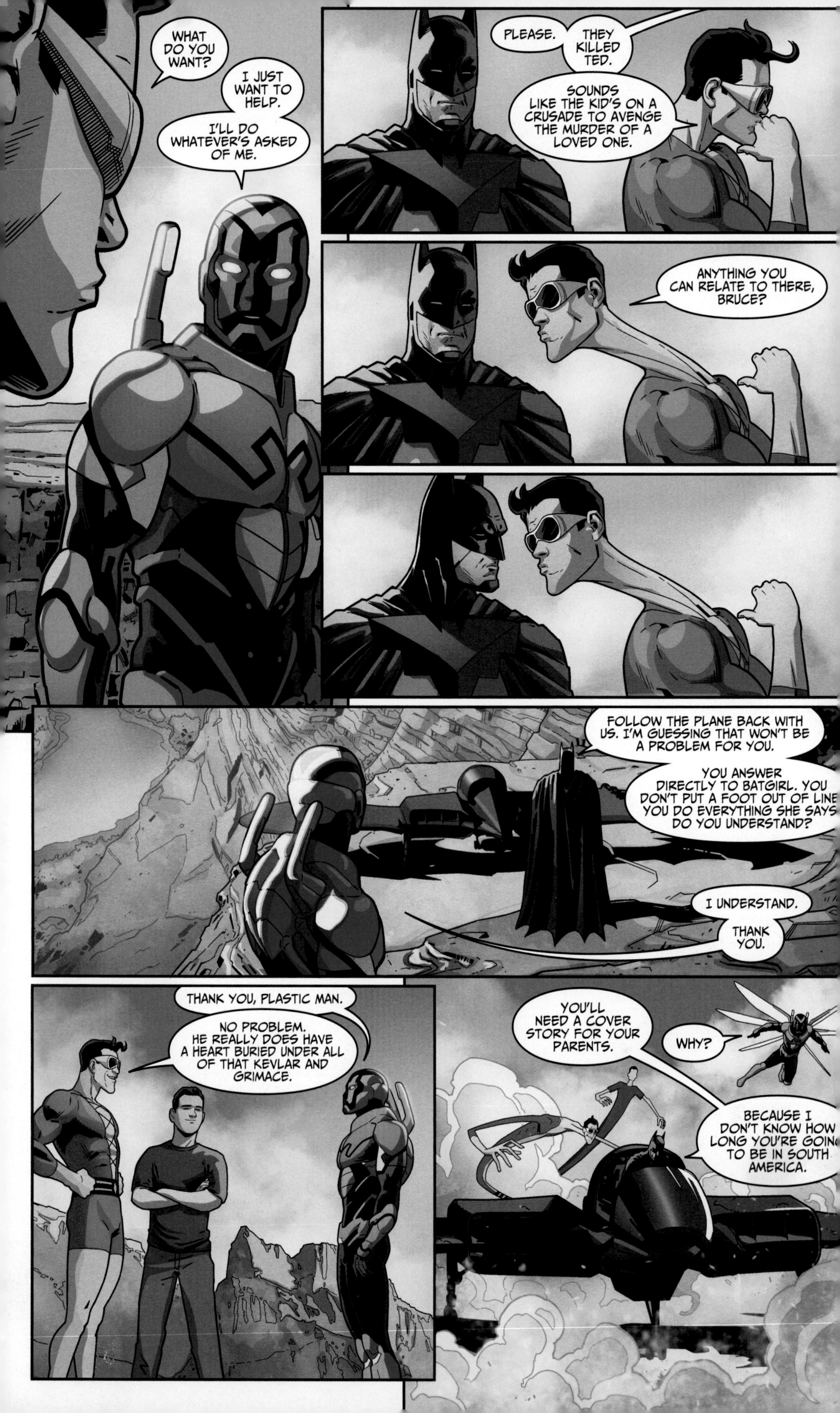
WHAT DO YOU WANT?
I JUST WANT TO HELP.
I'LL DO WHATEVER'S ASKED OF ME.
PLEASE.
THEY KILLED TED.
SOUNDS LIKE THE KID'S ON A CRUSADE TO AVENGE THE MURDER OF A LOVED ONE.
ANYTHING YOU CAN RELATE TO THERE, BRUCE?
FOLLOW THE PLANE BACK WITH US. I'M GUESSING THAT WON'T BE A PROBLEM FOR YOU.
YOU ANSWER DIRECTLY TO BATGIRL. YOU DON'T PUT A FOOT OUT OF LINE. YOU DO EVERYTHING SHE SAYS. DO YOU UNDERSTAND?
I UNDERSTAND.
THANK YOU.
THANK YOU, PLASTIC MAN.
NO PROBLEM. HE REALLY DOES HAVE A HEART BURIED UNDER ALL OF THAT KEVLAR AND GRIMACE.
YOU'LL NEED A COVER STORY FOR YOUR PARENTS.
WHY?
BECAUSE I DON'T KNOW HOW LONG YOU'RE GOING TO BE IN SOUTH AMERICA.

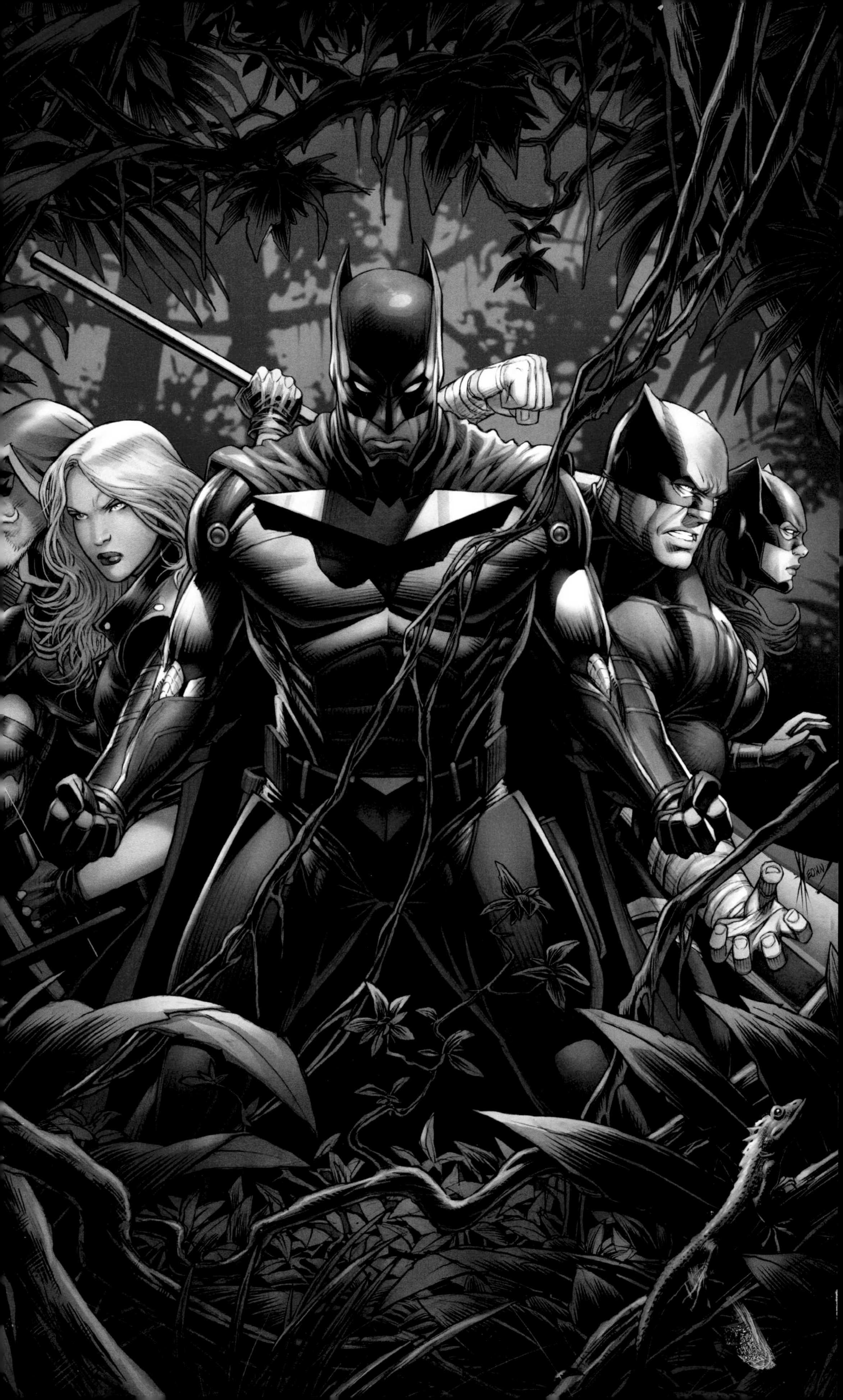

"Extinction"

Tom Taylor Writer **Daniel Sampere** Penciller **Juan Albarran** Inker **Rex Lokus** Colorist
Wes Abbott Letterer Cover art by **Dale Keown** and **Jason Keith**

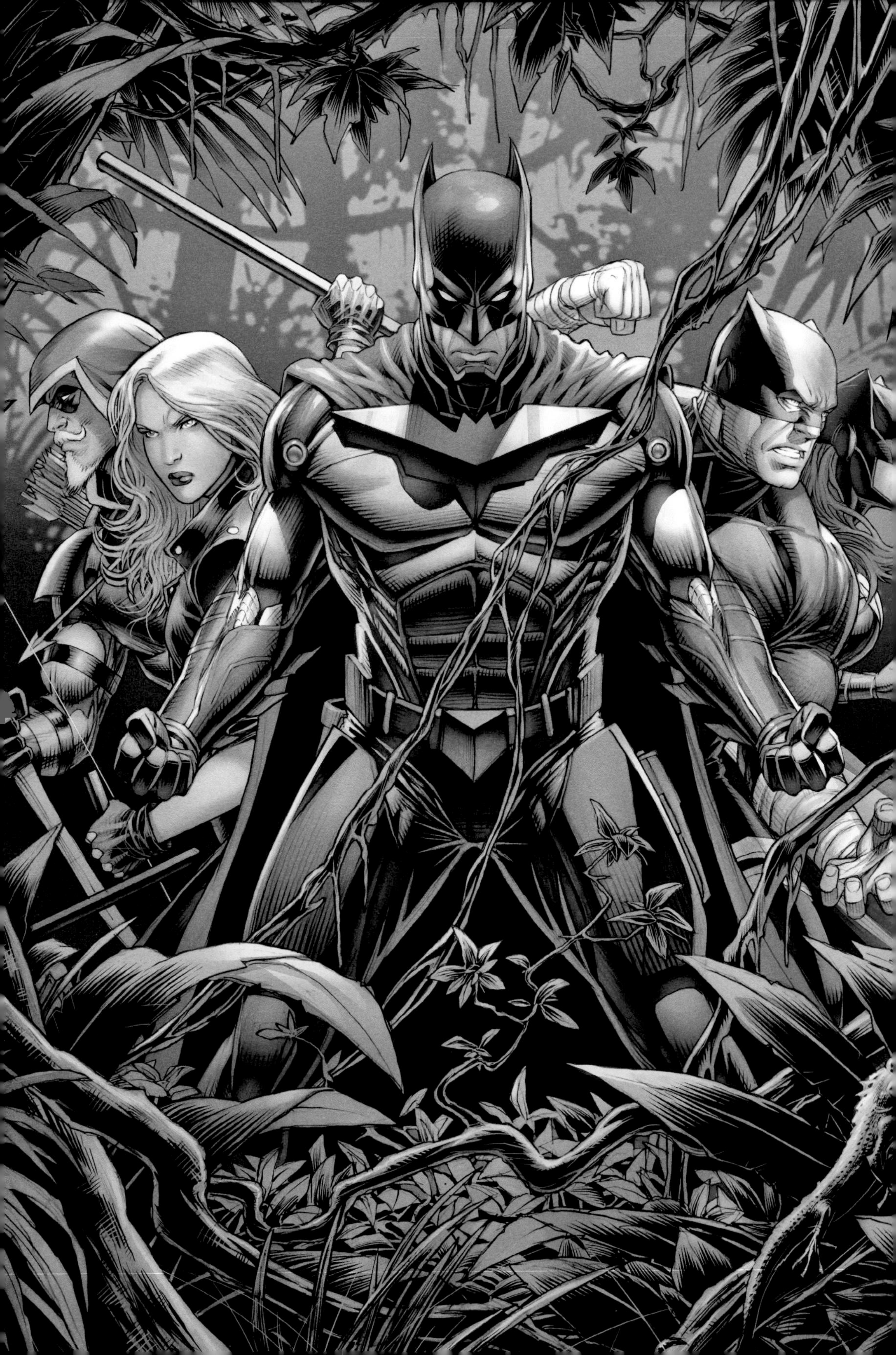

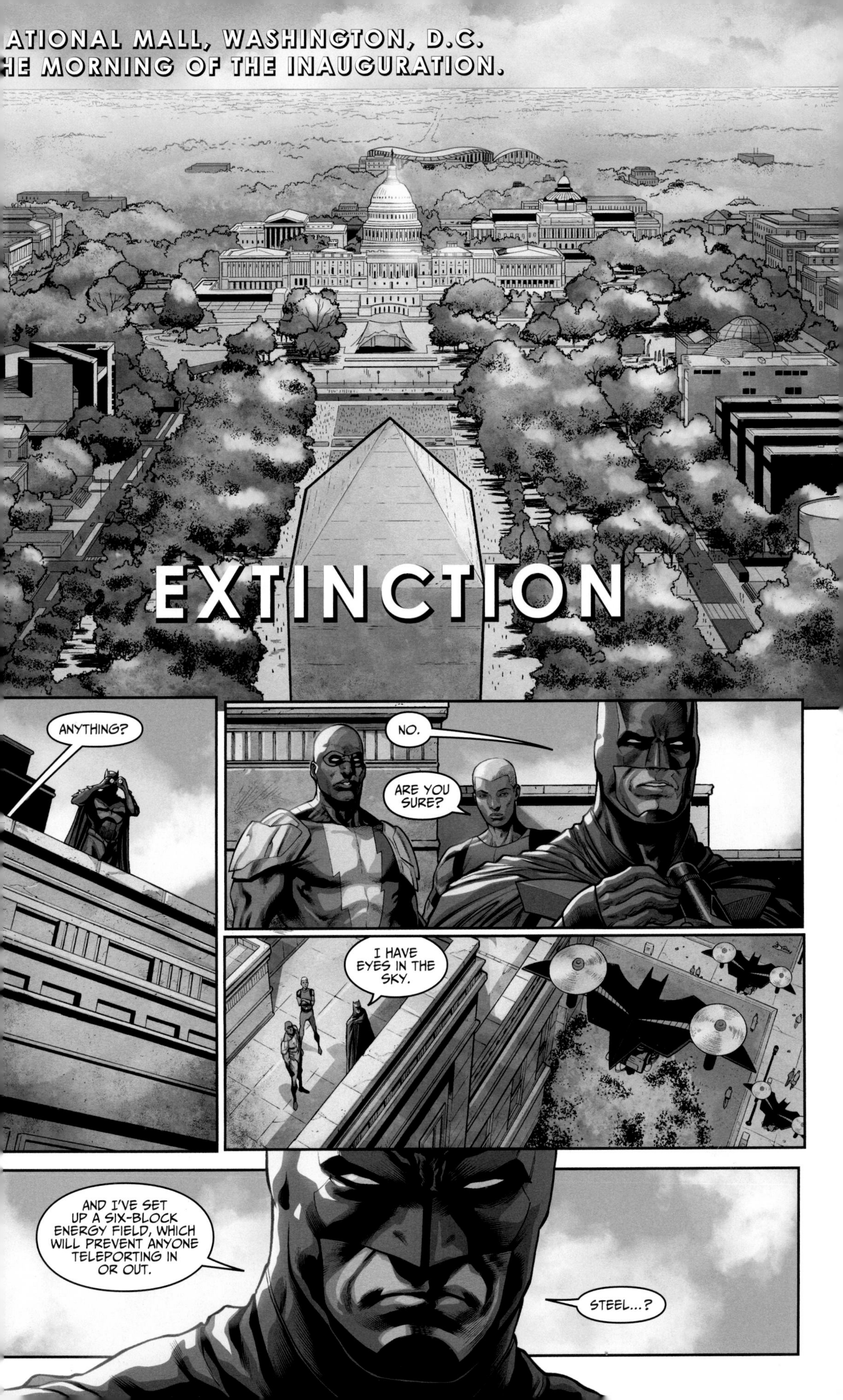
ATIONAL MALL, WASHINGTON, D.C.
HE MORNING OF THE INAUGURATION.
EXTINCTION
ANYTHING?
NO.
ARE YOU SURE?
I HAVE EYES IN THE SKY.
AND I'VE SET UP A SIX-BLOCK ENERGY FIELD, WHICH WILL PREVENT ANYONE TELEPORTING IN OR OUT.
STEEL...?

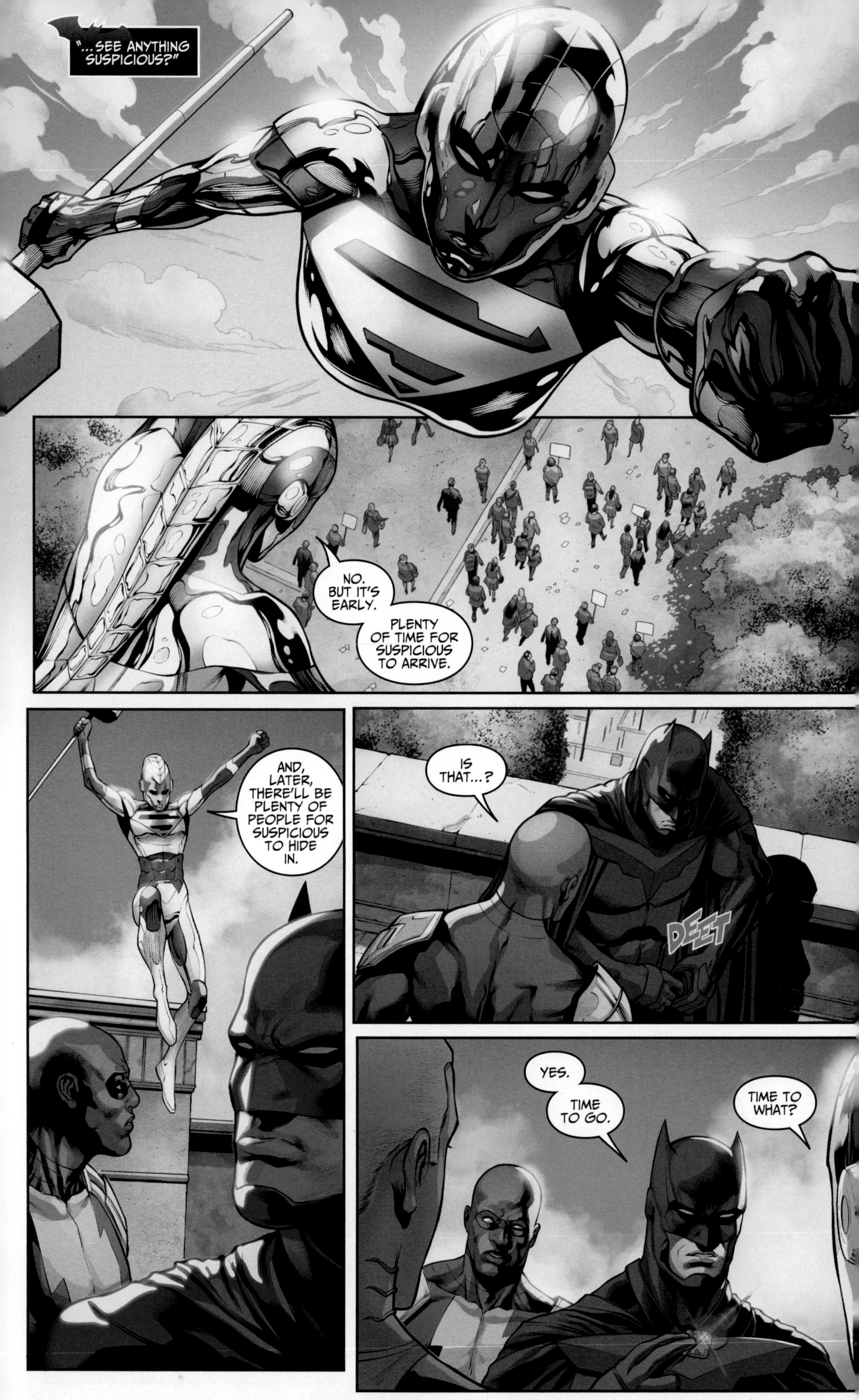
"...SEE ANYTHING SUSPICIOUS?"
NO. BUT IT'S EARLY.
PLENTY OF TIME FOR SUSPICIOUS TO ARRIVE.
AND, LATER, THERE'LL BE PLENTY OF PEOPLE FOR SUSPICIOUS TO HIDE IN.
IS THAT...?
DEET
YES.
TIME TO GO.
TIME TO WHAT?

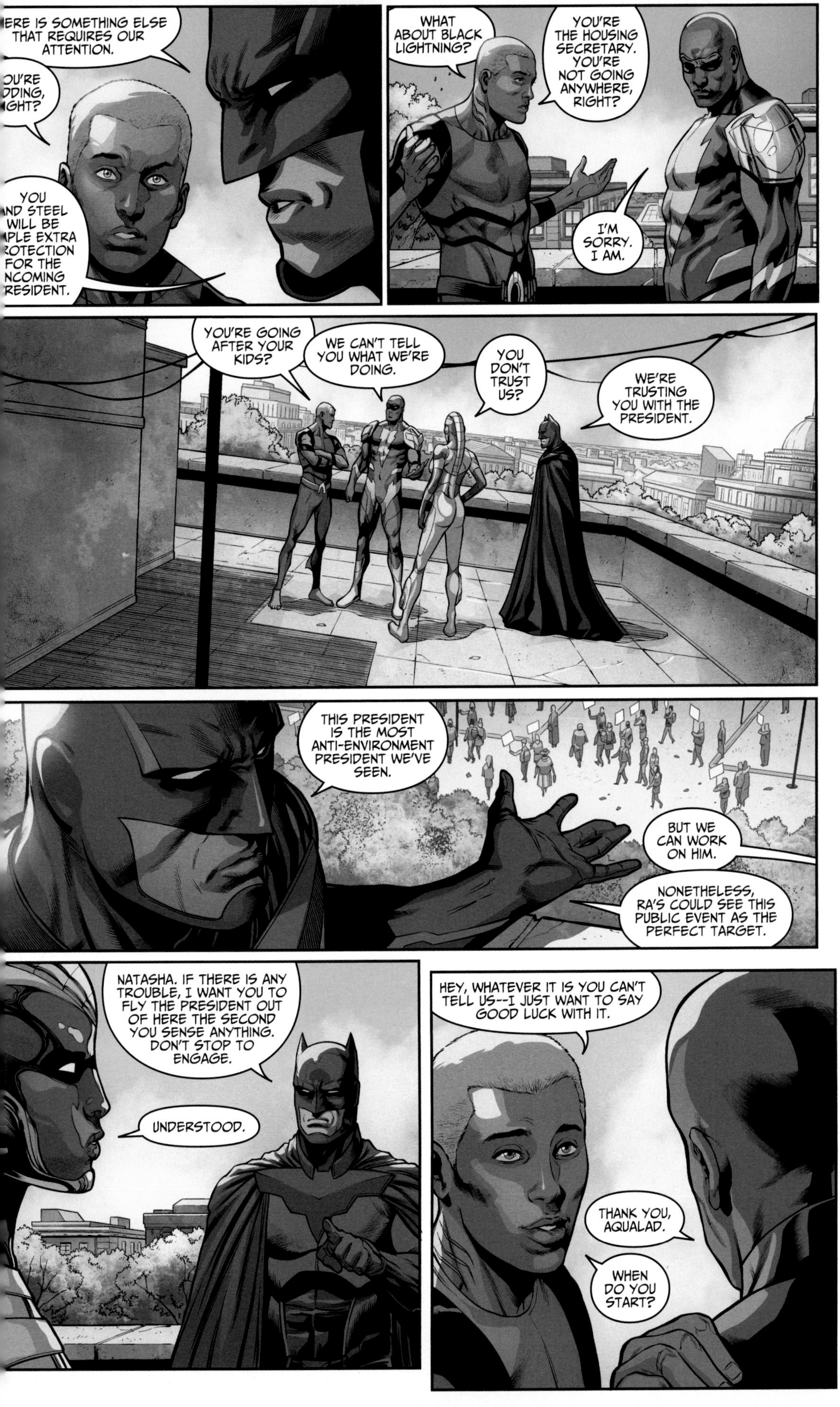
ERE IS SOMETHING ELSE THAT REQUIRES OUR ATTENTION.
OU'RE ODDING, GHT?
YOU ND STEEL WILL BE PLE EXTRA ROTECTION FOR THE NCOMING RESIDENT.
WHAT ABOUT BLACK LIGHTNING?
YOU'RE THE HOUSING SECRETARY. YOU'RE NOT GOING ANYWHERE, RIGHT?
I'M SORRY. I AM.
YOU'RE GOING AFTER YOUR KIDS?
WE CAN'T TELL YOU WHAT WE'RE DOING.
YOU DON'T TRUST US?
WE'RE TRUSTING YOU WITH THE PRESIDENT.
THIS PRESIDENT IS THE MOST ANTI-ENVIRONMENT PRESIDENT WE'VE SEEN.
BUT WE CAN WORK ON HIM.
NONETHELESS, RA'S COULD SEE THIS PUBLIC EVENT AS THE PERFECT TARGET.
NATASHA. IF THERE IS ANY TROUBLE, I WANT YOU TO FLY THE PRESIDENT OUT OF HERE THE SECOND YOU SENSE ANYTHING. DON'T STOP TO ENGAGE.
UNDERSTOOD.
HEY, WHATEVER IT IS YOU CAN'T TELL US--I JUST WANT TO SAY GOOD LUCK WITH IT.
THANK YOU, AQUALAD.
WHEN DO YOU START?

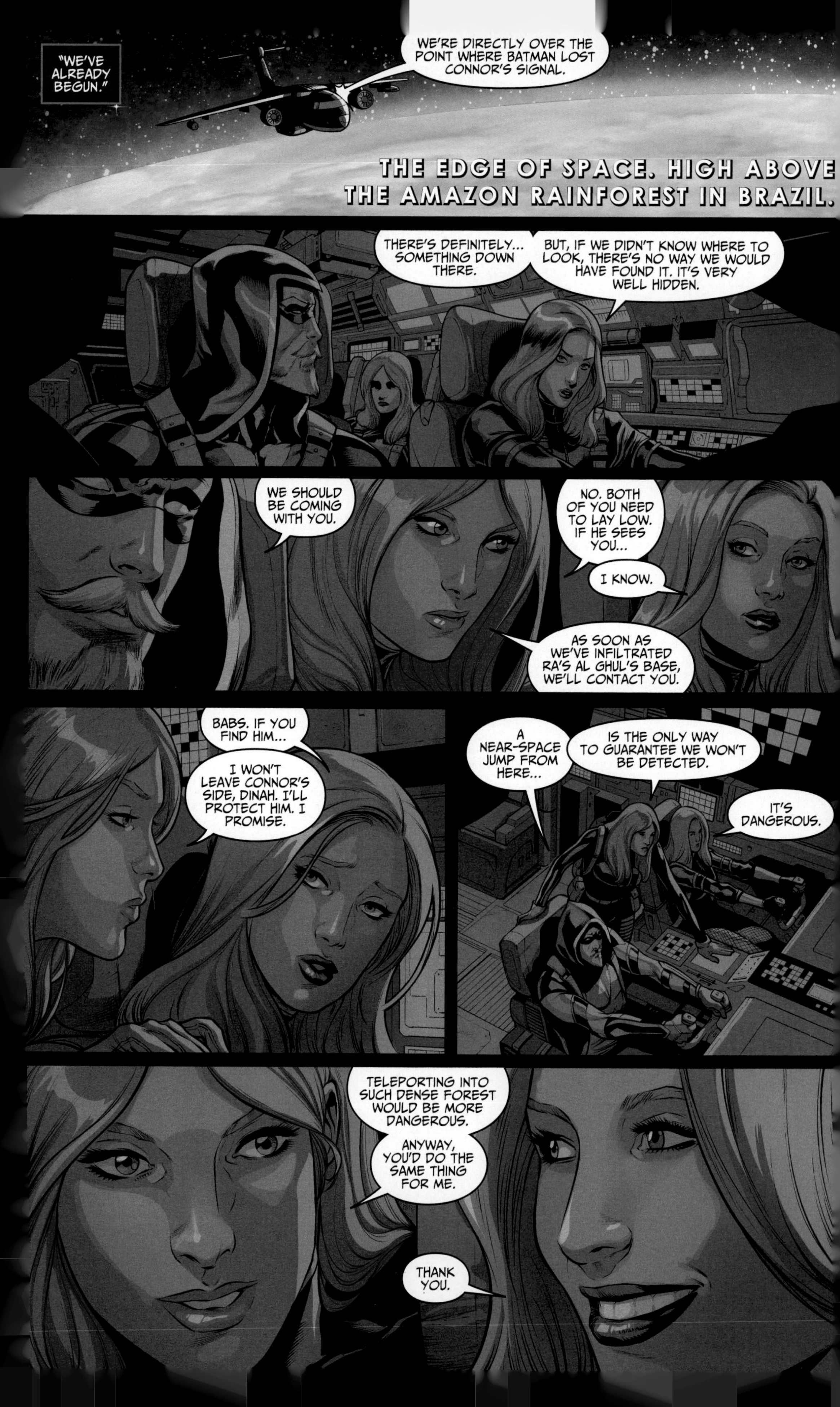
"WE'VE ALREADY BEGUN."
WE'RE DIRECTLY OVER THE POINT WHERE BATMAN LOST CONNOR'S SIGNAL.
THE EDGE OF SPACE. HIGH ABOVE THE AMAZON RAINFOREST IN BRAZIL.
THERE'S DEFINITELY... SOMETHING DOWN THERE.
BUT, IF WE DIDN'T KNOW WHERE TO LOOK, THERE'S NO WAY WE WOULD HAVE FOUND IT. IT'S VERY WELL HIDDEN.
WE SHOULD BE COMING WITH YOU.
NO. BOTH OF YOU NEED TO LAY LOW. IF HE SEES YOU...
I KNOW.
AS SOON AS WE'VE INFILTRATED RA'S AL GHUL'S BASE, WE'LL CONTACT YOU.
BABS. IF YOU FIND HIM...
I WON'T LEAVE CONNOR'S SIDE, DINAH. I'LL PROTECT HIM. I PROMISE.
A NEAR-SPACE JUMP FROM HERE...
IS THE ONLY WAY TO GUARANTEE WE WON'T BE DETECTED.
IT'S DANGEROUS.
TELEPORTING INTO SUCH DENSE FOREST WOULD BE MORE DANGEROUS.
ANYWAY, YOU'D DO THE SAME THING FOR ME.
THANK YOU.

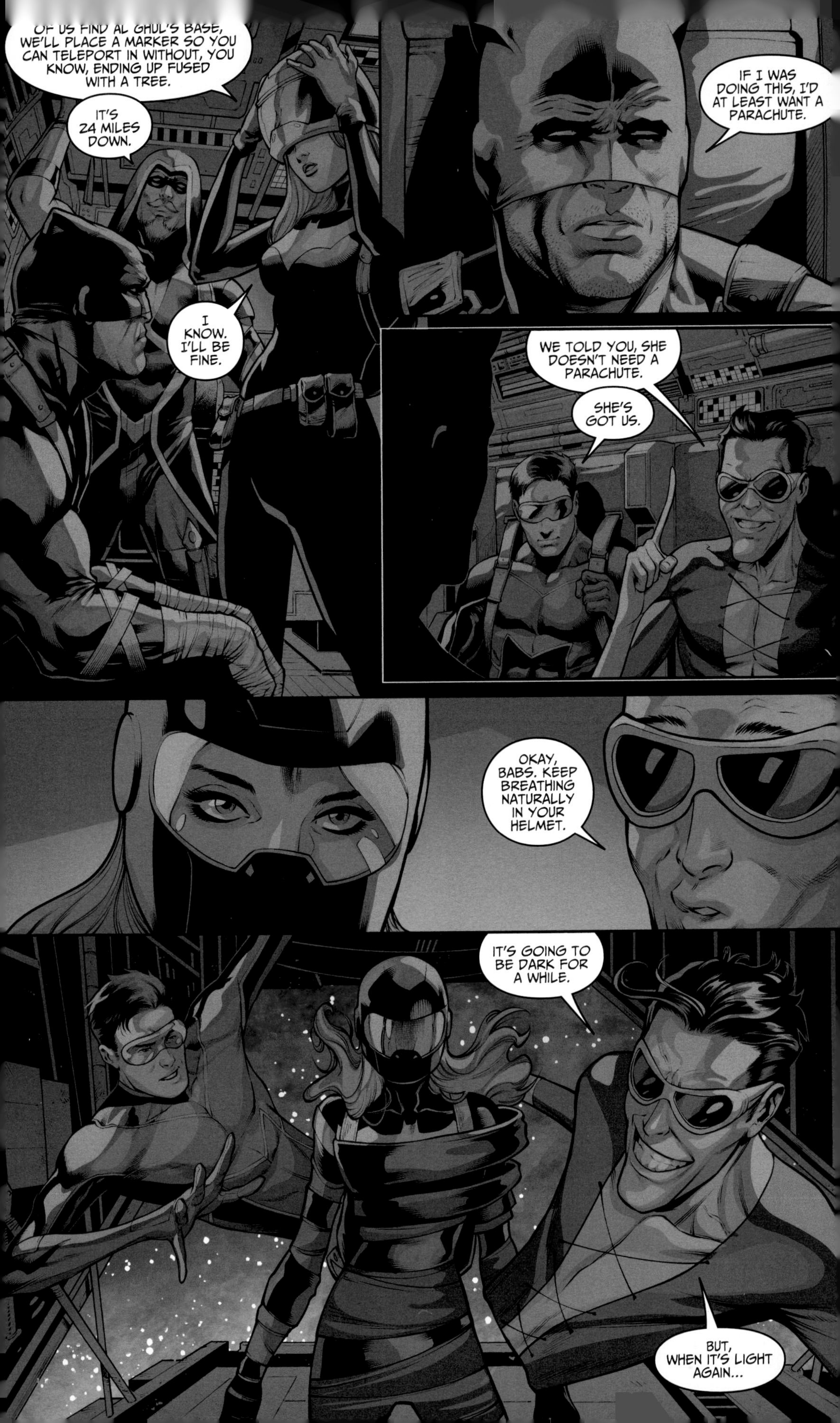
OF US FIND AL GHUL'S BASE, WE'LL PLACE A MARKER SO YOU CAN TELEPORT IN WITHOUT, YOU KNOW, ENDING UP FUSED WITH A TREE.
IT'S 24 MILES DOWN.
IF I WAS DOING THIS, I'D AT LEAST WANT A PARACHUTE.
I KNOW. I'LL BE FINE.
WE TOLD YOU, SHE DOESN'T NEED A PARACHUTE.
SHE'S GOT US.
OKAY, BABS. KEEP BREATHING NATURALLY IN YOUR HELMET.
IT'S GOING TO BE DARK FOR A WHILE.
BUT, WHEN IT'S LIGHT AGAIN...

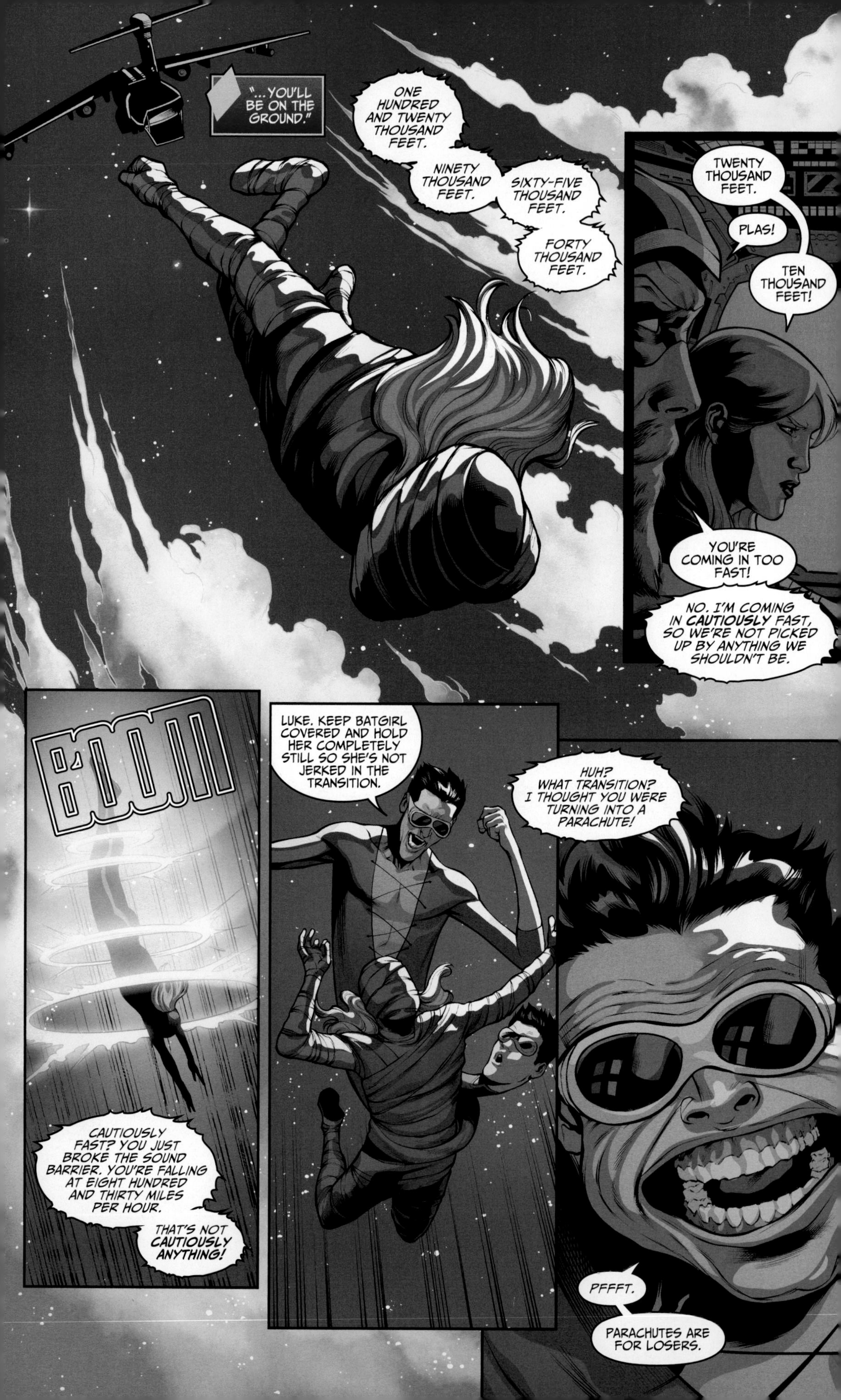
"...YOU'LL BE ON THE GROUND."
ONE HUNDRED AND TWENTY THOUSAND FEET.
NINETY THOUSAND FEET.
SIXTY-FIVE THOUSAND FEET.
FORTY THOUSAND FEET.
TWENTY THOUSAND FEET.
PLAS!
TEN THOUSAND FEET!
YOU'RE COMING IN TOO FAST!
NO. I'M COMING IN **CAUTIOUSLY** FAST, SO WE'RE NOT PICKED UP BY ANYTHING WE SHOULDN'T BE.
BOOM
CAUTIOUSLY FAST? YOU JUST BROKE THE SOUND BARRIER. YOU'RE FALLING AT EIGHT HUNDRED AND THIRTY MILES PER HOUR.
THAT'S NOT **CAUTIOUSLY** ANYTHING!
LUKE. KEEP BATGIRL COVERED AND HOLD HER COMPLETELY STILL SO SHE'S NOT JERKED IN THE TRANSITION.
HUH? WHAT TRANSITION? I THOUGHT YOU WERE TURNING INTO A PARACHUTE!
PFFFT.
PARACHUTES ARE FOR LOSERS.

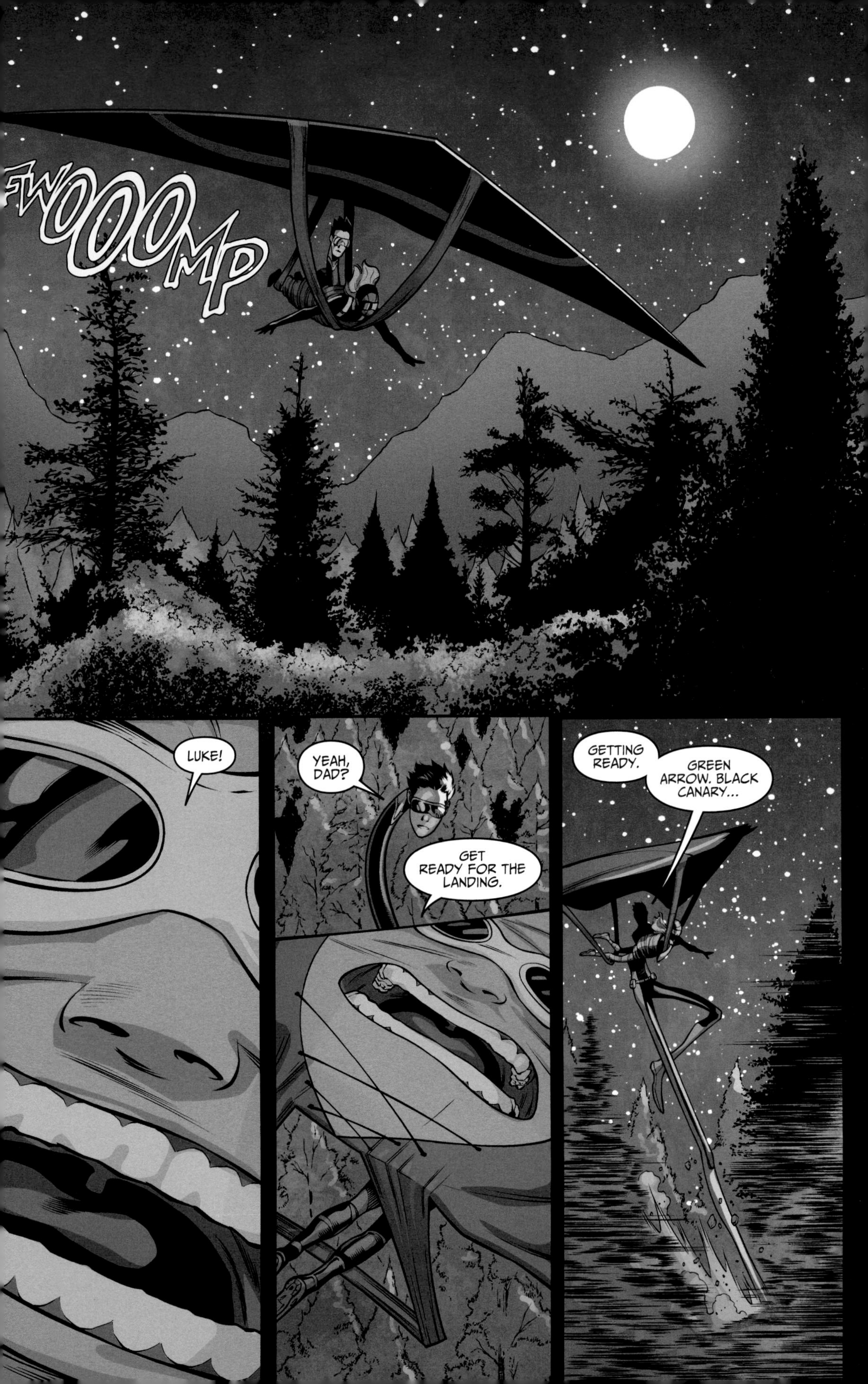

FWOOOMP
LUKE!
YEAH, DAD?
GET READY FOR THE LANDING.
GETTING READY.
GREEN ARROW. BLACK CANARY...

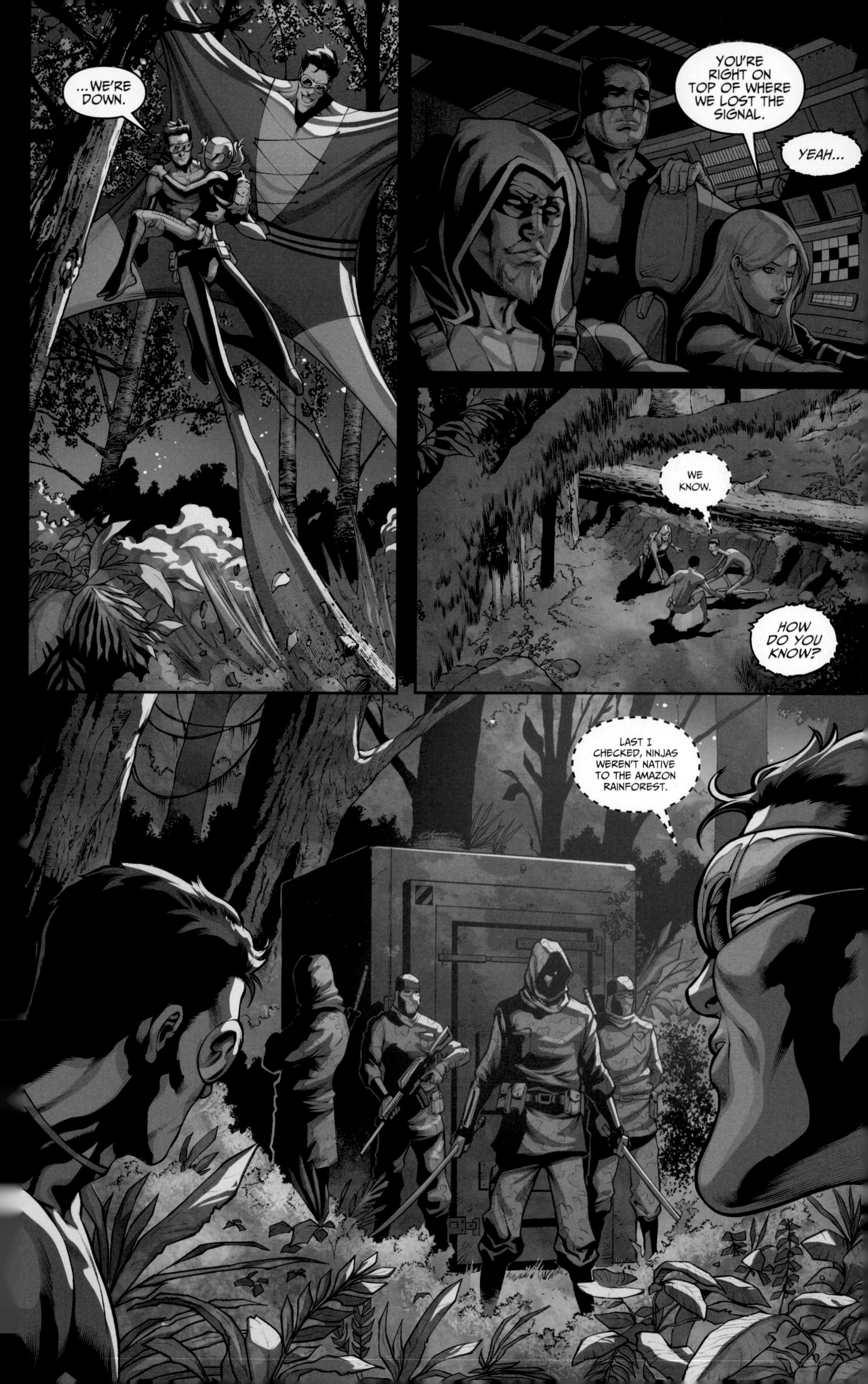
...WE'RE DOWN.
YOU'RE RIGHT ON TOP OF WHERE WE LOST THE SIGNAL.
YEAH...
WE KNOW.
HOW DO YOU KNOW?
LAST I CHECKED, NINJAS WEREN'T NATIVE TO THE AMAZON RAINFOREST.

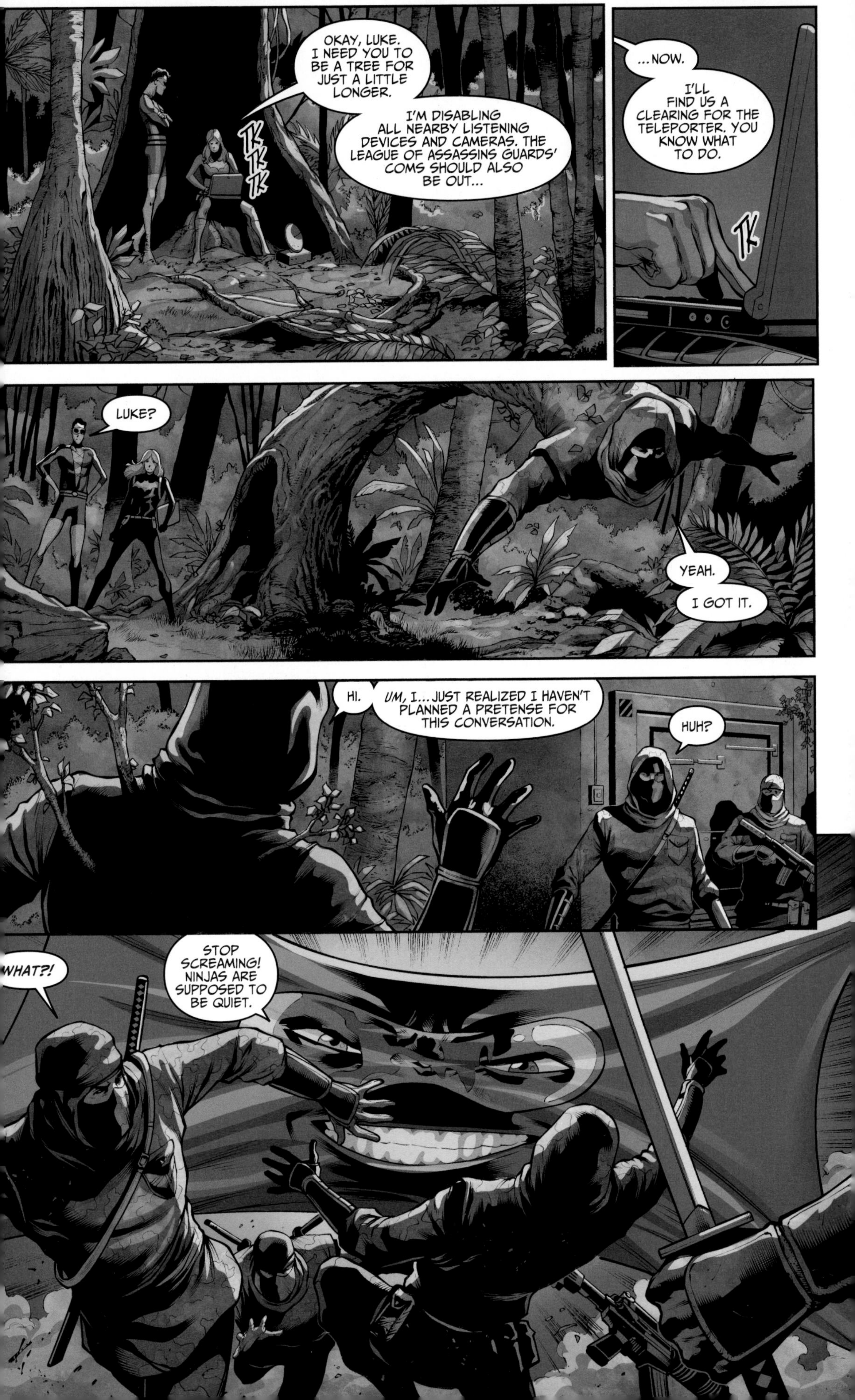
OKAY, LUKE. I NEED YOU TO BE A TREE FOR JUST A LITTLE LONGER.
I'M DISABLING ALL NEARBY LISTENING DEVICES AND CAMERAS. THE LEAGUE OF ASSASSINS GUARDS' COMS SHOULD ALSO BE OUT...
TK TK TK
...NOW.
I'LL FIND US A CLEARING FOR THE TELEPORTER. YOU KNOW WHAT TO DO.
TK
LUKE?
YEAH.
I GOT IT.
HI.
UM, I...JUST REALIZED I HAVEN'T PLANNED A PRETENSE FOR THIS CONVERSATION.
HUH?
WHAT?!
STOP SCREAMING! NINJAS ARE SUPPOSED TO BE QUIET.

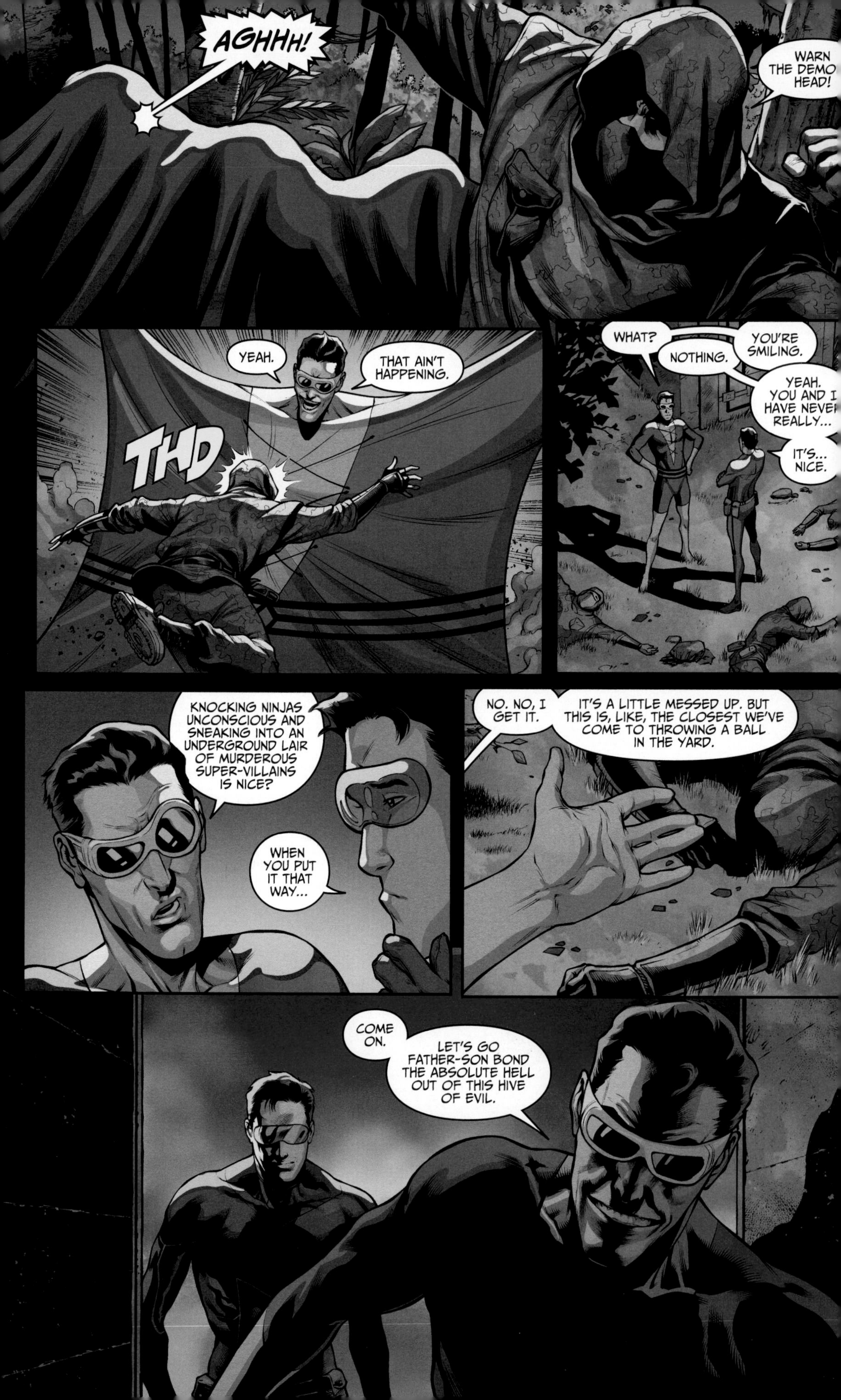
AGHHH!
WARN THE DEMO HEAD!
YEAH.
THAT AIN'T HAPPENING.
THD
WHAT?
YOU'RE SMILING.
NOTHING.
YEAH. YOU AND I HAVE NEVE REALLY...
IT'S... NICE.
KNOCKING NINJAS UNCONSCIOUS AND SNEAKING INTO AN UNDERGROUND LAIR OF MURDEROUS SUPER-VILLAINS IS NICE?
WHEN YOU PUT IT THAT WAY...
NO. NO, I GET IT.
IT'S A LITTLE MESSED UP. BUT THIS IS, LIKE, THE CLOSEST WE'VE COME TO THROWING A BALL IN THE YARD.
COME ON.
LET'S GO FATHER-SON BOND THE ABSOLUTE HELL OUT OF THIS HIVE OF EVIL.

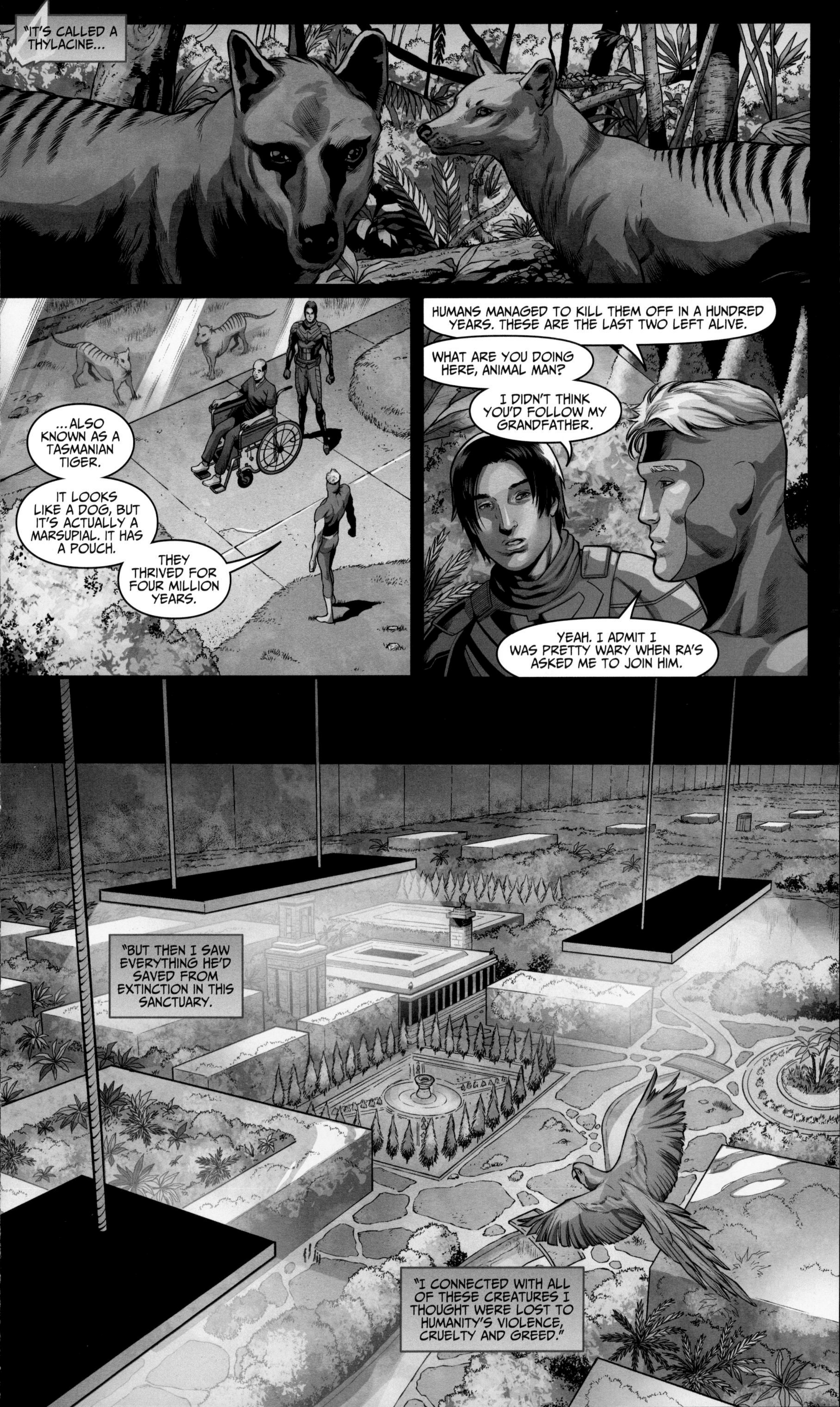
"IT'S CALLED A THYLACINE...
...ALSO KNOWN AS A TASMANIAN TIGER.
IT LOOKS LIKE A DOG, BUT IT'S ACTUALLY A MARSUPIAL. IT HAS A POUCH.
THEY THRIVED FOR FOUR MILLION YEARS.
HUMANS MANAGED TO KILL THEM OFF IN A HUNDRED YEARS. THESE ARE THE LAST TWO LEFT ALIVE.
WHAT ARE YOU DOING HERE, ANIMAL MAN?
I DIDN'T THINK YOU'D FOLLOW MY GRANDFATHER.
YEAH. I ADMIT I WAS PRETTY WARY WHEN RA'S ASKED ME TO JOIN HIM.
"BUT THEN I SAW EVERYTHING HE'D SAVED FROM EXTINCTION IN THIS SANCTUARY.
"I CONNECTED WITH ALL OF THESE CREATURES I THOUGHT WERE LOST TO HUMANITY'S VIOLENCE, CRUELTY AND GREED."

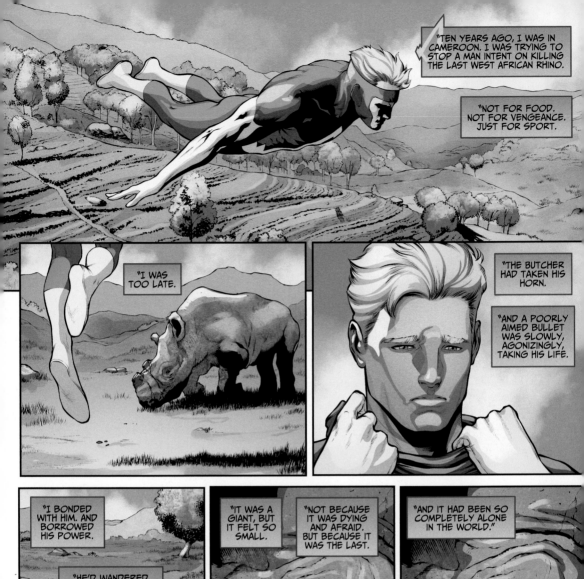

"TEN YEARS AGO, I WAS IN CAMEROON. I WAS TRYING TO STOP A MAN INTENT ON KILLING THE LAST WEST AFRICAN RHINO.

"NOT FOR FOOD. NOT FOR VENGEANCE. JUST FOR SPORT.

"I WAS TOO LATE.

"THE BUTCHER HAD TAKEN HIS HORN.

"AND A POORLY AIMED BULLET WAS SLOWLY, AGONIZINGLY, TAKING HIS LIFE.

"I BONDED WITH HIM. AND BORROWED HIS POWER.

"HE'D WANDERED FOR A YEAR, MAYBE MORE. CALLING WITH NO ANSWER.

"I SAT WITH IT... AS IT LEFT.

"IT WAS A GIANT, BUT IT FELT SO SMALL.

"NOT BECAUSE IT WAS DYING AND AFRAID. BUT BECAUSE IT WAS THE LAST.

"AND IT HAD BEEN SO COMPLETELY ALONE IN THE WORLD."

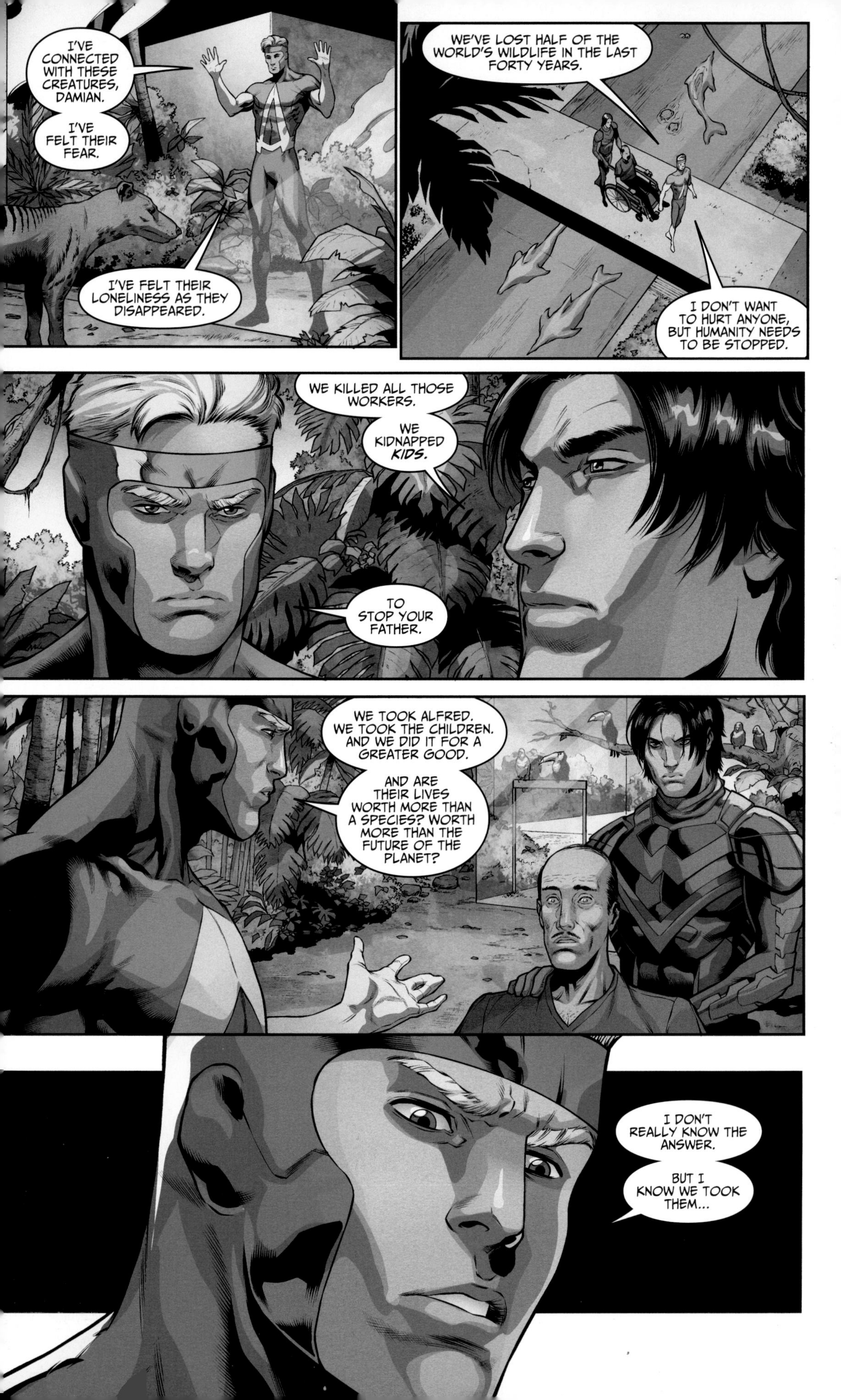
I'VE CONNECTED WITH THESE CREATURES, DAMIAN.
I'VE FELT THEIR FEAR.
I'VE FELT THEIR LONELINESS AS THEY DISAPPEARED.
WE'VE LOST HALF OF THE WORLD'S WILDLIFE IN THE LAST FORTY YEARS.
I DON'T WANT TO HURT ANYONE, BUT HUMANITY NEEDS TO BE STOPPED.
WE KILLED ALL THOSE WORKERS.
WE KIDNAPPED *KIDS*.
TO STOP YOUR FATHER.
WE TOOK ALFRED. WE TOOK THE CHILDREN. AND WE DID IT FOR A GREATER GOOD.
AND ARE THEIR LIVES WORTH MORE THAN A SPECIES? WORTH MORE THAN THE FUTURE OF THE PLANET?
I DON'T REALLY KNOW THE ANSWER.
BUT I KNOW WE TOOK THEM...

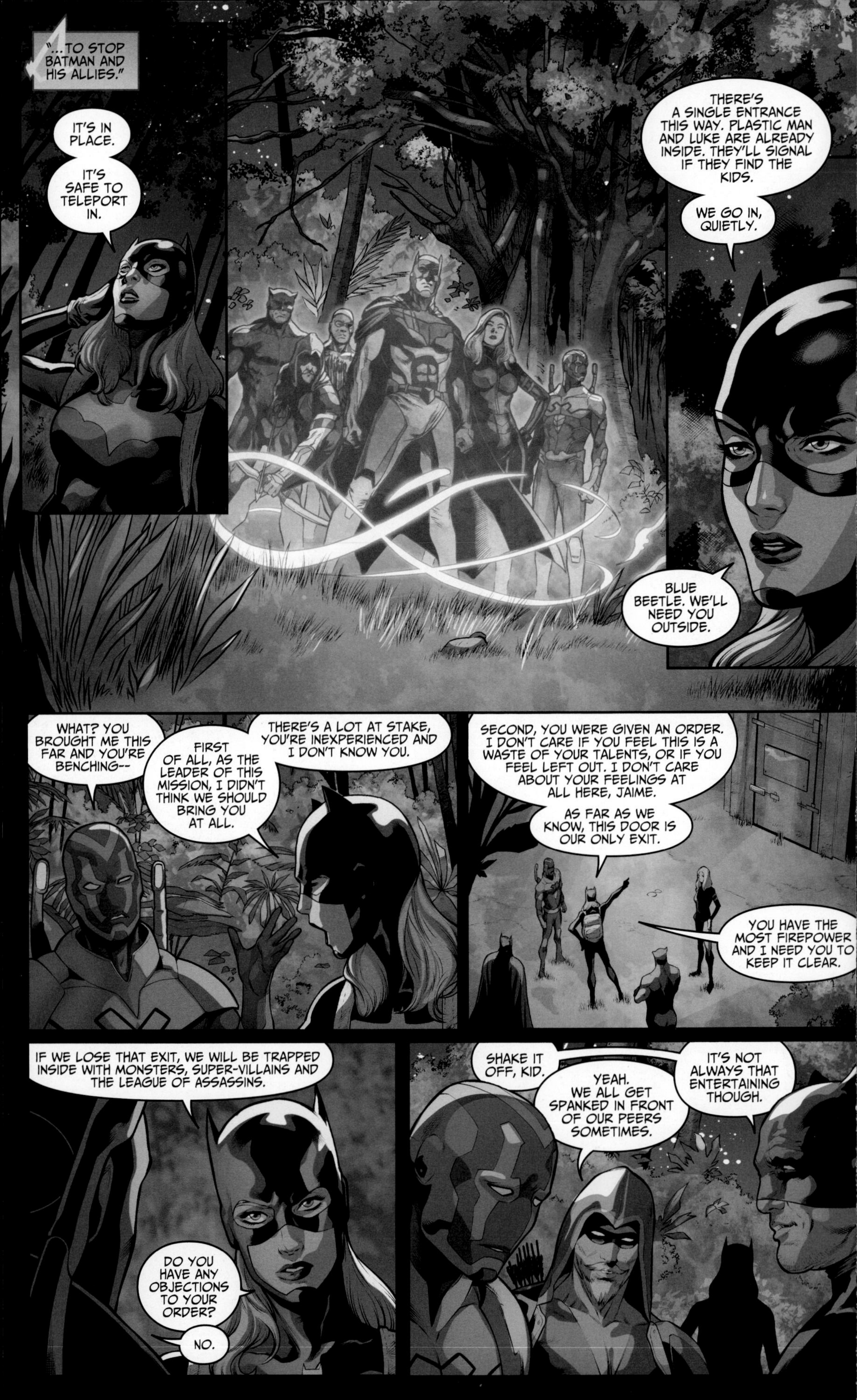
"...TO STOP BATMAN AND HIS ALLIES."
IT'S IN PLACE.
IT'S SAFE TO TELEPORT IN.
THERE'S A SINGLE ENTRANCE THIS WAY. PLASTIC MAN AND LUKE ARE ALREADY INSIDE. THEY'LL SIGNAL IF THEY FIND THE KIDS.
WE GO IN, QUIETLY.
BLUE BEETLE. WE'LL NEED YOU OUTSIDE.
WHAT? YOU BROUGHT ME THIS FAR AND YOU'RE BENCHING--
FIRST OF ALL, AS THE LEADER OF THIS MISSION, I DIDN'T THINK WE SHOULD BRING YOU AT ALL.
THERE'S A LOT AT STAKE, YOU'RE INEXPERIENCED AND I DON'T KNOW YOU.
SECOND, YOU WERE GIVEN AN ORDER. I DON'T CARE IF YOU FEEL THIS IS A WASTE OF YOUR TALENTS, OR IF YOU FEEL LEFT OUT. I DON'T CARE ABOUT YOUR FEELINGS AT ALL HERE, JAIME.
AS FAR AS WE KNOW, THIS DOOR IS OUR ONLY EXIT.
YOU HAVE THE MOST FIREPOWER AND I NEED YOU TO KEEP IT CLEAR.
IF WE LOSE THAT EXIT, WE WILL BE TRAPPED INSIDE WITH MONSTERS, SUPER-VILLAINS AND THE LEAGUE OF ASSASSINS.
DO YOU HAVE ANY OBJECTIONS TO YOUR ORDER?
NO.
SHAKE IT OFF, KID.
YEAH. WE ALL GET SPANKED IN FRONT OF OUR PEERS SOMETIMES.
IT'S NOT ALWAYS THAT ENTERTAINING THOUGH.

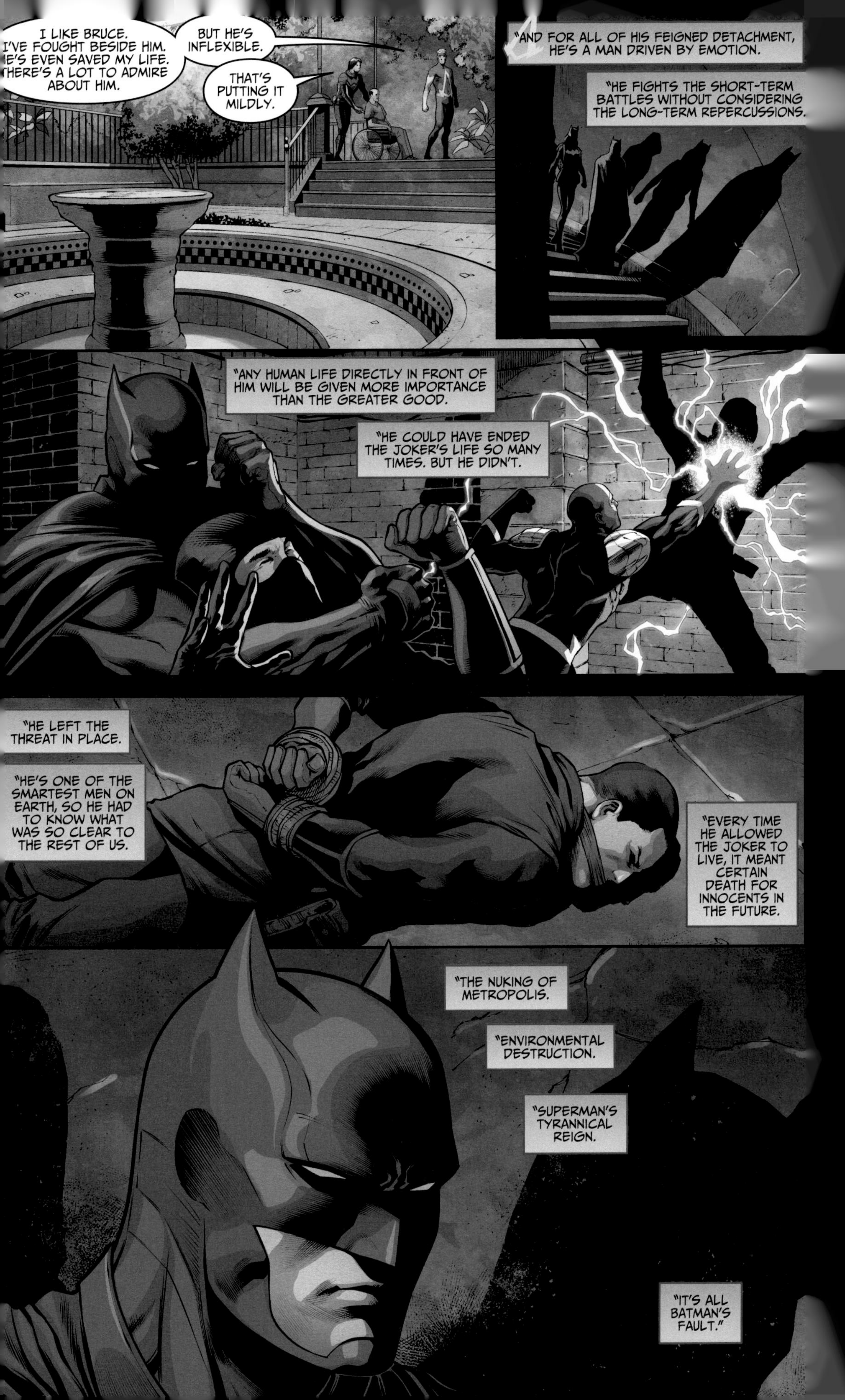
I LIKE BRUCE. I'VE FOUGHT BESIDE HIM. HE'S EVEN SAVED MY LIFE. THERE'S A LOT TO ADMIRE ABOUT HIM.
BUT HE'S INFLEXIBLE.
THAT'S PUTTING IT MILDLY.
"AND FOR ALL OF HIS FEIGNED DETACHMENT, HE'S A MAN DRIVEN BY EMOTION.
"HE FIGHTS THE SHORT-TERM BATTLES WITHOUT CONSIDERING THE LONG-TERM REPERCUSSIONS.
"ANY HUMAN LIFE DIRECTLY IN FRONT OF HIM WILL BE GIVEN MORE IMPORTANCE THAN THE GREATER GOOD.
"HE COULD HAVE ENDED THE JOKER'S LIFE SO MANY TIMES. BUT HE DIDN'T.
"HE LEFT THE THREAT IN PLACE.
"HE'S ONE OF THE SMARTEST MEN ON EARTH, SO HE HAD TO KNOW WHAT WAS SO CLEAR TO THE REST OF US.
"EVERY TIME HE ALLOWED THE JOKER TO LIVE, IT MEANT CERTAIN DEATH FOR INNOCENTS IN THE FUTURE.
"THE NUKING OF METROPOLIS.
"ENVIRONMENTAL DESTRUCTION.
"SUPERMAN'S TYRANNICAL REIGN.
"IT'S ALL BATMAN'S FAULT."

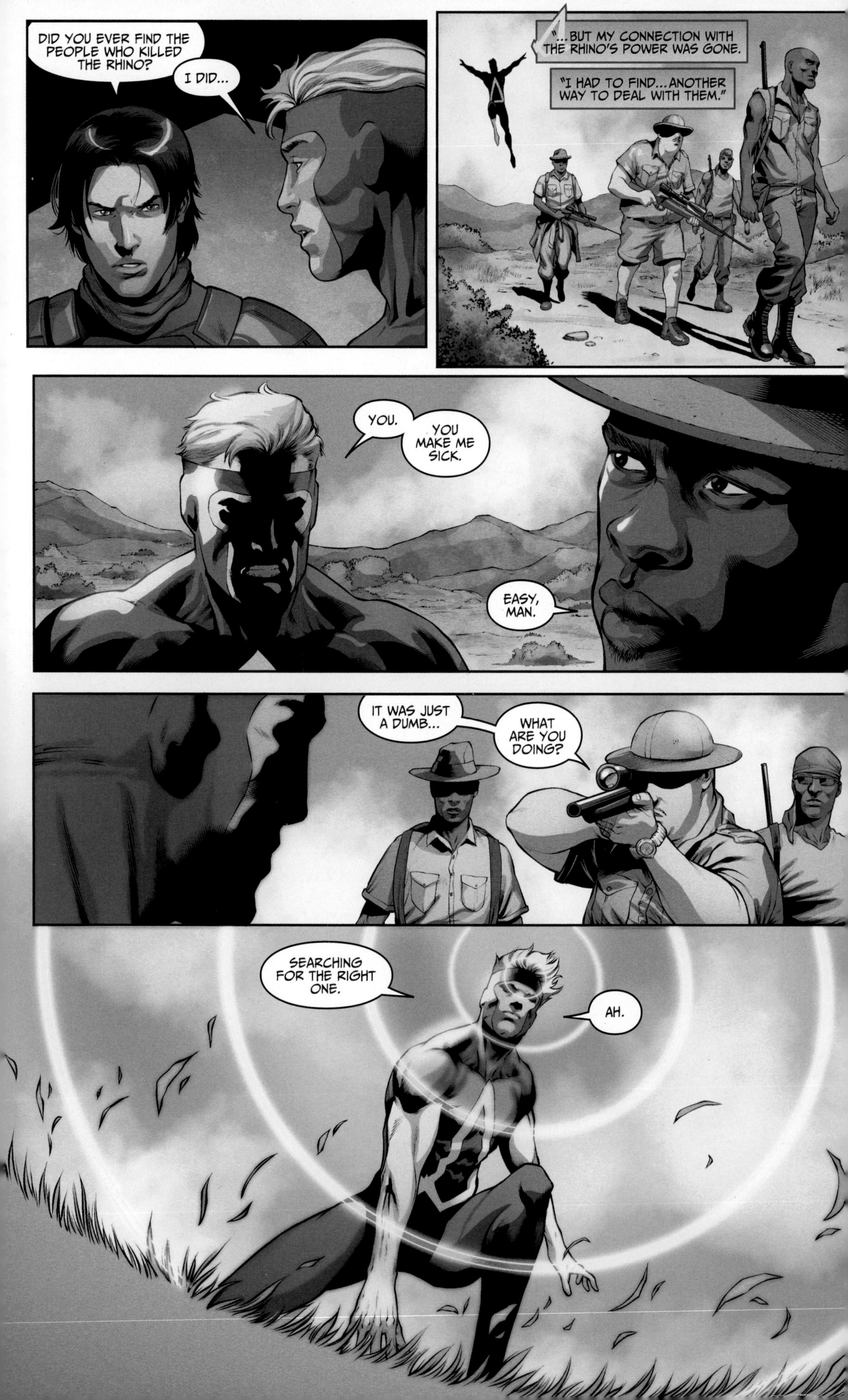

DID YOU EVER FIND THE PEOPLE WHO KILLED THE RHINO?
I DID...
"...BUT MY CONNECTION WITH THE RHINO'S POWER WAS GONE.
"I HAD TO FIND...ANOTHER WAY TO DEAL WITH THEM."
YOU.
YOU MAKE ME SICK.
EASY, MAN.
IT WAS JUST A DUMB...
WHAT ARE YOU DOING?
SEARCHING FOR THE RIGHT ONE.
AH.

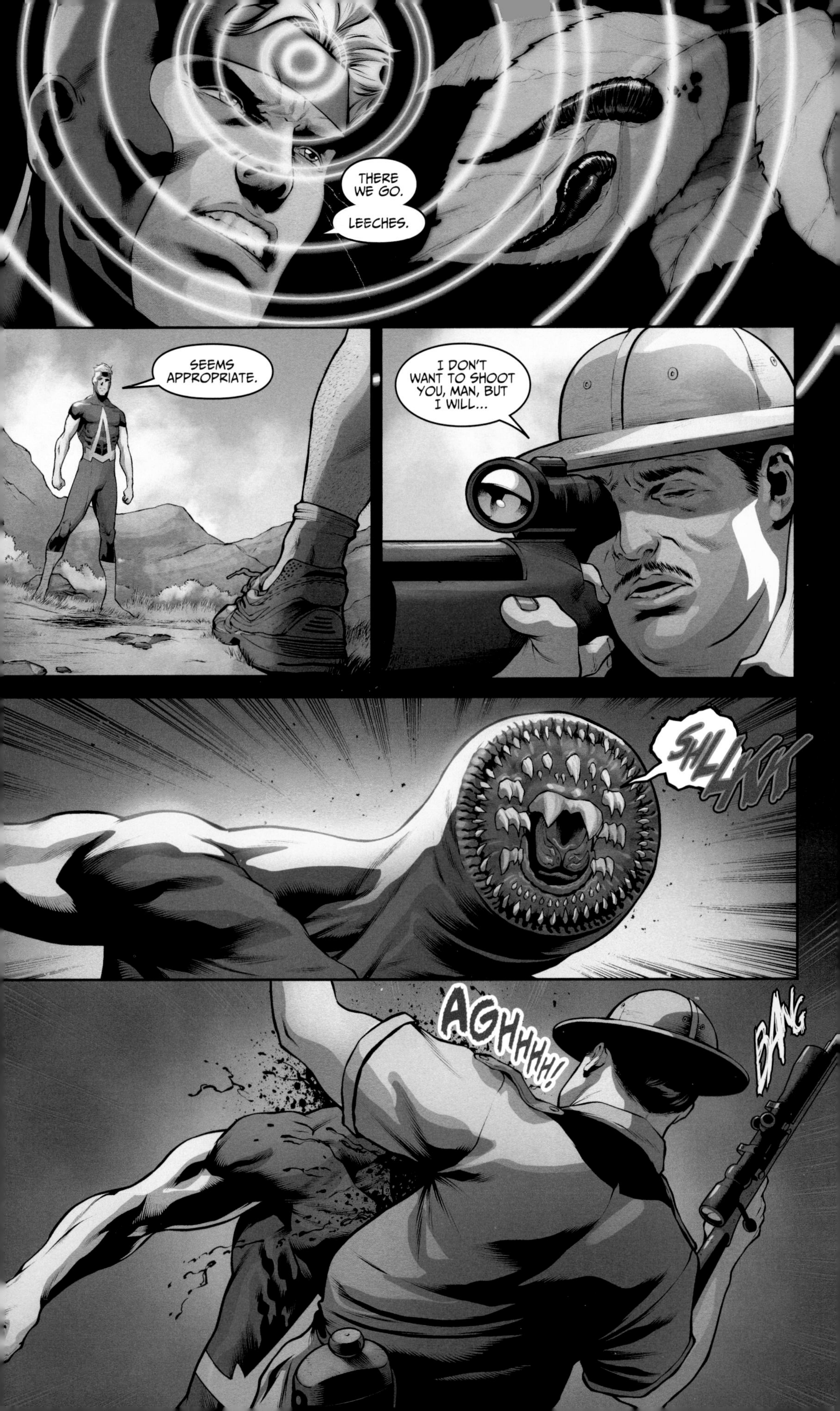
THERE WE GO.
LEECHES.
SEEMS APPROPRIATE.
I DON'T WANT TO SHOOT YOU, MAN, BUT I WILL...
SHLLKKK
AGHHHH!
BANG

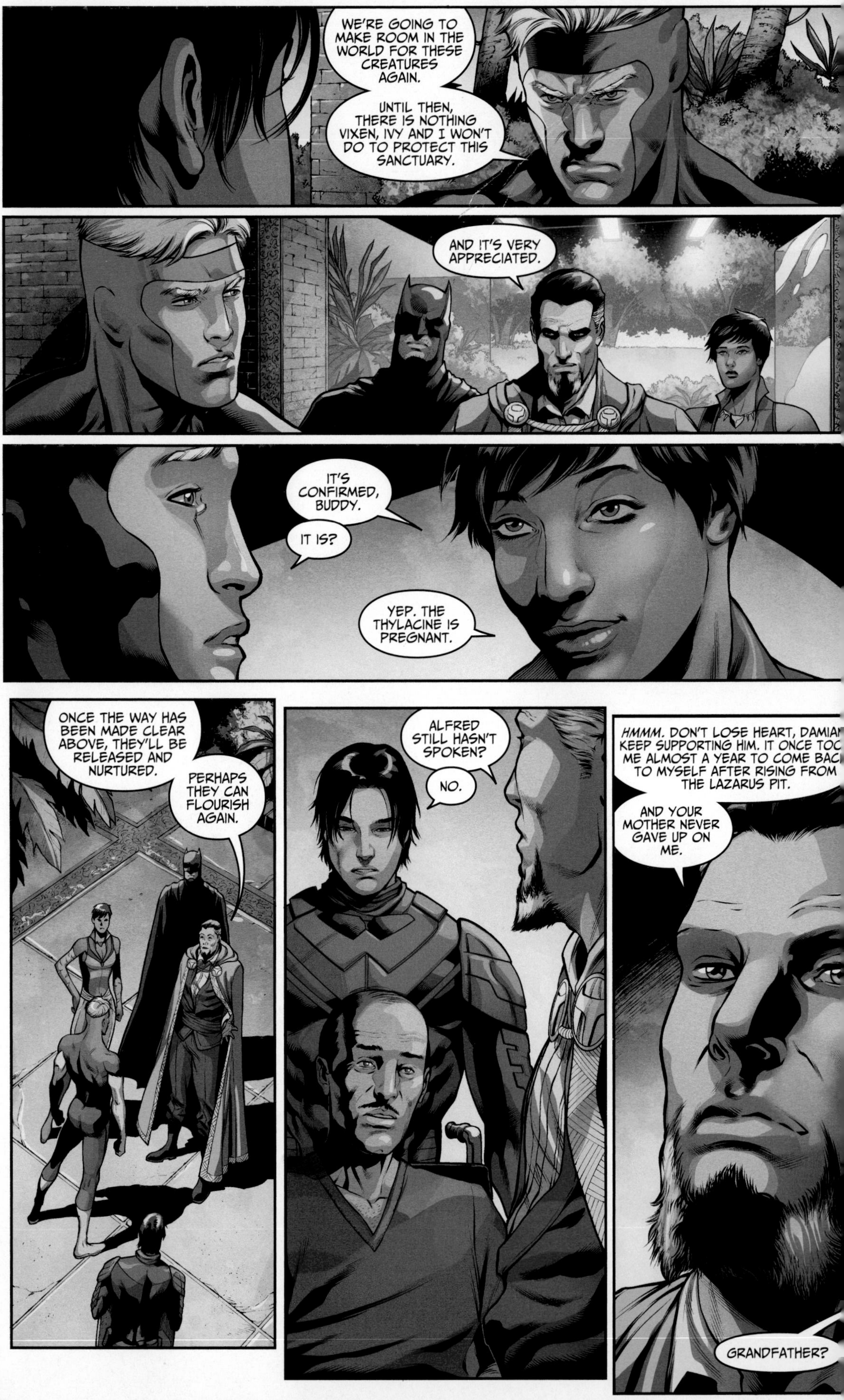

WE'RE GOING TO MAKE ROOM IN THE WORLD FOR THESE CREATURES AGAIN.
UNTIL THEN, THERE IS NOTHING VIXEN, IVY AND I WON'T DO TO PROTECT THIS SANCTUARY.
AND IT'S VERY APPRECIATED.
IT'S CONFIRMED, BUDDY.
IT IS?
YEP. THE THYLACINE IS PREGNANT.
ONCE THE WAY HAS BEEN MADE CLEAR ABOVE, THEY'LL BE RELEASED AND NURTURED.
PERHAPS THEY CAN FLOURISH AGAIN.
ALFRED STILL HASN'T SPOKEN?
NO.
HMMM. DON'T LOSE HEART, DAMIA
KEEP SUPPORTING HIM. IT ONCE TOO
ME ALMOST A YEAR TO COME BAC
TO MYSELF AFTER RISING FROM THE LAZARUS PIT.
AND YOUR MOTHER NEVER GAVE UP ON ME.
GRANDFATHER?

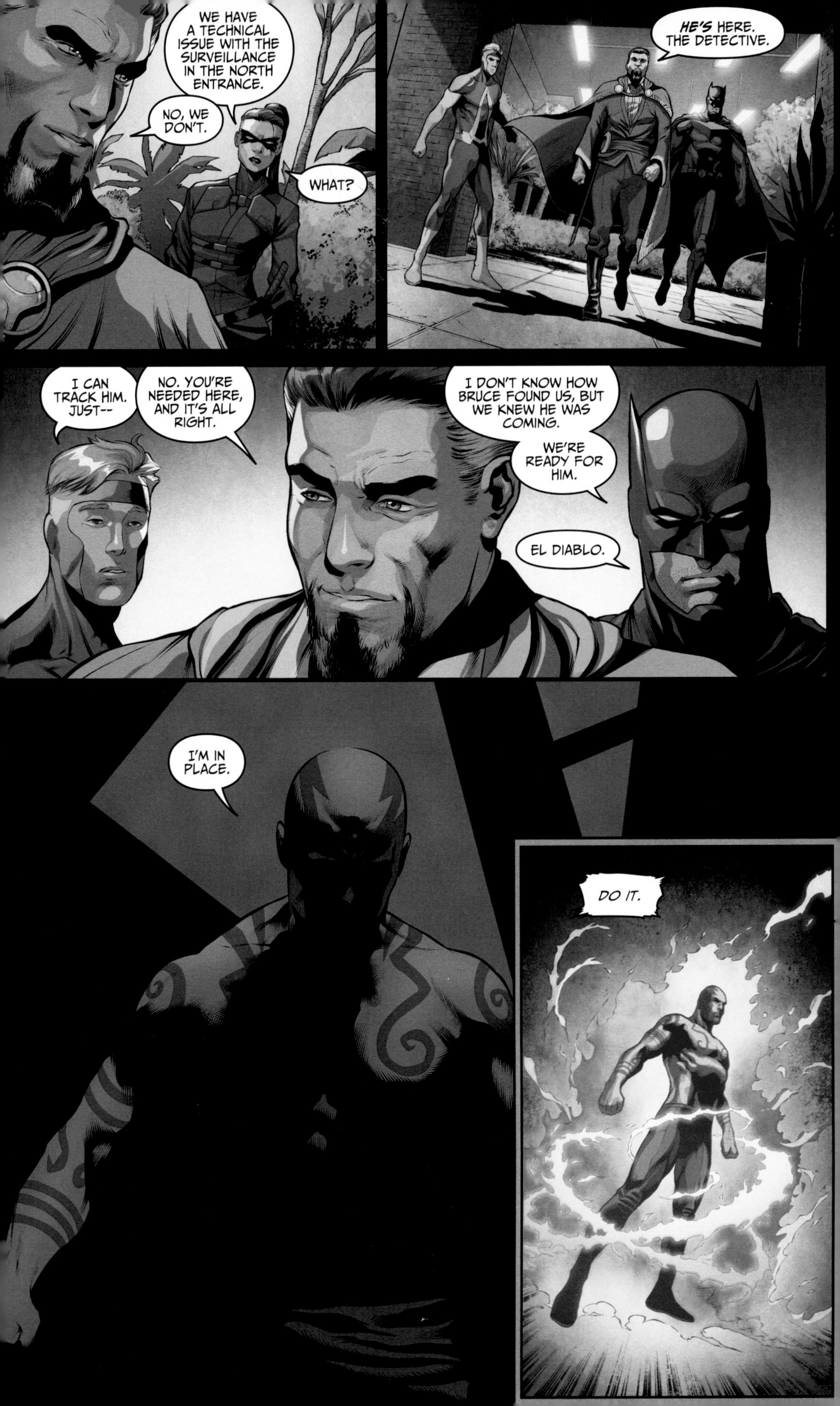
WE HAVE A TECHNICAL ISSUE WITH THE SURVEILLANCE IN THE NORTH ENTRANCE.
NO, WE DON'T.
WHAT?
HE'S HERE. THE DETECTIVE.
I CAN TRACK HIM. JUST--
NO. YOU'RE NEEDED HERE, AND IT'S ALL RIGHT.
I DON'T KNOW HOW BRUCE FOUND US, BUT WE KNEW HE WAS COMING.
WE'RE READY FOR HIM.
EL DIABLO.
I'M IN PLACE.
DO IT.

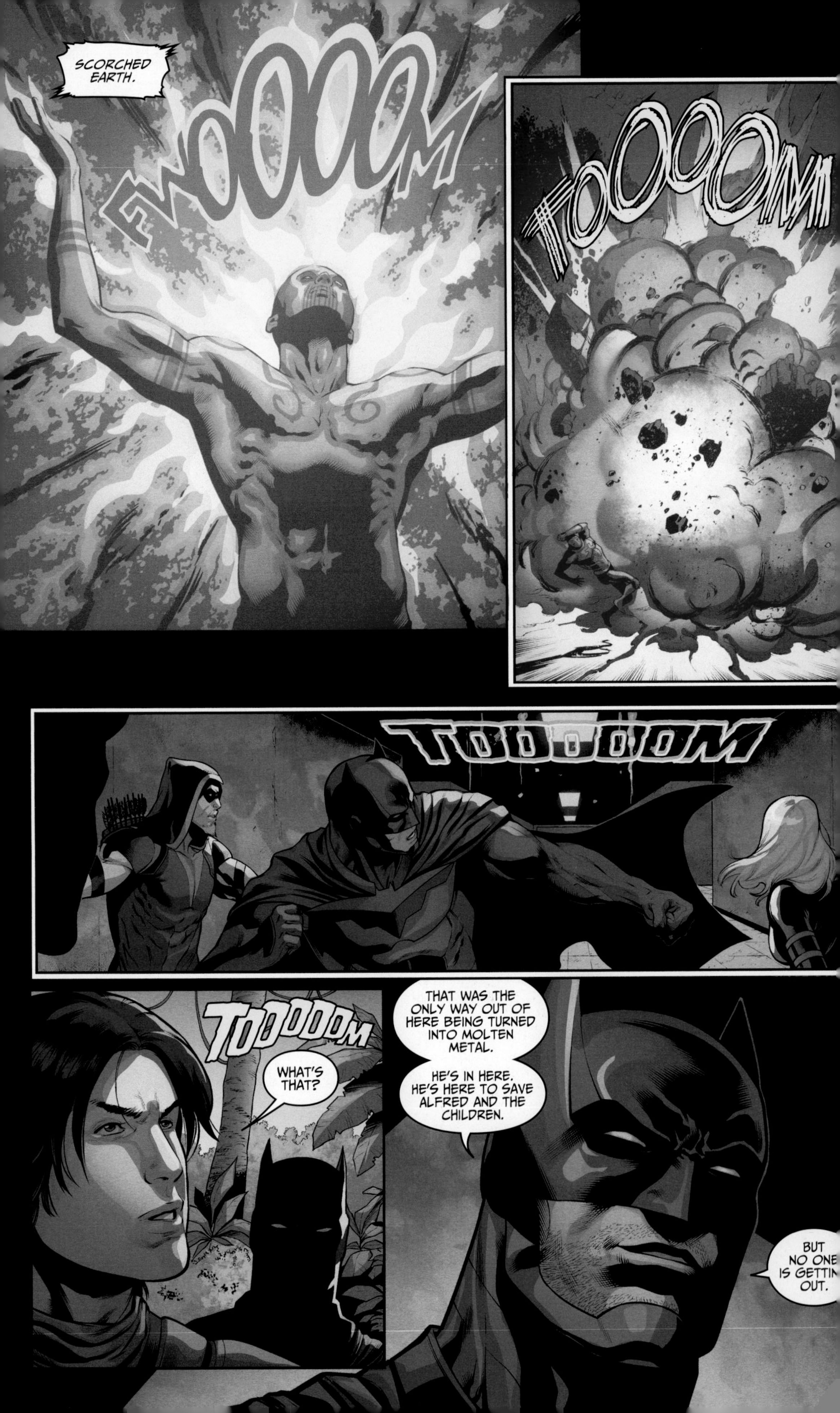
SCORCHED EARTH.
FWOOOOM
TOOOOOM
TOOOOOM
TOOOOOM
WHAT'S THAT?
THAT WAS THE ONLY WAY OUT OF HERE BEING TURNED INTO MOLTEN METAL.
HE'S IN HERE. HE'S HERE TO SAVE ALFRED AND THE CHILDREN.
BUT NO ONE IS GETTIN OUT.

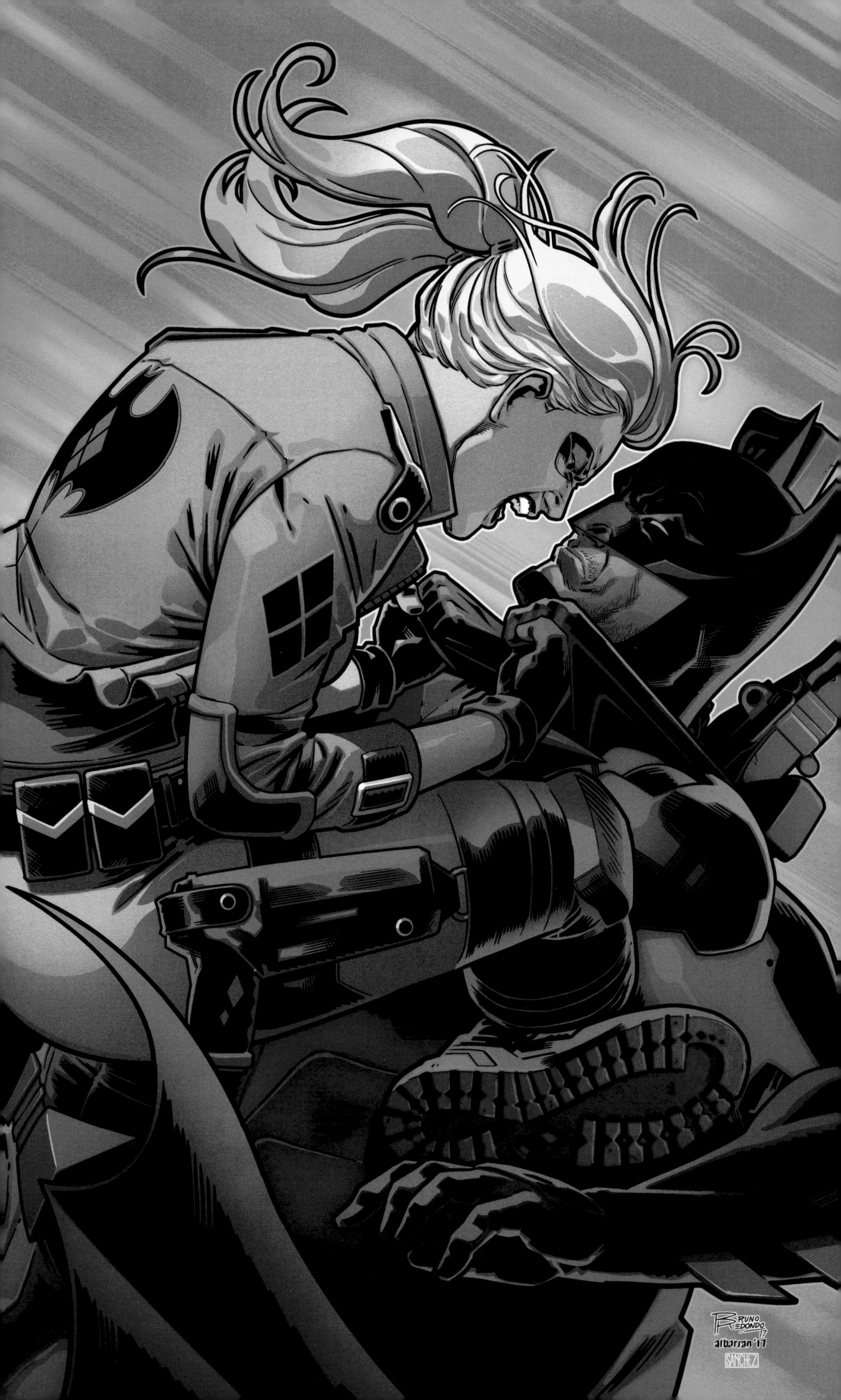
BRUNO REDONDO 17
albarran '17
SÁNCHEZ

"Scorched Earth"

Tom Taylor Writer **Daniel Sampere** Penciller **Juan Albarran** Inker **Rex Lokus** Colorist
Wes Abbott Letterer Cover art by **Bruno Redondo, Juan Albarran** and **Alejandro Sanchez**

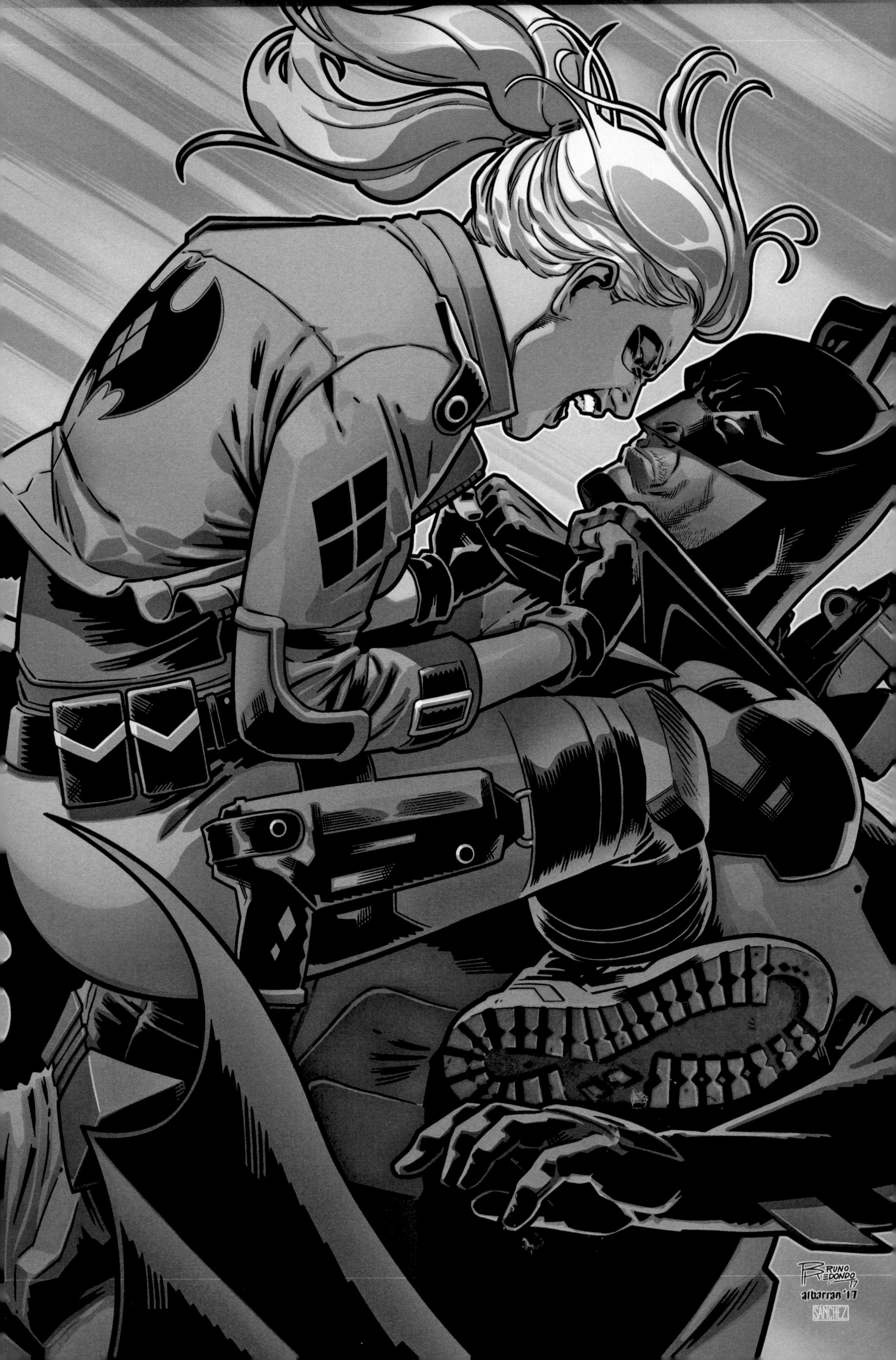
BRUNO REDONDO '17
albarran '17
SANCHEZ

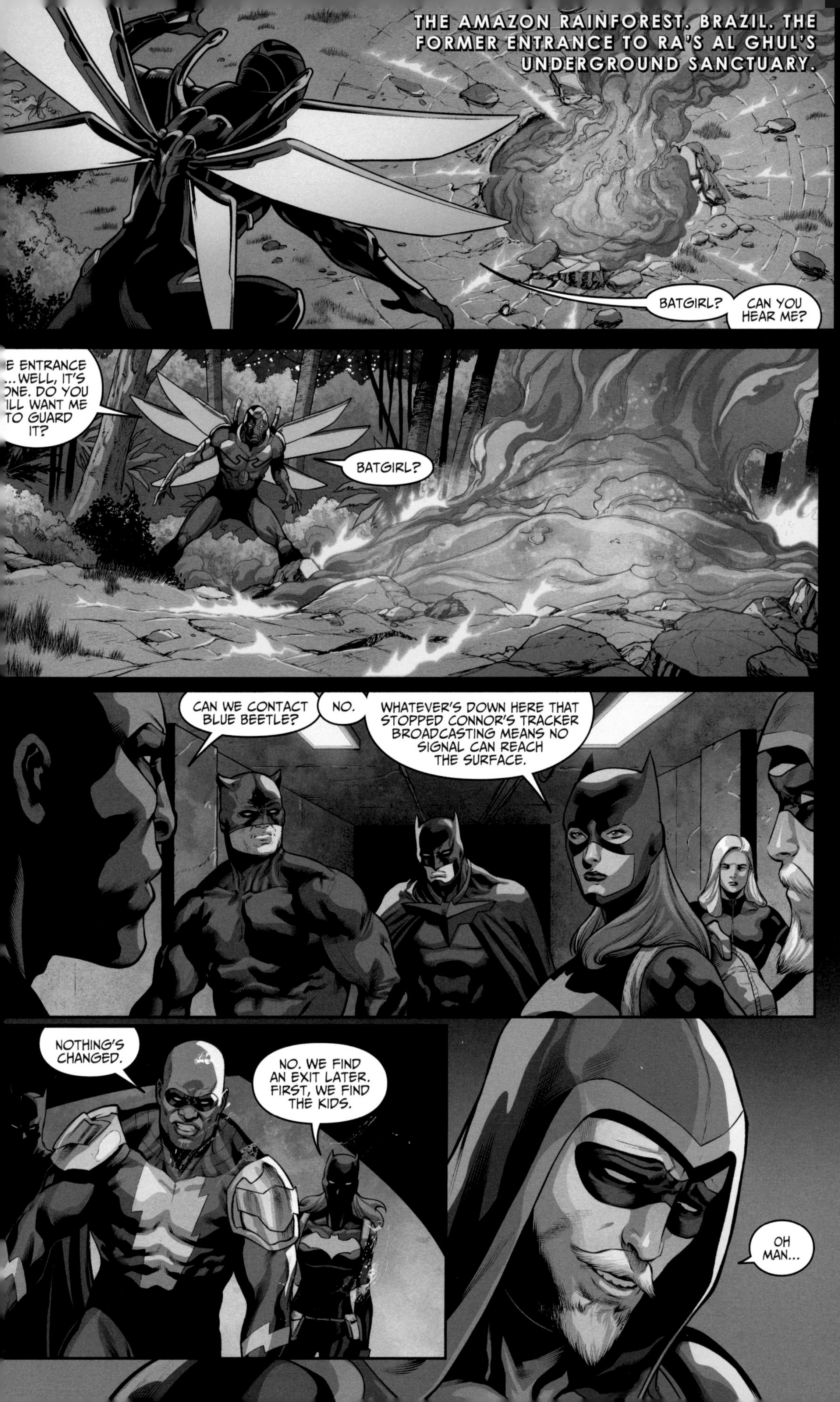
THE AMAZON RAINFOREST. BRAZIL. THE FORMER ENTRANCE TO RA'S AL GHUL'S UNDERGROUND SANCTUARY.
BATGIRL?
CAN YOU HEAR ME?
E ENTRANCE ...WELL, IT'S ONE. DO YOU ILL WANT ME TO GUARD IT?
BATGIRL?
CAN WE CONTACT BLUE BEETLE?
NO.
WHATEVER'S DOWN HERE THAT STOPPED CONNOR'S TRACKER BROADCASTING MEANS NO SIGNAL CAN REACH THE SURFACE.
NOTHING'S CHANGED.
NO. WE FIND AN EXIT LATER. FIRST, WE FIND THE KIDS.
OH MAN...

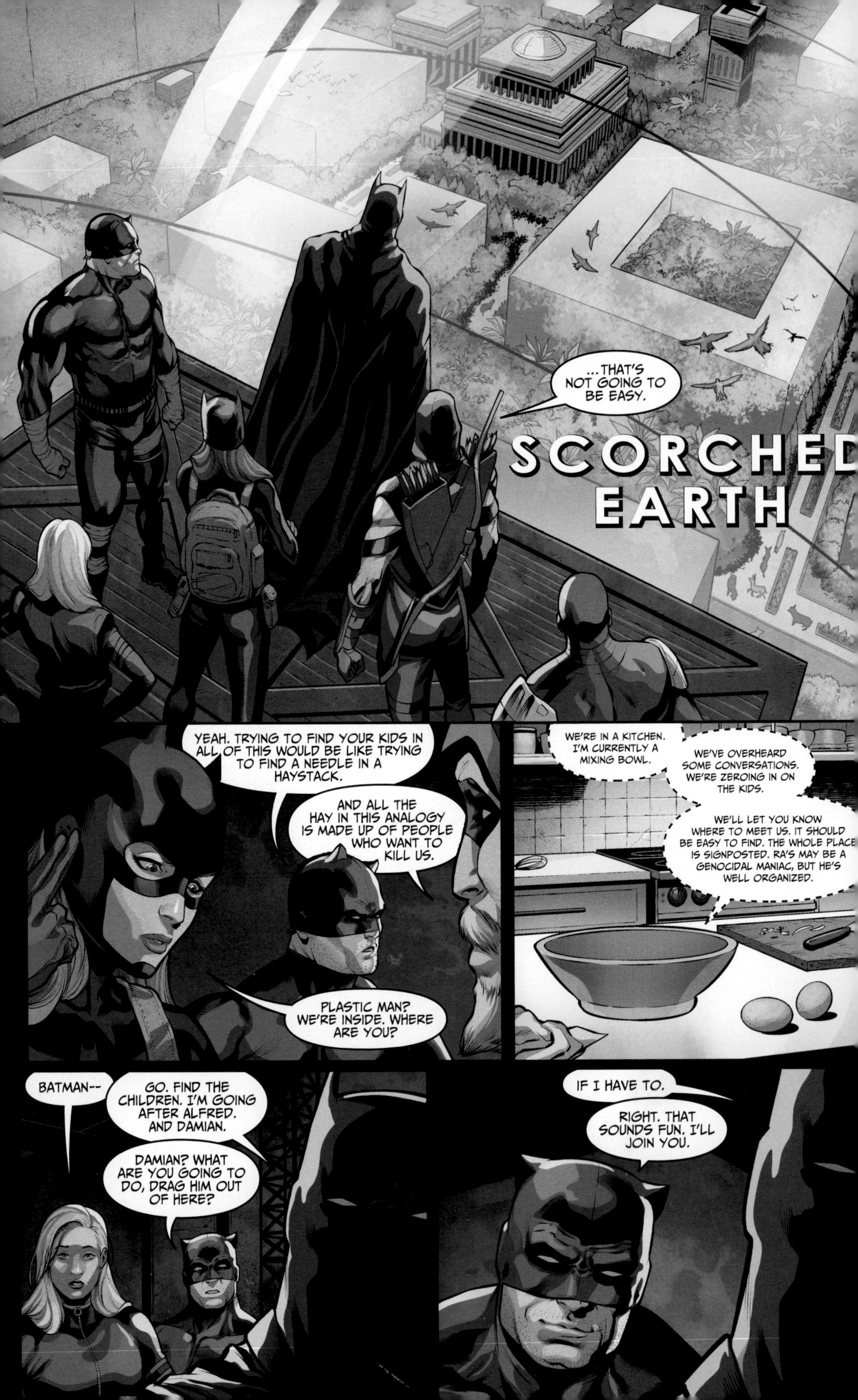
...THAT'S NOT GOING TO BE EASY.
SCORCHED EARTH
YEAH. TRYING TO FIND YOUR KIDS IN ALL OF THIS WOULD BE LIKE TRYING TO FIND A NEEDLE IN A HAYSTACK.
AND ALL THE HAY IN THIS ANALOGY IS MADE UP OF PEOPLE WHO WANT TO KILL US.
PLASTIC MAN? WE'RE INSIDE. WHERE ARE YOU?
WE'RE IN A KITCHEN. I'M CURRENTLY A MIXING BOWL.
WE'VE OVERHEARD SOME CONVERSATIONS. WE'RE ZEROING IN ON THE KIDS.
WE'LL LET YOU KNOW WHERE TO MEET US. IT SHOULD BE EASY TO FIND. THE WHOLE PLACE IS SIGNPOSTED. RA'S MAY BE A GENOCIDAL MANIAC, BUT HE'S WELL ORGANIZED.
BATMAN--
GO. FIND THE CHILDREN. I'M GOING AFTER ALFRED. AND DAMIAN.
DAMIAN? WHAT ARE YOU GOING TO DO, DRAG HIM OUT OF HERE?
IF I HAVE TO.
RIGHT. THAT SOUNDS FUN. I'LL JOIN YOU.

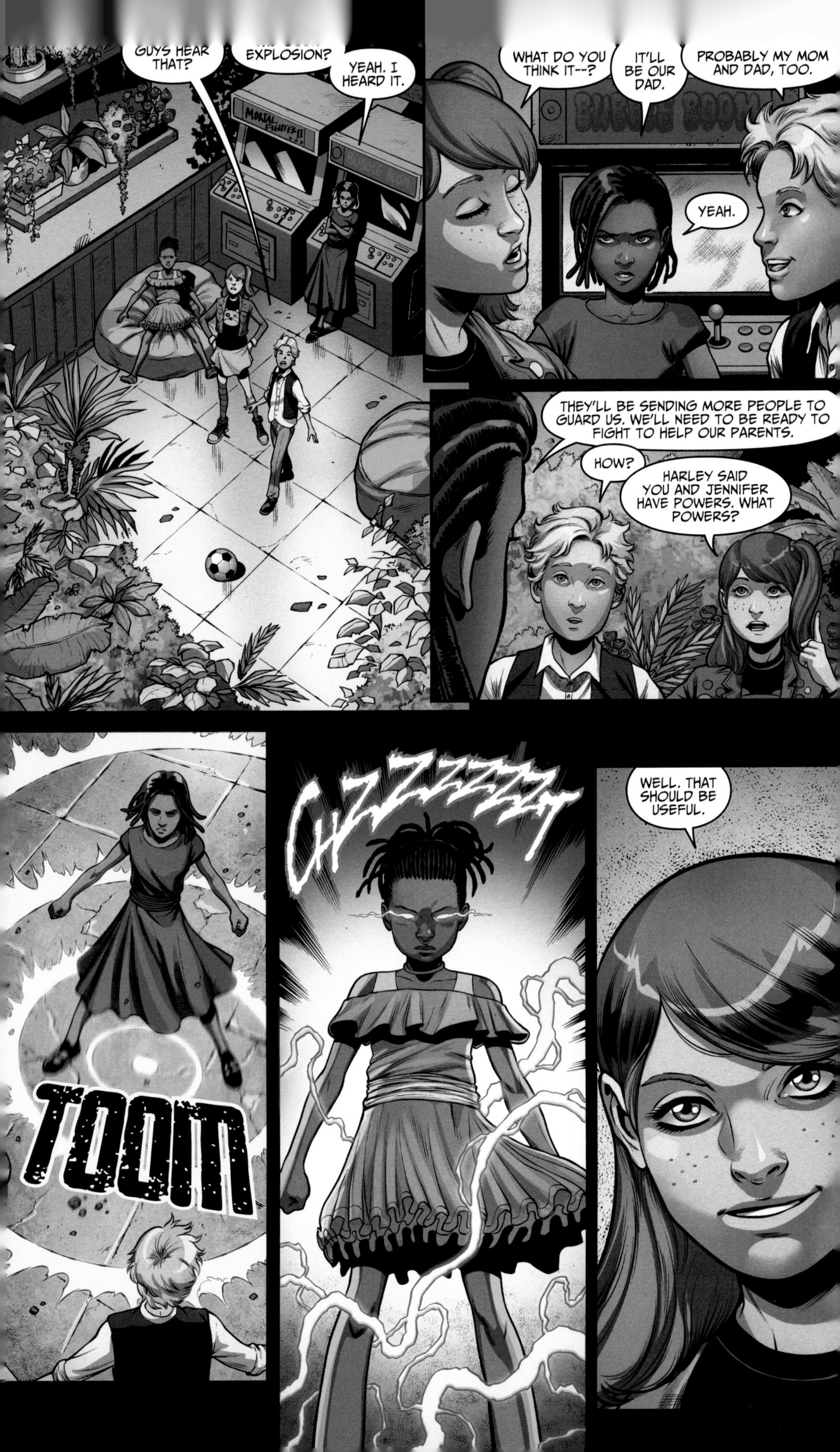
GUYS HEAR THAT?
EXPLOSION?
YEAH. I HEARD IT.
MORTAL FIGHTER II
WHAT DO YOU THINK IT--?
IT'LL BE OUR DAD.
PROBABLY MY MOM AND DAD, TOO.
YEAH.
THEY'LL BE SENDING MORE PEOPLE TO GUARD US. WE'LL NEED TO BE READY TO FIGHT TO HELP OUR PARENTS.
HOW?
HARLEY SAID YOU AND JENNIFER HAVE POWERS. WHAT POWERS?
TOOM
CHZZZZZZT
WELL. THAT SHOULD BE USEFUL.

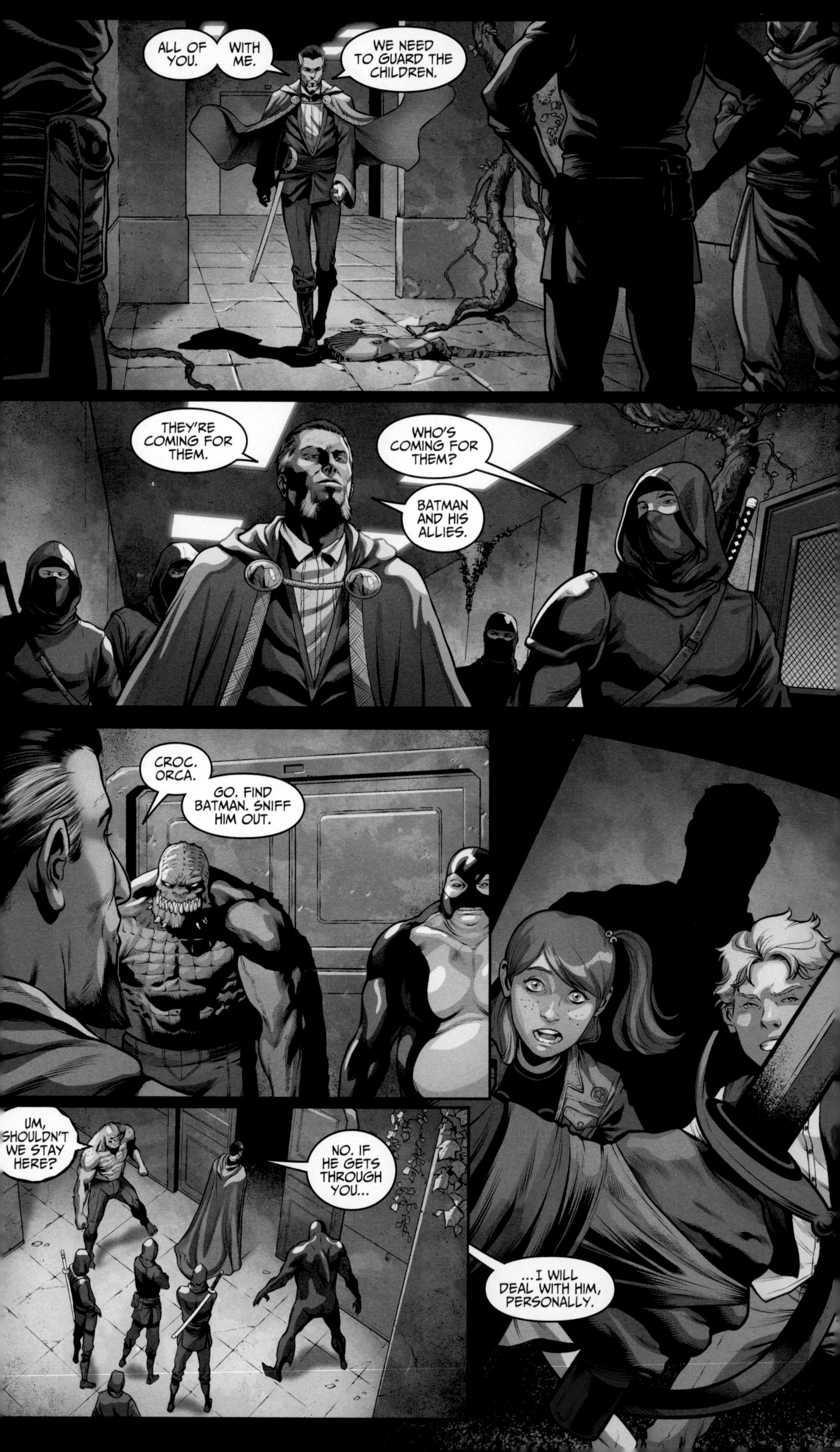
ALL OF YOU.
WITH ME.
WE NEED TO GUARD THE CHILDREN.
THEY'RE COMING FOR THEM.
WHO'S COMING FOR THEM?
BATMAN AND HIS ALLIES.
CROC. ORCA.
GO. FIND BATMAN. SNIFF HIM OUT.
UM, SHOULDN'T WE STAY HERE?
NO. IF HE GETS THROUGH YOU...
...I WILL DEAL WITH HIM, PERSONALLY.

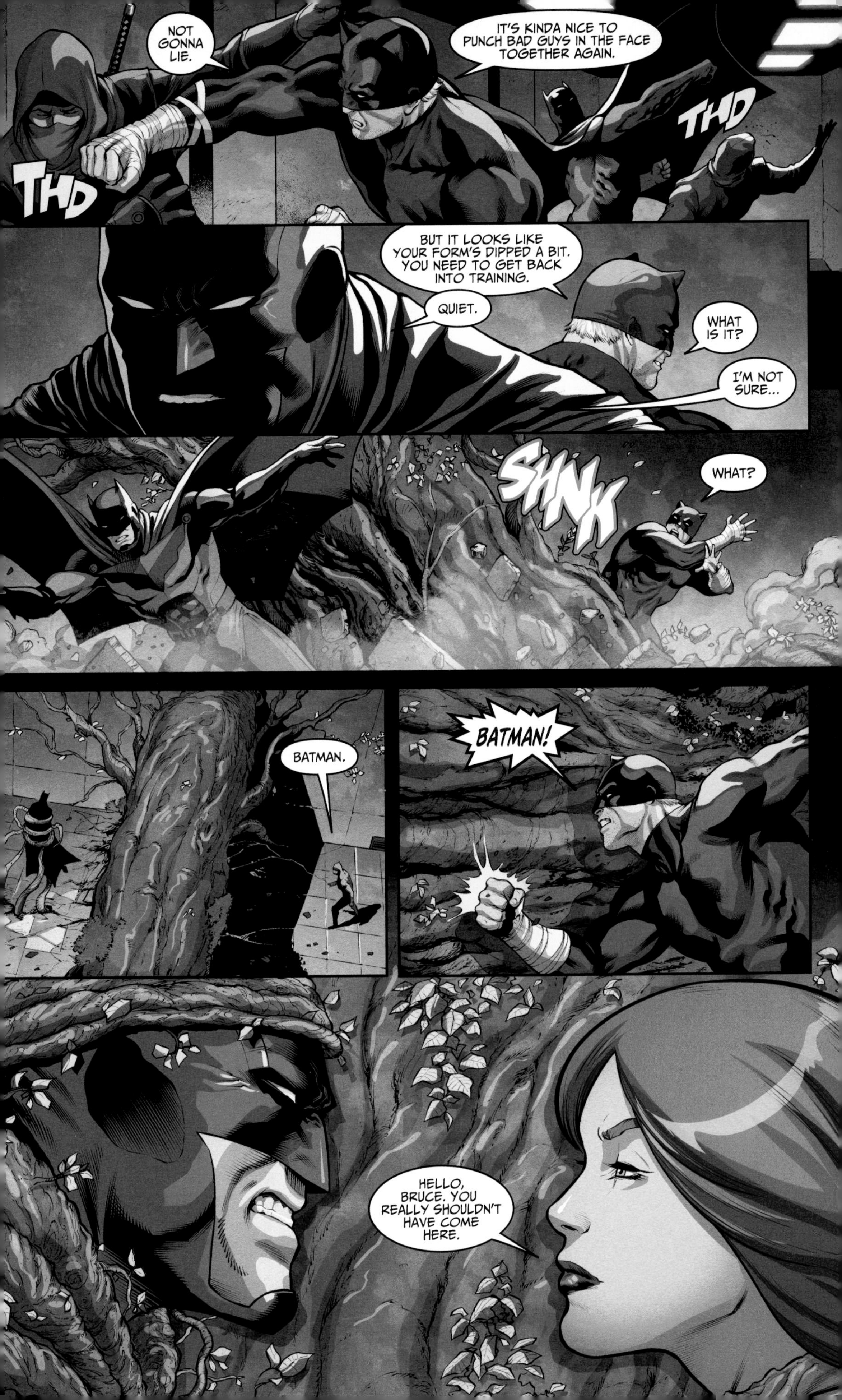

NOT GONNA LIE.
IT'S KINDA NICE TO PUNCH BAD GUYS IN THE FACE TOGETHER AGAIN.
THD
THD
BUT IT LOOKS LIKE YOUR FORM'S DIPPED A BIT. YOU NEED TO GET BACK INTO TRAINING.
QUIET.
WHAT IS IT?
I'M NOT SURE...
SHNK
WHAT?
BATMAN.
BATMAN!
HELLO, BRUCE. YOU REALLY SHOULDN'T HAVE COME HERE.

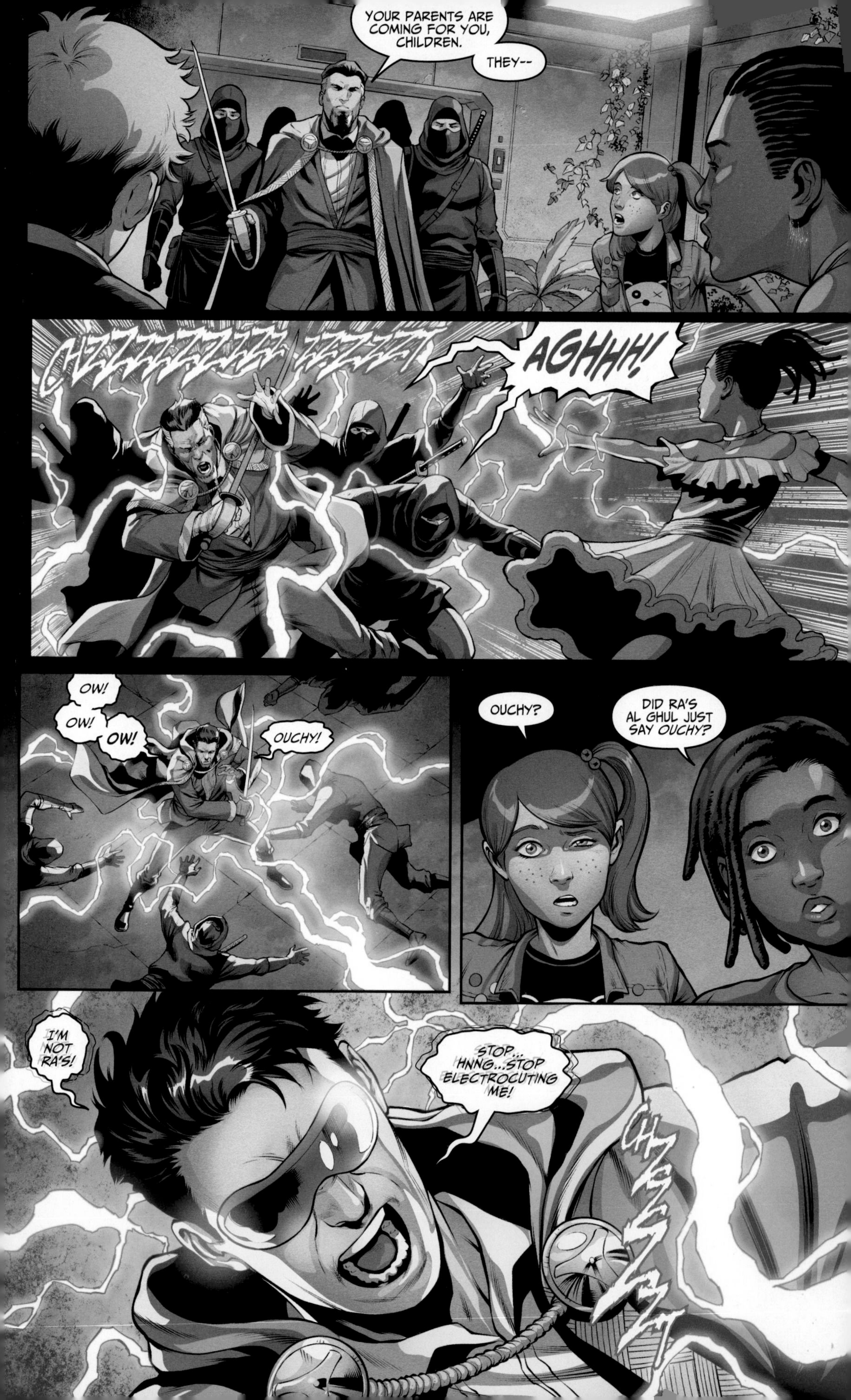
YOUR PARENTS ARE COMING FOR YOU, CHILDREN.
THEY--
CHZZZZZZZZZT
AGHHH!
OW!
OW!
OW!
OUCHY!
OUCHY?
DID RA'S AL GHUL JUST SAY OUCHY?
I'M NOT RA'S!
STOP... HNNG...STOP ELECTROCUTING ME!

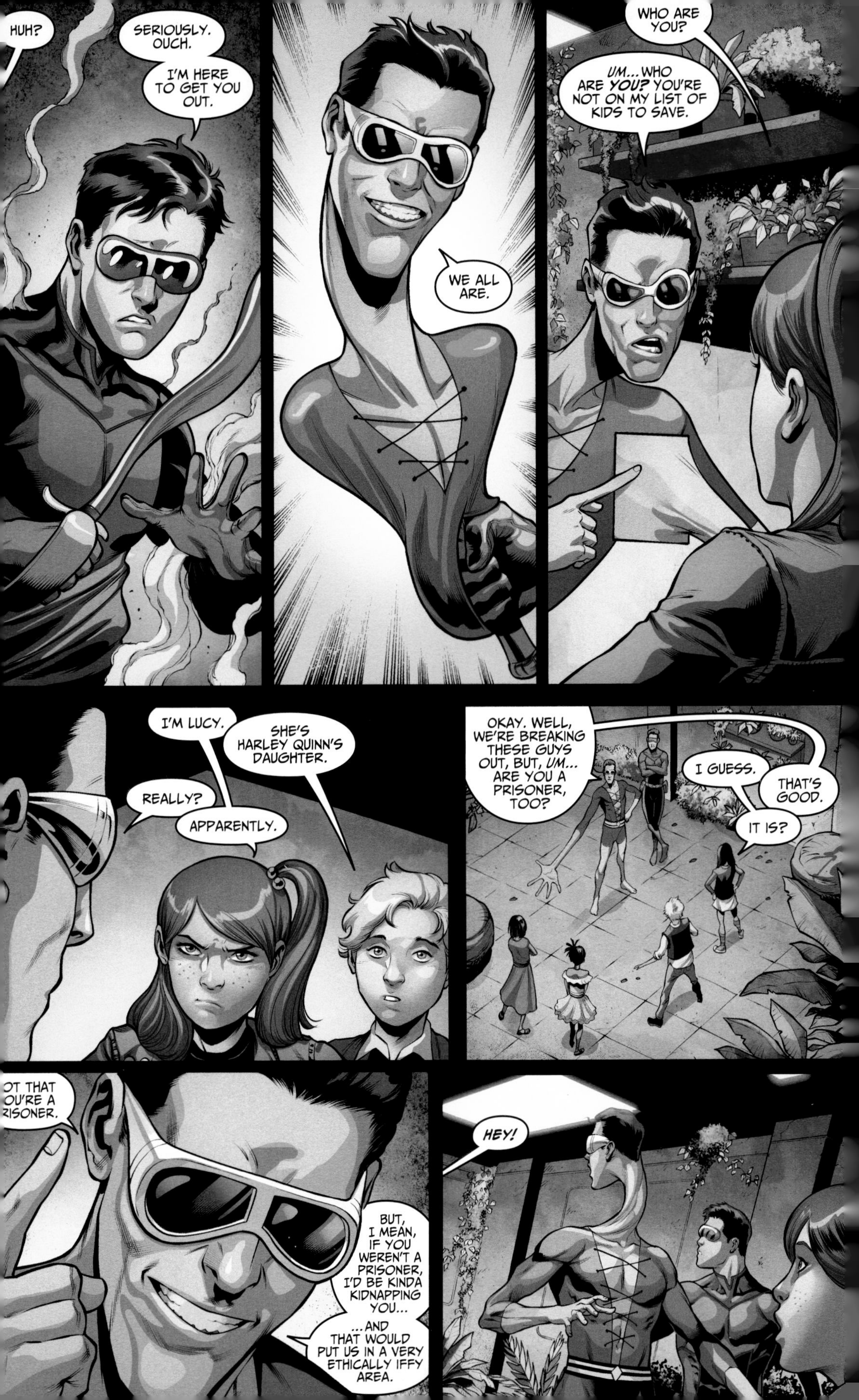
HUH?
SERIOUSLY. OUCH.
I'M HERE TO GET YOU OUT.
WE ALL ARE.
WHO ARE YOU?
UM... WHO ARE YOU? YOU'RE NOT ON MY LIST OF KIDS TO SAVE.
I'M LUCY.
SHE'S HARLEY QUINN'S DAUGHTER.
REALLY?
APPARENTLY.
OKAY. WELL, WE'RE BREAKING THESE GUYS OUT, BUT, UM... ARE YOU A PRISONER, TOO?
I GUESS.
THAT'S GOOD.
IT IS?
OT THAT OU'RE A RISONER.
BUT, I MEAN, IF YOU WEREN'T A PRISONER, I'D BE KINDA KIDNAPPING YOU...
...AND THAT WOULD PUT US IN A VERY ETHICALLY IFFY AREA.
HEY!

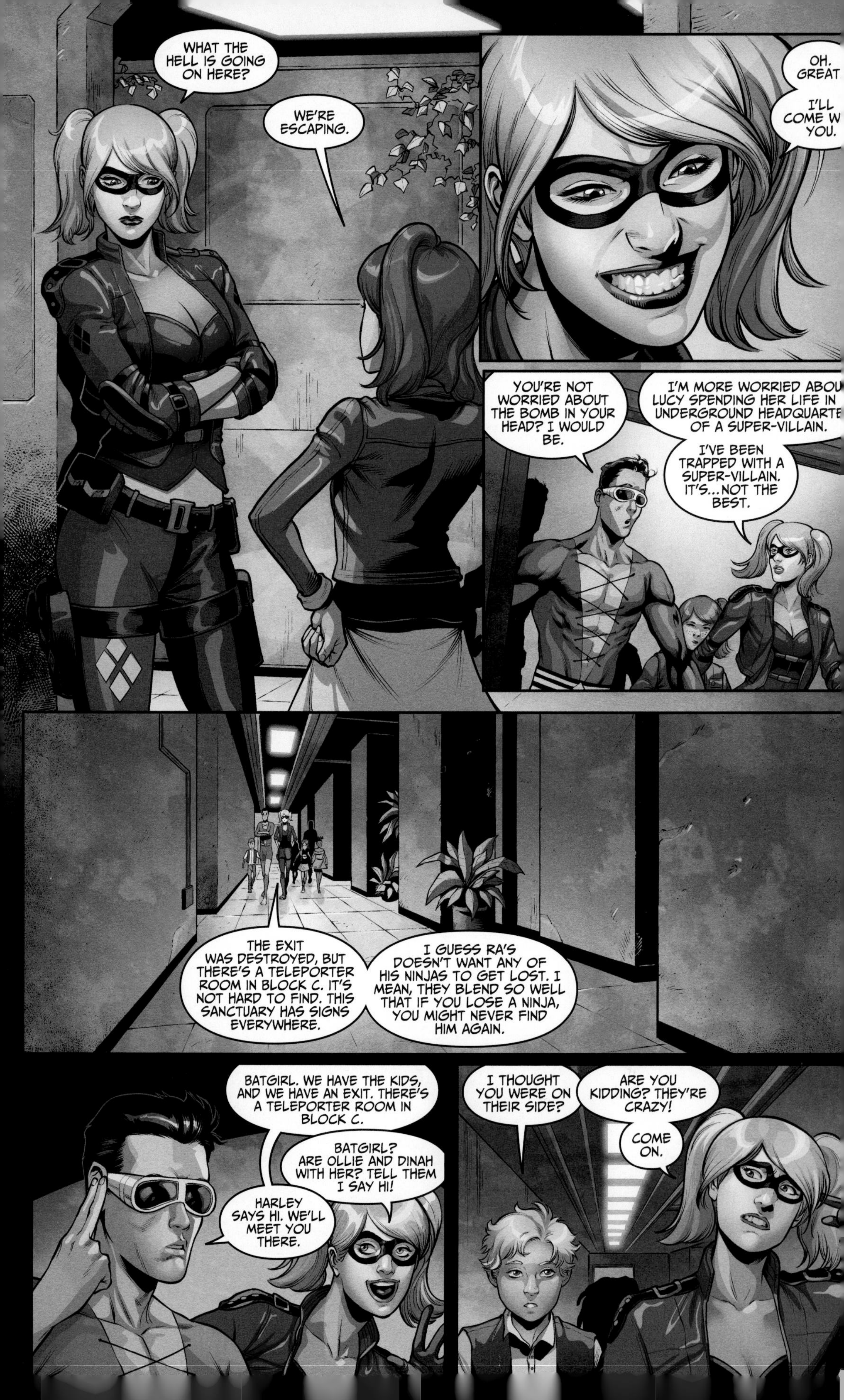
WHAT THE HELL IS GOING ON HERE?
WE'RE ESCAPING.
OH. GREAT
I'LL COME W YOU.
YOU'RE NOT WORRIED ABOUT THE BOMB IN YOUR HEAD? I WOULD BE.
I'M MORE WORRIED ABOU LUCY SPENDING HER LIFE IN UNDERGROUND HEADQUARTE OF A SUPER-VILLAIN.
I'VE BEEN TRAPPED WITH A SUPER-VILLAIN. IT'S...NOT THE BEST.
THE EXIT WAS DESTROYED, BUT THERE'S A TELEPORTER ROOM IN BLOCK C. IT'S NOT HARD TO FIND. THIS SANCTUARY HAS SIGNS EVERYWHERE.
I GUESS RA'S DOESN'T WANT ANY OF HIS NINJAS TO GET LOST. I MEAN, THEY BLEND SO WELL THAT IF YOU LOSE A NINJA, YOU MIGHT NEVER FIND HIM AGAIN.
BATGIRL. WE HAVE THE KIDS, AND WE HAVE AN EXIT. THERE'S A TELEPORTER ROOM IN BLOCK C.
BATGIRL? ARE OLLIE AND DINAH WITH HER? TELL THEM I SAY HI!
HARLEY SAYS HI. WE'LL MEET YOU THERE.
I THOUGHT YOU WERE ON THEIR SIDE?
ARE YOU KIDDING? THEY'RE CRAZY!
COME ON.

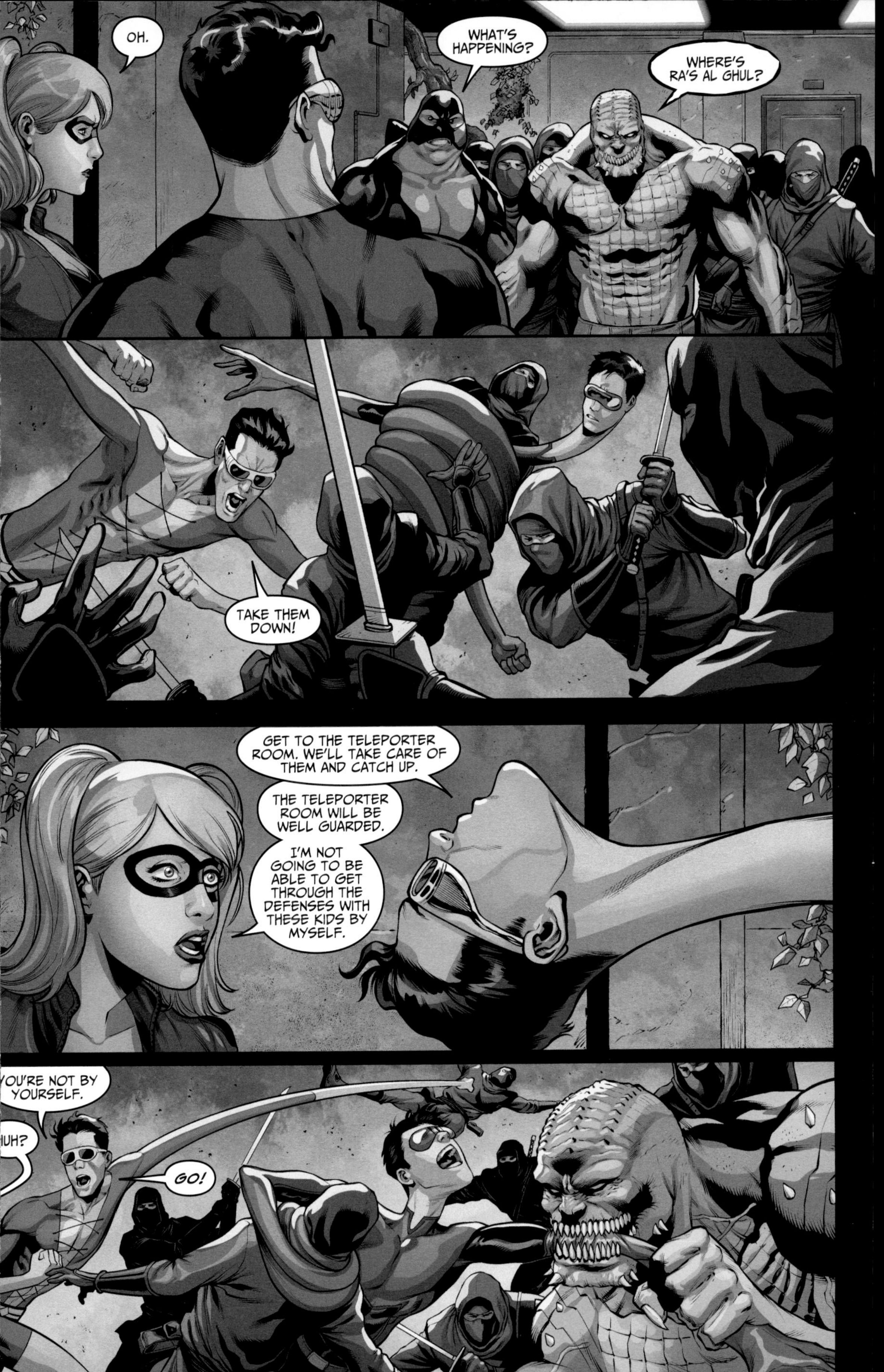
OH.
WHAT'S HAPPENING?
WHERE'S RA'S AL GHUL?
TAKE THEM DOWN!
GET TO THE TELEPORTER ROOM. WE'LL TAKE CARE OF THEM AND CATCH UP.
THE TELEPORTER ROOM WILL BE WELL GUARDED.
I'M NOT GOING TO BE ABLE TO GET THROUGH THE DEFENSES WITH THESE KIDS BY MYSELF.
YOU'RE NOT BY YOURSELF.
HUH?
GO!

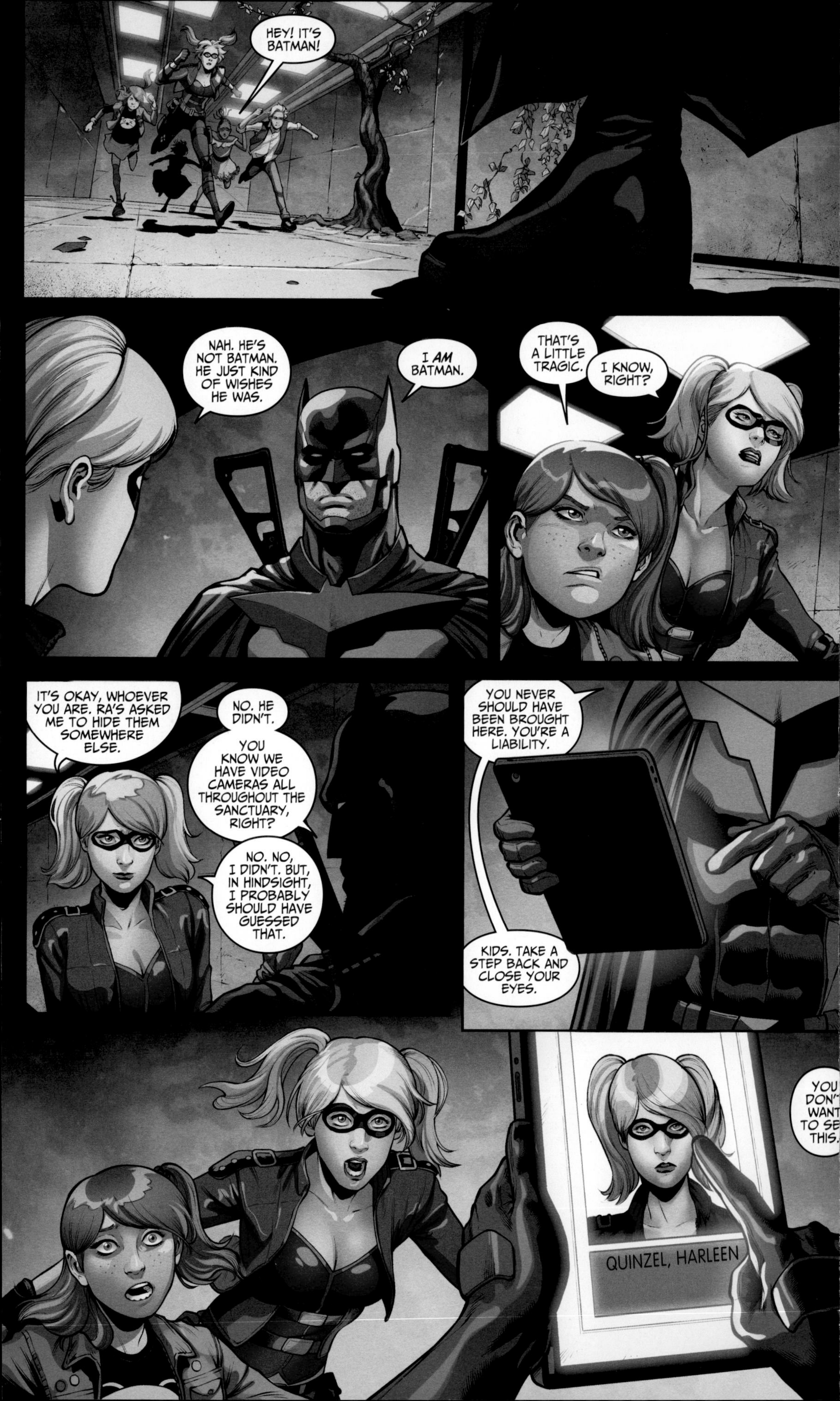

HEY! IT'S BATMAN!
NAH. HE'S NOT BATMAN. HE JUST KIND OF WISHES HE WAS.
I *AM* BATMAN.
THAT'S A LITTLE TRAGIC.
I KNOW, RIGHT?
IT'S OKAY, WHOEVER YOU ARE. RA'S ASKED ME TO HIDE THEM SOMEWHERE ELSE.
NO. HE DIDN'T.
YOU KNOW WE HAVE VIDEO CAMERAS ALL THROUGHOUT THE SANCTUARY, RIGHT?
NO. NO, I DIDN'T. BUT, IN HINDSIGHT, I PROBABLY SHOULD HAVE GUESSED THAT.
YOU NEVER SHOULD HAVE BEEN BROUGHT HERE. YOU'RE A LIABILITY.
KIDS. TAKE A STEP BACK AND CLOSE YOUR EYES.
QUINZEL, HARLEEN

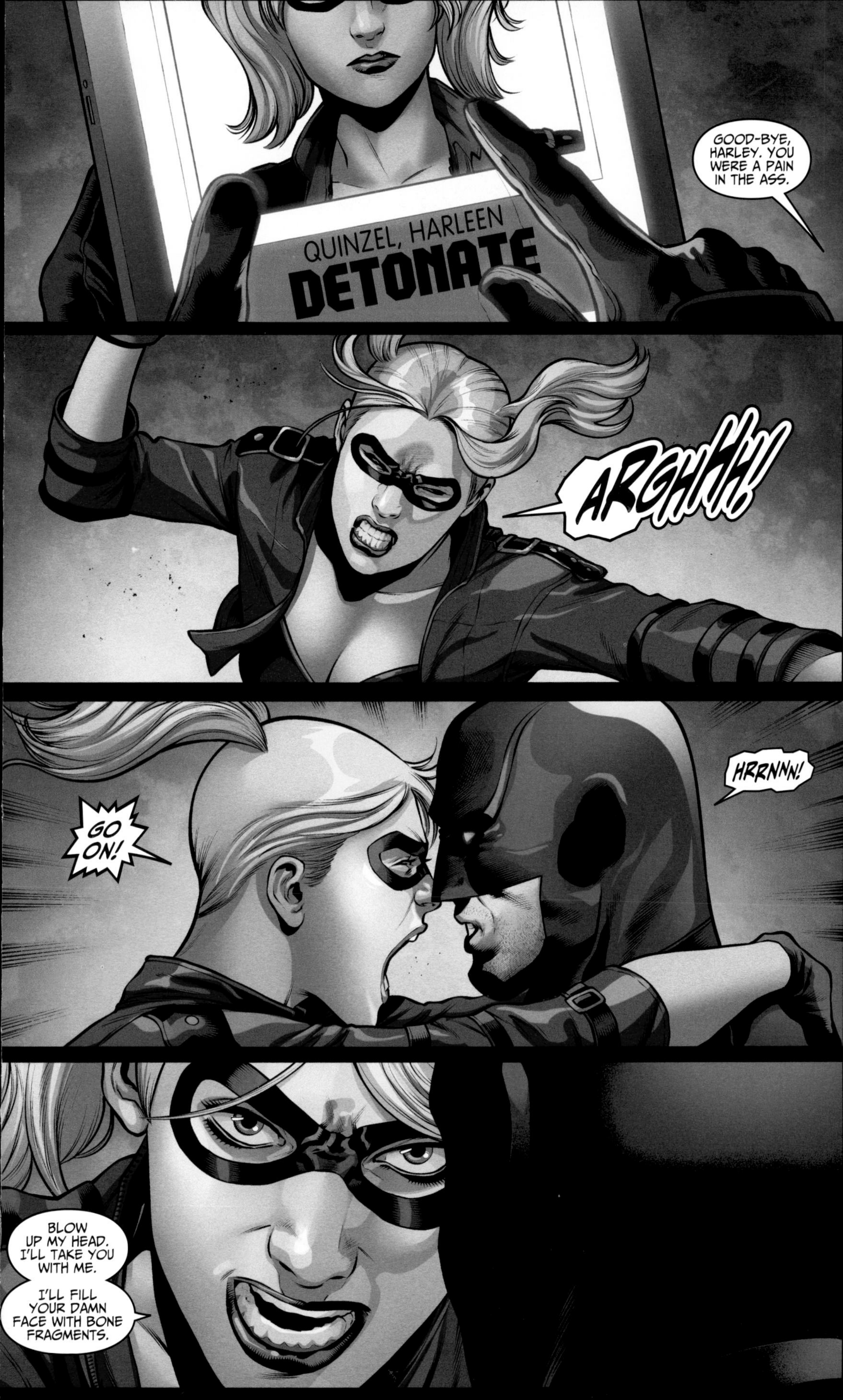
QUINZEL, HARLEEN
DETONATE
GOOD-BYE, HARLEY. YOU WERE A PAIN IN THE ASS.
ARGHHH!
HRRNNN!
GO ON!
BLOW UP MY HEAD. I'LL TAKE YOU WITH ME.
I'LL FILL YOUR DAMN FACE WITH BONE FRAGMENTS.

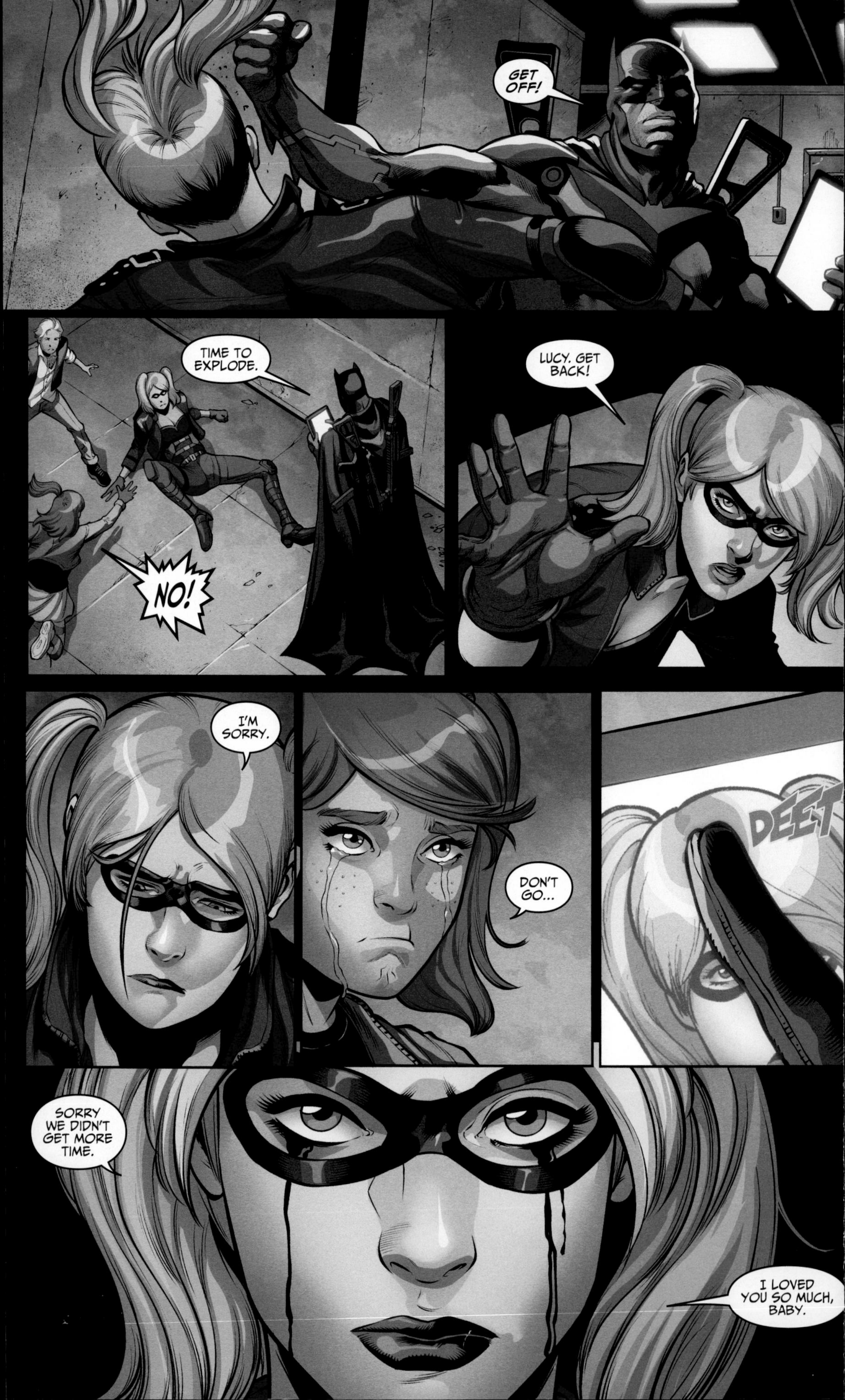
GET OFF!
TIME TO EXPLODE.
NO!
LUCY. GET BACK!
I'M SORRY.
DON'T GO...
DEET
SORRY WE DIDN'T GET MORE TIME.
I LOVED YOU SO MUCH, BABY.

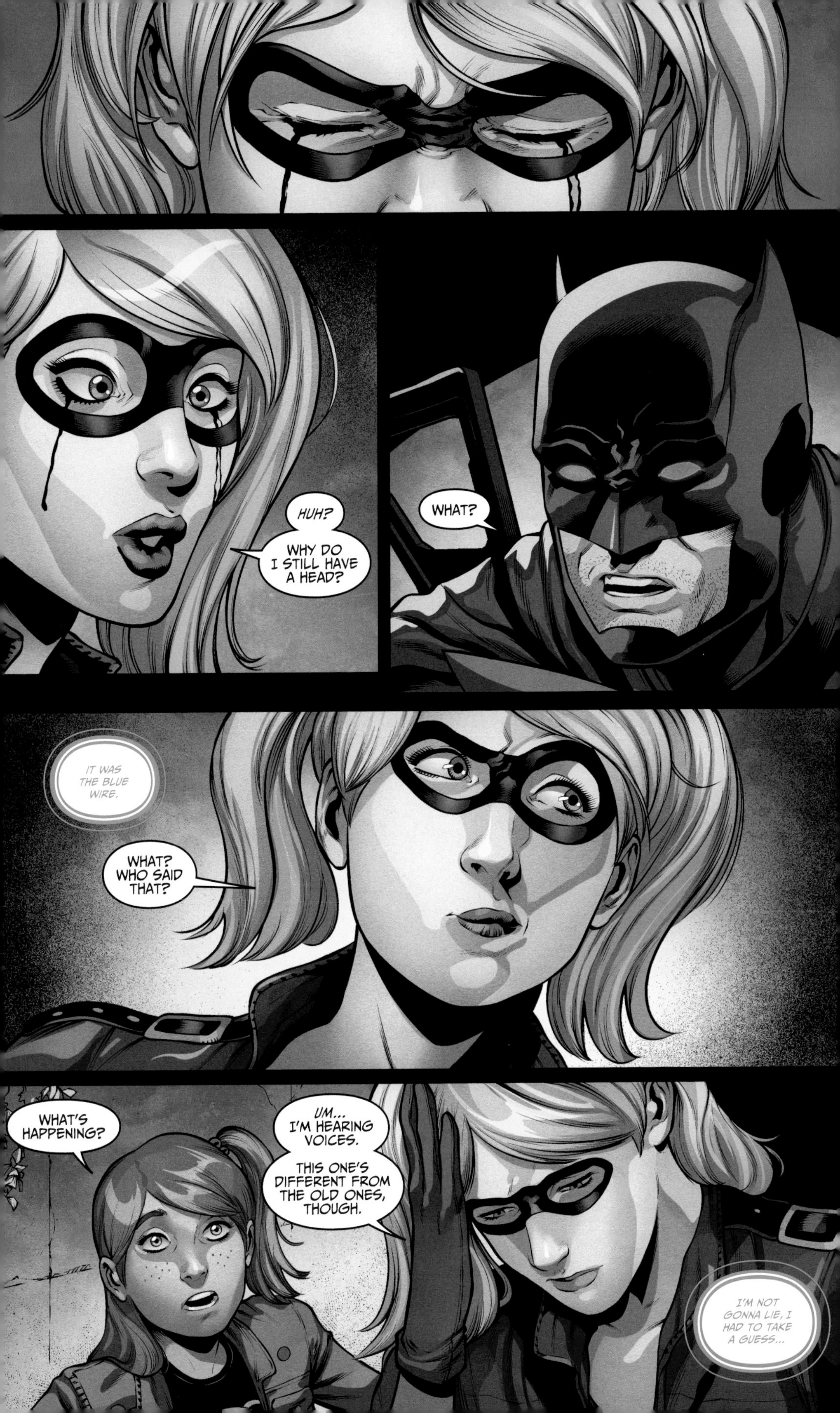
HUH?
WHY DO I STILL HAVE A HEAD?
WHAT?
IT WAS THE BLUE WIRE.
WHAT? WHO SAID THAT?
WHAT'S HAPPENING?
UM... I'M HEARING VOICES.
THIS ONE'S DIFFERENT FROM THE OLD ONES, THOUGH.
I'M NOT GONNA LIE, I HAD TO TAKE A GUESS...

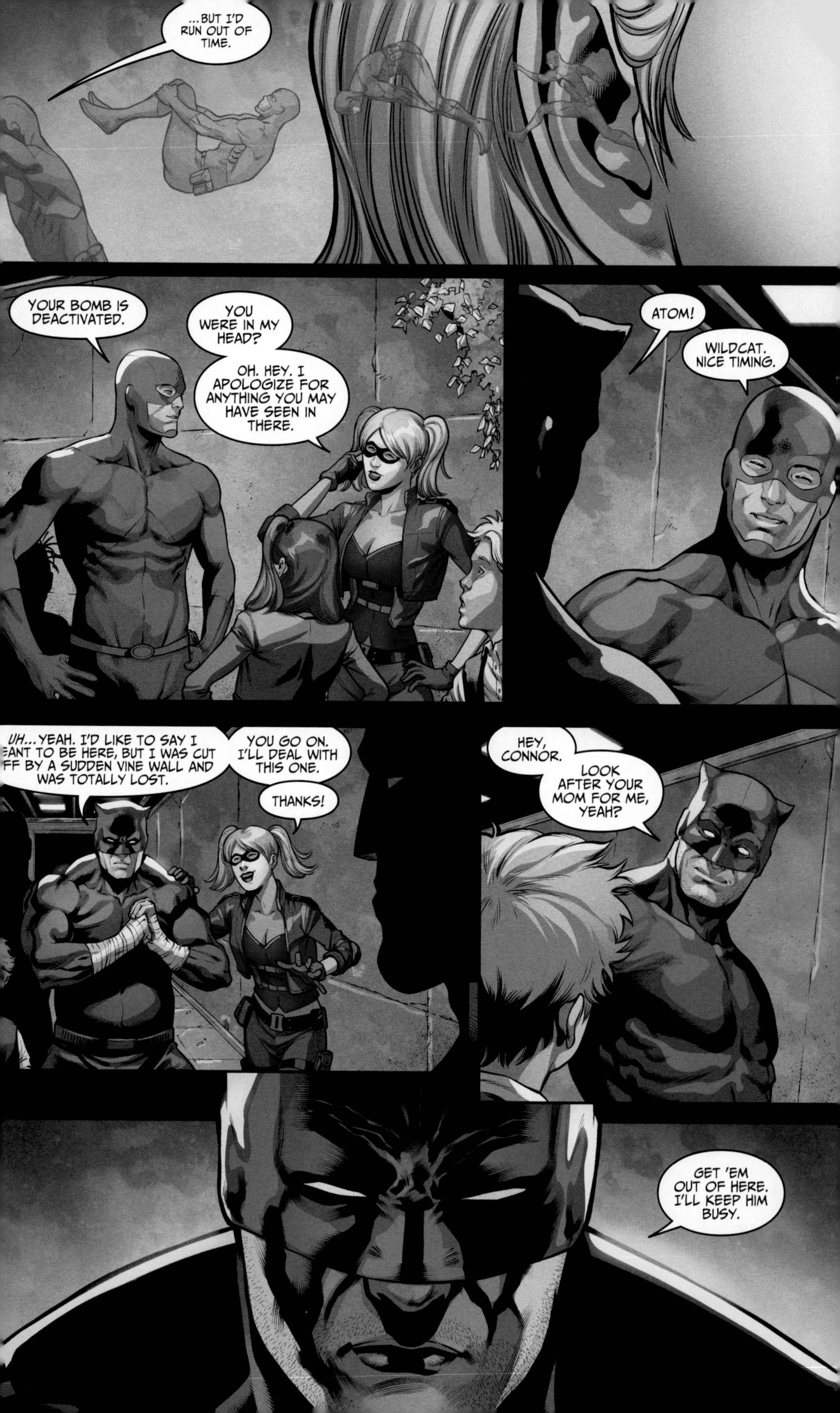
...BUT I'D RUN OUT OF TIME.
YOUR BOMB IS DEACTIVATED.
YOU WERE IN MY HEAD?
OH. HEY. I APOLOGIZE FOR ANYTHING YOU MAY HAVE SEEN IN THERE.
ATOM!
WILDCAT. NICE TIMING.
UH... YEAH. I'D LIKE TO SAY I
EANT TO BE HERE, BUT I WAS CUT
FF BY A SUDDEN VINE WALL AND WAS TOTALLY LOST.
YOU GO ON. I'LL DEAL WITH THIS ONE.
THANKS!
HEY, CONNOR.
LOOK AFTER YOUR MOM FOR ME, YEAH?
GET 'EM OUT OF HERE. I'LL KEEP HIM BUSY.

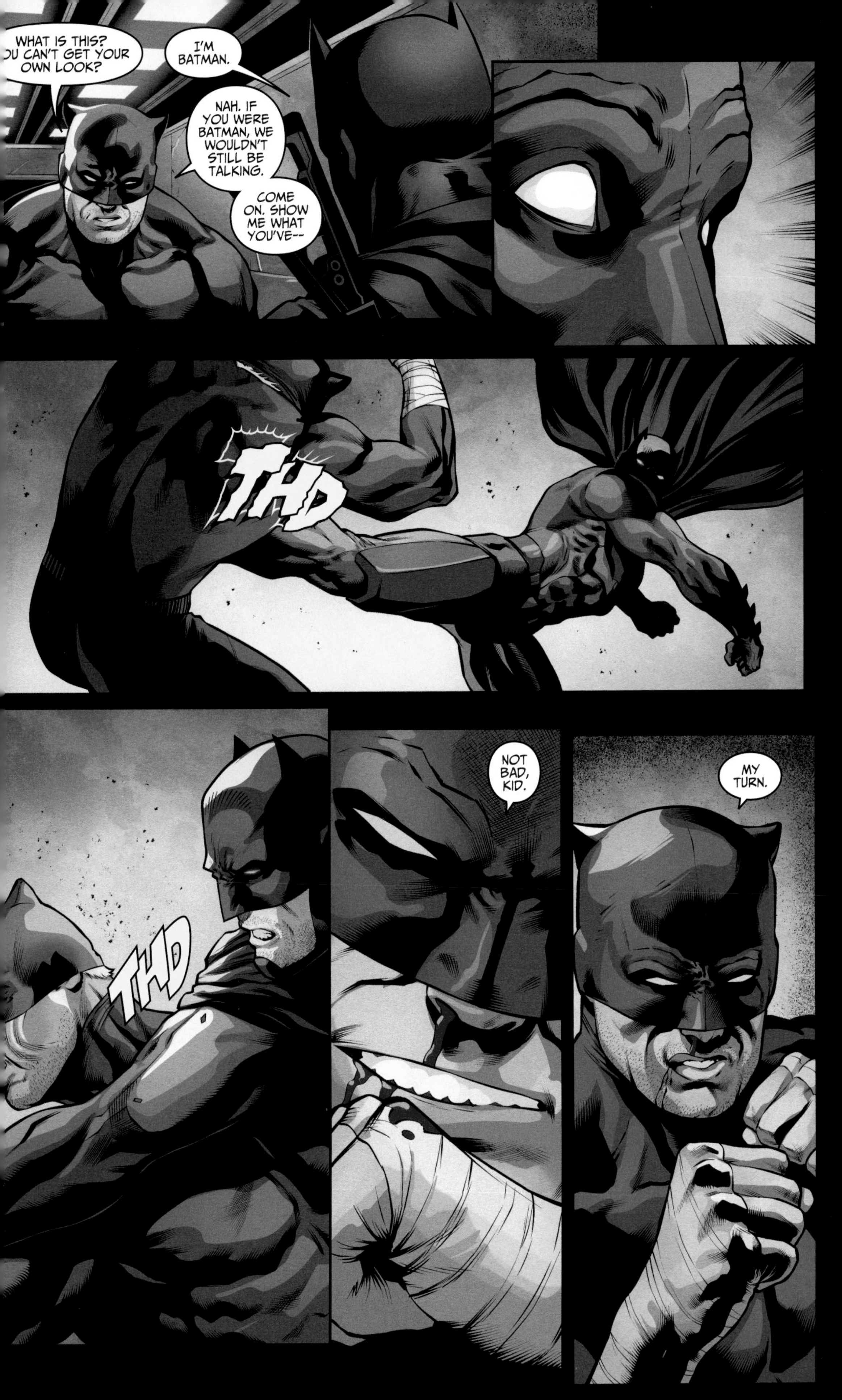
WHAT IS THIS? OU CAN'T GET YOUR OWN LOOK?
I'M BATMAN.
NAH. IF YOU WERE BATMAN, WE WOULDN'T STILL BE TALKING.
COME ON. SHOW ME WHAT YOU'VE--
THD
THD
NOT BAD, KID.
MY TURN.

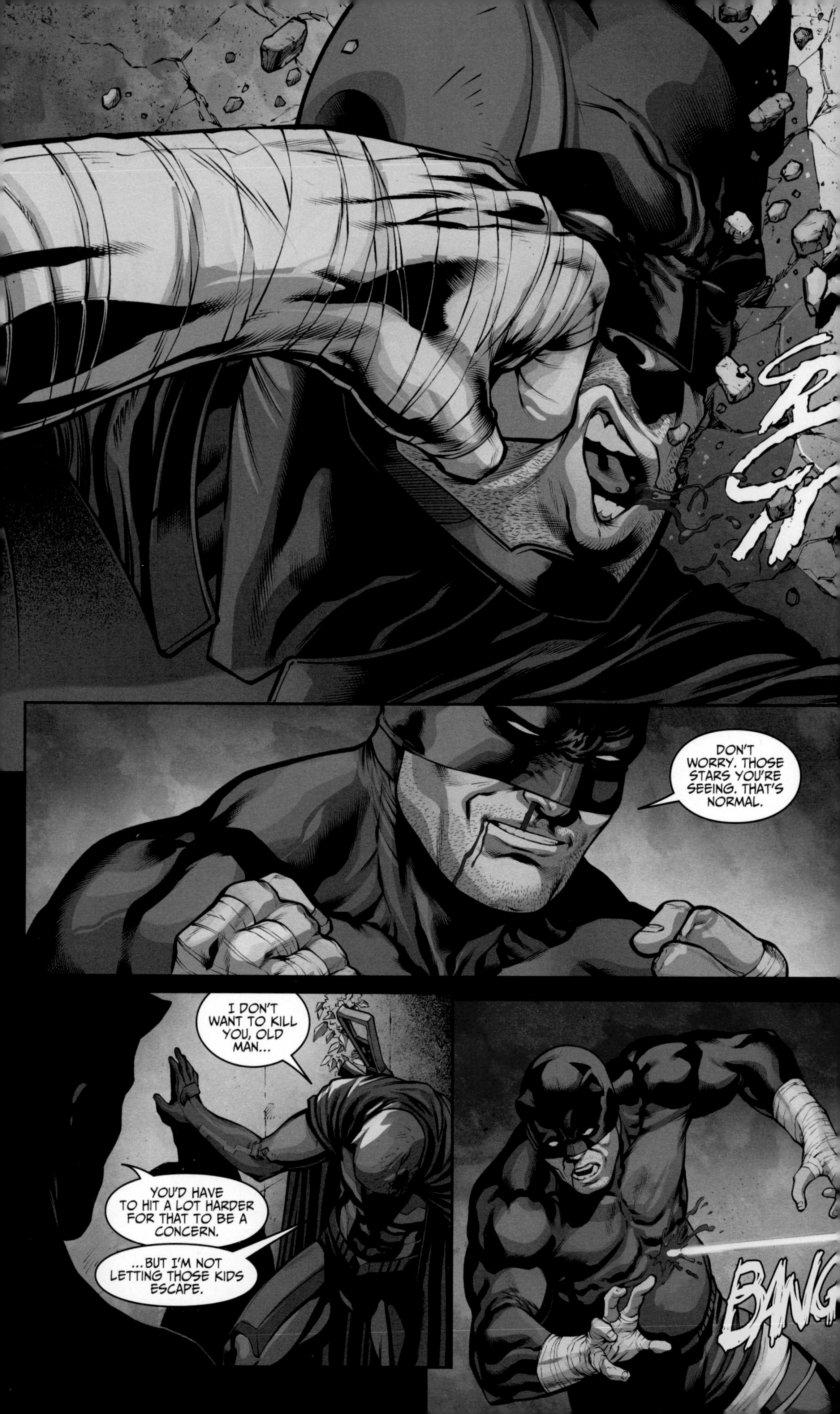

CRACK
DON'T WORRY. THOSE STARS YOU'RE SEEING. THAT'S NORMAL.
I DON'T WANT TO KILL YOU, OLD MAN...
YOU'D HAVE TO HIT A LOT HARDER FOR THAT TO BE A CONCERN.
...BUT I'M NOT LETTING THOSE KIDS ESCAPE.
BANG

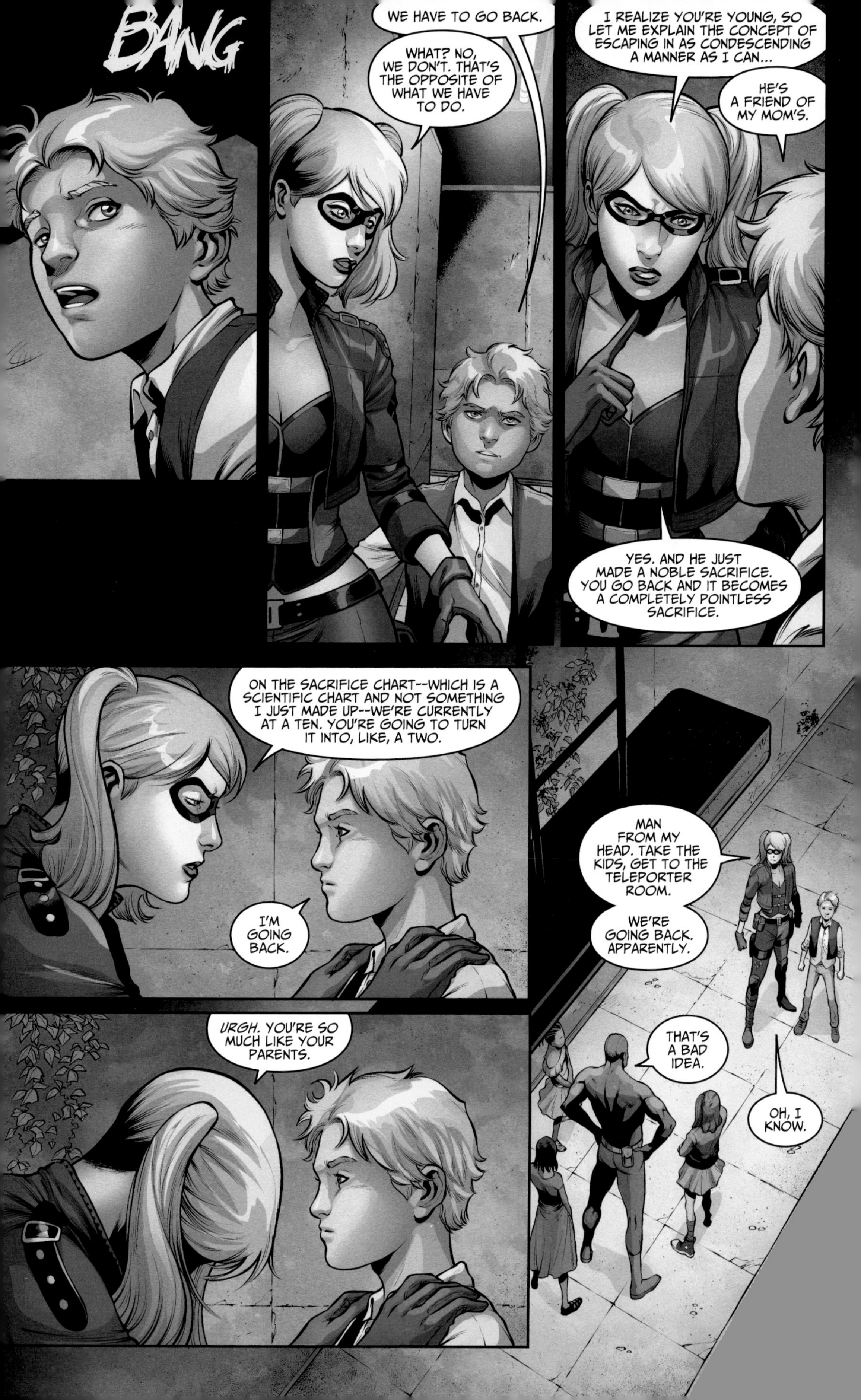
BANG
WE HAVE TO GO BACK.
WHAT? NO, WE DON'T. THAT'S THE OPPOSITE OF WHAT WE HAVE TO DO.
I REALIZE YOU'RE YOUNG, SO LET ME EXPLAIN THE CONCEPT OF ESCAPING IN AS CONDESCENDING A MANNER AS I CAN...
HE'S A FRIEND OF MY MOM'S.
YES. AND HE JUST MADE A NOBLE SACRIFICE. YOU GO BACK AND IT BECOMES A COMPLETELY POINTLESS SACRIFICE.
ON THE SACRIFICE CHART--WHICH IS A SCIENTIFIC CHART AND NOT SOMETHING I JUST MADE UP--WE'RE CURRENTLY AT A TEN. YOU'RE GOING TO TURN IT INTO, LIKE, A TWO.
I'M GOING BACK.
URGH. YOU'RE SO MUCH LIKE YOUR PARENTS.
MAN FROM MY HEAD. TAKE THE KIDS, GET TO THE TELEPORTER ROOM.
WE'RE GOING BACK. APPARENTLY.
THAT'S A BAD IDEA.
OH, I KNOW.

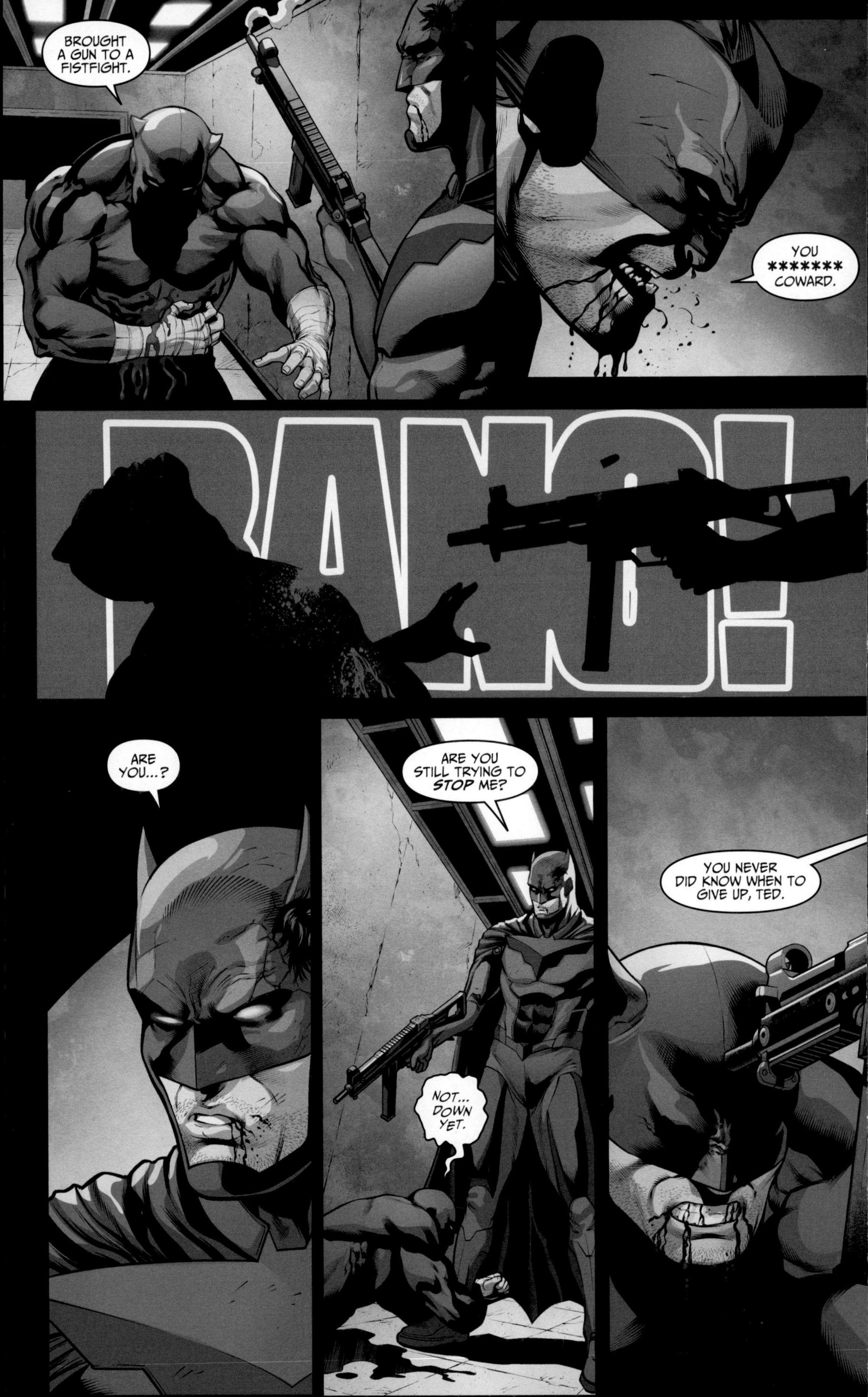
BROUGHT A GUN TO A FISTFIGHT.
YOU ******* COWARD.
BANG!
ARE YOU...?
ARE YOU STILL TRYING TO STOP ME?
NOT... DOWN YET.
YOU NEVER DID KNOW WHEN TO GIVE UP, TED.

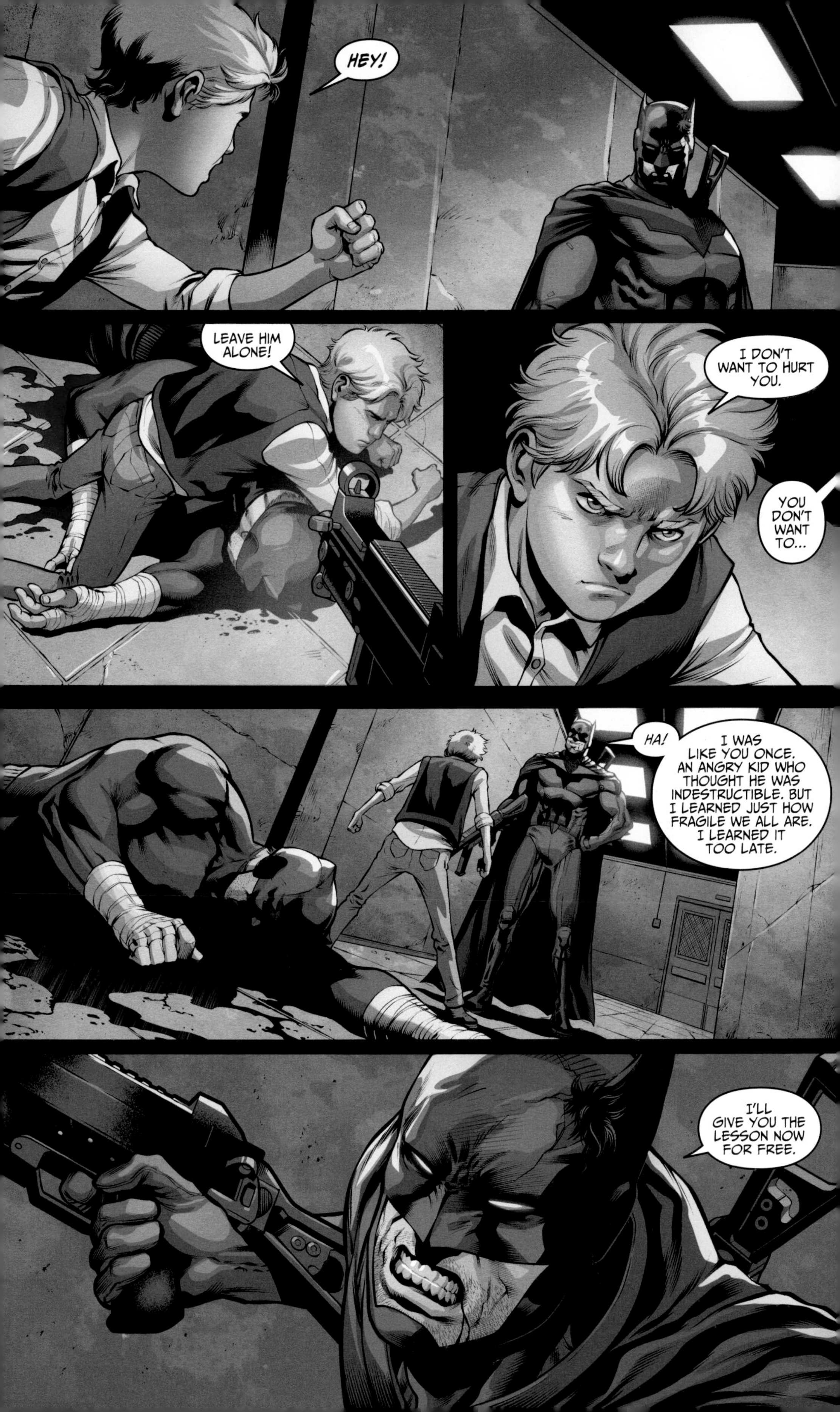
HEY!
LEAVE HIM ALONE!
I DON'T WANT TO HURT YOU.
YOU DON'T WANT TO...
HA!
I WAS LIKE YOU ONCE. AN ANGRY KID WHO THOUGHT HE WAS INDESTRUCTIBLE. BUT I LEARNED JUST HOW FRAGILE WE ALL ARE. I LEARNED IT TOO LATE.
I'LL GIVE YOU THE LESSON NOW FOR FREE.

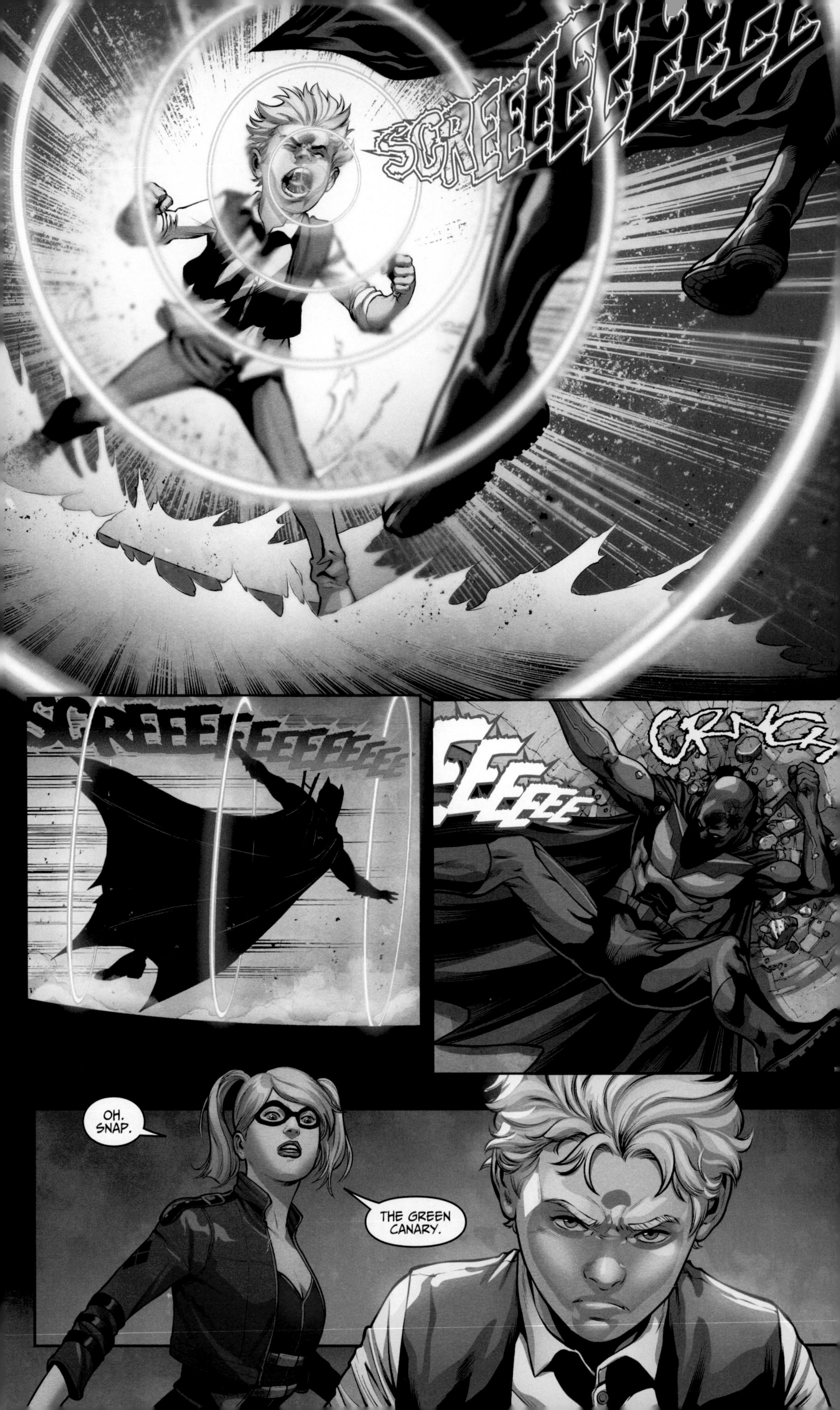
SCREEEEEEEEEE
SCREEEEEEEEEEEEEE
EEEEEE
CRNCH
OH. SNAP.
THE GREEN CANARY.

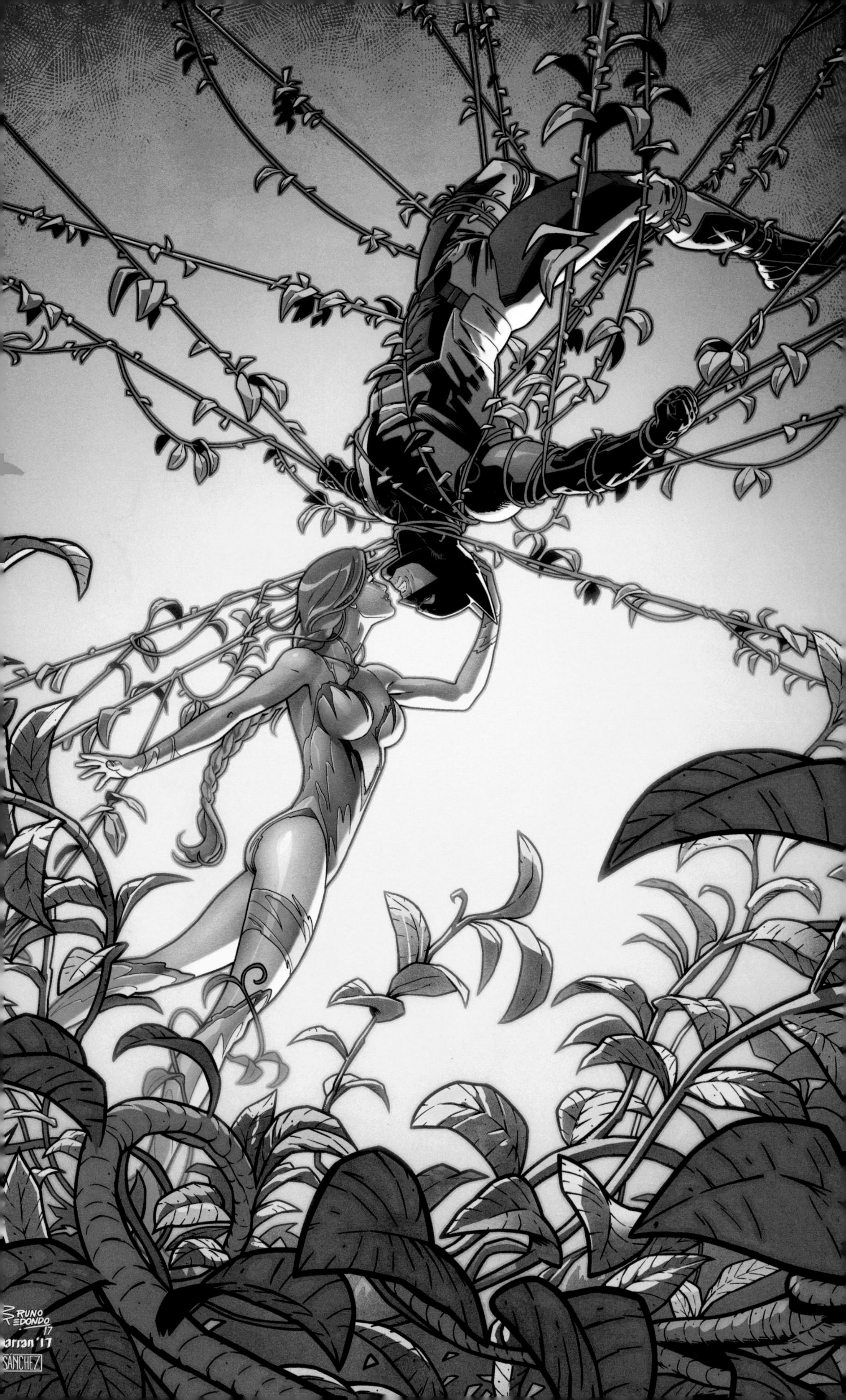
BRUNO REDONDO 17
arran '17
SÁNCHEZ

"Sanctuary"

Tom Taylor Writer **Bruno Redondo** Penciller **Juan Albarran** Inker **Rex Lokus** Colorist
Wes Abbott Letterer Cover art by **Bruno Redondo, Juan Albarran** and **Alejandro Sanchez**

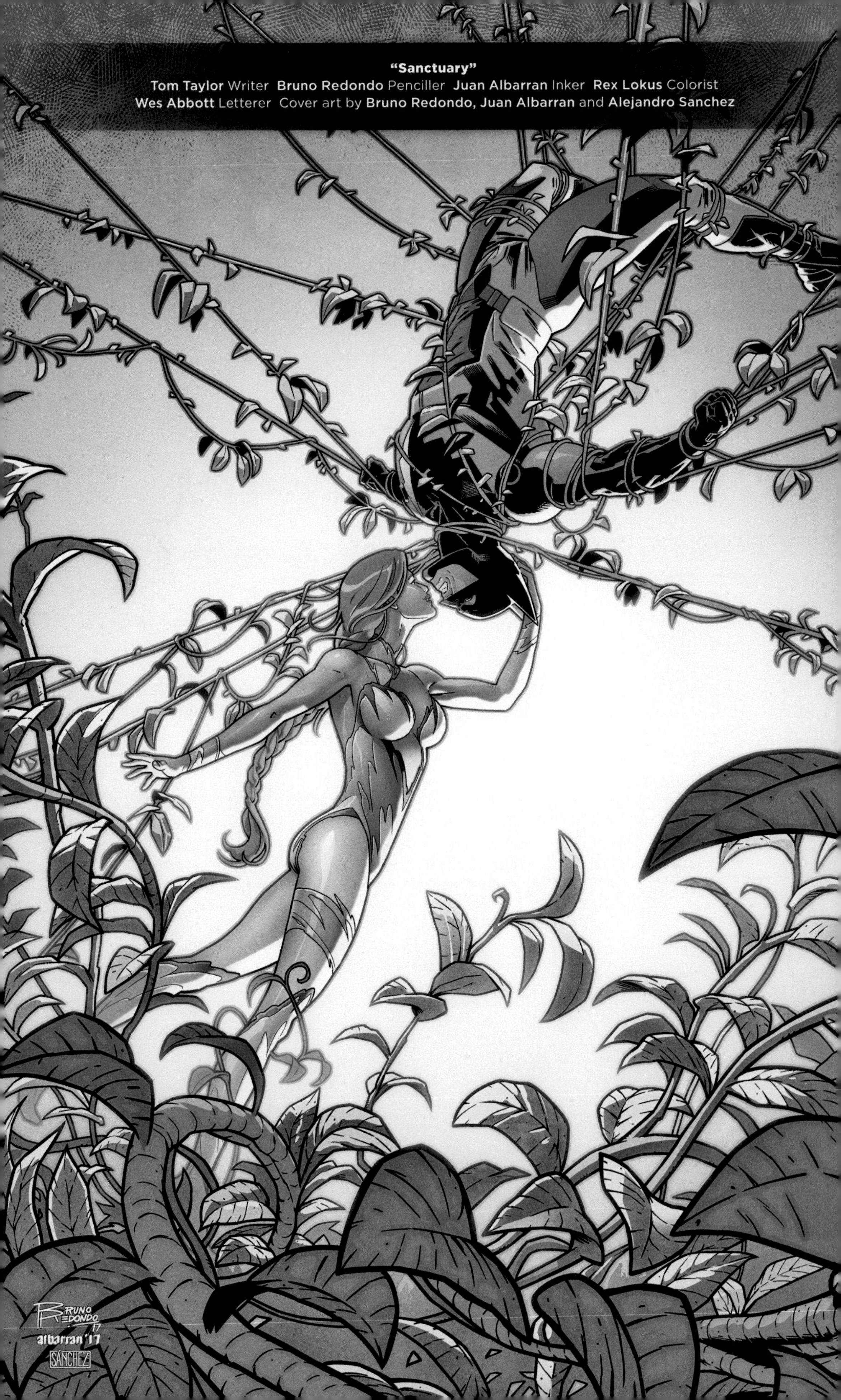
BRUNO REDONDO '17
albarran '17
SÁNCHEZ

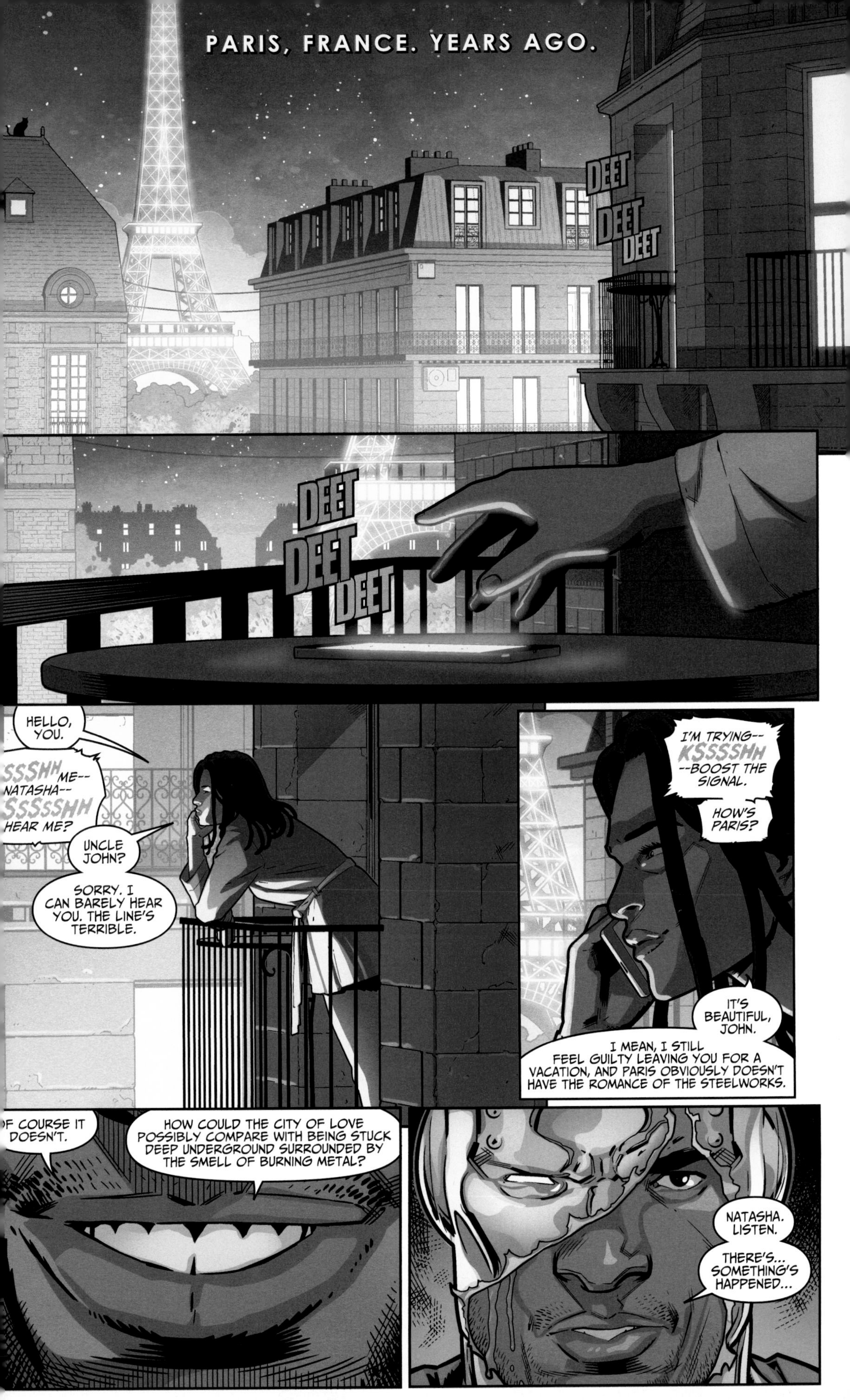
PARIS, FRANCE. YEARS AGO.
DEET DEET DEET
DEET DEET DEET
HELLO, YOU.
SSSSHH ME-- NATASHA-- SSSSSHH HEAR ME?
UNCLE JOHN?
SORRY. I CAN BARELY HEAR YOU. THE LINE'S TERRIBLE.
I'M TRYING-- KSSSSHH --BOOST THE SIGNAL.
HOW'S PARIS?
IT'S BEAUTIFUL, JOHN.
I MEAN, I STILL FEEL GUILTY LEAVING YOU FOR A VACATION, AND PARIS OBVIOUSLY DOESN'T HAVE THE ROMANCE OF THE STEELWORKS.
OF COURSE IT DOESN'T.
HOW COULD THE CITY OF LOVE POSSIBLY COMPARE WITH BEING STUCK DEEP UNDERGROUND SURROUNDED BY THE SMELL OF BURNING METAL?
NATASHA. LISTEN.
THERE'S... SOMETHING'S HAPPENED...

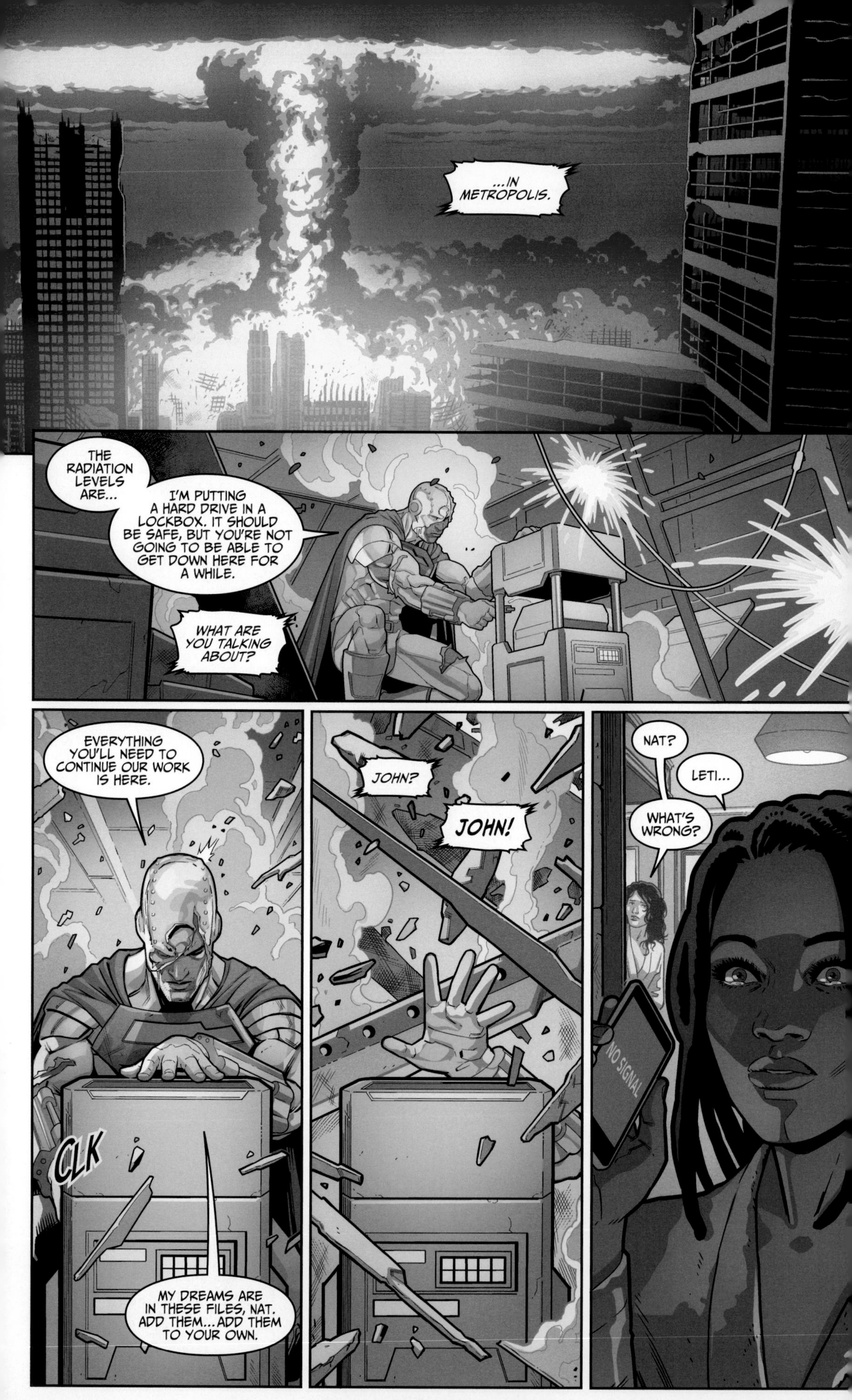

...IN METROPOLIS.
THE RADIATION LEVELS ARE...
I'M PUTTING A HARD DRIVE IN A LOCKBOX. IT SHOULD BE SAFE, BUT YOU'RE NOT GOING TO BE ABLE TO GET DOWN HERE FOR A WHILE.
WHAT ARE YOU TALKING ABOUT?
EVERYTHING YOU'LL NEED TO CONTINUE OUR WORK IS HERE.
CLK
MY DREAMS ARE IN THESE FILES, NAT. ADD THEM... ADD THEM TO YOUR OWN.
JOHN?
JOHN!
NAT?
LETI...
WHAT'S WRONG?
NO SIGNAL

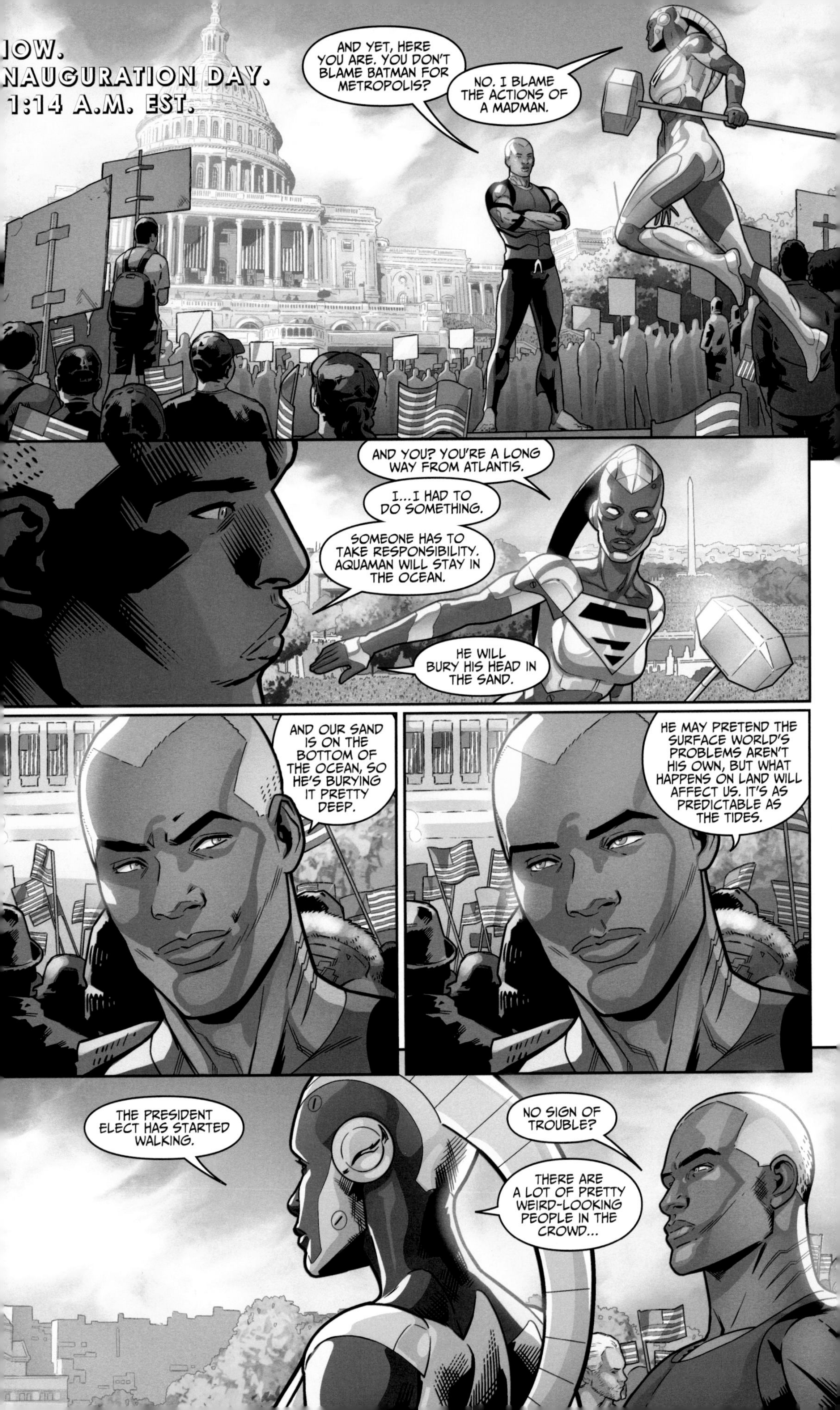

IOW.
NAUGURATION DAY.
1:14 A.M. EST.
AND YET, HERE YOU ARE. YOU DON'T BLAME BATMAN FOR METROPOLIS?
NO. I BLAME THE ACTIONS OF A MADMAN.
AND YOU? YOU'RE A LONG WAY FROM ATLANTIS.
I...I HAD TO DO SOMETHING.
SOMEONE HAS TO TAKE RESPONSIBILITY. AQUAMAN WILL STAY IN THE OCEAN.
HE WILL BURY HIS HEAD IN THE SAND.
AND OUR SAND IS ON THE BOTTOM OF THE OCEAN, SO HE'S BURYING IT PRETTY DEEP.
HE MAY PRETEND THE SURFACE WORLD'S PROBLEMS AREN'T HIS OWN, BUT WHAT HAPPENS ON LAND WILL AFFECT US. IT'S AS PREDICTABLE AS THE TIDES.
THE PRESIDENT ELECT HAS STARTED WALKING.
NO SIGN OF TROUBLE?
THERE ARE A LOT OF PRETTY WEIRD-LOOKING PEOPLE IN THE CROWD...

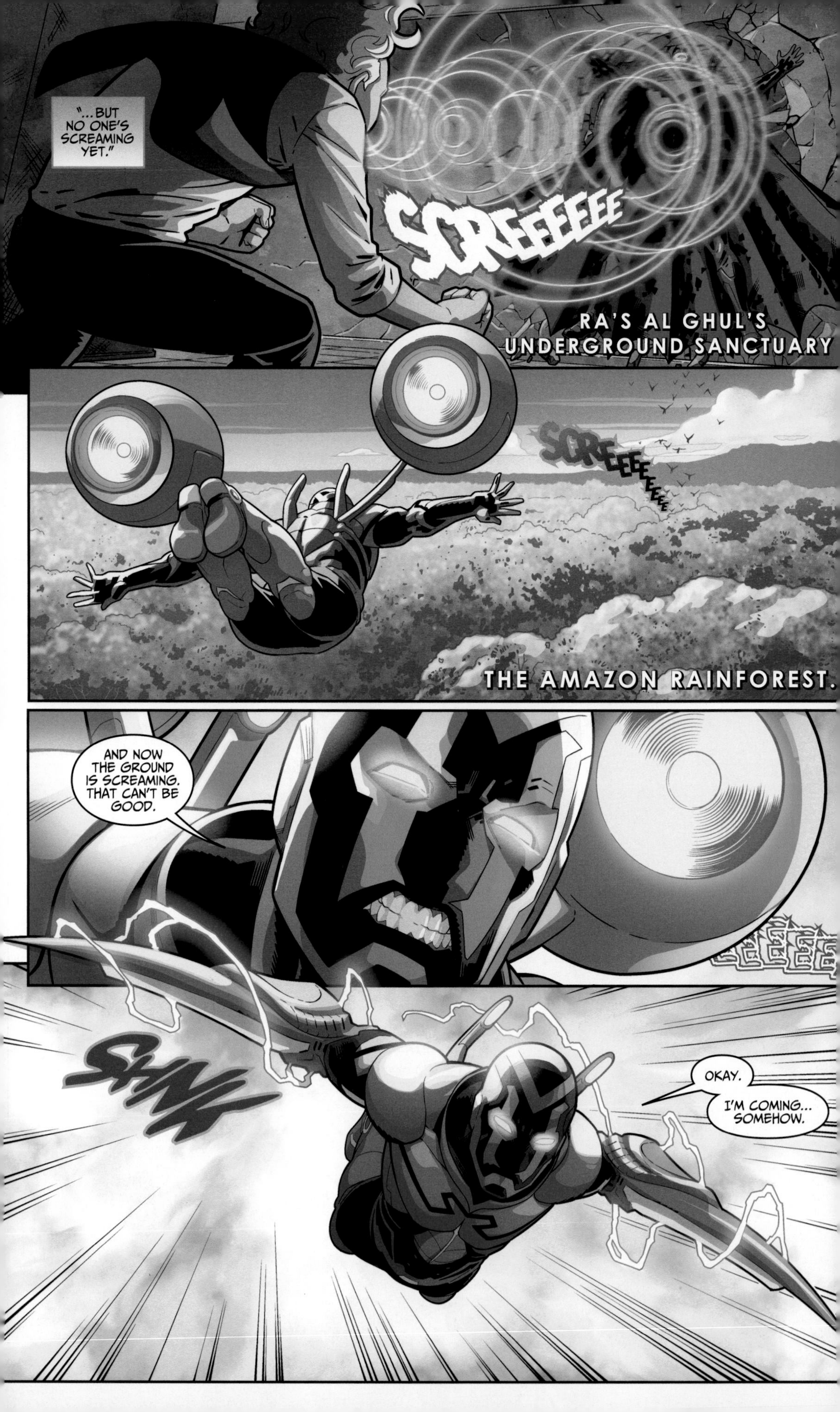
"...BUT NO ONE'S SCREAMING YET."
SCREEEEEEE
RA'S AL GHUL'S UNDERGROUND SANCTUARY
SCREEEEEEEEE
THE AMAZON RAINFOREST.
AND NOW THE GROUND IS SCREAMING. THAT CAN'T BE GOOD.
SHNK
OKAY.
I'M COMING... SOMEHOW.

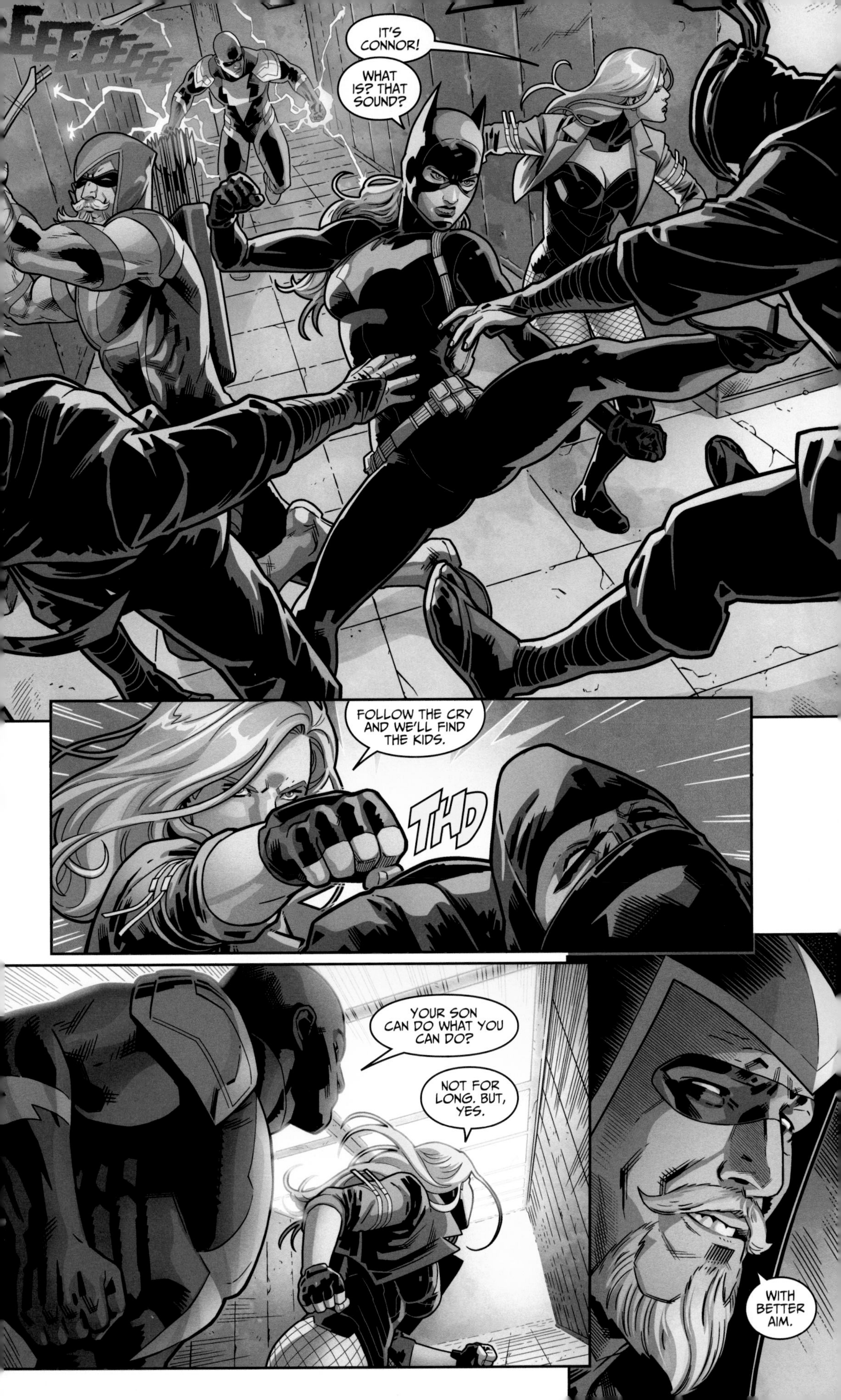
EEEEEEEE
IT'S CONNOR!
WHAT IS? THAT SOUND?
FOLLOW THE CRY AND WE'LL FIND THE KIDS.
THD
YOUR SON CAN DO WHAT YOU CAN DO?
NOT FOR LONG. BUT, YES.
WITH BETTER AIM.

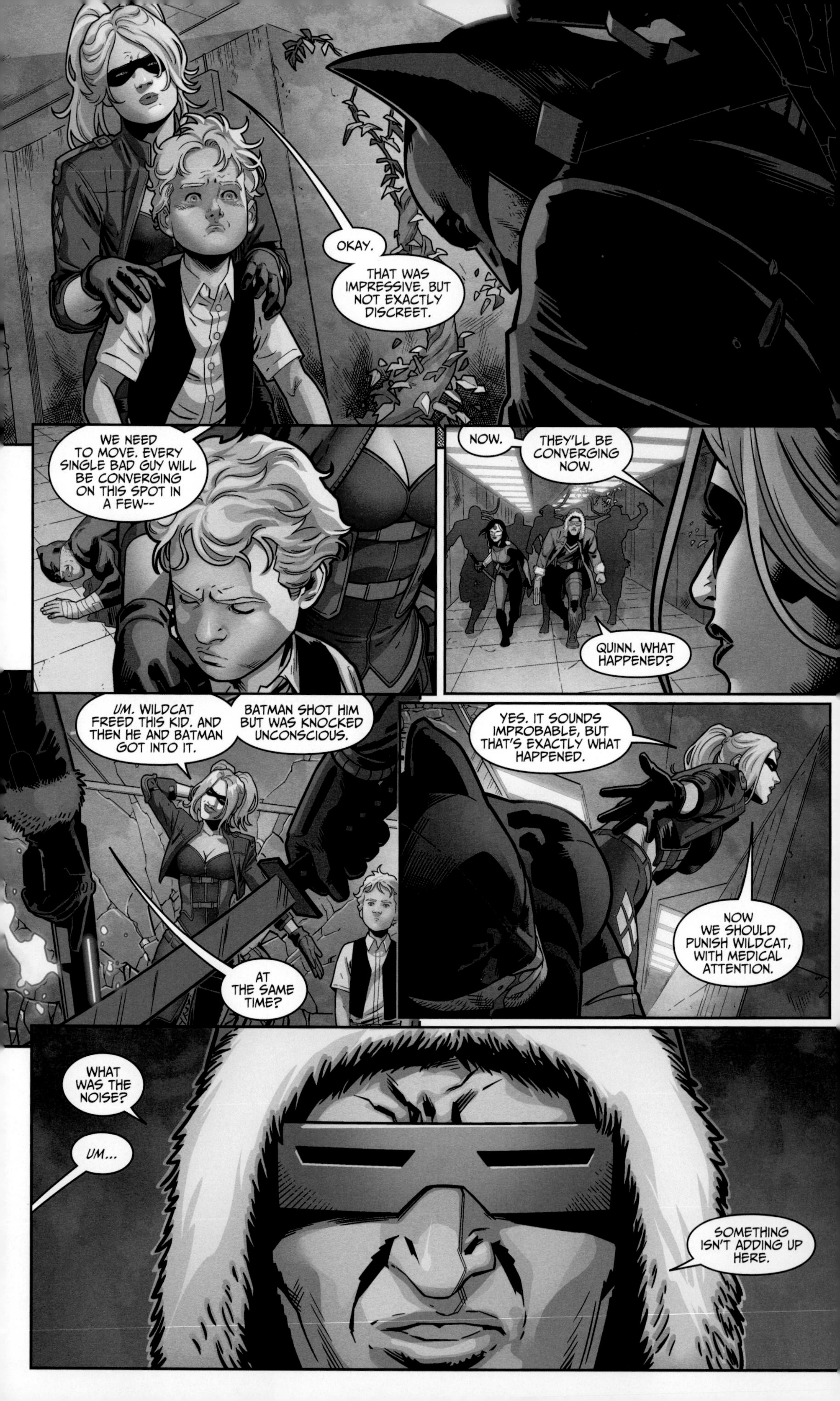
OKAY.
THAT WAS IMPRESSIVE. BUT NOT EXACTLY DISCREET.
WE NEED TO MOVE. EVERY SINGLE BAD GUY WILL BE CONVERGING ON THIS SPOT IN A FEW--
NOW.
THEY'LL BE CONVERGING NOW.
QUINN. WHAT HAPPENED?
UM. WILDCAT FREED THIS KID. AND THEN HE AND BATMAN GOT INTO IT.
BATMAN SHOT HIM BUT WAS KNOCKED UNCONSCIOUS.
AT THE SAME TIME?
YES. IT SOUNDS IMPROBABLE, BUT THAT'S EXACTLY WHAT HAPPENED.
NOW WE SHOULD PUNISH WILDCAT, WITH MEDICAL ATTENTION.
WHAT WAS THE NOISE?
UM...
SOMETHING ISN'T ADDING UP HERE.

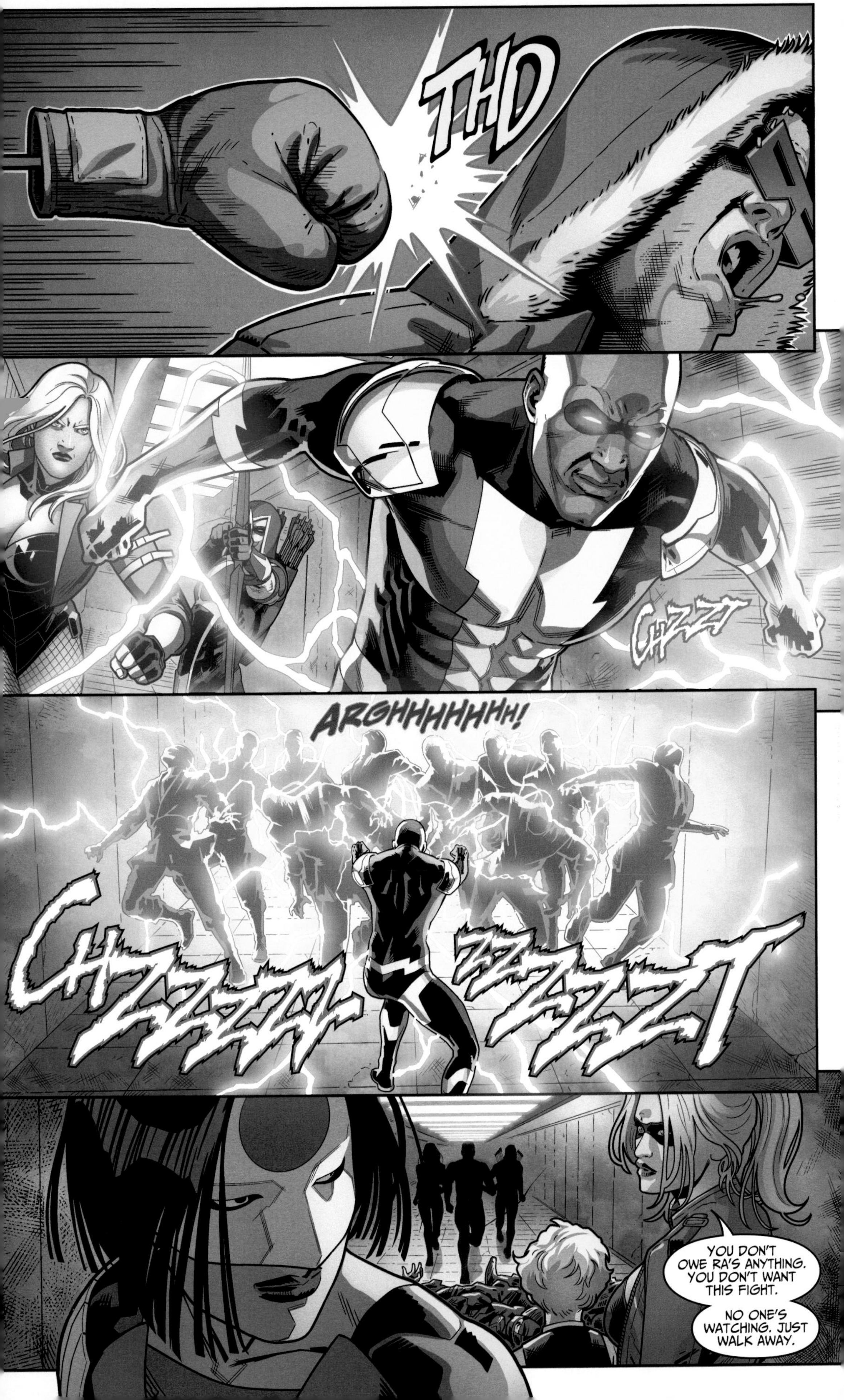
THD
CHZZT
ARGHHHHHHH!
CHZZZZZZZZZZZZT
YOU DON'T OWE RA'S ANYTHING. YOU DON'T WANT THIS FIGHT.
NO ONE'S WATCHING. JUST WALK AWAY.

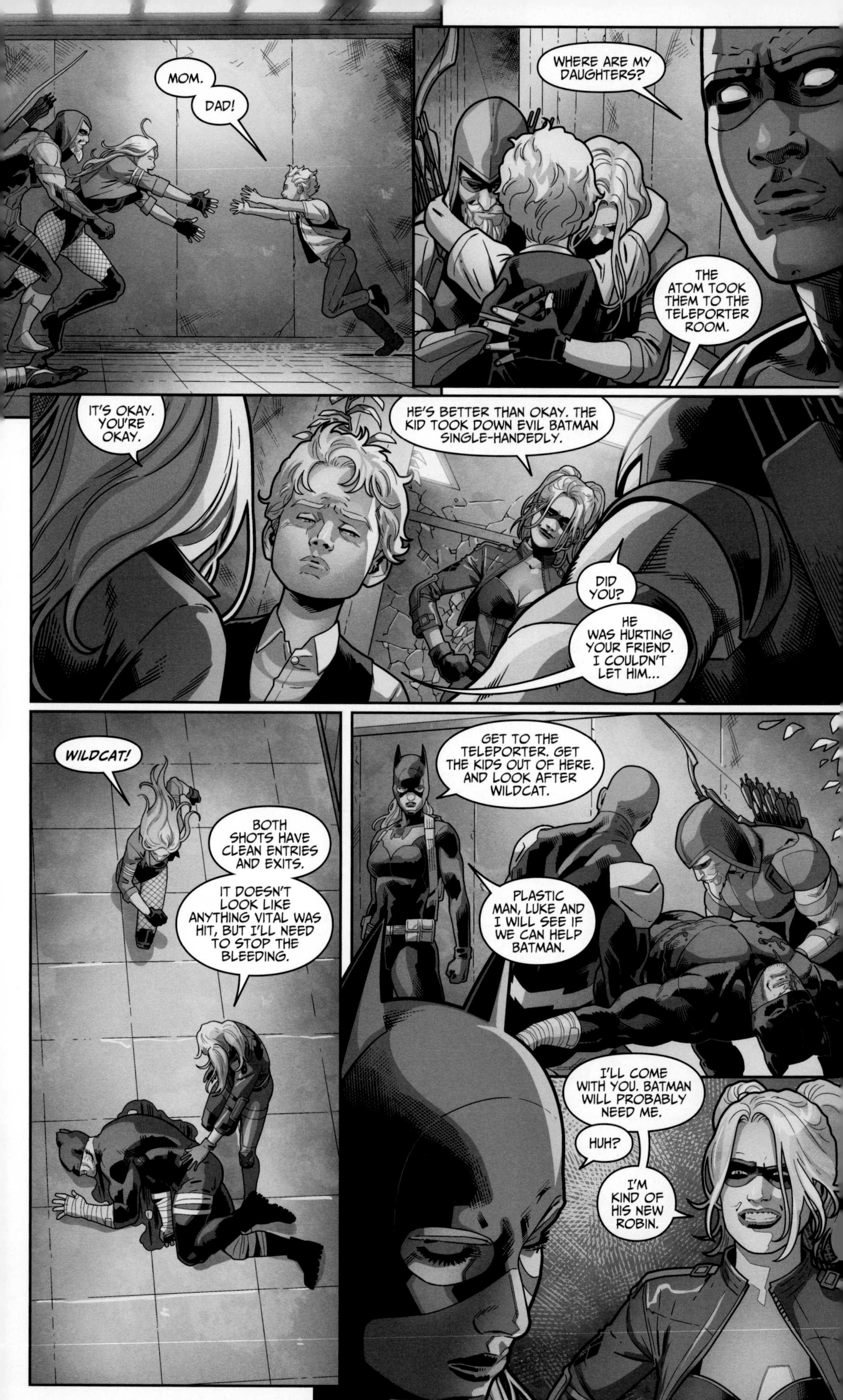
MOM.
DAD!
WHERE ARE MY DAUGHTERS?
THE ATOM TOOK THEM TO THE TELEPORTER ROOM.
IT'S OKAY. YOU'RE OKAY.
HE'S BETTER THAN OKAY. THE KID TOOK DOWN EVIL BATMAN SINGLE-HANDEDLY.
DID YOU?
HE WAS HURTING YOUR FRIEND. I COULDN'T LET HIM...
WILDCAT!
BOTH SHOTS HAVE CLEAN ENTRIES AND EXITS.
IT DOESN'T LOOK LIKE ANYTHING VITAL WAS HIT, BUT I'LL NEED TO STOP THE BLEEDING.
GET TO THE TELEPORTER. GET THE KIDS OUT OF HERE. AND LOOK AFTER WILDCAT.
PLASTIC MAN, LUKE AND I WILL SEE IF WE CAN HELP BATMAN.
I'LL COME WITH YOU. BATMAN WILL PROBABLY NEED ME.
HUH?
I'M KIND OF HIS NEW ROBIN.

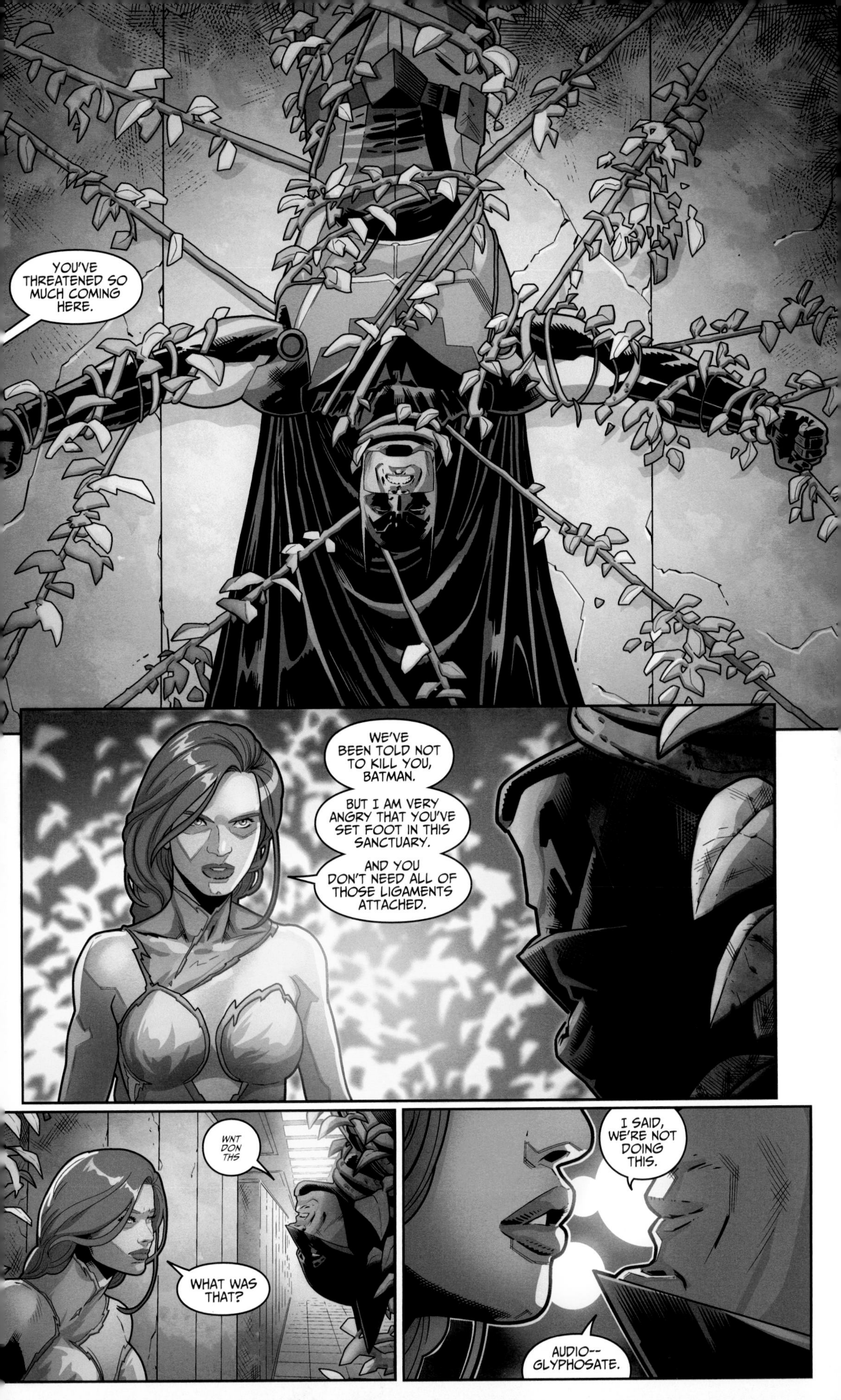

YOU'VE THREATENED SO MUCH COMING HERE.
WE'VE BEEN TOLD NOT TO KILL YOU, BATMAN.
BUT I AM VERY ANGRY THAT YOU'VE SET FOOT IN THIS SANCTUARY.
AND YOU DON'T NEED ALL OF THOSE LIGAMENTS ATTACHED.
WNT DON THS
WHAT WAS THAT?
I SAID, WE'RE NOT DOING THIS.
AUDIO-- GLYPHOSATE.

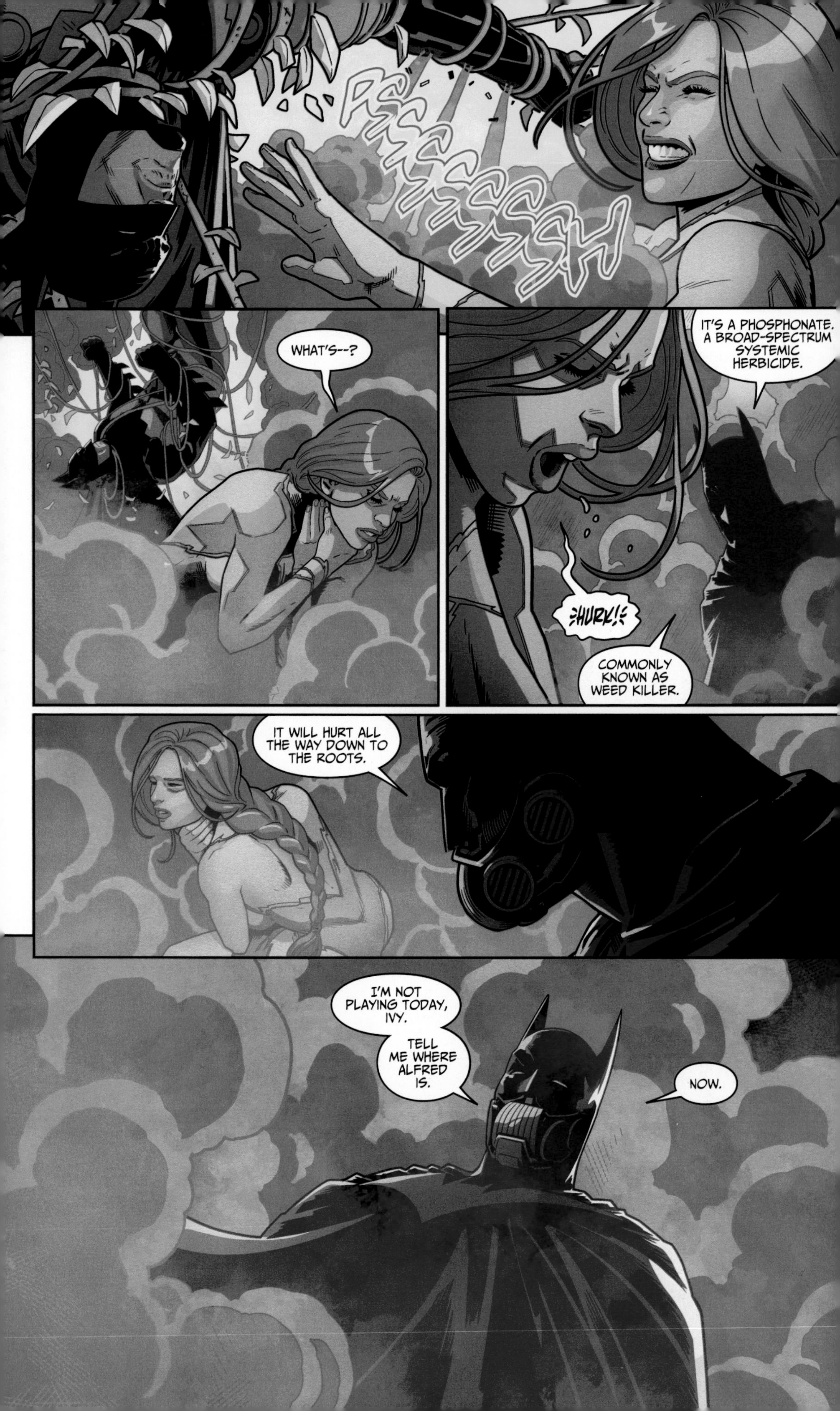
PSSSSSSSHHH
WHAT'S--?
IT'S A PHOSPHONATE. A BROAD-SPECTRUM SYSTEMIC HERBICIDE.
HURK!
COMMONLY KNOWN AS WEED KILLER.
IT WILL HURT ALL THE WAY DOWN TO THE ROOTS.
I'M NOT PLAYING TODAY, IVY.
TELL ME WHERE ALFRED IS.
NOW.

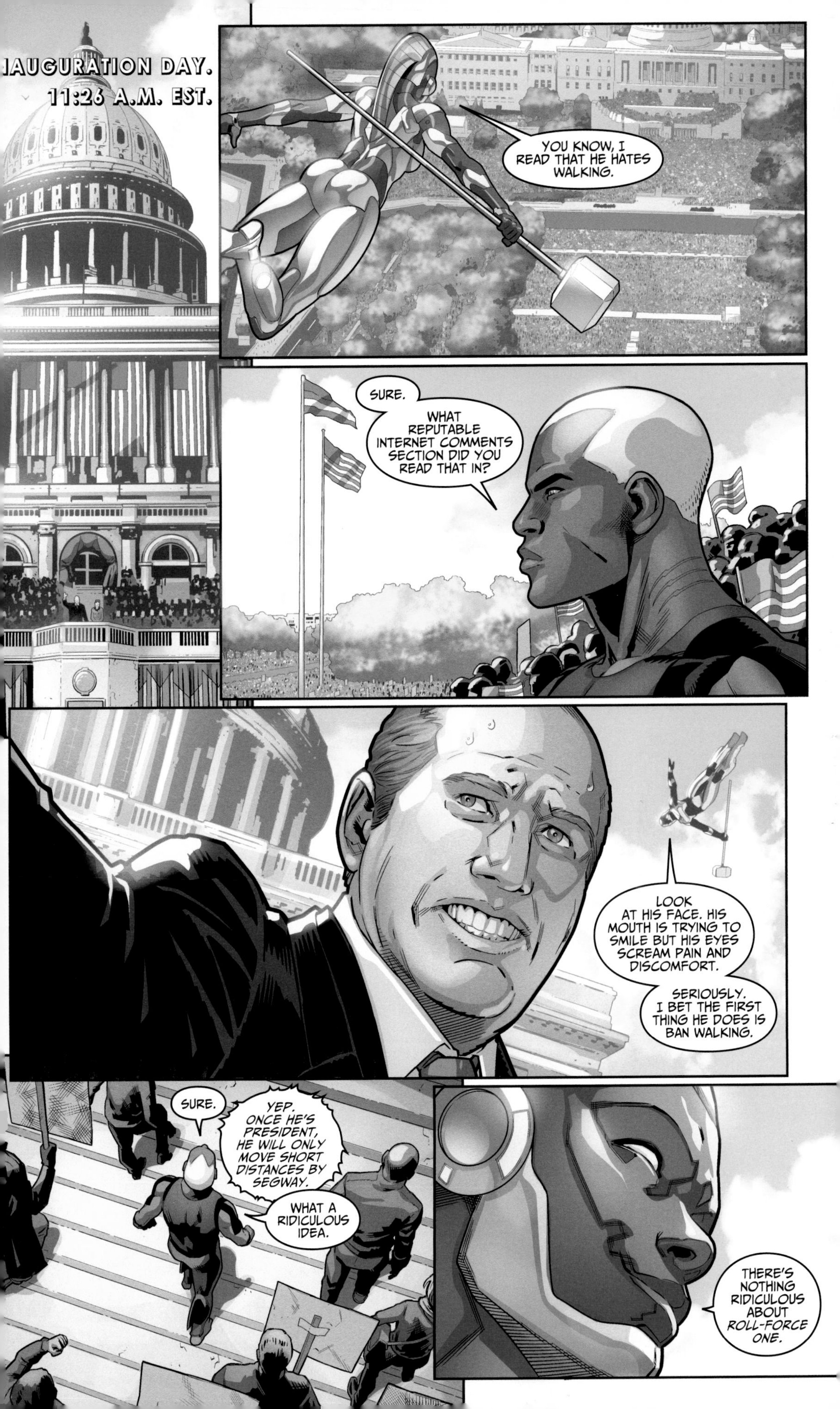

IAUGURATION DAY. 11:26 A.M. EST.
YOU KNOW, I READ THAT HE HATES WALKING.
SURE.
WHAT REPUTABLE INTERNET COMMENTS SECTION DID YOU READ THAT IN?
LOOK AT HIS FACE. HIS MOUTH IS TRYING TO SMILE BUT HIS EYES SCREAM PAIN AND DISCOMFORT.
SERIOUSLY. I BET THE FIRST THING HE DOES IS BAN WALKING.
SURE.
YEP. ONCE HE'S PRESIDENT, HE WILL ONLY MOVE SHORT DISTANCES BY SEGWAY.
WHAT A RIDICULOUS IDEA.
THERE'S NOTHING RIDICULOUS ABOUT ROLL-FORCE ONE.

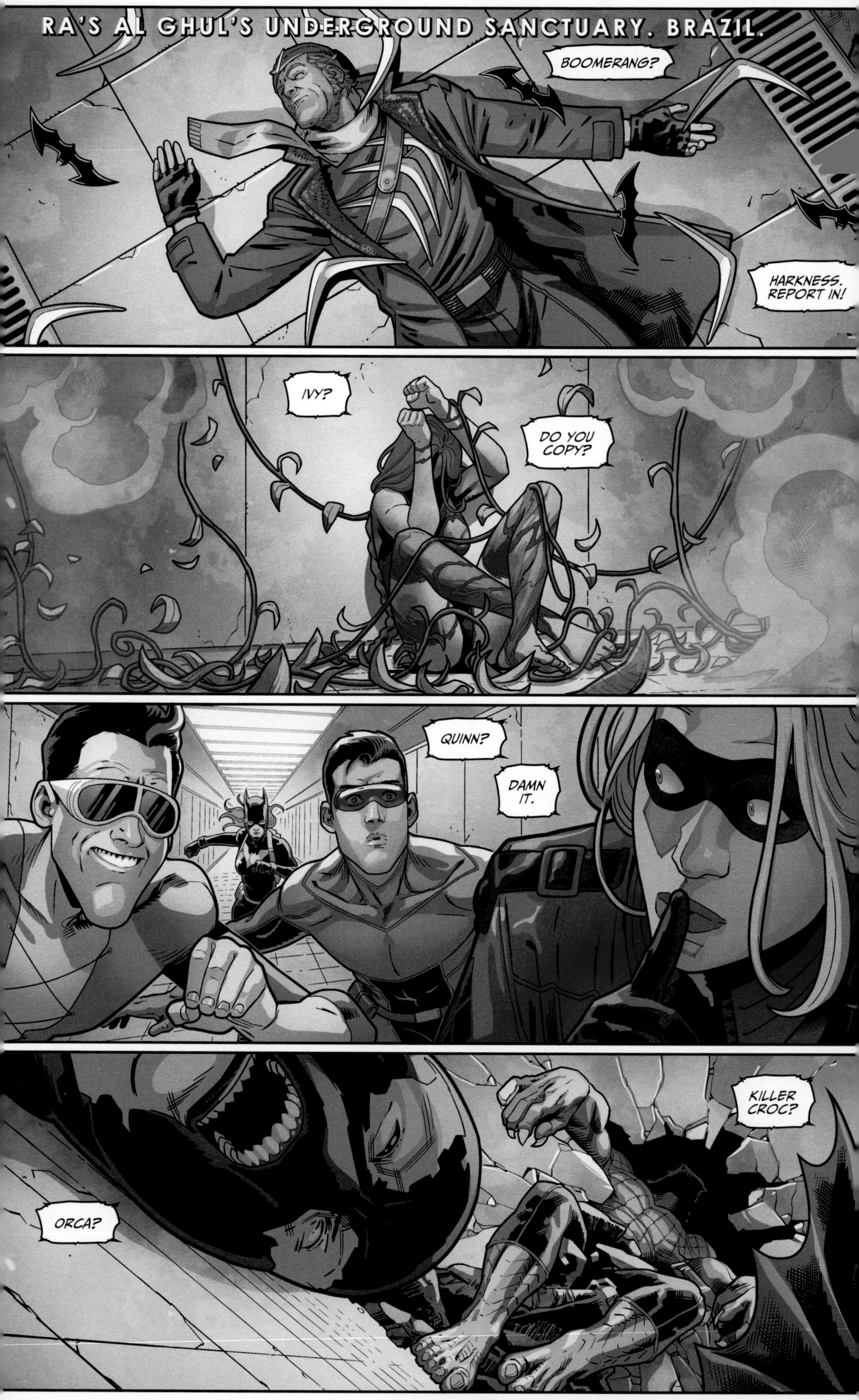
RA'S AL GHUL'S UNDERGROUND SANCTUARY. BRAZIL.
BOOMERANG?
HARKNESS. REPORT IN!
IVY?
DO YOU COPY?
QUINN?
DAMN IT.
KILLER CROC?
ORCA?

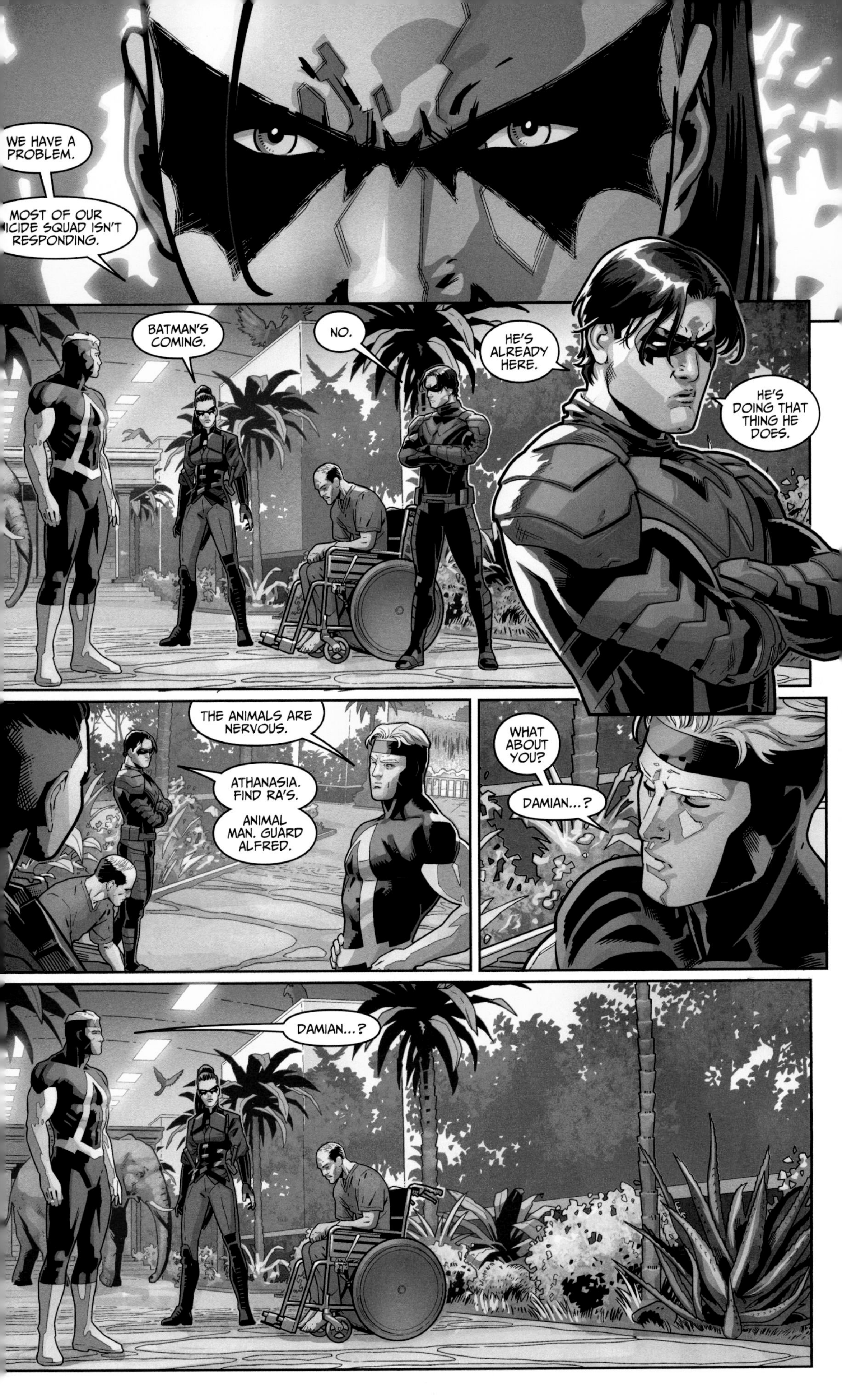
WE HAVE A PROBLEM.
MOST OF OUR ICIDE SQUAD ISN'T RESPONDING.
BATMAN'S COMING.
NO.
HE'S ALREADY HERE.
HE'S DOING THAT THING HE DOES.
THE ANIMALS ARE NERVOUS.
ATHANASIA. FIND RA'S.
ANIMAL MAN. GUARD ALFRED.
WHAT ABOUT YOU?
DAMIAN...?
DAMIAN...?

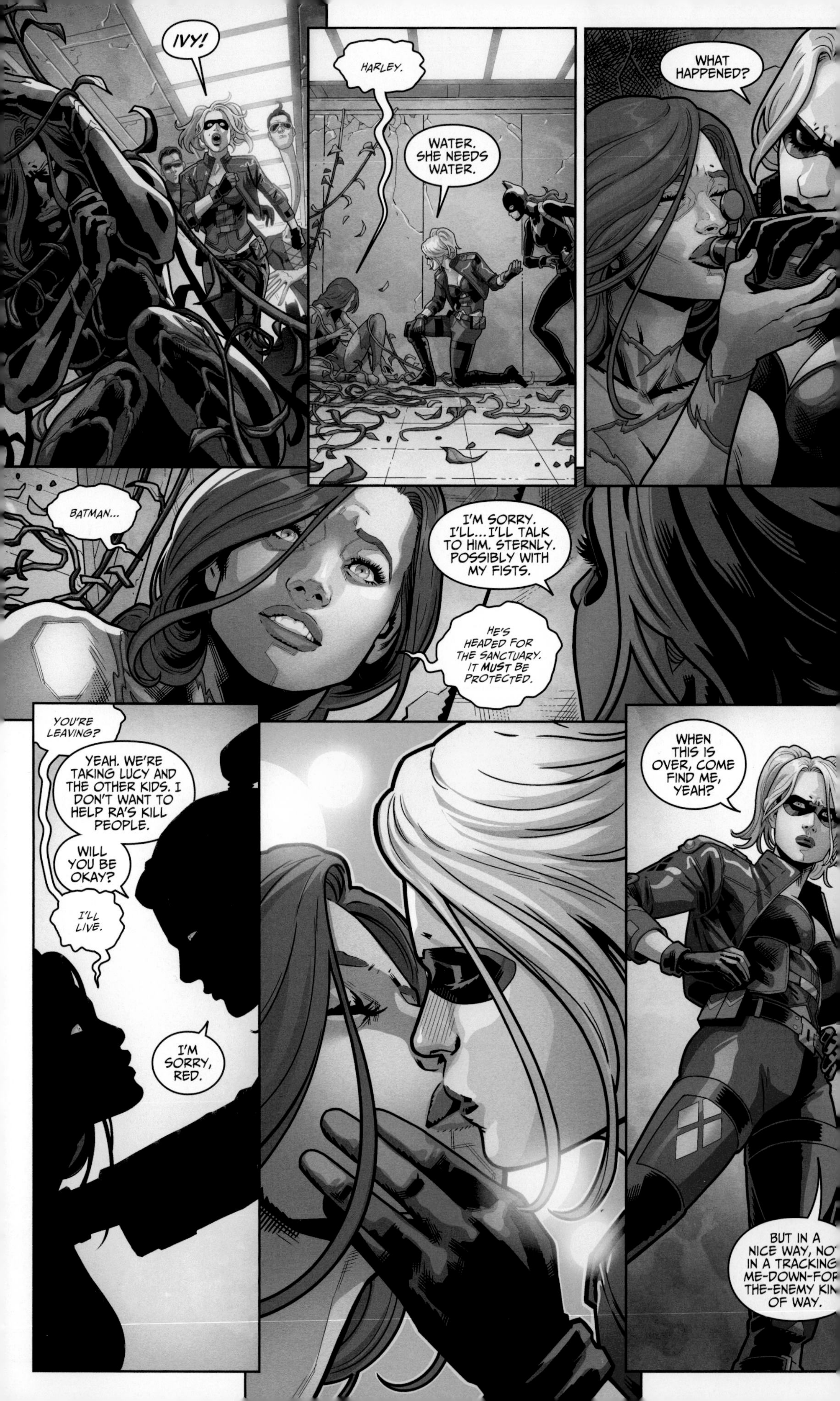
IVY!
HARLEY.
WATER. SHE NEEDS WATER.
WHAT HAPPENED?
BATMAN...
I'M SORRY. I'LL...I'LL TALK TO HIM. STERNLY. POSSIBLY WITH MY FISTS.
HE'S HEADED FOR THE SANCTUARY. IT MUST BE PROTECTED.
YOU'RE LEAVING?
YEAH. WE'RE TAKING LUCY AND THE OTHER KIDS. I DON'T WANT TO HELP RA'S KILL PEOPLE.
WILL YOU BE OKAY?
I'LL LIVE.
I'M SORRY, RED.
WHEN THIS IS OVER, COME FIND ME, YEAH?
BUT IN A NICE WAY, NO IN A TRACKING ME-DOWN-FOR THE-ENEMY KIN OF WAY.

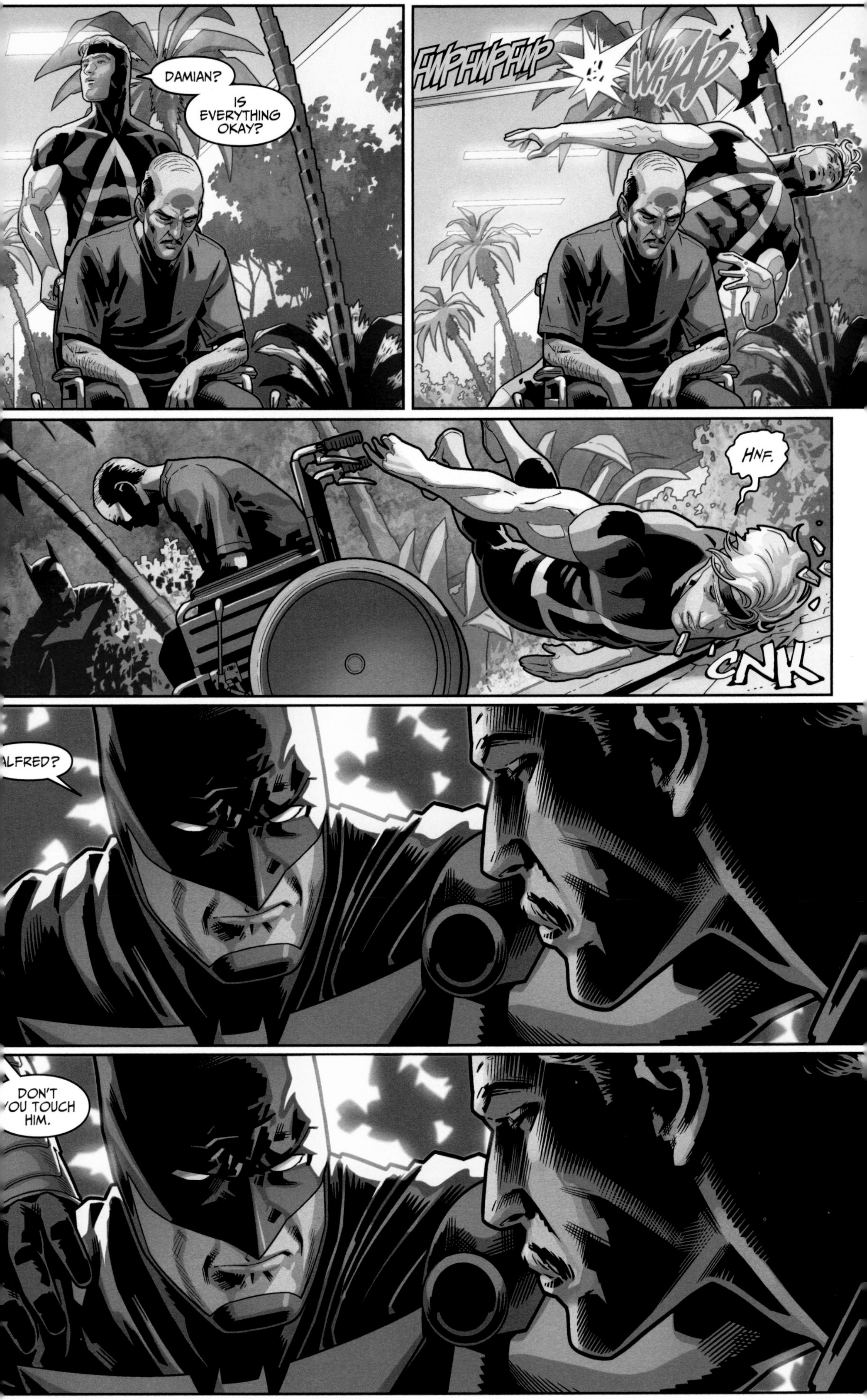

DAMIAN?
IS EVERYTHING OKAY?
FWPFWPFWP
WHAP
HNF.
CNK
ALFRED?
DON'T YOU TOUCH HIM.

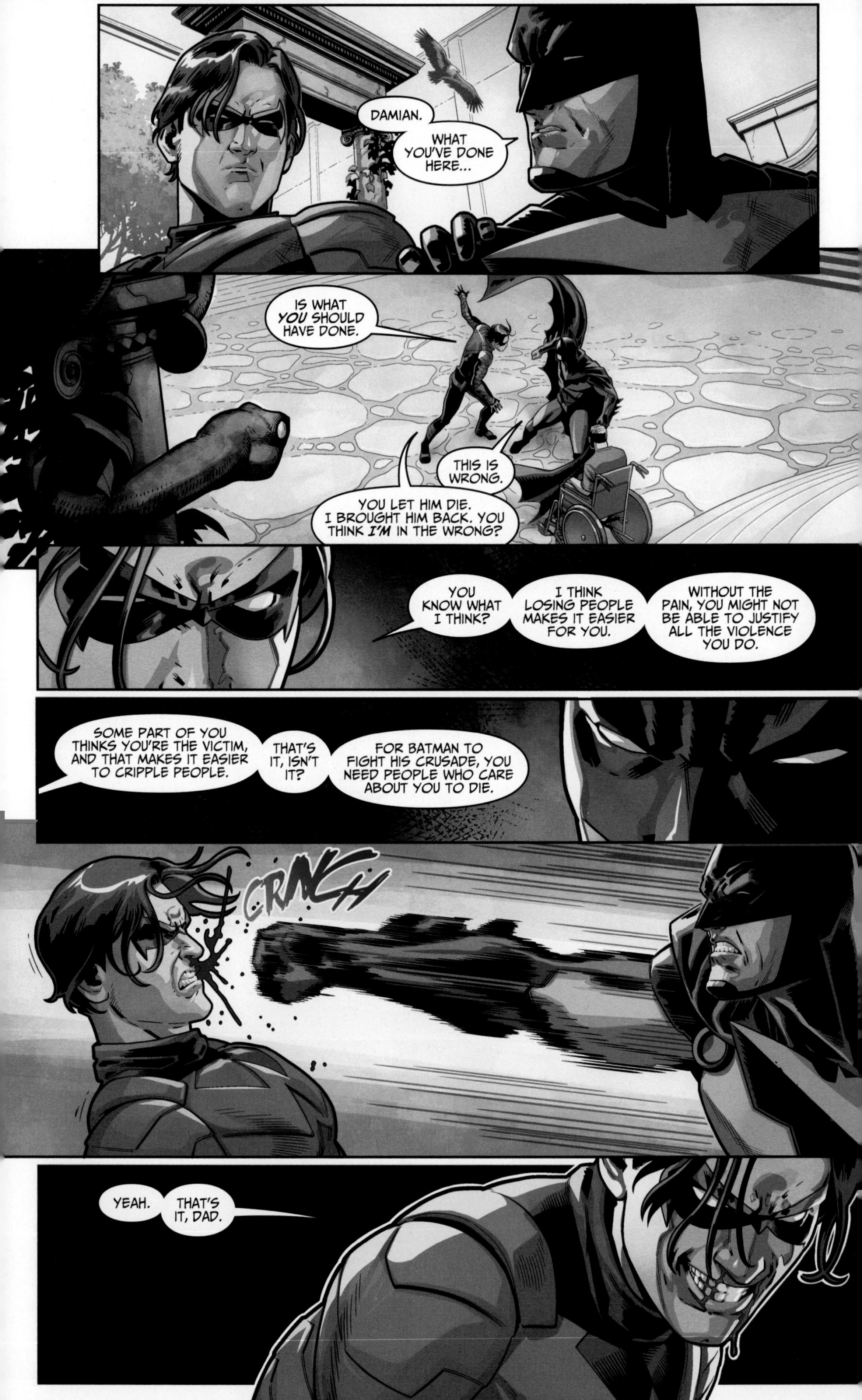
DAMIAN.
WHAT YOU'VE DONE HERE...
IS WHAT *YOU* SHOULD HAVE DONE.
THIS IS WRONG.
YOU LET HIM DIE. I BROUGHT HIM BACK. YOU THINK *I'M* IN THE WRONG?
YOU KNOW WHAT I THINK?
I THINK LOSING PEOPLE MAKES IT EASIER FOR YOU.
WITHOUT THE PAIN, YOU MIGHT NOT BE ABLE TO JUSTIFY ALL THE VIOLENCE YOU DO.
SOME PART OF YOU THINKS YOU'RE THE VICTIM, AND THAT MAKES IT EASIER TO CRIPPLE PEOPLE.
THAT'S IT, ISN'T IT?
FOR BATMAN TO FIGHT HIS CRUSADE, YOU NEED PEOPLE WHO CARE ABOUT YOU TO DIE.
CRNCH
YEAH.
THAT'S IT, DAD.

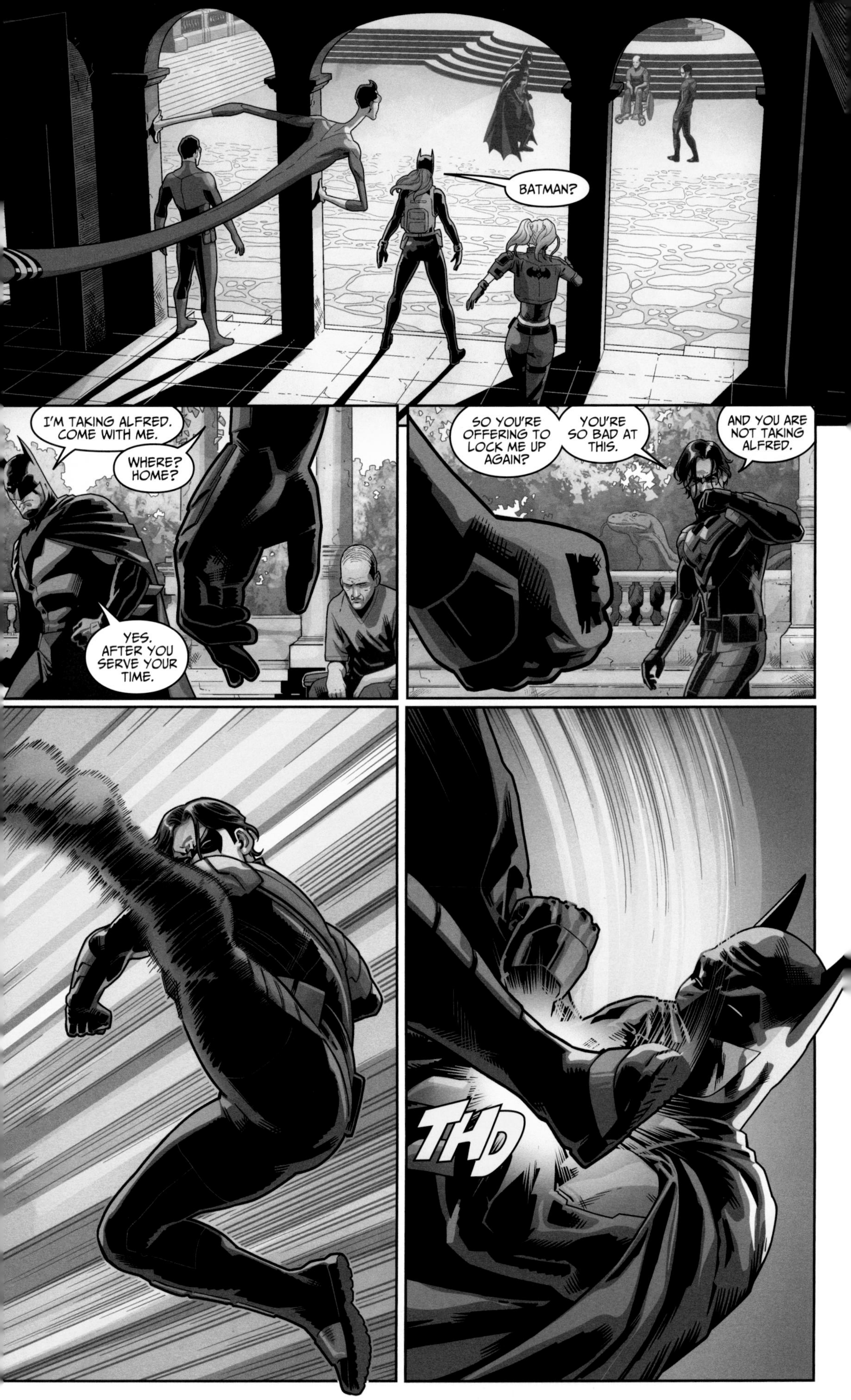
BATMAN?
I'M TAKING ALFRED. COME WITH ME.
WHERE? HOME?
YES. AFTER YOU SERVE YOUR TIME.
SO YOU'RE OFFERING TO LOCK ME UP AGAIN?
YOU'RE SO BAD AT THIS.
AND YOU ARE NOT TAKING ALFRED.
THD

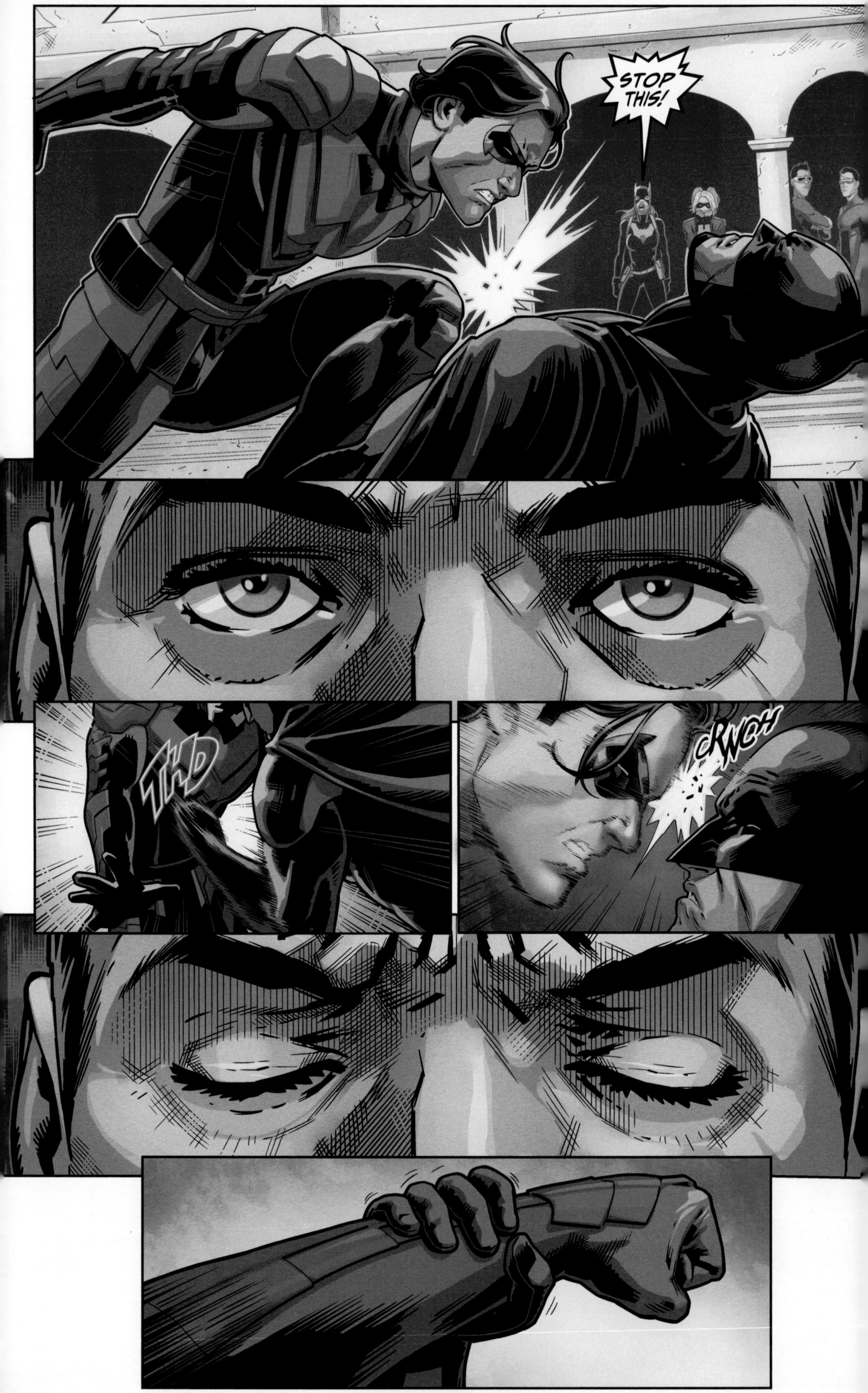
STOP THIS!
THD
CRNCH

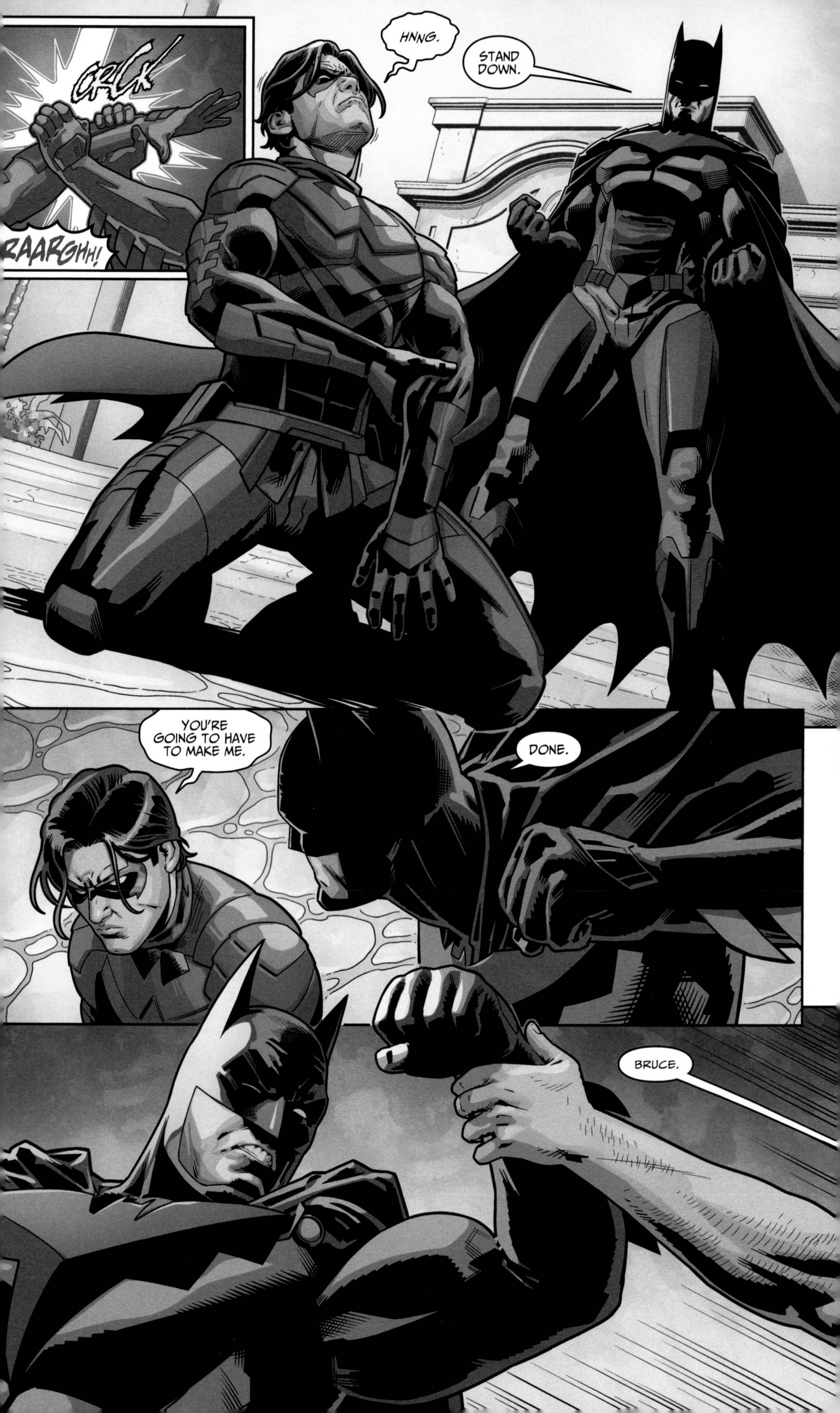
CRCK!
RAARGHH!
HNNG.
STAND DOWN.
YOU'RE GOING TO HAVE TO MAKE ME.
DONE.
BRUCE.

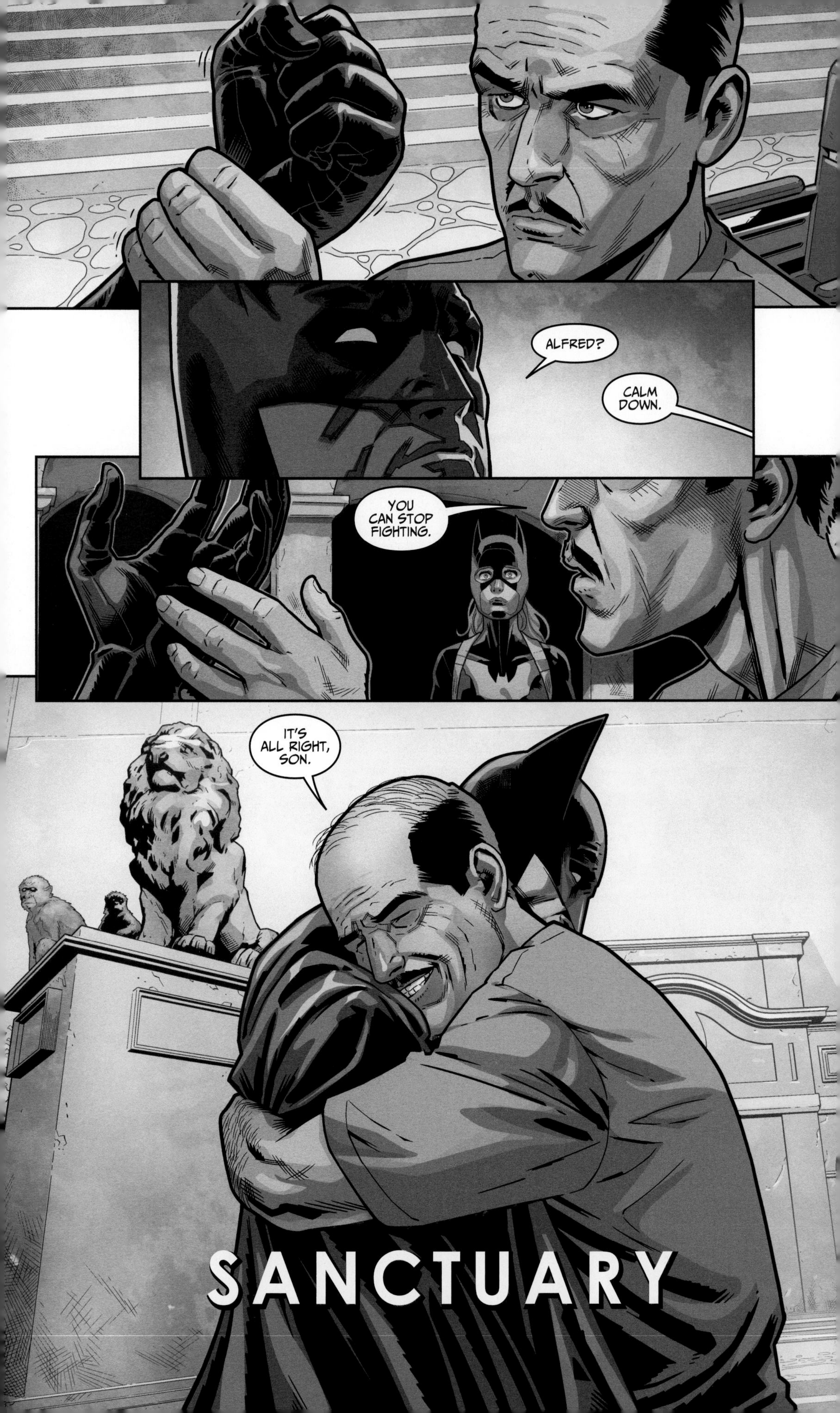
ALFRED?
CALM DOWN.
YOU CAN STOP FIGHTING.
IT'S ALL RIGHT, SON.
SANCTUARY

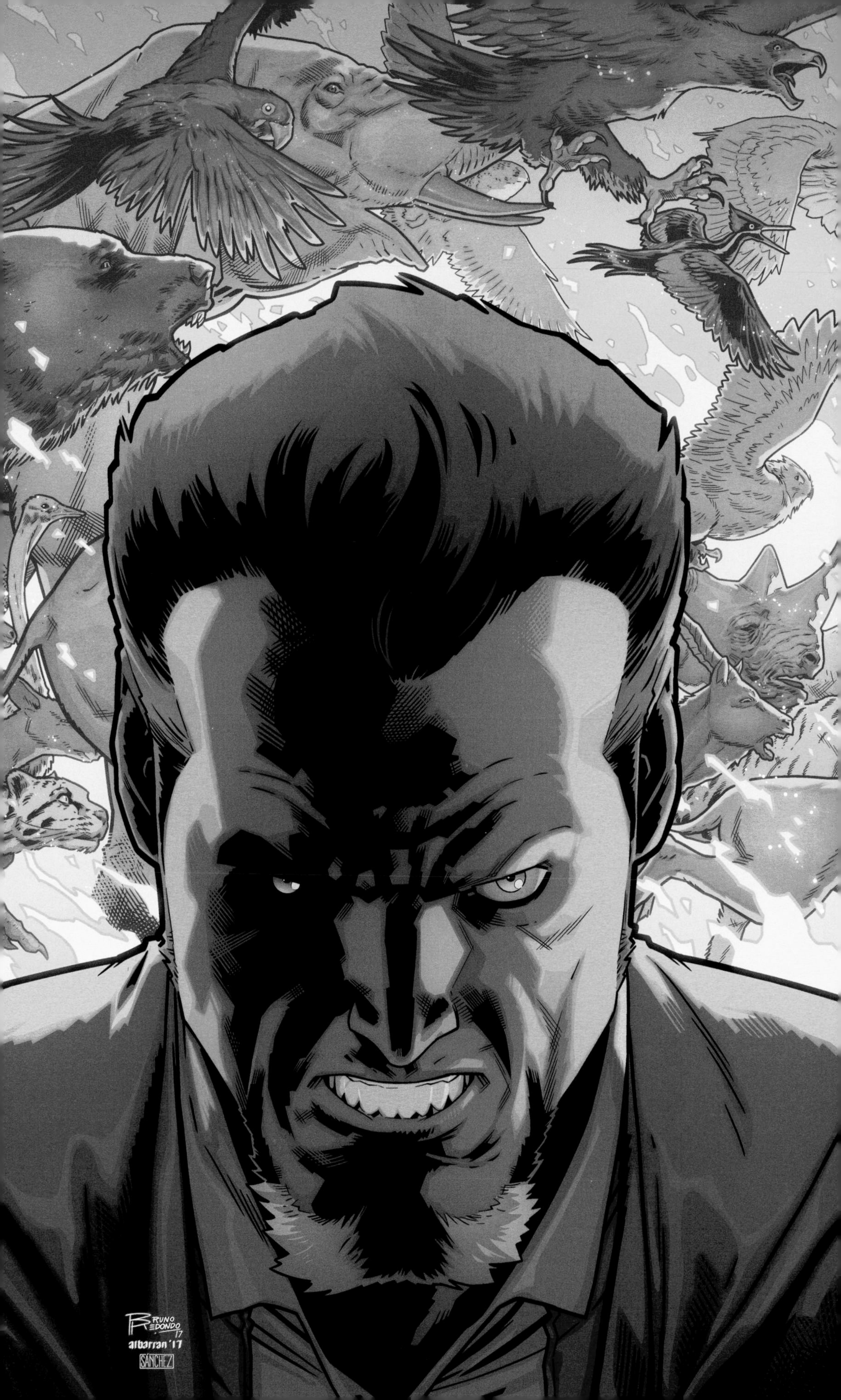
BRUNO REDONDO 17
albarran '17
SÁNCHEZ

"Endangered Species"

Tom Taylor Writer **Daniel Sampere** (p. 1-10) **Bruno Redondo** (p. 11-20) Pencillers **Juan Albarran** Inker
Rex Lokus Colorist **Wes Abbott** Letterer Cover art by **Bruno Redondo, Juan Albarran** and **Alejandro Sanchez**

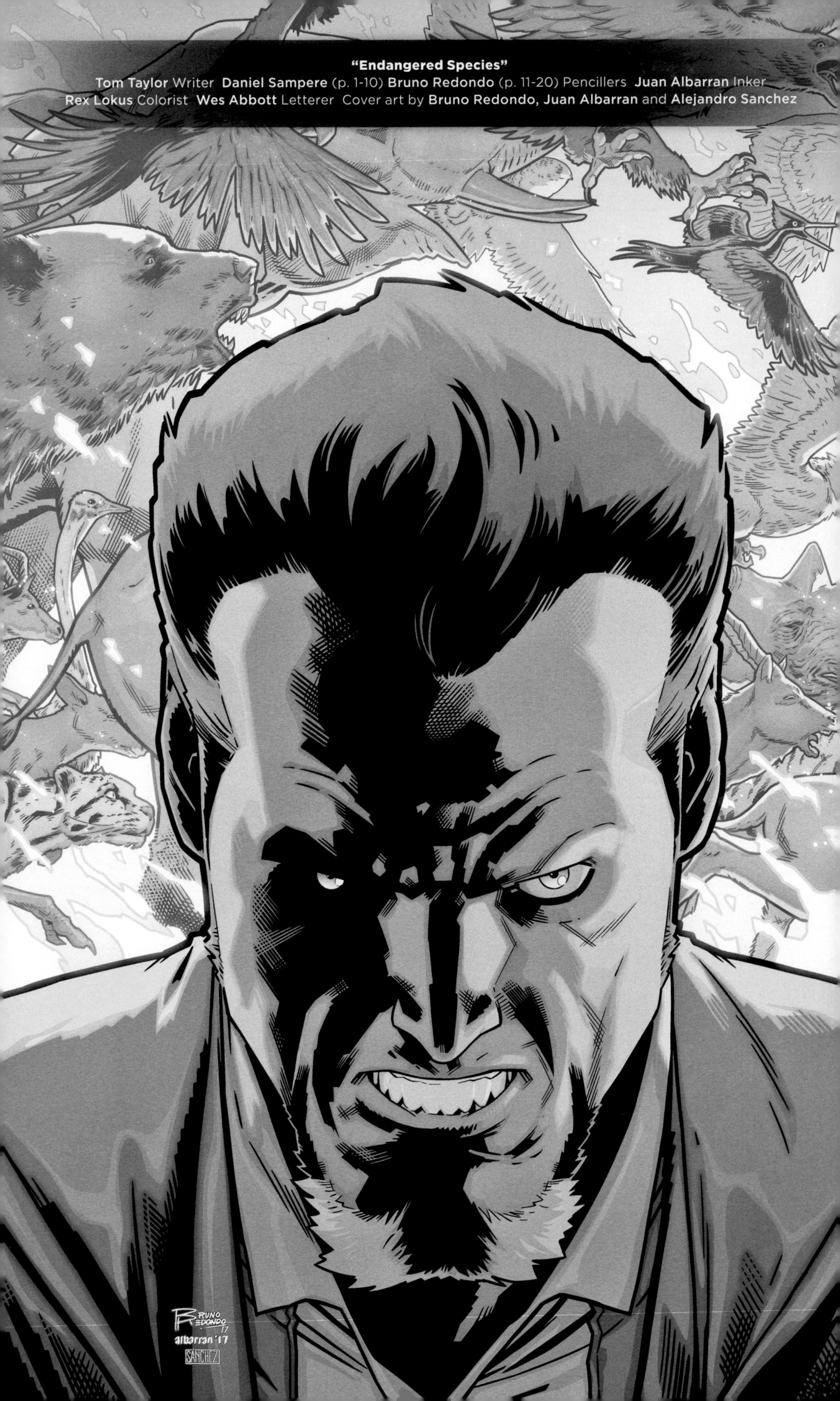
BRUNO REDONDO '17
albarran '17
SANCHEZ

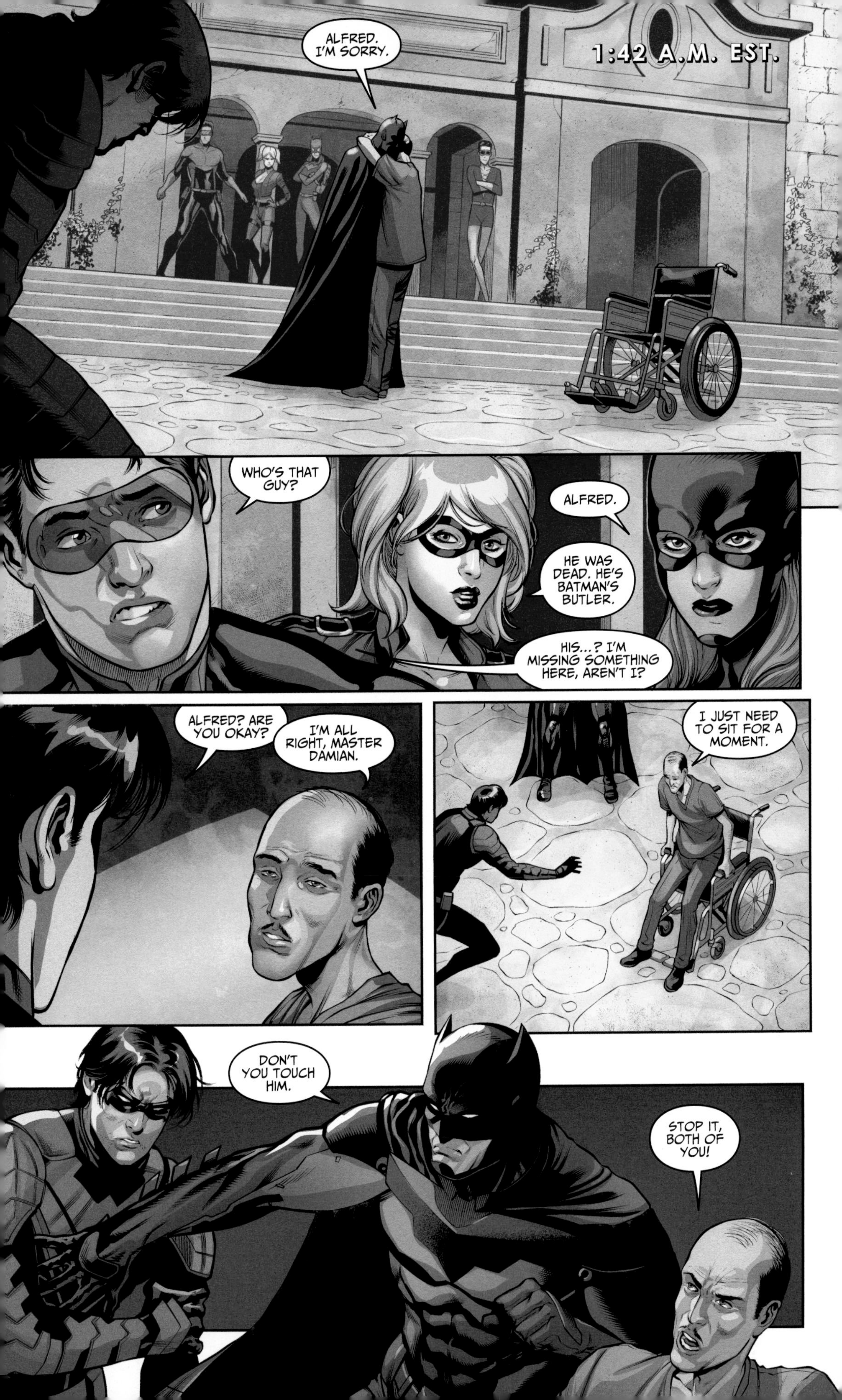
1:42 A.M. EST.
ALFRED. I'M SORRY.
WHO'S THAT GUY?
ALFRED.
HE WAS DEAD. HE'S BATMAN'S BUTLER.
HIS...? I'M MISSING SOMETHING HERE, AREN'T I?
ALFRED? ARE YOU OKAY?
I'M ALL RIGHT, MASTER DAMIAN.
I JUST NEED TO SIT FOR A MOMENT.
DON'T YOU TOUCH HIM.
STOP IT, BOTH OF YOU!

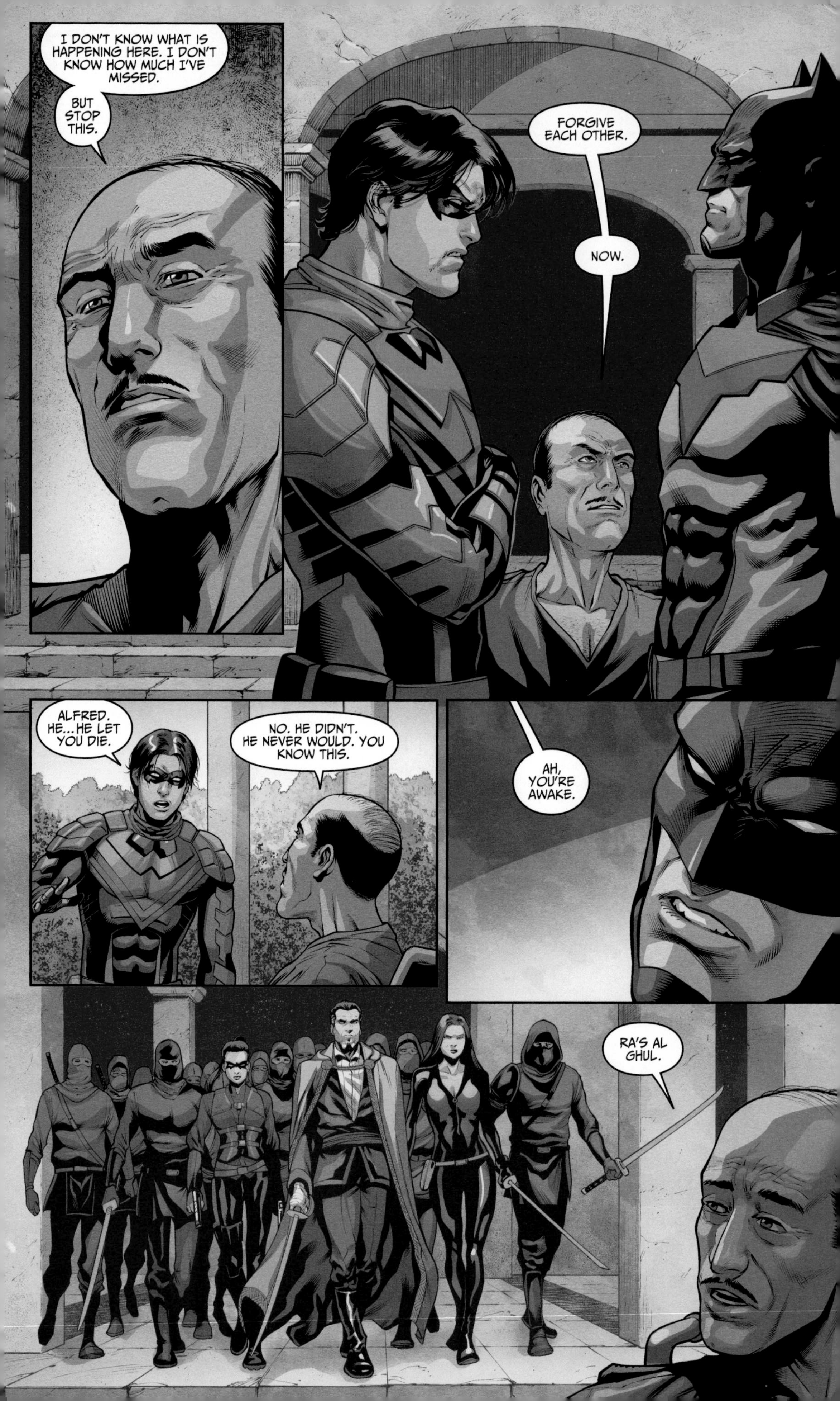
I DON'T KNOW WHAT IS HAPPENING HERE. I DON'T KNOW HOW MUCH I'VE MISSED.
BUT STOP THIS.
FORGIVE EACH OTHER.
NOW.
ALFRED. HE...HE LET YOU DIE.
NO. HE DIDN'T. HE NEVER WOULD. YOU KNOW THIS.
AH, YOU'RE AWAKE.
RA'S AL GHUL.

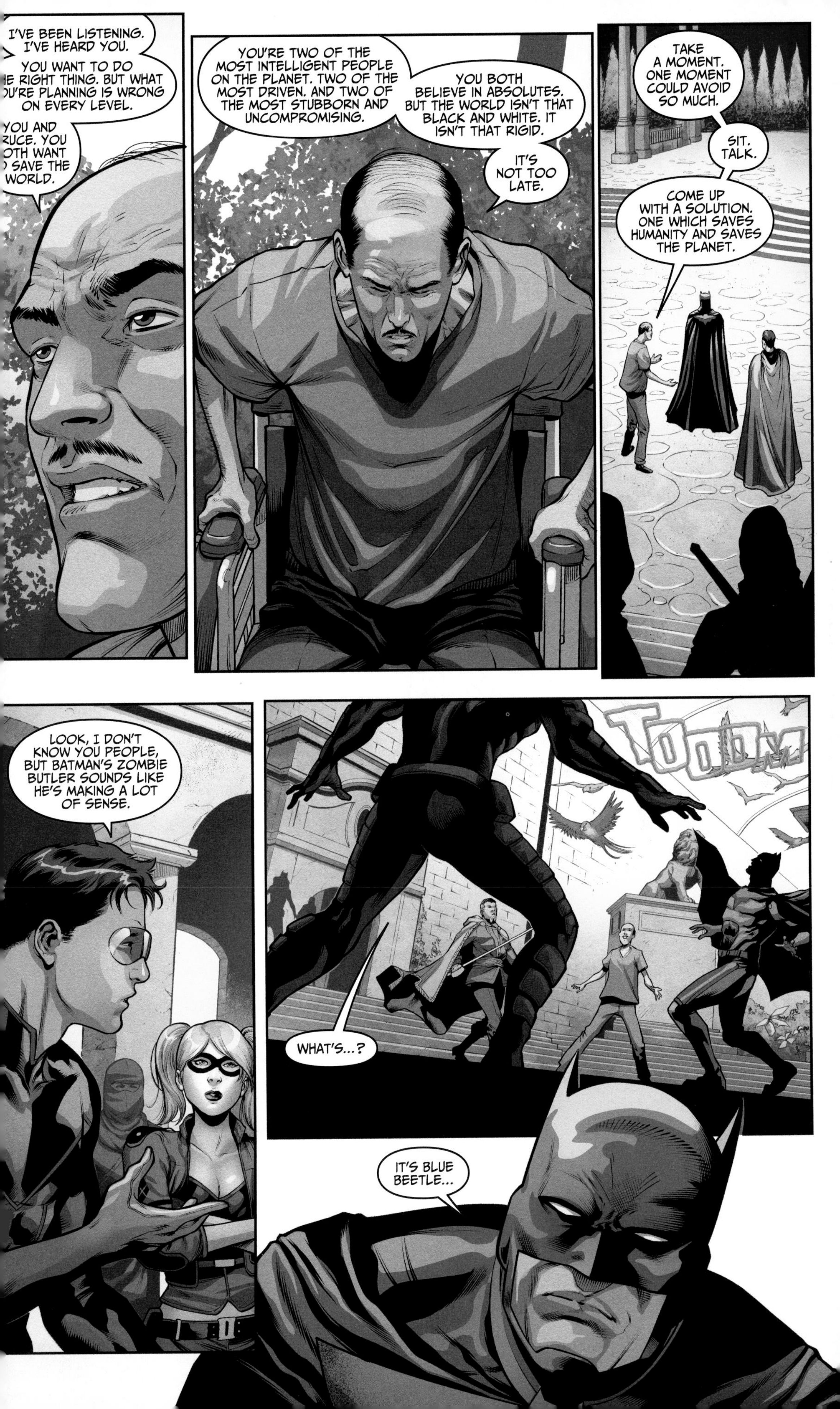
I'VE BEEN LISTENING. I'VE HEARD YOU.
YOU WANT TO DO THE RIGHT THING. BUT WHAT YOU'RE PLANNING IS WRONG ON EVERY LEVEL.
YOU AND BRUCE. YOU BOTH WANT TO SAVE THE WORLD.
YOU'RE TWO OF THE MOST INTELLIGENT PEOPLE ON THE PLANET. TWO OF THE MOST DRIVEN. AND TWO OF THE MOST STUBBORN AND UNCOMPROMISING.
YOU BOTH BELIEVE IN ABSOLUTES. BUT THE WORLD ISN'T THAT BLACK AND WHITE. IT ISN'T THAT RIGID.
IT'S NOT TOO LATE.
TAKE A MOMENT. ONE MOMENT COULD AVOID SO MUCH.
SIT. TALK.
COME UP WITH A SOLUTION. ONE WHICH SAVES HUMANITY AND SAVES THE PLANET.
LOOK, I DON'T KNOW YOU PEOPLE, BUT BATMAN'S ZOMBIE BUTLER SOUNDS LIKE HE'S MAKING A LOT OF SENSE.
TOOOM
WHAT'S...?
IT'S BLUE BEETLE...

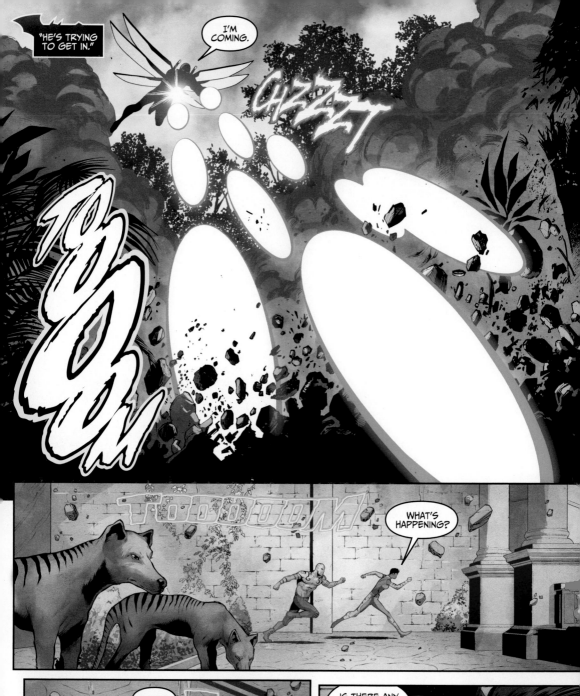

"HE'S TRYING TO GET IN."

I'M COMING.

GZZZZT

TOOOOM

WHAT'S HAPPENING?

VIXEN?

TOOOM

LOOK AROUND YOU. LOOK WHAT RA'S HAS DONE HERE. WHAT HE'S SAVED.

YOU CAN'T THREATEN THIS.

WHATEVER THIS IS, STOP IT!

IS THERE ANY WAY TO GET A SIGNAL OUT OF HERE?

IF I CAN TALK TO HIM, I CAN STOP HIM!

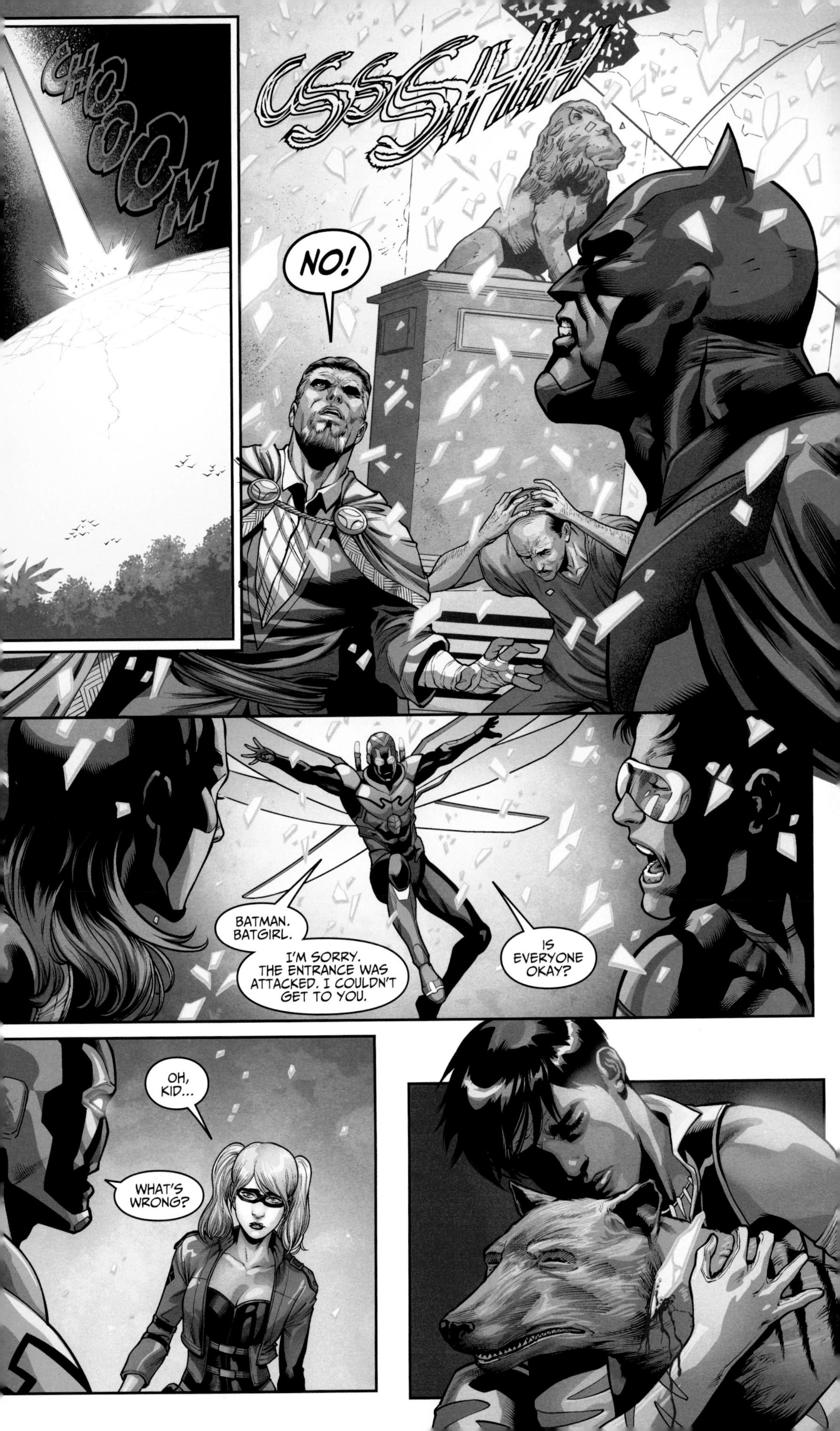
CHOOOOM
CSSSSHHH
NO!
BATMAN. BATGIRL.
I'M SORRY. THE ENTRANCE WAS ATTACKED. I COULDN'T GET TO YOU.
IS EVERYONE OKAY?
OH, KID...
WHAT'S WRONG?

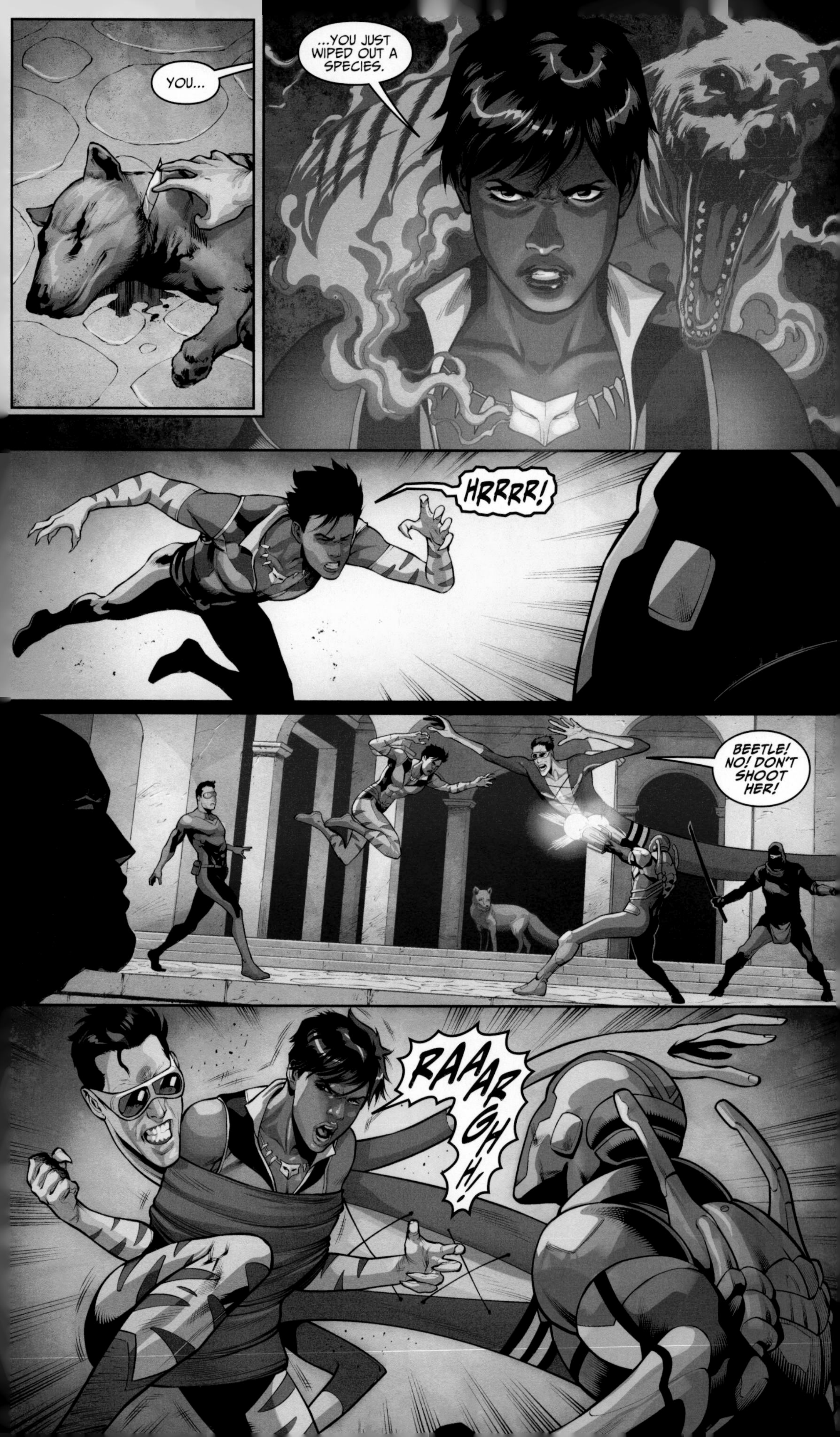
YOU...
...YOU JUST WIPED OUT A SPECIES.
HRRRR!
BEETLE! NO! DON'T SHOOT HER!
RAAARGHHH!

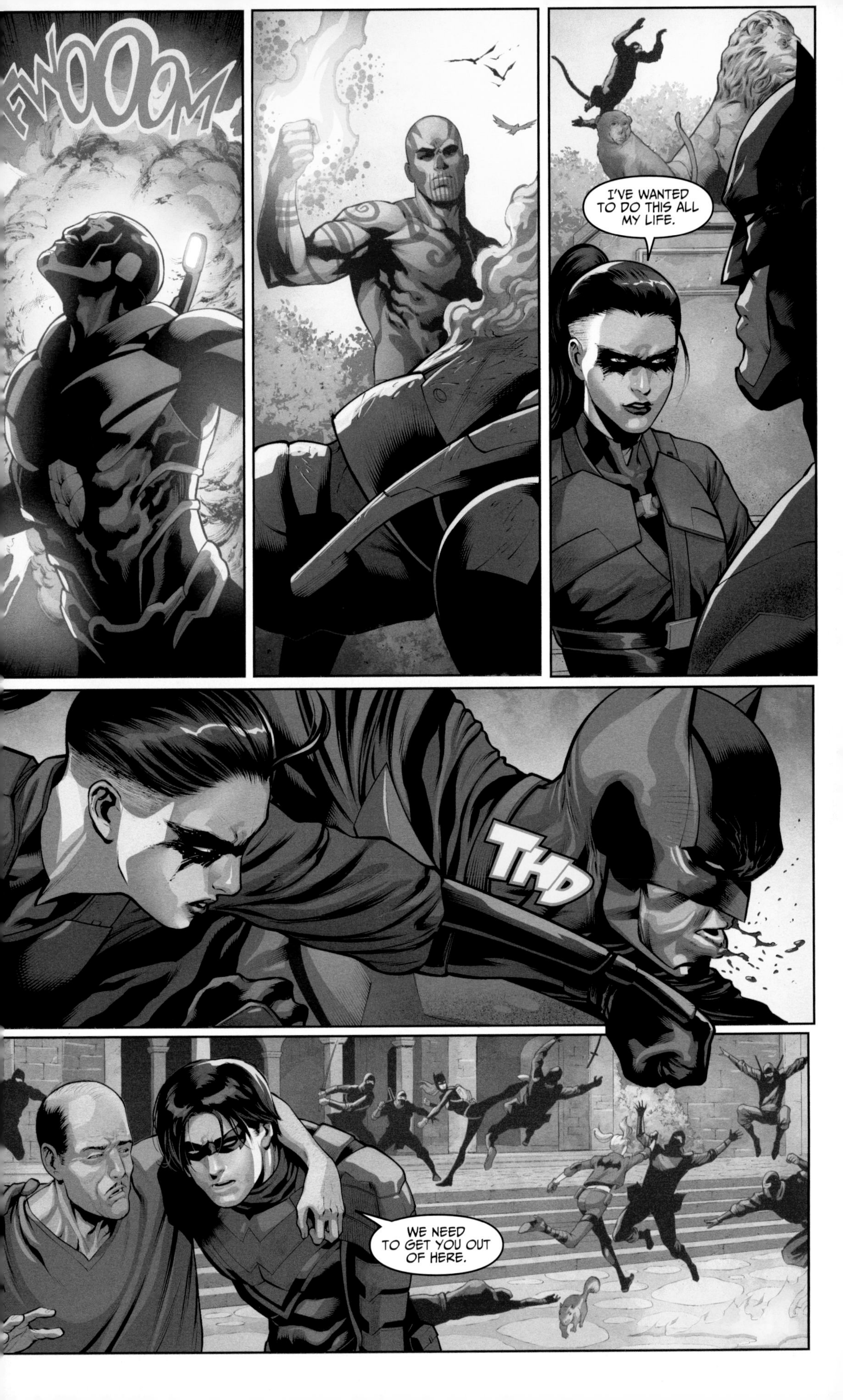
FWOOOM
I'VE WANTED TO DO THIS ALL MY LIFE.
THD
WE NEED TO GET YOU OUT OF HERE.

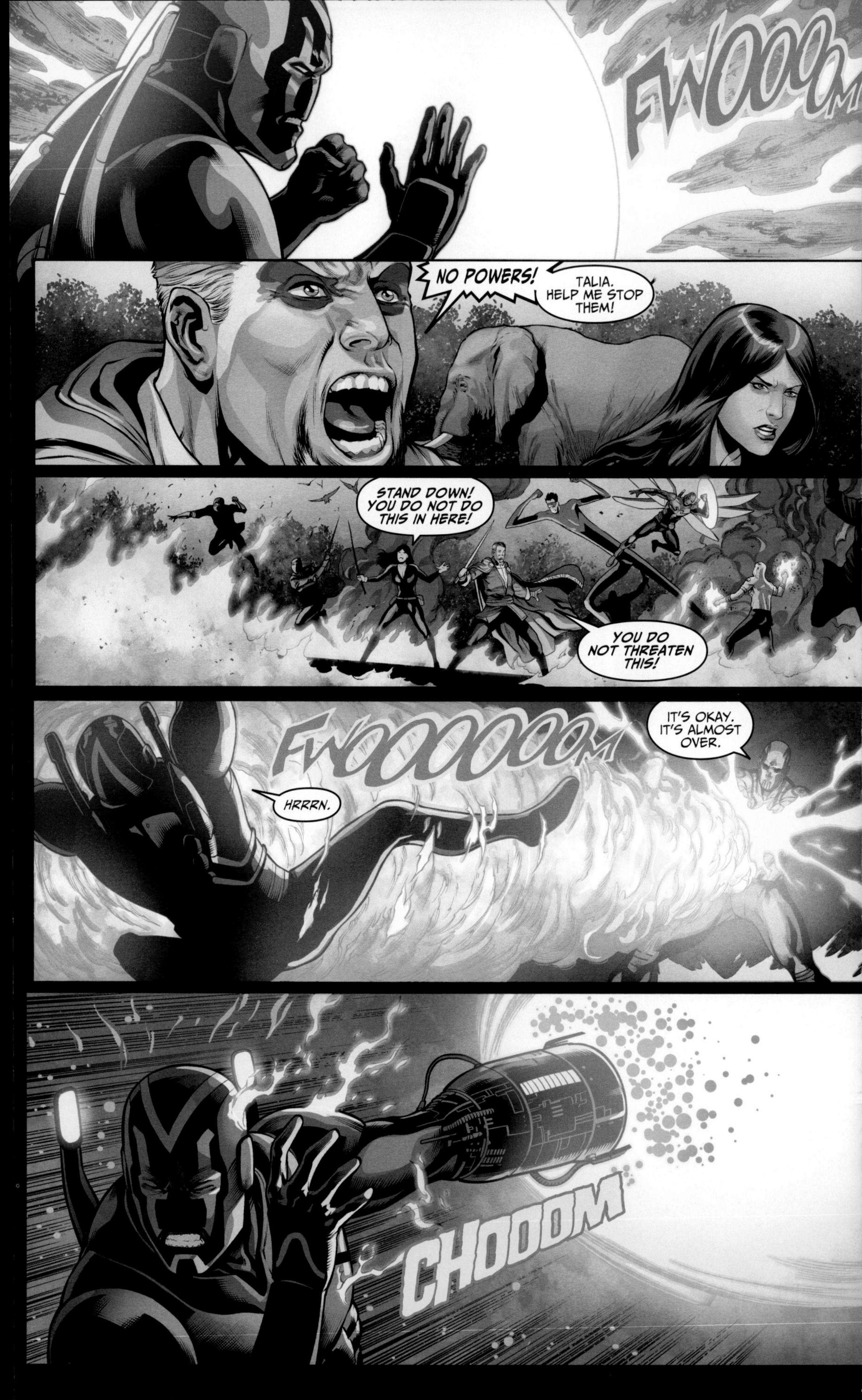
FWOOOM
NO POWERS!
TALIA. HELP ME STOP THEM!
STAND DOWN! YOU DO NOT DO THIS IN HERE!
YOU DO NOT THREATEN THIS!
FWOOOOOOM
IT'S OKAY. IT'S ALMOST OVER.
HRRRN.
CHOOOM

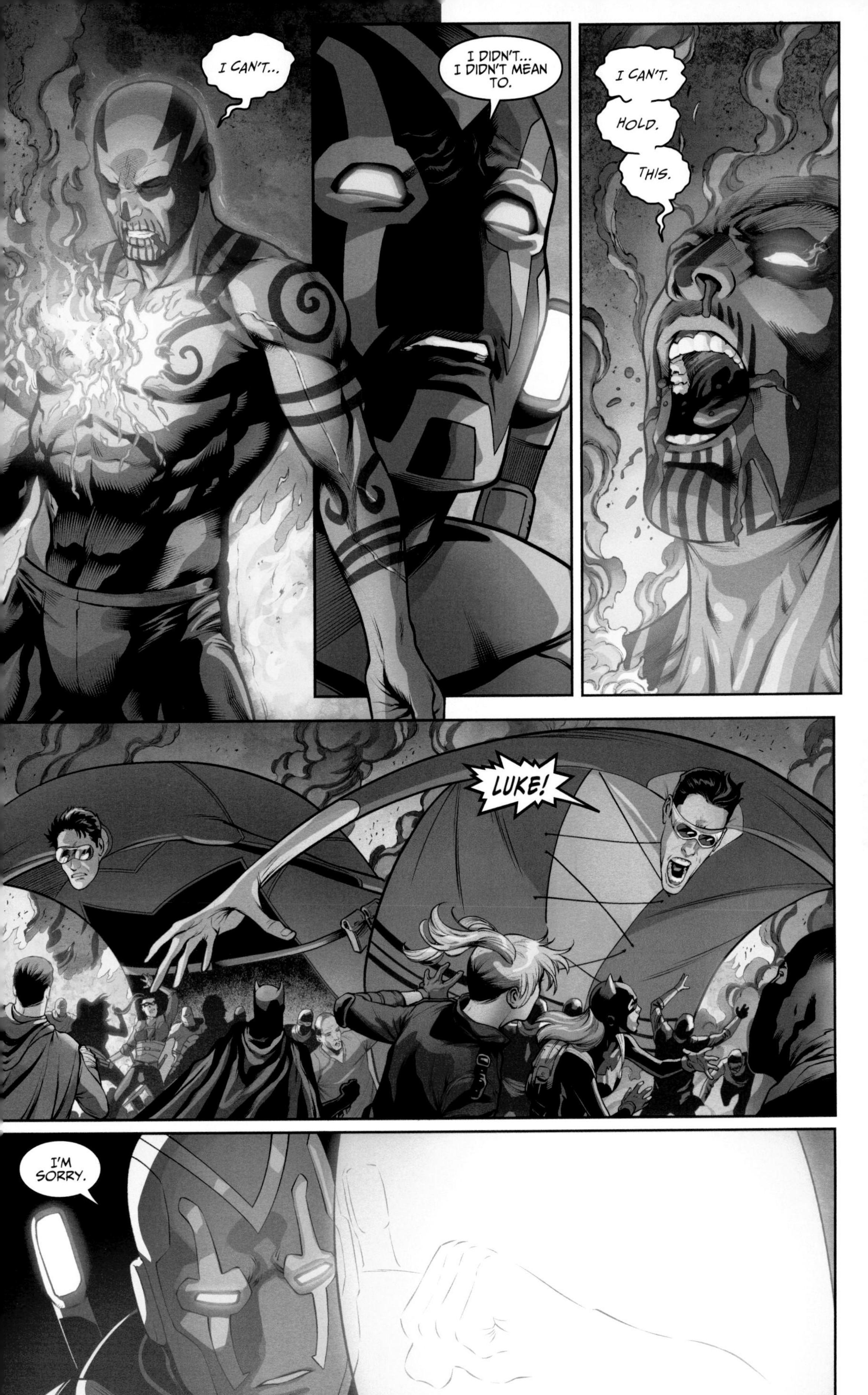
I CAN'T...
I DIDN'T... I DIDN'T MEAN TO.
I CAN'T.
HOLD.
THIS.
LUKE!
I'M SORRY.

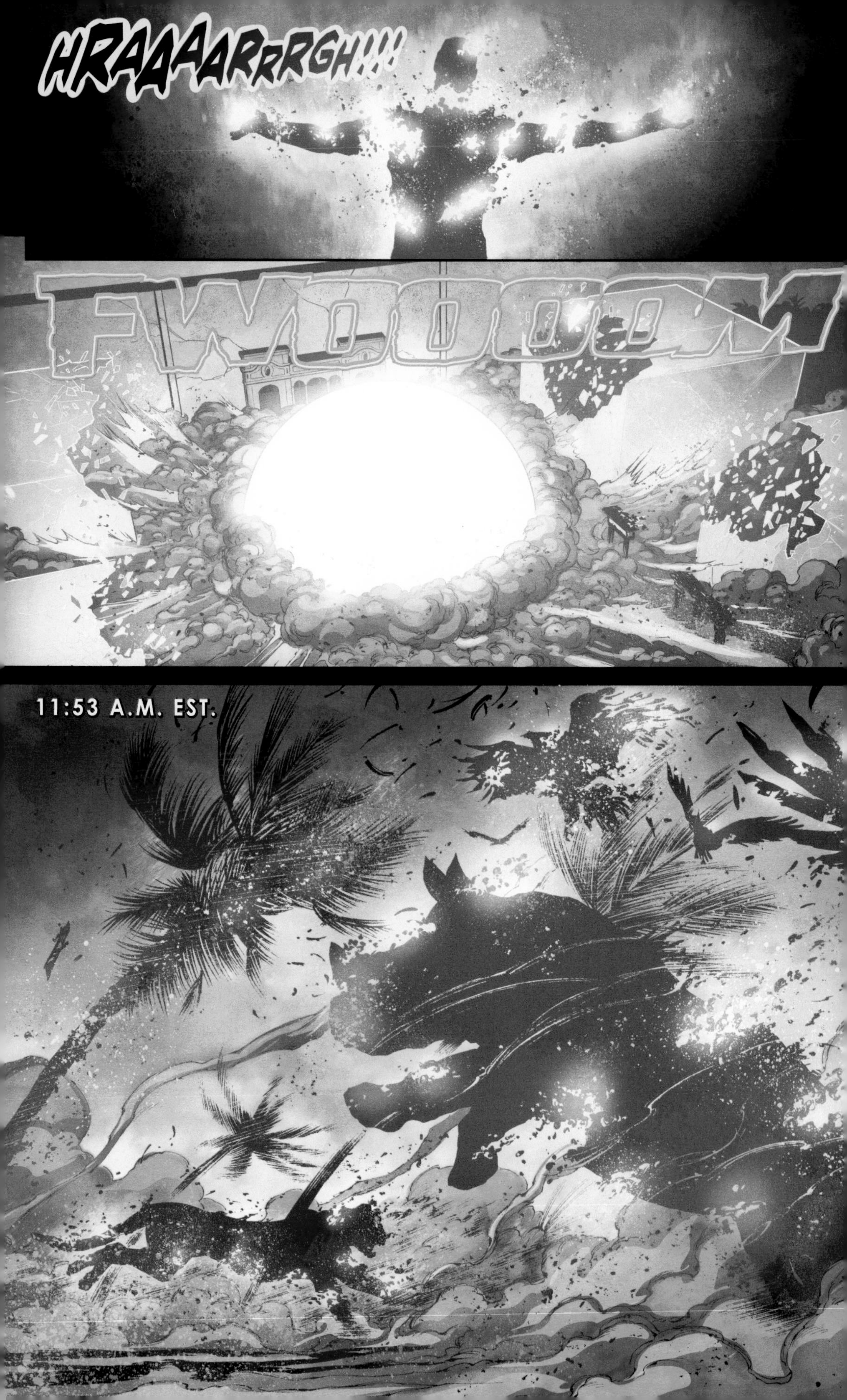
HRAAAARRRGH!!!
FWOOOOM
11:53 A.M. EST.

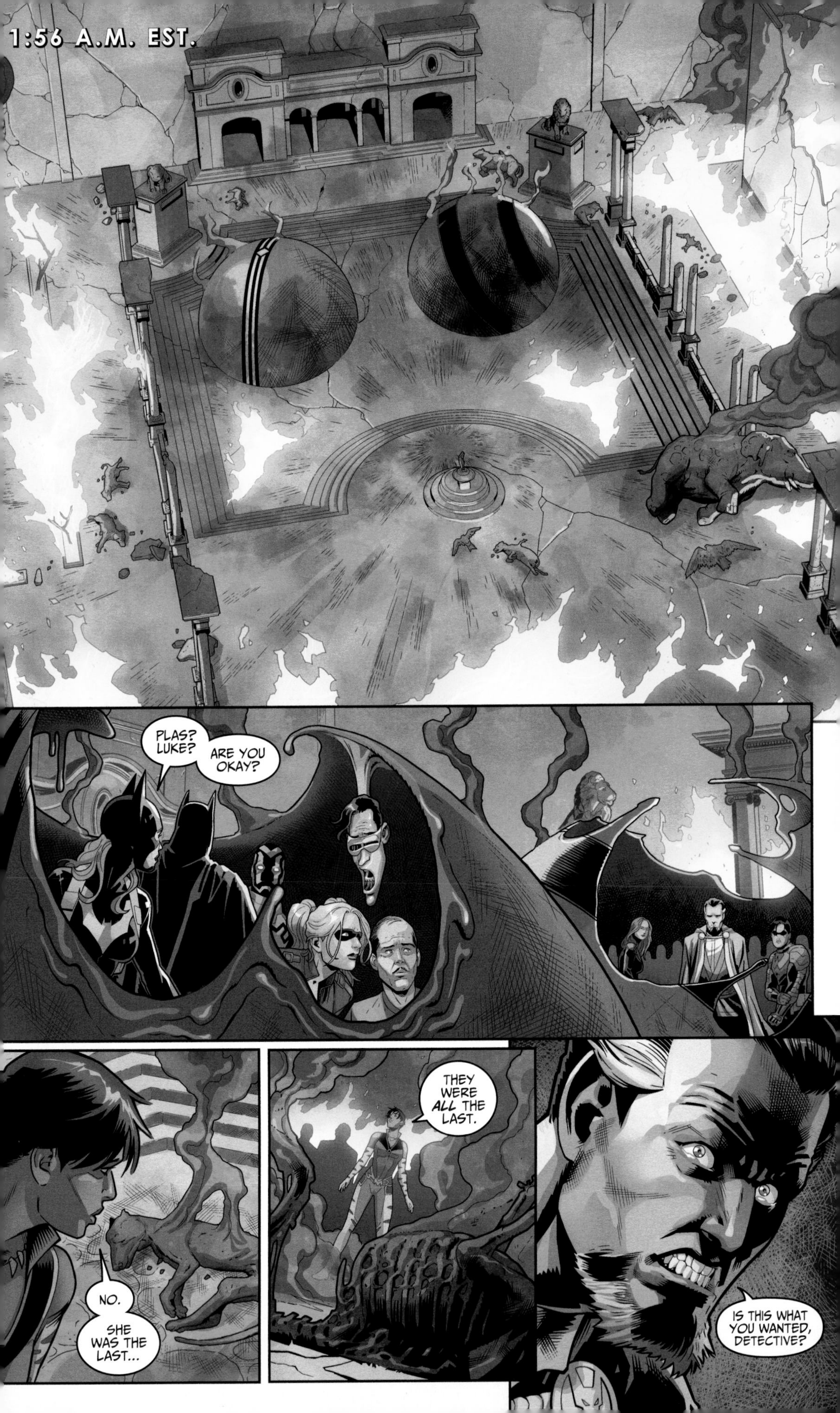
1:56 A.M. EST.
PLAS? LUKE?
ARE YOU OKAY?
NO.
SHE WAS THE LAST...
THEY WERE ALL THE LAST.
IS THIS WHAT YOU WANTED, DETECTIVE?

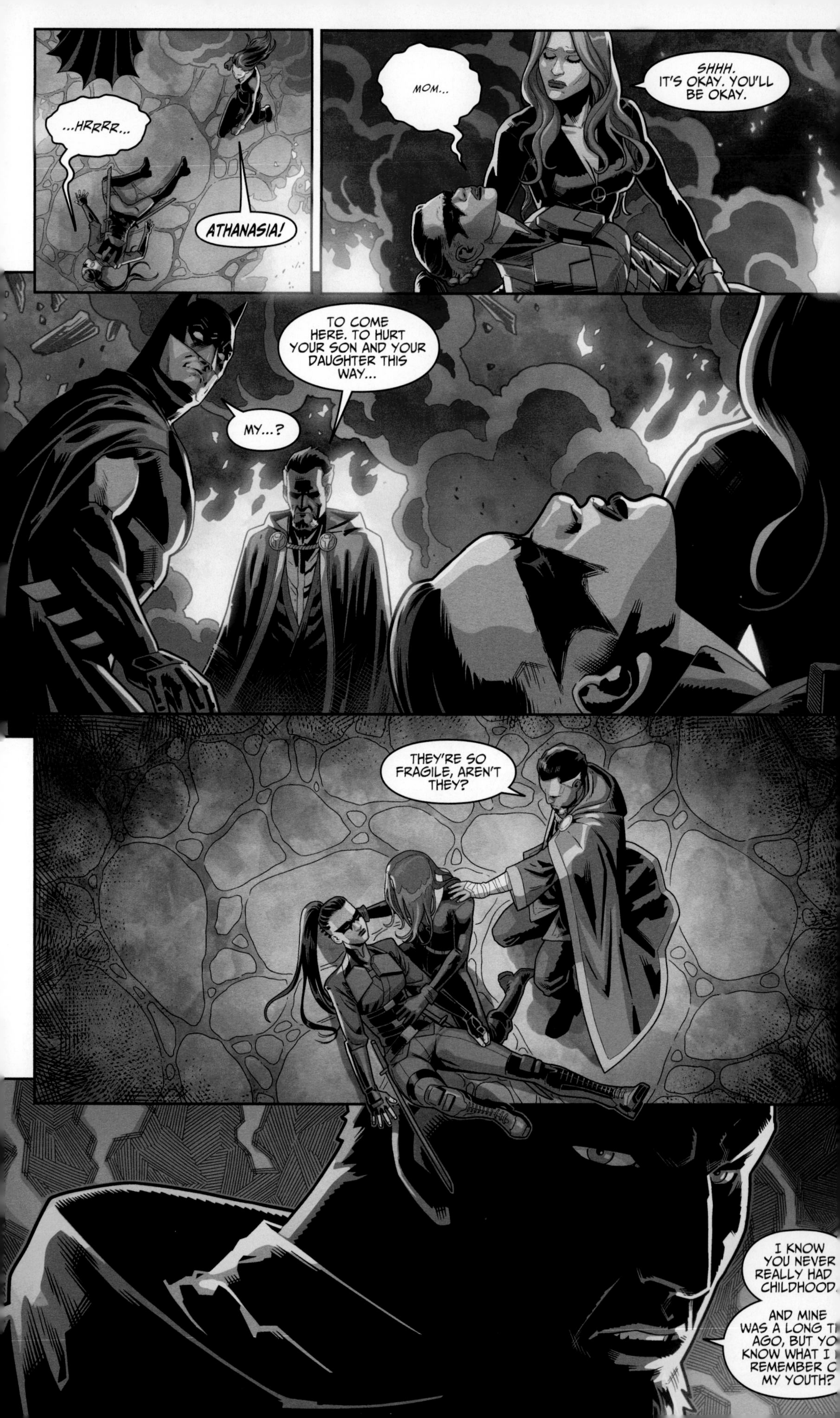

...HRRRR...
ATHANASIA!
MOM...
SHHH. IT'S OKAY. YOU'LL BE OKAY.
TO COME HERE. TO HURT YOUR SON AND YOUR DAUGHTER THIS WAY...
MY...?
THEY'RE SO FRAGILE, AREN'T THEY?
I KNOW YOU NEVER REALLY HAD CHILDHOOD.
AND MINE WAS A LONG T AGO, BUT YO KNOW WHAT I REMEMBER O MY YOUTH?

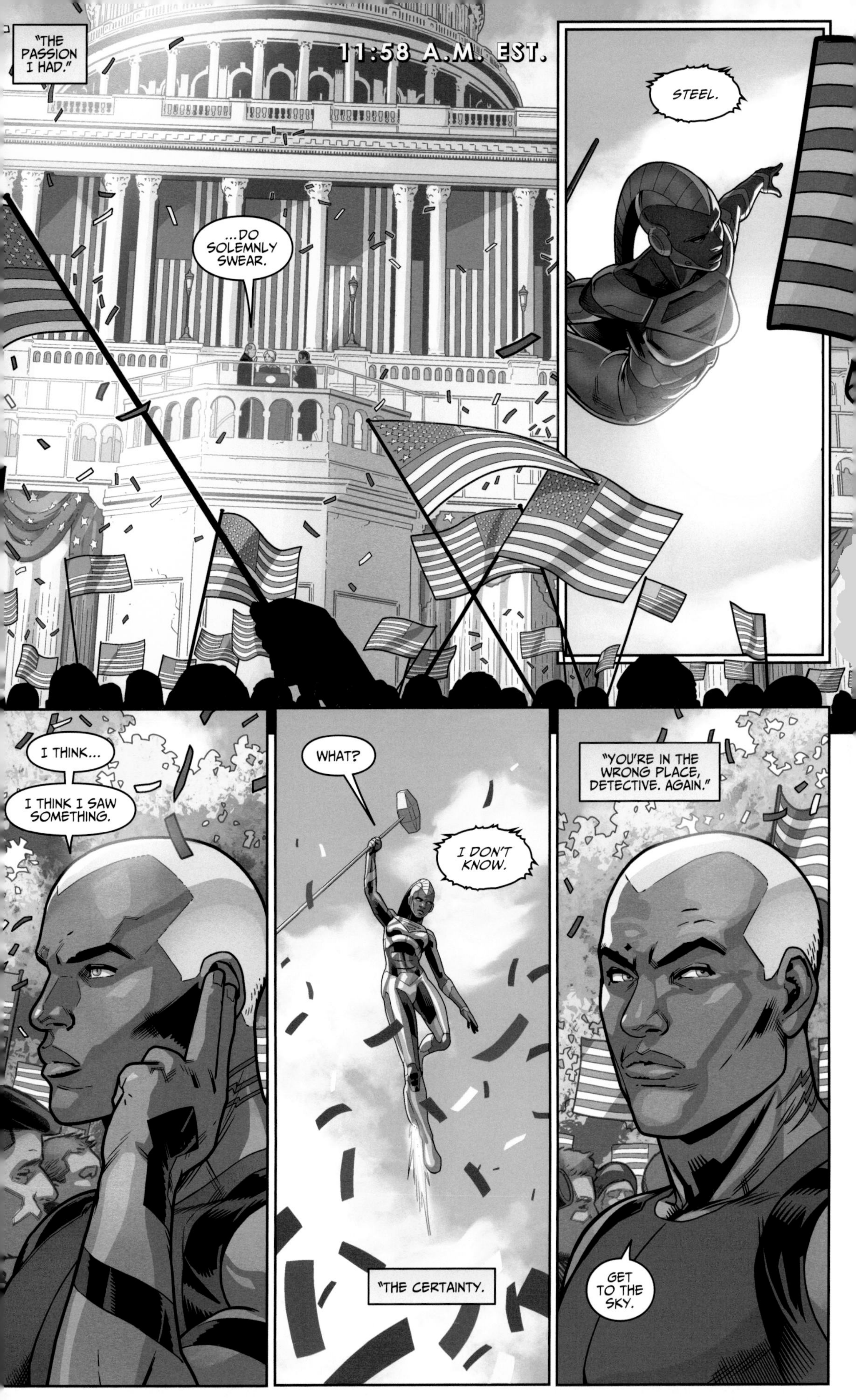
"THE PASSION I HAD."
11:58 A.M. EST.
...DO SOLEMNLY SWEAR.
STEEL.
I THINK...
I THINK I SAW SOMETHING.
WHAT?
I DON'T KNOW.
"THE CERTAINTY.
"YOU'RE IN THE WRONG PLACE, DETECTIVE. AGAIN."
GET TO THE SKY.

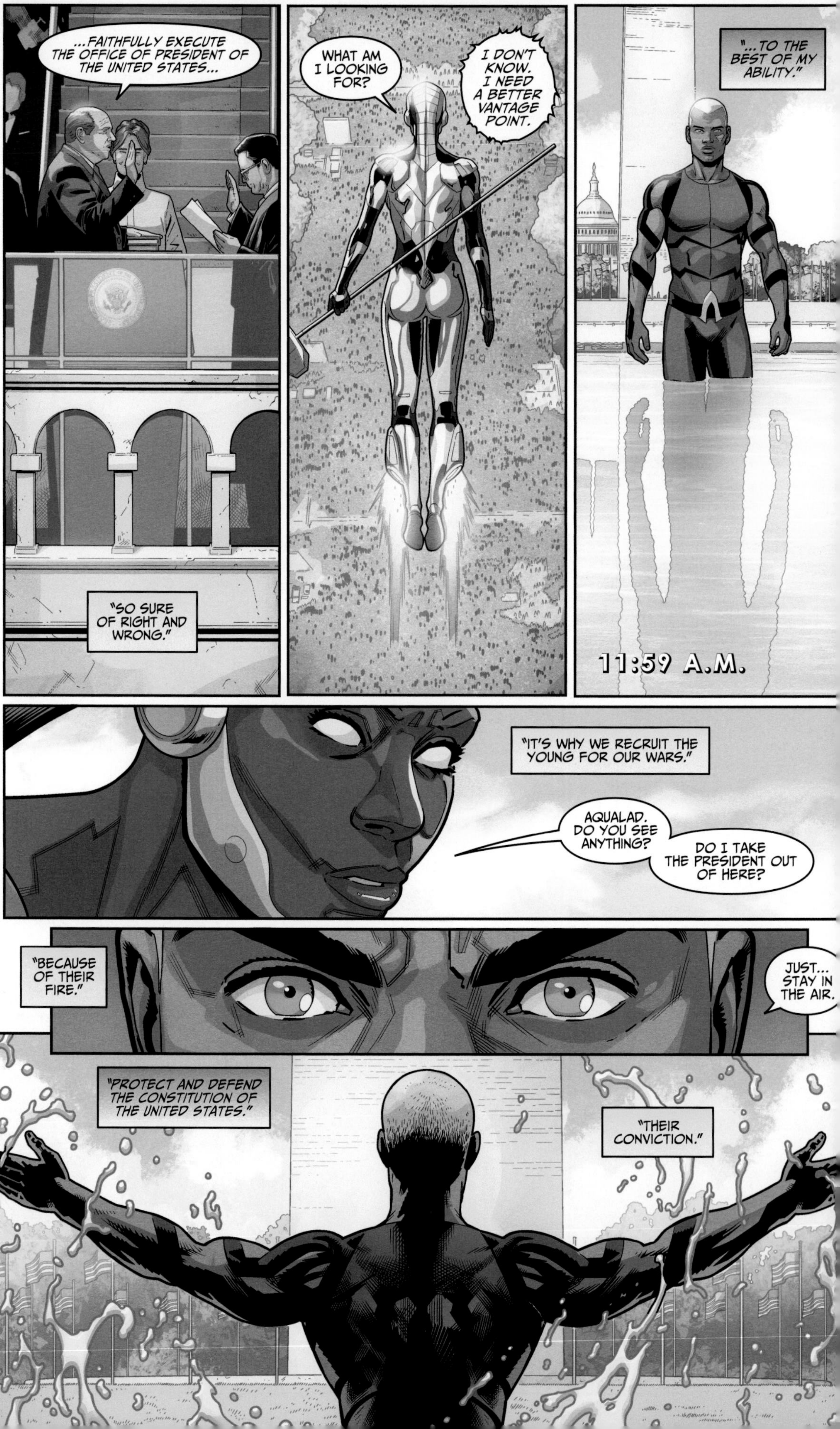
...FAITHFULLY EXECUTE THE OFFICE OF PRESIDENT OF THE UNITED STATES...
"SO SURE OF RIGHT AND WRONG."
WHAT AM I LOOKING FOR?
I DON'T KNOW. I NEED A BETTER VANTAGE POINT.
"...TO THE BEST OF MY ABILITY."
11:59 A.M.
"IT'S WHY WE RECRUIT THE YOUNG FOR OUR WARS."
AQUALAD. DO YOU SEE ANYTHING?
DO I TAKE THE PRESIDENT OUT OF HERE?
"BECAUSE OF THEIR FIRE."
JUST... STAY IN THE AIR.
"PROTECT AND DEFEND THE CONSTITUTION OF THE UNITED STATES."
"THEIR CONVICTION."

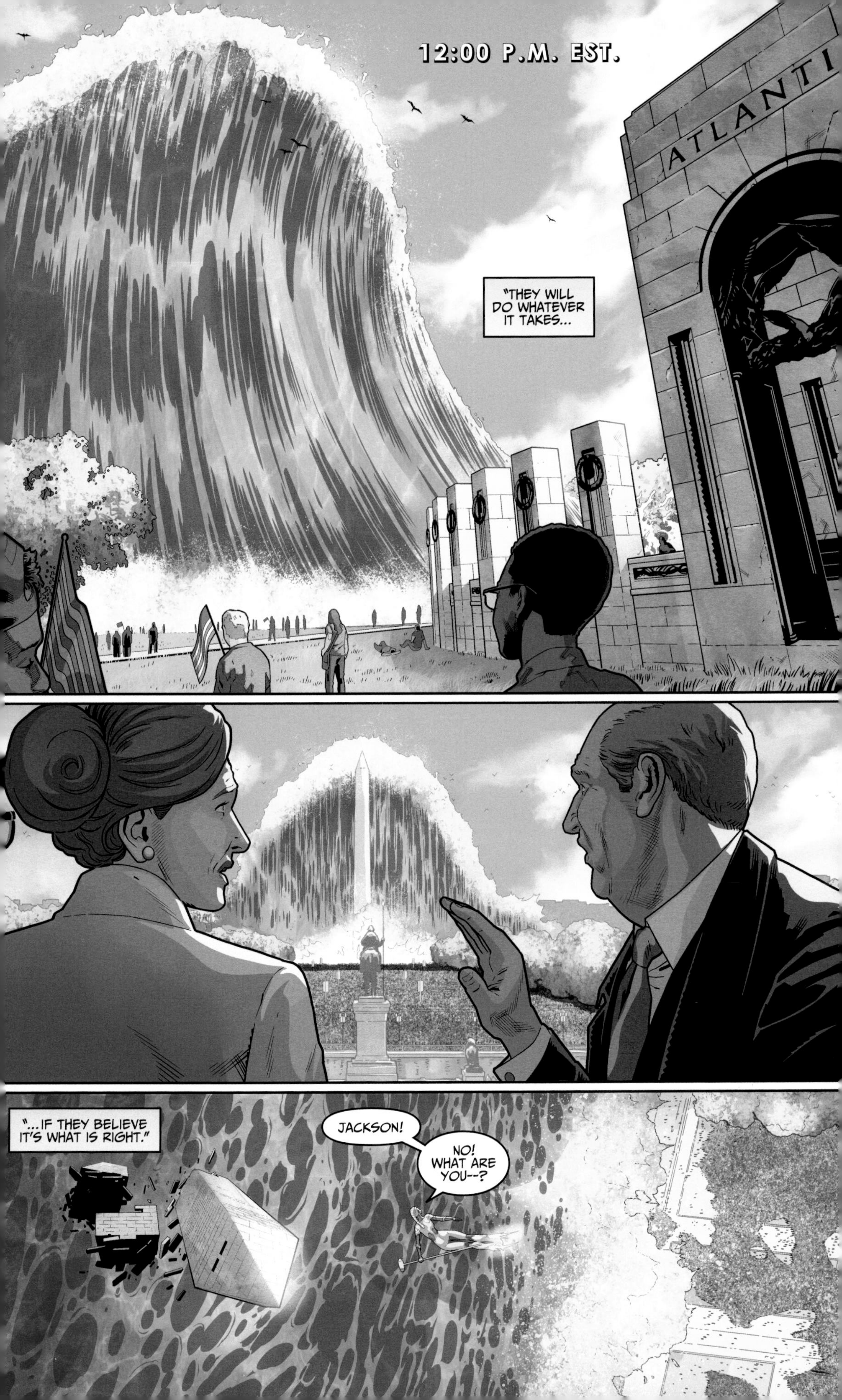
12:00 P.M. EST.
ATLANTI
"THEY WILL DO WHATEVER IT TAKES...
"...IF THEY BELIEVE IT'S WHAT IS RIGHT."
JACKSON!
NO! WHAT ARE YOU--?

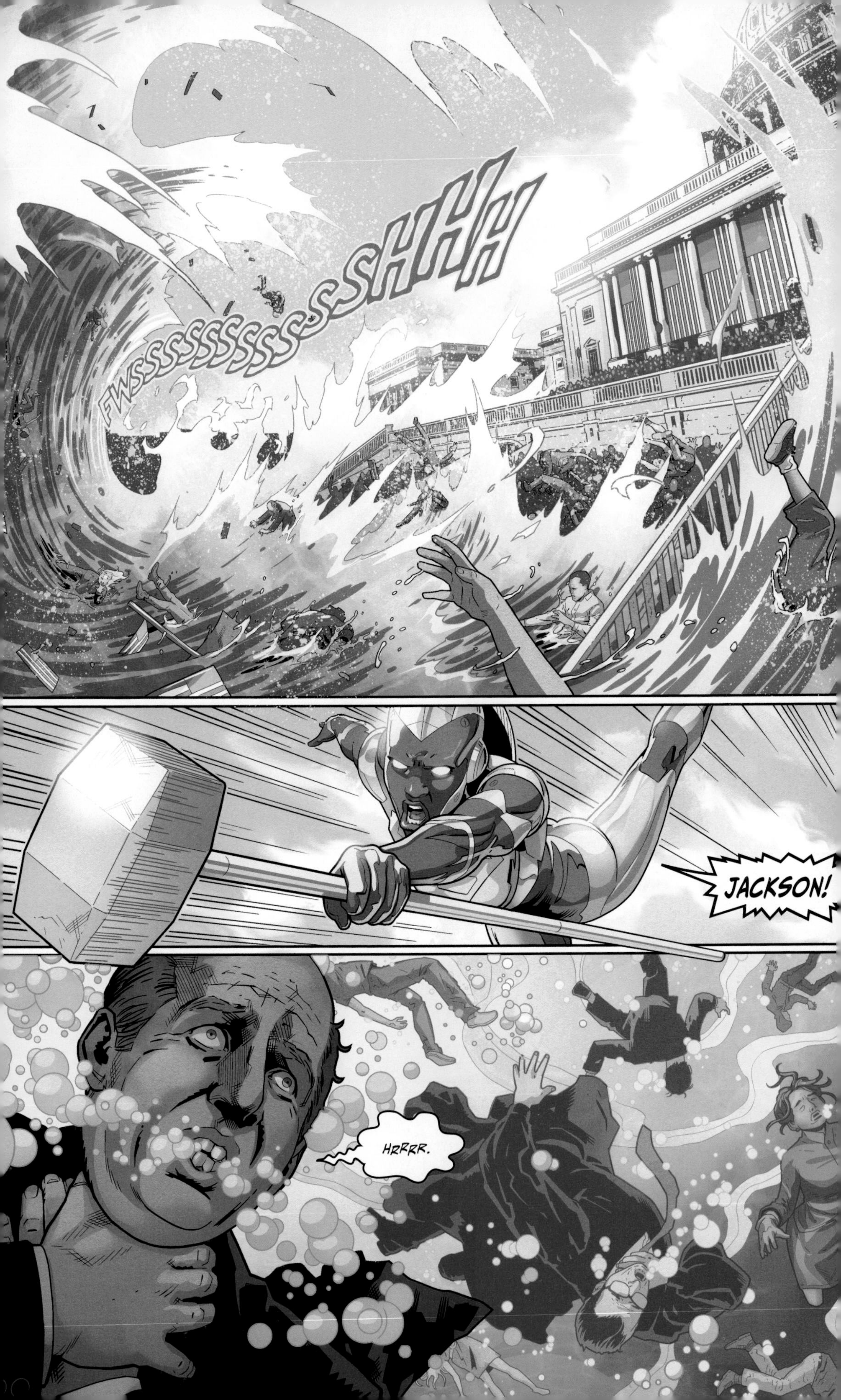
FWSSSSSSSSSSSSHHH
JACKSON!
HRRRR.

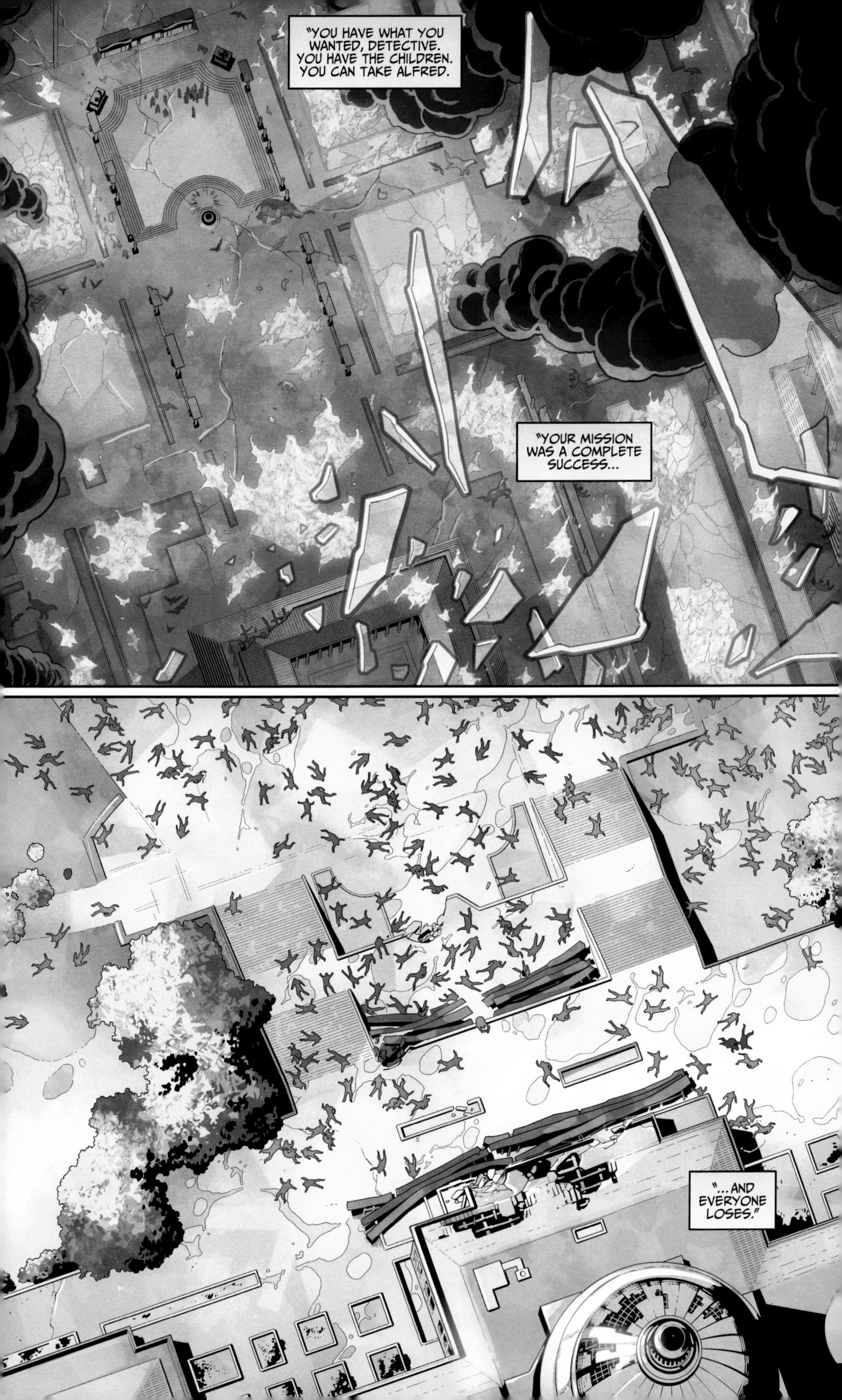
"YOU HAVE WHAT YOU WANTED, DETECTIVE. YOU HAVE THE CHILDREN. YOU CAN TAKE ALFRED.
"YOUR MISSION WAS A COMPLETE SUCCESS...
"...AND EVERYONE LOSES."

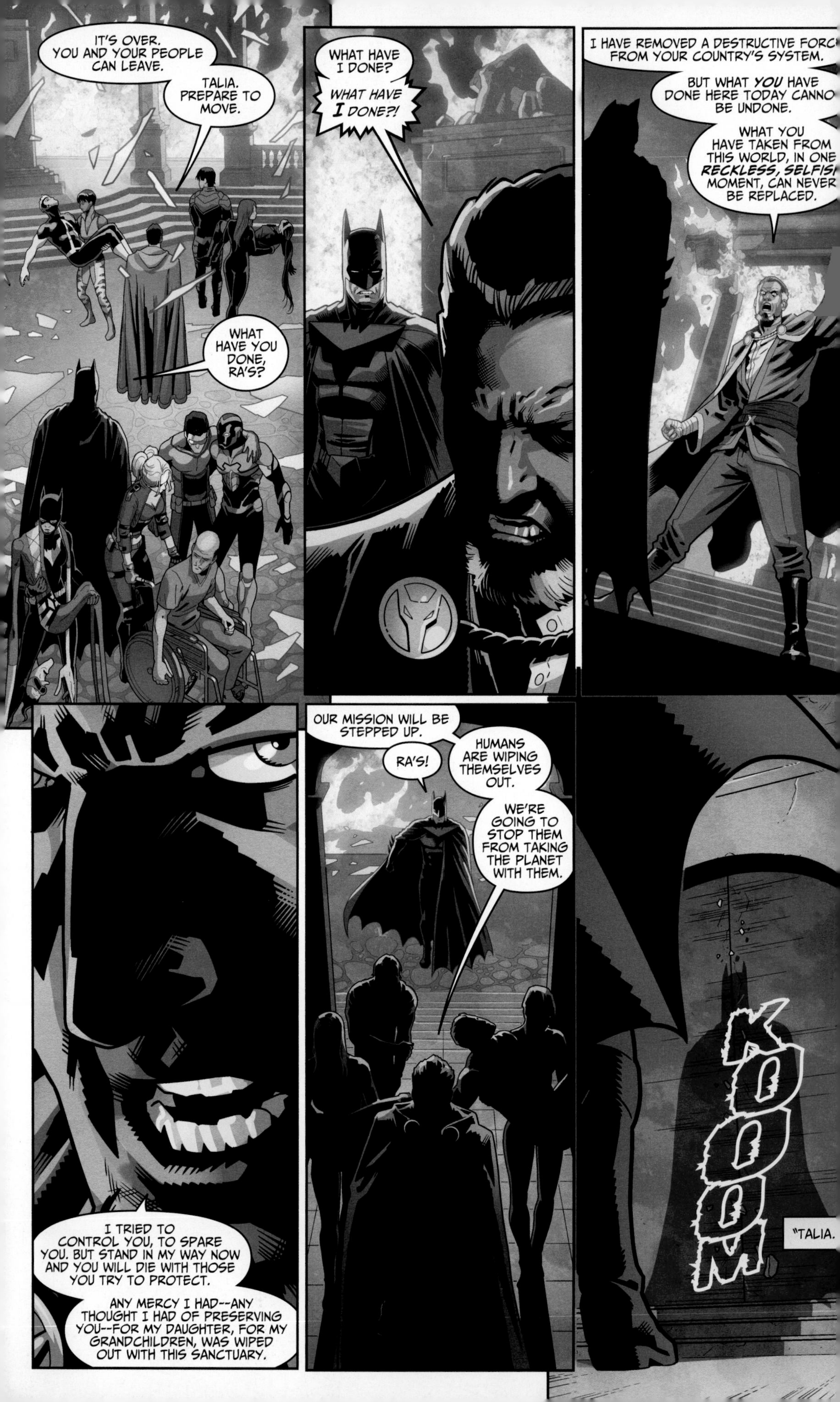
IT'S OVER. YOU AND YOUR PEOPLE CAN LEAVE.
TALIA. PREPARE TO MOVE.
WHAT HAVE YOU DONE, RA'S?
WHAT HAVE I DONE?
WHAT HAVE I DONE?!
I HAVE REMOVED A DESTRUCTIVE FORC FROM YOUR COUNTRY'S SYSTEM.
BUT WHAT YOU HAVE DONE HERE TODAY CANNO BE UNDONE.
WHAT YOU HAVE TAKEN FROM THIS WORLD, IN ONE RECKLESS, SELFIS MOMENT, CAN NEVER BE REPLACED.
I TRIED TO CONTROL YOU, TO SPARE YOU. BUT STAND IN MY WAY NOW AND YOU WILL DIE WITH THOSE YOU TRY TO PROTECT.
ANY MERCY I HAD--ANY THOUGHT I HAD OF PRESERVING YOU--FOR MY DAUGHTER, FOR MY GRANDCHILDREN, WAS WIPED OUT WITH THIS SANCTUARY.
OUR MISSION WILL BE STEPPED UP.
RA'S!
HUMANS ARE WIPING THEMSELVES OUT.
WE'RE GOING TO STOP THEM FROM TAKING THE PLANET WITH THEM.
KDOOOM
"TALIA.

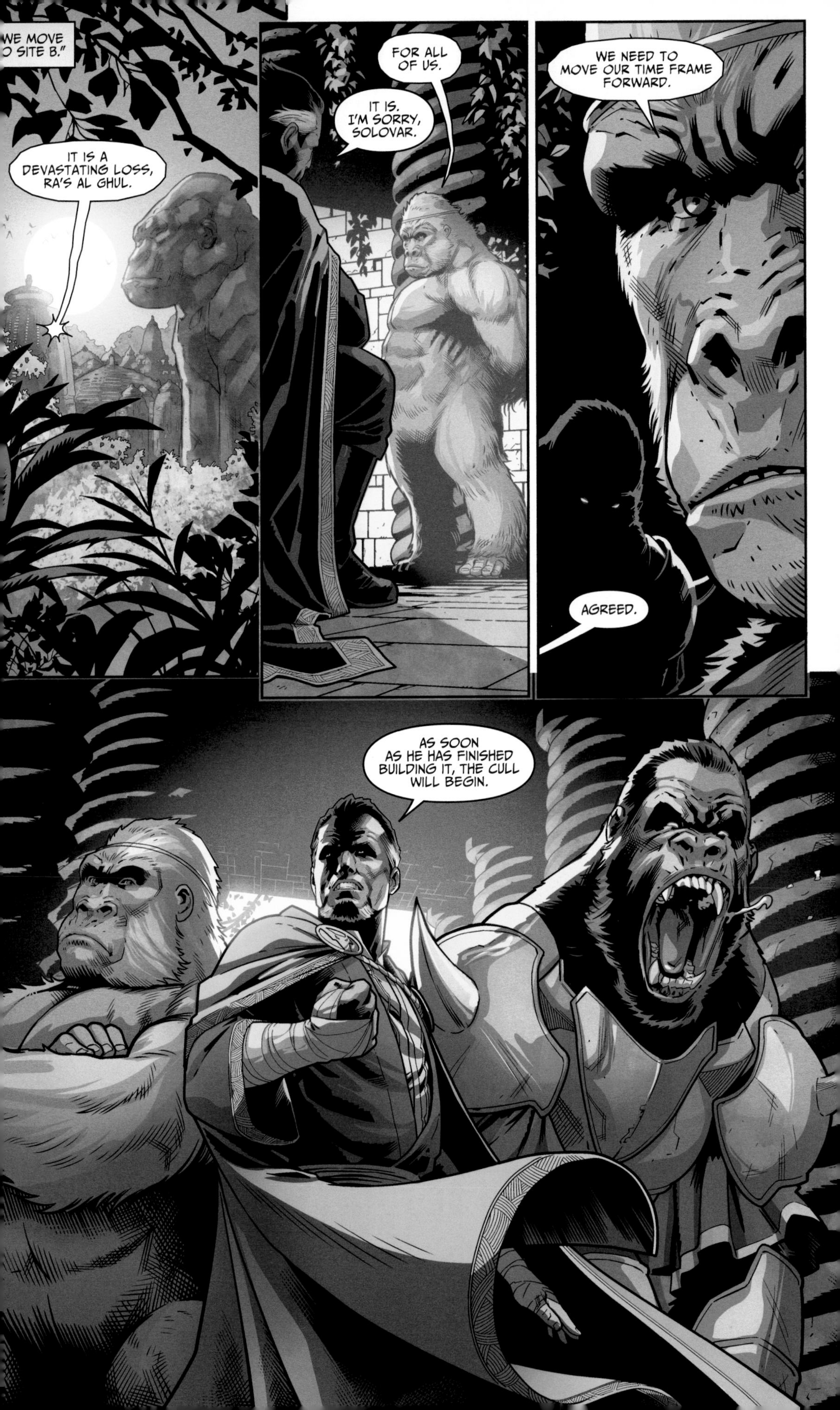

WE MOVE
O SITE B."
IT IS A DEVASTATING LOSS, RA'S AL GHUL.
IT IS. I'M SORRY, SOLOVAR.
FOR ALL OF US.
WE NEED TO MOVE OUR TIME FRAME FORWARD.
AGREED.
AS SOON AS HE HAS FINISHED BUILDING IT, THE CULL WILL BEGIN.

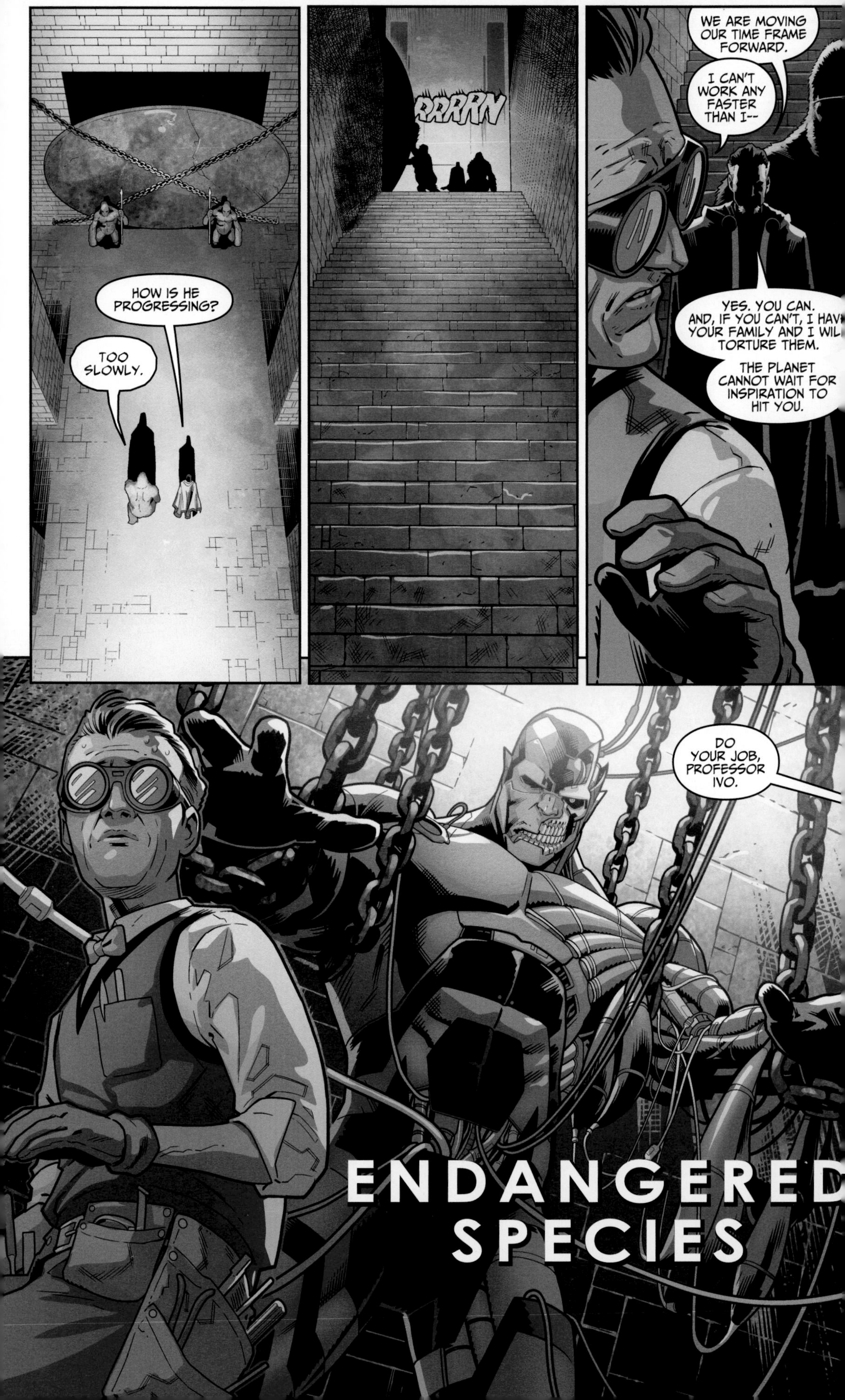
HOW IS HE PROGRESSING?
TOO SLOWLY.
RRRRN
WE ARE MOVING OUR TIME FRAME FORWARD.
I CAN'T WORK ANY FASTER THAN I--
YES. YOU CAN. AND, IF YOU CAN'T, I HAV YOUR FAMILY AND I WIL TORTURE THEM.
THE PLANET CANNOT WAIT FOR INSPIRATION TO HIT YOU.
DO YOUR JOB, PROFESSOR IVO.
ENDANGERED SPECIES

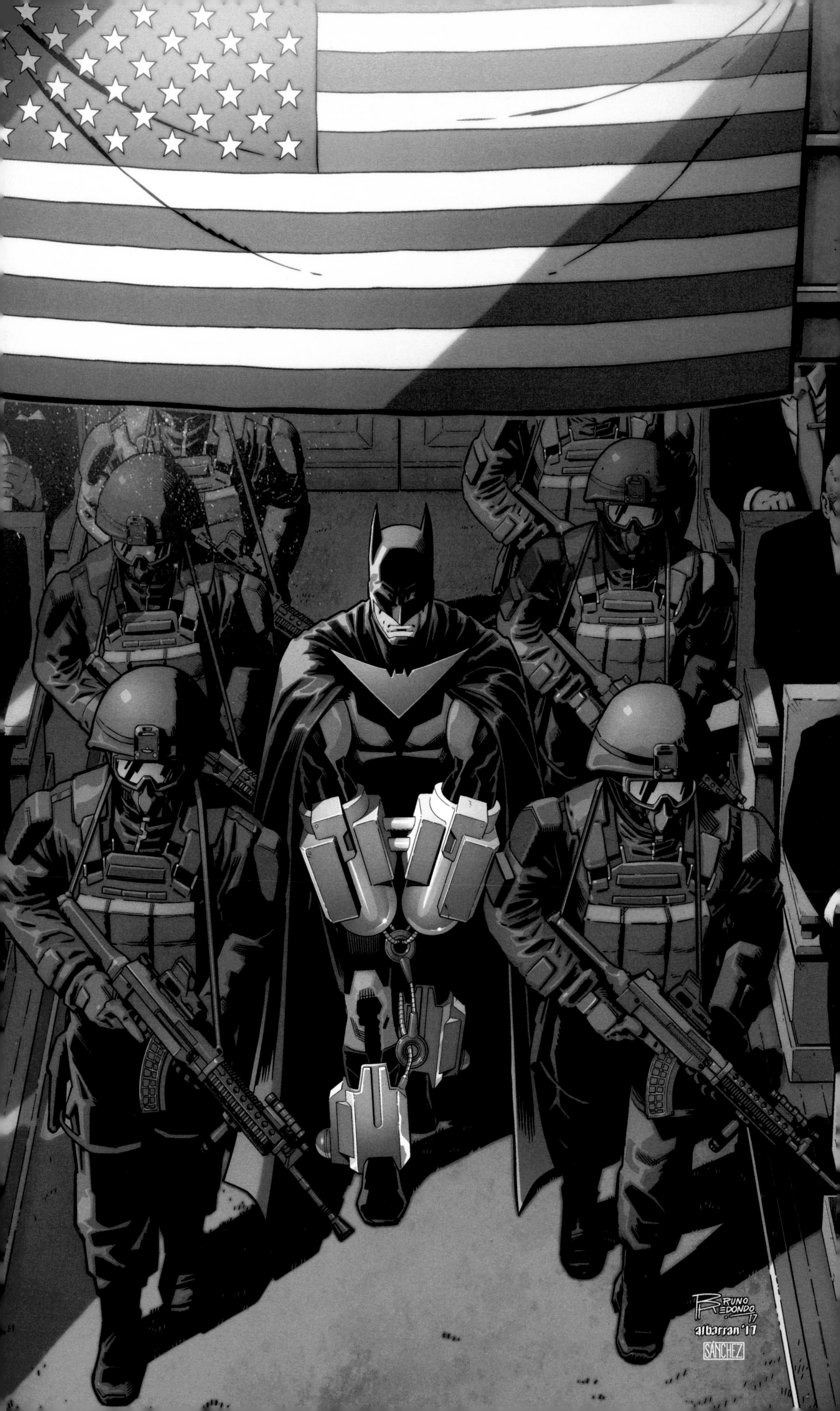
BRUNO REDONDO '17
albarran '17
SANCHEZ

"The Trial of Bruce Wayne"

Tom Taylor Writer **Daniel Sampere** Penciller **Juan Albarran** Inker **Rex Lokus** Colorist
Wes Abbott Letterer Cover art by **Bruno Redondo, Juan Albarran** and **Alejandro Sanchez**

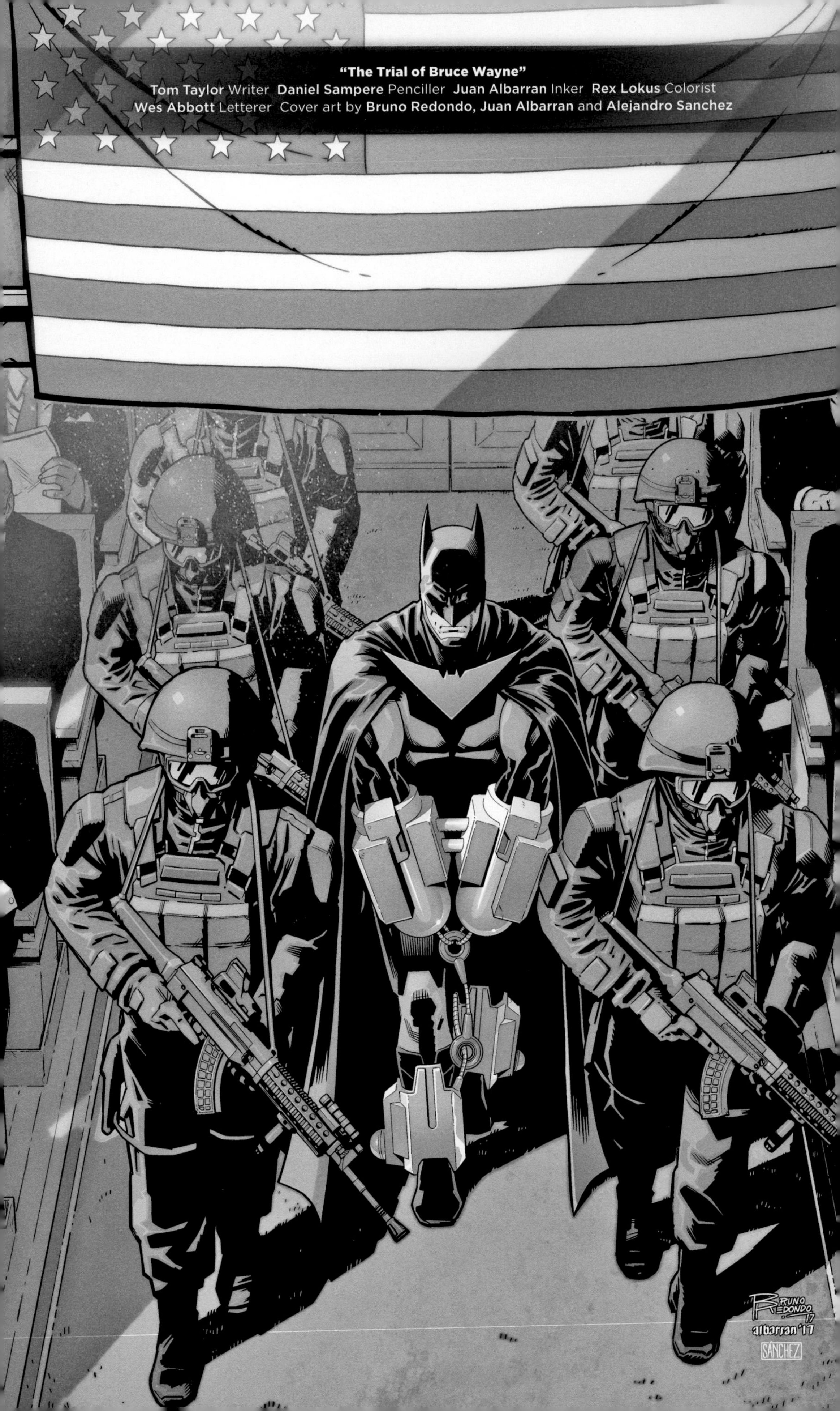

BRUNO REDONDO '17
albarran '17
SÁNCHEZ

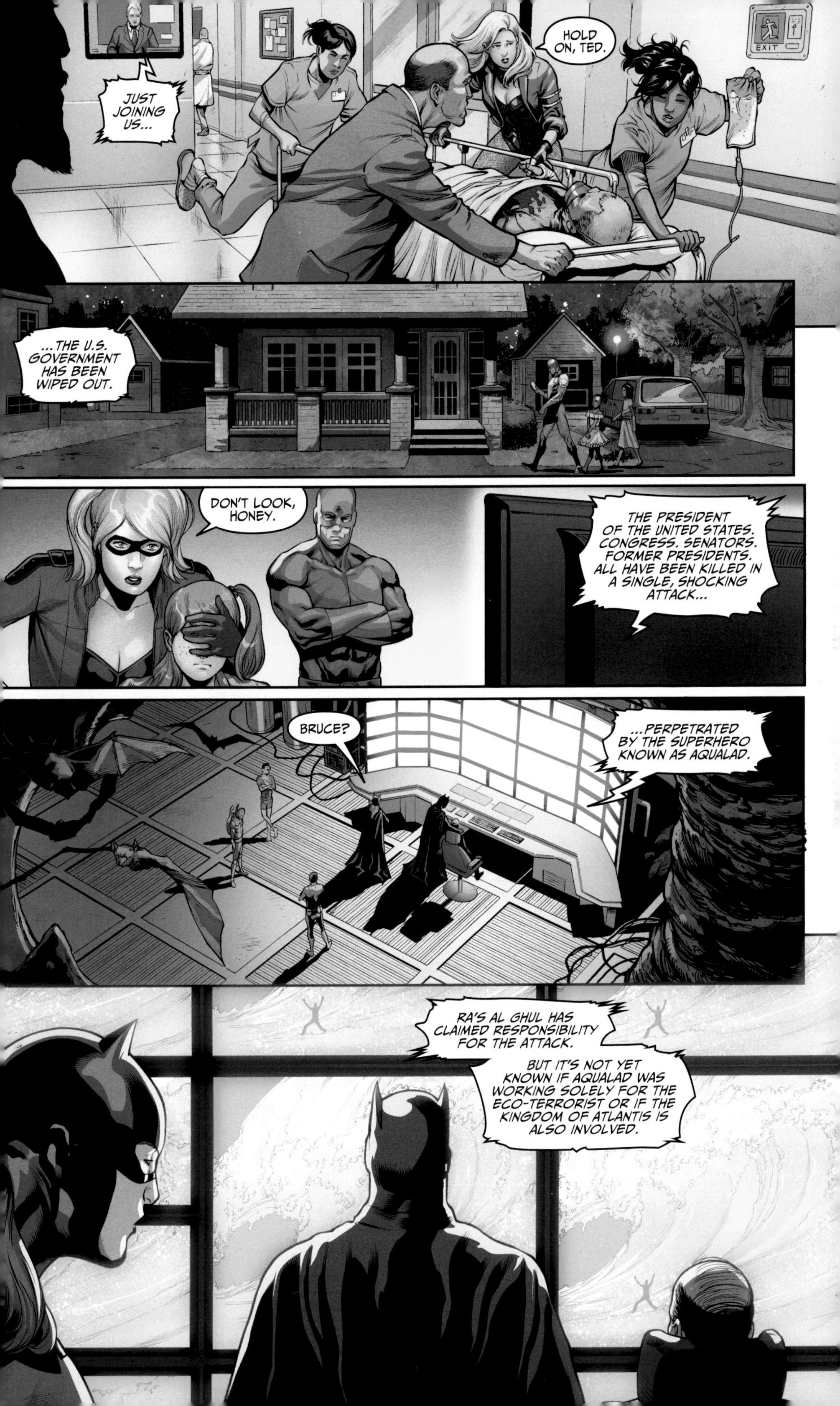
JUST JOINING US...
HOLD ON, TED.
...THE U.S. GOVERNMENT HAS BEEN WIPED OUT.
DON'T LOOK, HONEY.
THE PRESIDENT OF THE UNITED STATES. CONGRESS. SENATORS. FORMER PRESIDENTS. ALL HAVE BEEN KILLED IN A SINGLE, SHOCKING ATTACK...
BRUCE?
...PERPETRATED BY THE SUPERHERO KNOWN AS AQUALAD.
RA'S AL GHUL HAS CLAIMED RESPONSIBILITY FOR THE ATTACK.
BUT IT'S NOT YET KNOWN IF AQUALAD WAS WORKING SOLELY FOR THE ECO-TERRORIST OR IF THE KINGDOM OF ATLANTIS IS ALSO INVOLVED.
EXIT

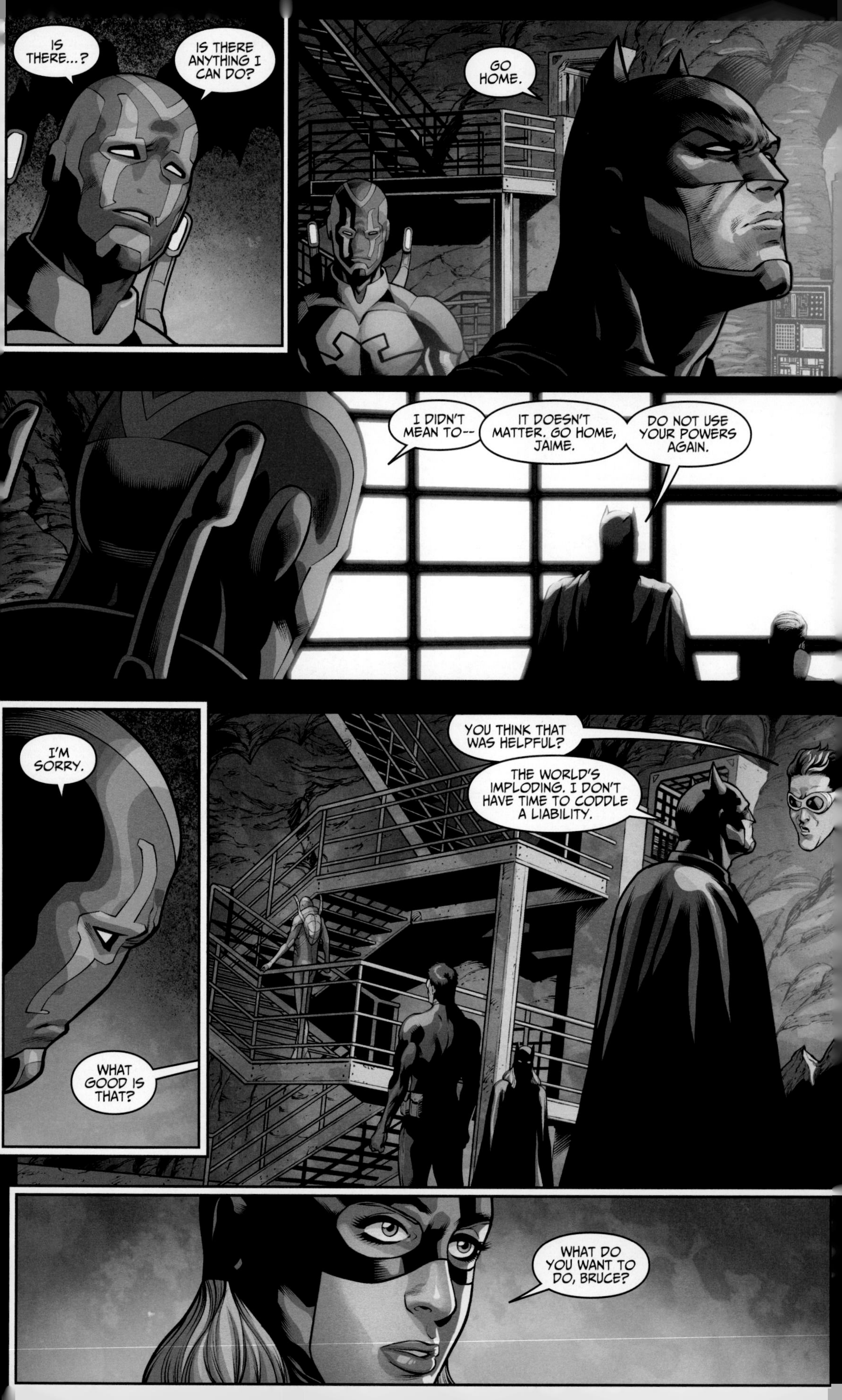

IS THERE...?
IS THERE ANYTHING I CAN DO?
GO HOME.
I DIDN'T MEAN TO--
IT DOESN'T MATTER. GO HOME, JAIME.
DO NOT USE YOUR POWERS AGAIN.
I'M SORRY.
WHAT GOOD IS THAT?
YOU THINK THAT WAS HELPFUL?
THE WORLD'S IMPLODING. I DON'T HAVE TIME TO CODDLE A LIABILITY.
WHAT DO YOU WANT TO DO, BRUCE?

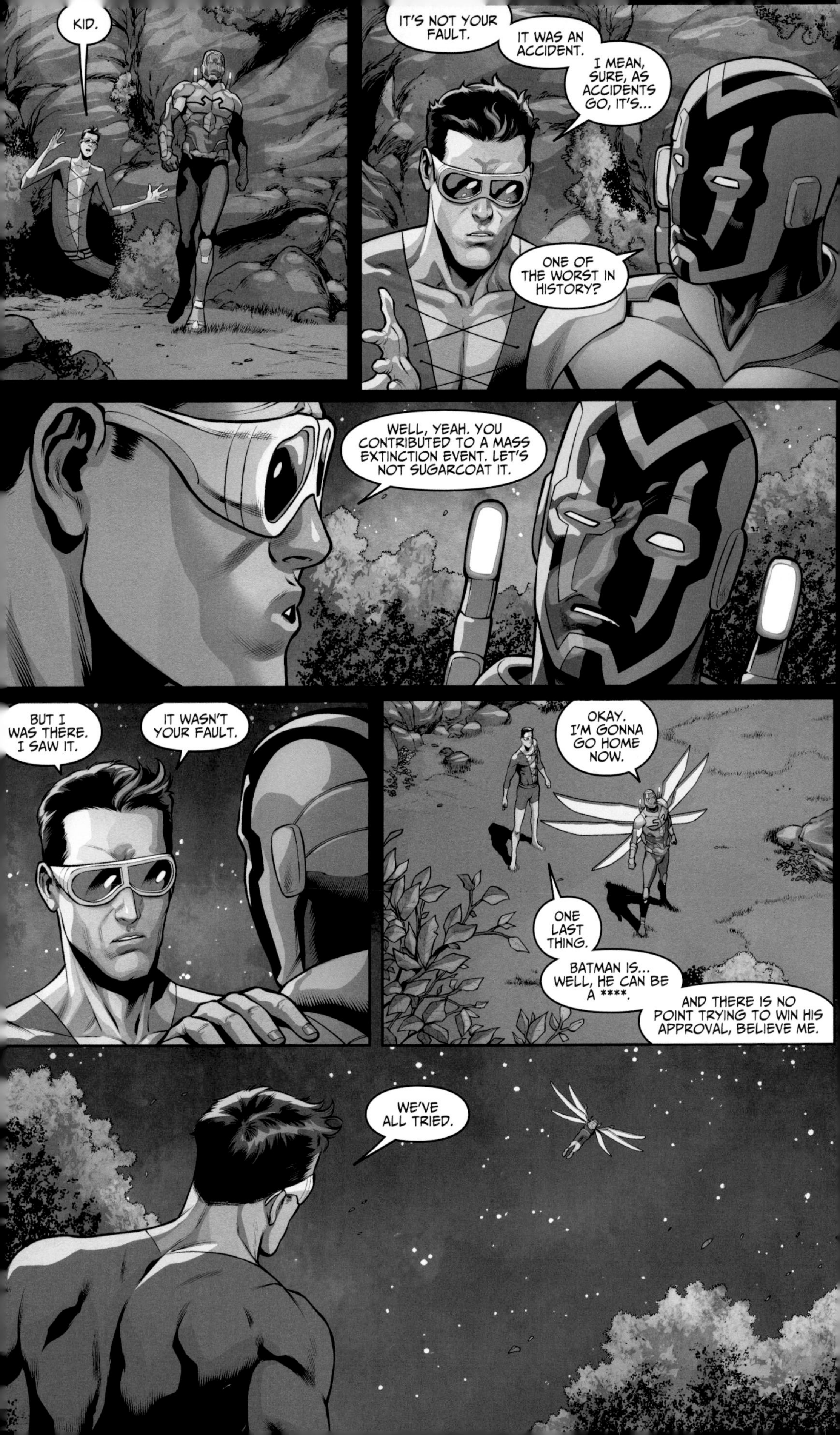
KID.
IT'S NOT YOUR FAULT.
IT WAS AN ACCIDENT.
I MEAN, SURE, AS ACCIDENTS GO, IT'S...
ONE OF THE WORST IN HISTORY?
WELL, YEAH. YOU CONTRIBUTED TO A MASS EXTINCTION EVENT. LET'S NOT SUGARCOAT IT.
BUT I WAS THERE. I SAW IT.
IT WASN'T YOUR FAULT.
OKAY. I'M GONNA GO HOME NOW.
ONE LAST THING.
BATMAN IS... WELL, HE CAN BE A ****.
AND THERE IS NO POINT TRYING TO WIN HIS APPROVAL, BELIEVE ME.
WE'VE ALL TRIED.

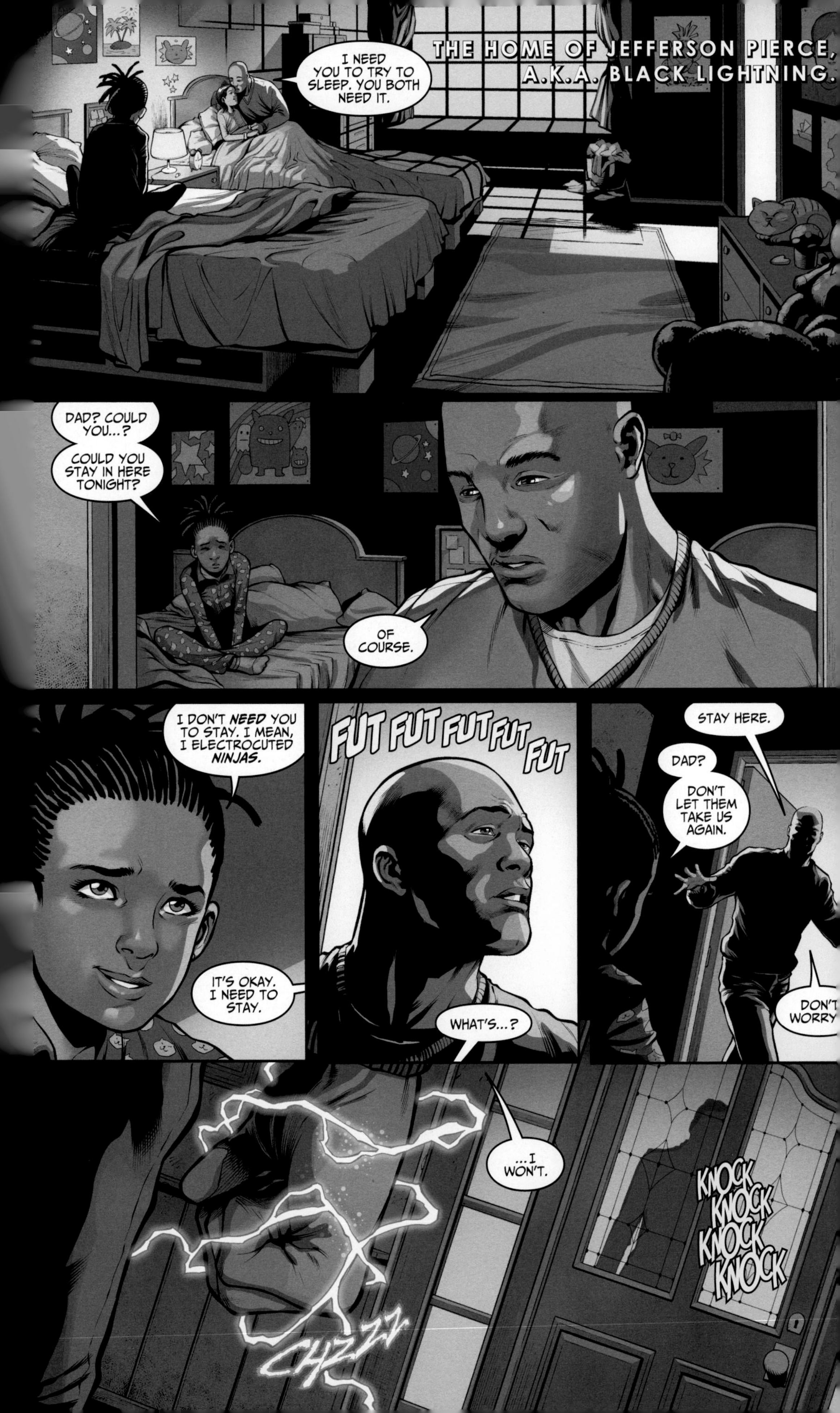
THE HOME OF JEFFERSON PIERCE, A.K.A. BLACK LIGHTNING.
I NEED YOU TO TRY TO SLEEP. YOU BOTH NEED IT.
DAD? COULD YOU...?
COULD YOU STAY IN HERE TONIGHT?
OF COURSE.
I DON'T NEED YOU TO STAY. I MEAN, I ELECTROCUTED NINJAS.
IT'S OKAY. I NEED TO STAY.
FUT FUT FUT FUT FUT
WHAT'S...?
STAY HERE.
DAD?
DON'T LET THEM TAKE US AGAIN.
DON'T WORRY
...I WON'T.
KNOCK KNOCK KNOCK KNOCK
CHZZZ

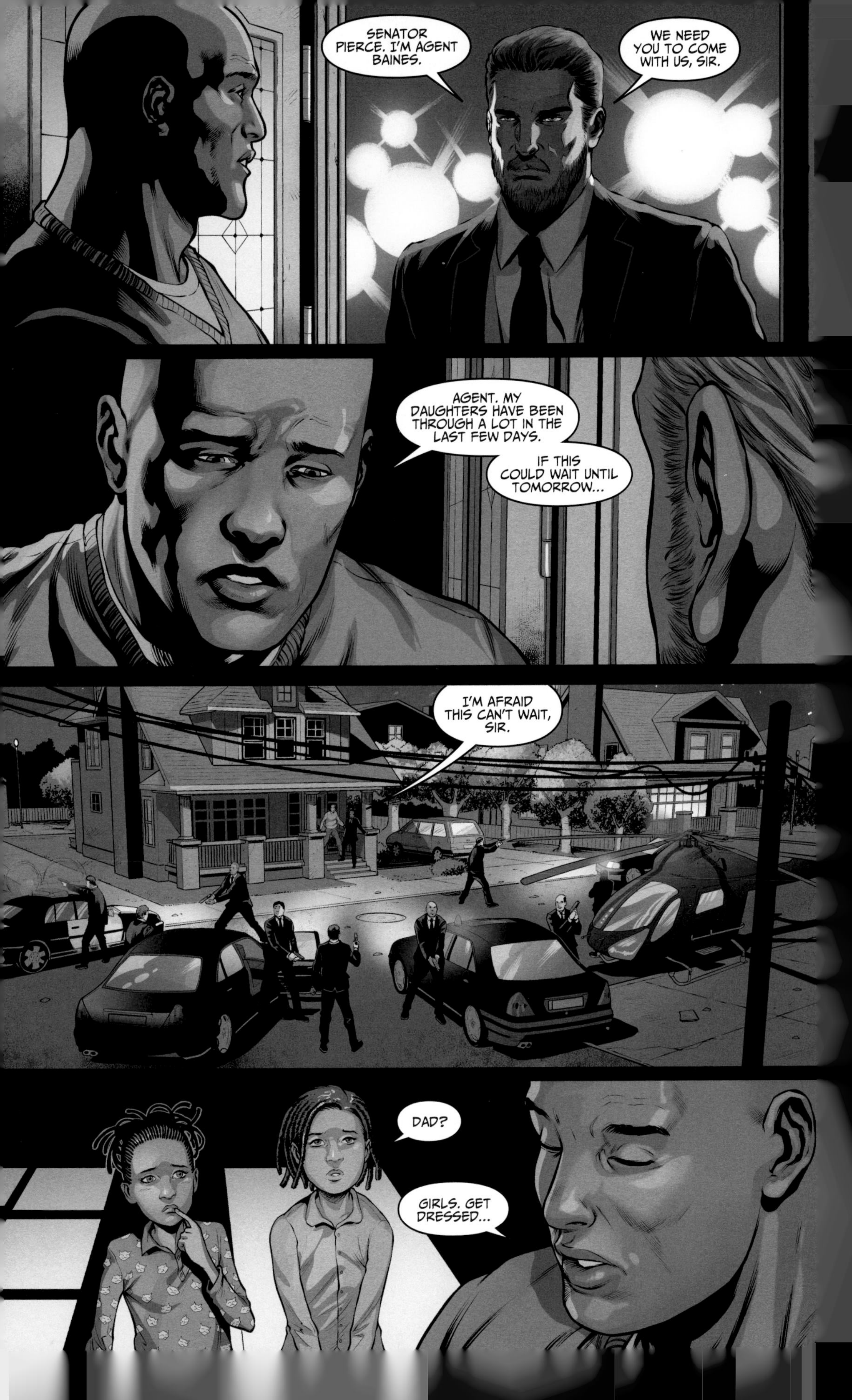
SENATOR PIERCE. I'M AGENT BAINES.
WE NEED YOU TO COME WITH US, SIR.
AGENT. MY DAUGHTERS HAVE BEEN THROUGH A LOT IN THE LAST FEW DAYS.
IF THIS COULD WAIT UNTIL TOMORROW...
I'M AFRAID THIS CAN'T WAIT, SIR.
DAD?
GIRLS. GET DRESSED...

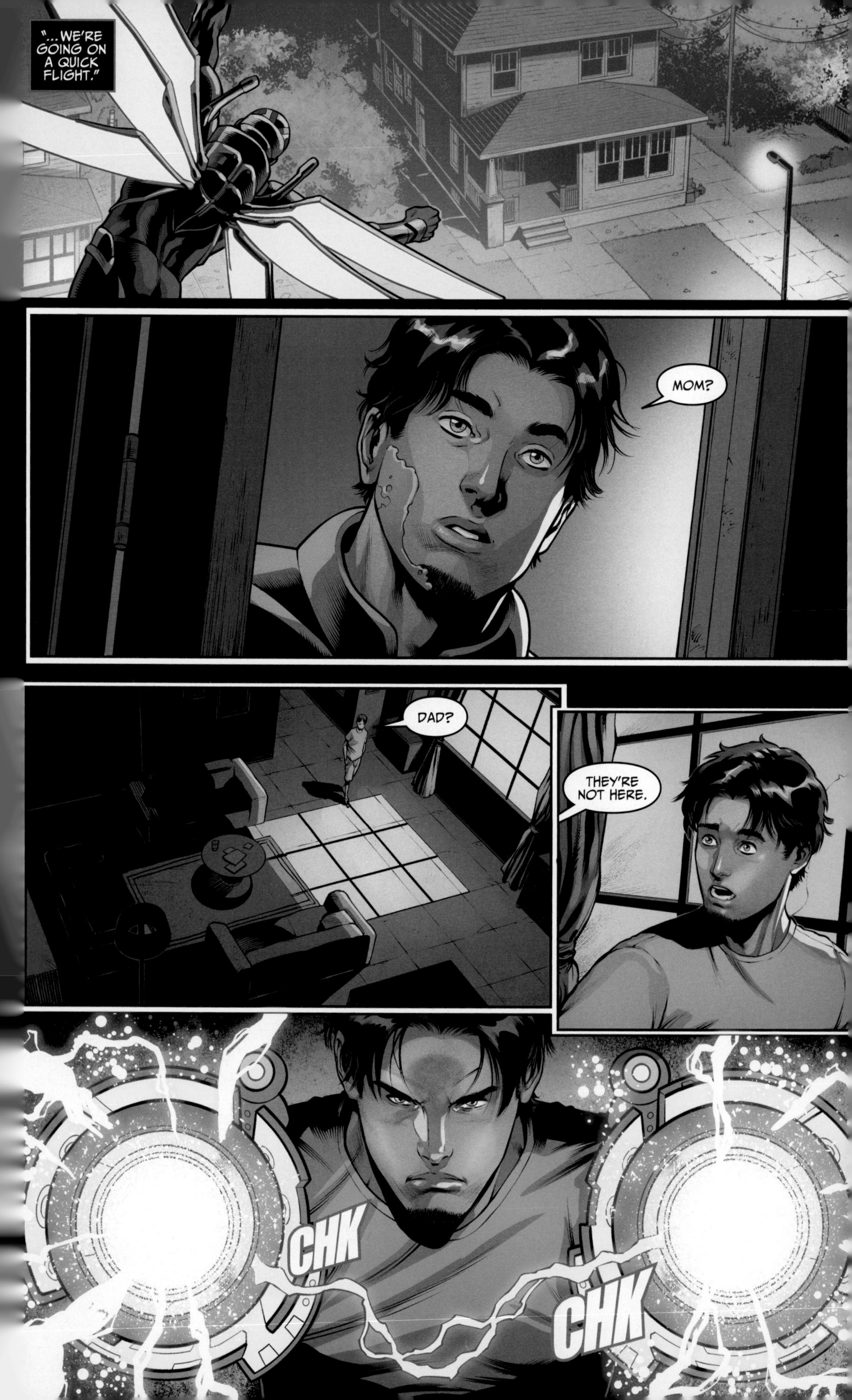
"...WE'RE GOING ON A QUICK FLIGHT."
MOM?
DAD?
THEY'RE NOT HERE.
CHK
CHK

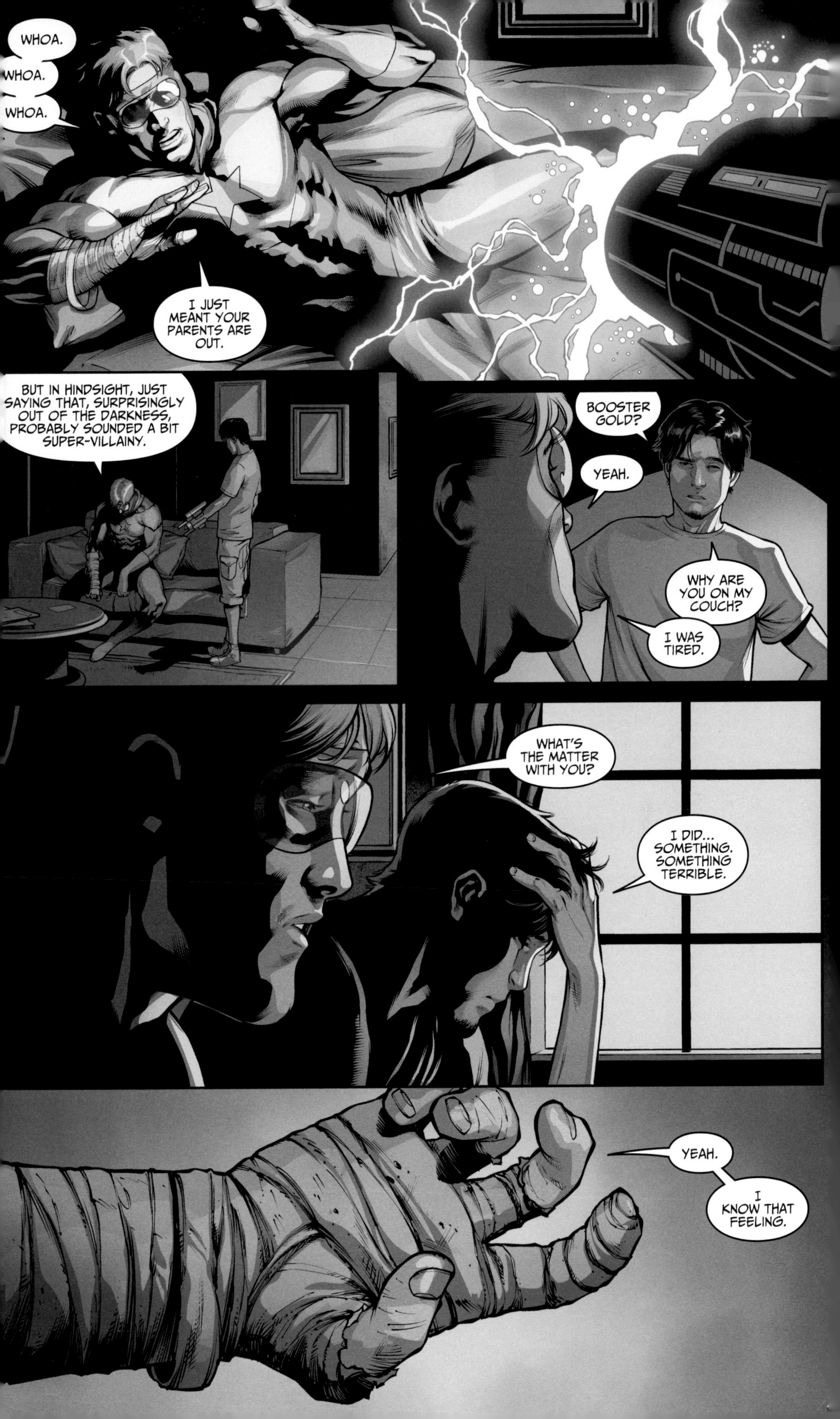
WHOA.
WHOA.
WHOA.
I JUST MEANT YOUR PARENTS ARE OUT.
BUT IN HINDSIGHT, JUST SAYING THAT, SURPRISINGLY OUT OF THE DARKNESS, PROBABLY SOUNDED A BIT SUPER-VILLAINY.
BOOSTER GOLD?
YEAH.
WHY ARE YOU ON MY COUCH?
I WAS TIRED.
WHAT'S THE MATTER WITH YOU?
I DID... SOMETHING. SOMETHING TERRIBLE.
YEAH.
I KNOW THAT FEELING.

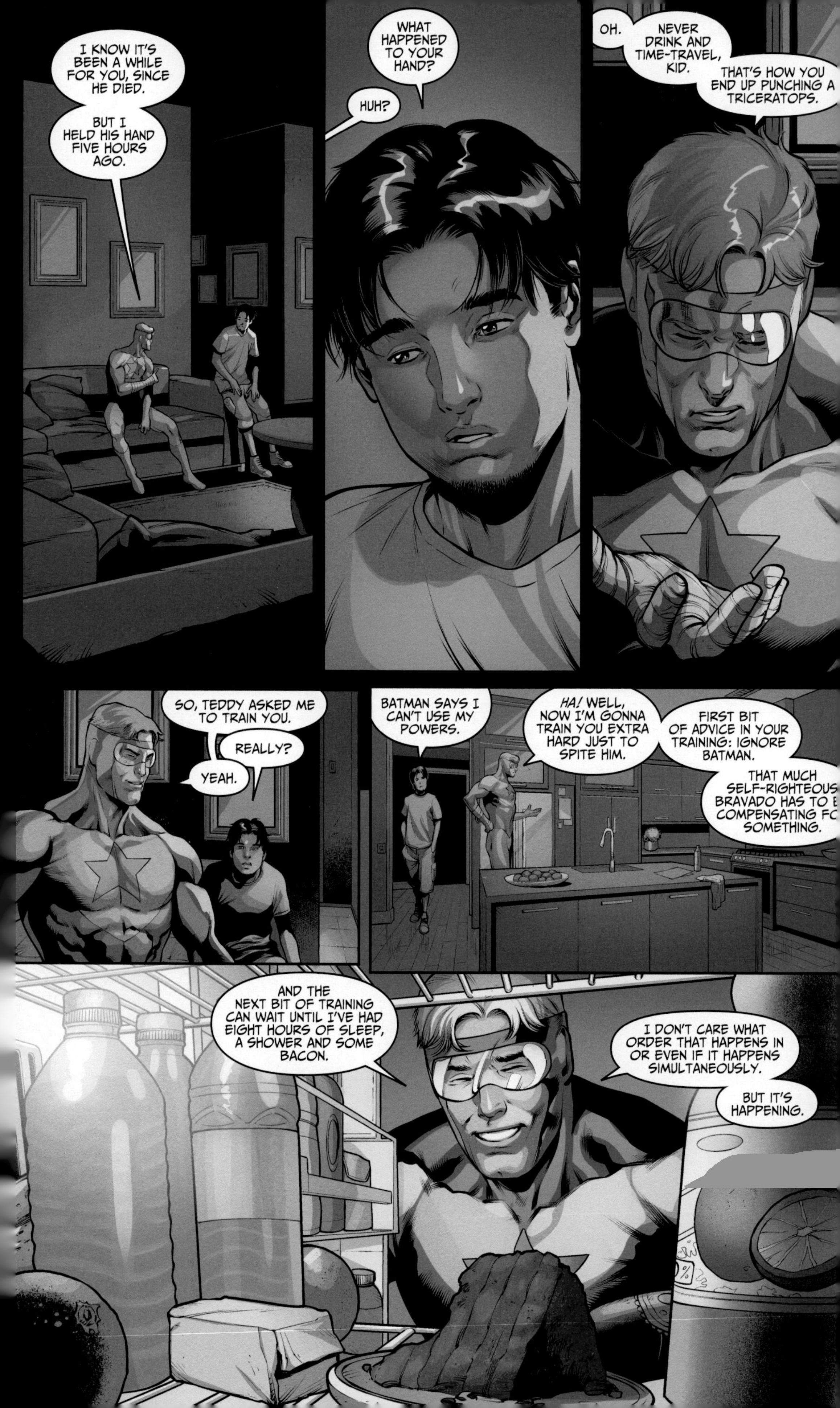

I KNOW IT'S BEEN A WHILE FOR YOU, SINCE HE DIED.
BUT I HELD HIS HAND FIVE HOURS AGO.
WHAT HAPPENED TO YOUR HAND?
HUH?
OH.
NEVER DRINK AND TIME-TRAVEL, KID.
THAT'S HOW YOU END UP PUNCHING A TRICERATOPS.
SO, TEDDY ASKED ME TO TRAIN YOU.
REALLY?
YEAH.
BATMAN SAYS I CAN'T USE MY POWERS.
HA! WELL, NOW I'M GONNA TRAIN YOU EXTRA HARD JUST TO SPITE HIM.
FIRST BIT OF ADVICE IN YOUR TRAINING: IGNORE BATMAN.
THAT MUCH SELF-RIGHTEOUS BRAVADO HAS TO B COMPENSATING FO SOMETHING.
AND THE NEXT BIT OF TRAINING CAN WAIT UNTIL I'VE HAD EIGHT HOURS OF SLEEP, A SHOWER AND SOME BACON.
I DON'T CARE WHAT ORDER THAT HAPPENS IN OR EVEN IF IT HAPPENS SIMULTANEOUSLY.
BUT IT'S HAPPENING.

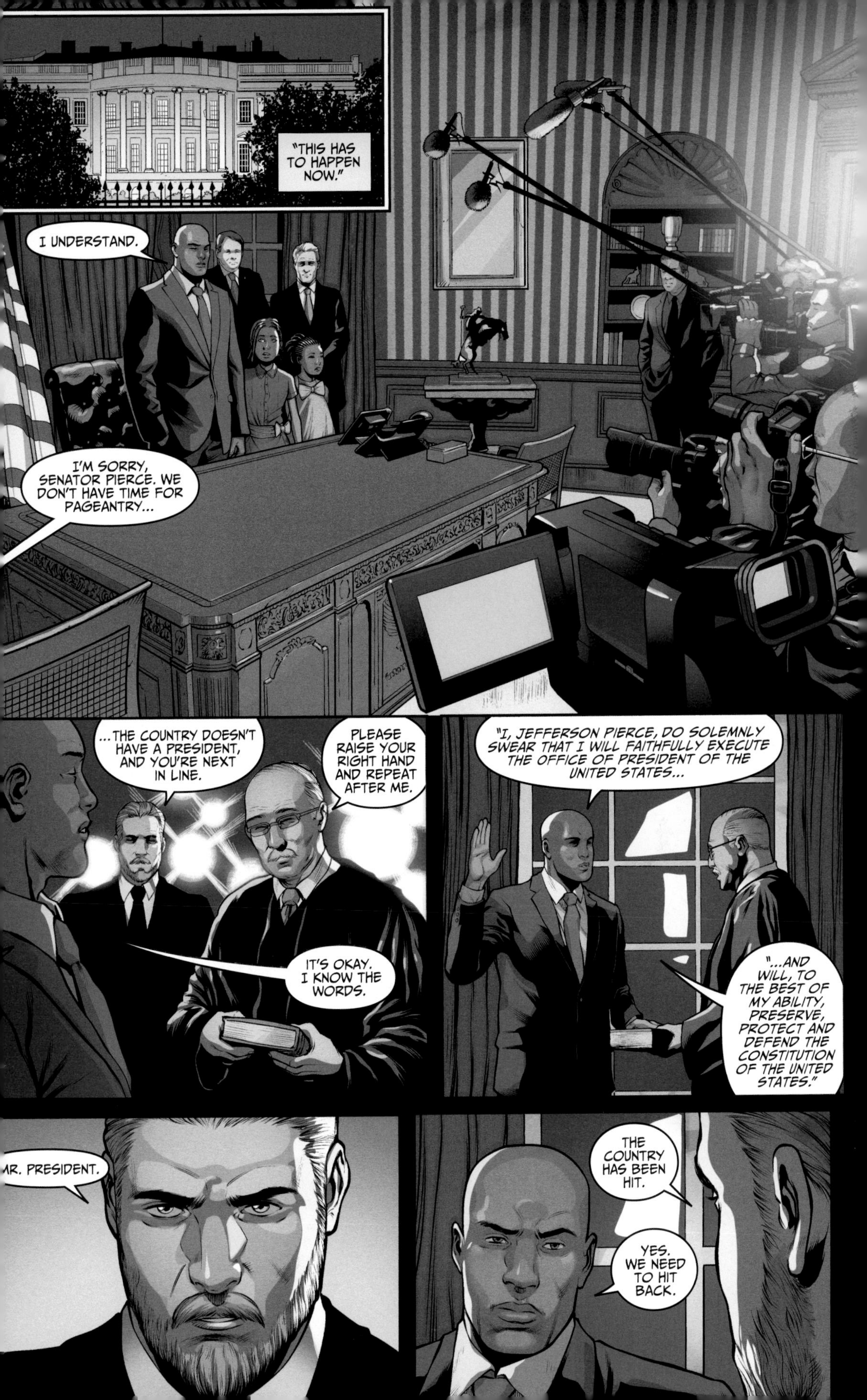
"THIS HAS TO HAPPEN NOW."
I UNDERSTAND.
I'M SORRY, SENATOR PIERCE. WE DON'T HAVE TIME FOR PAGEANTRY...
...THE COUNTRY DOESN'T HAVE A PRESIDENT, AND YOU'RE NEXT IN LINE.
PLEASE RAISE YOUR RIGHT HAND AND REPEAT AFTER ME.
IT'S OKAY. I KNOW THE WORDS.
"I, JEFFERSON PIERCE, DO SOLEMNLY SWEAR THAT I WILL FAITHFULLY EXECUTE THE OFFICE OF PRESIDENT OF THE UNITED STATES...
"...AND WILL, TO THE BEST OF MY ABILITY, PRESERVE, PROTECT AND DEFEND THE CONSTITUTION OF THE UNITED STATES."
MR. PRESIDENT.
THE COUNTRY HAS BEEN HIT.
YES. WE NEED TO HIT BACK.

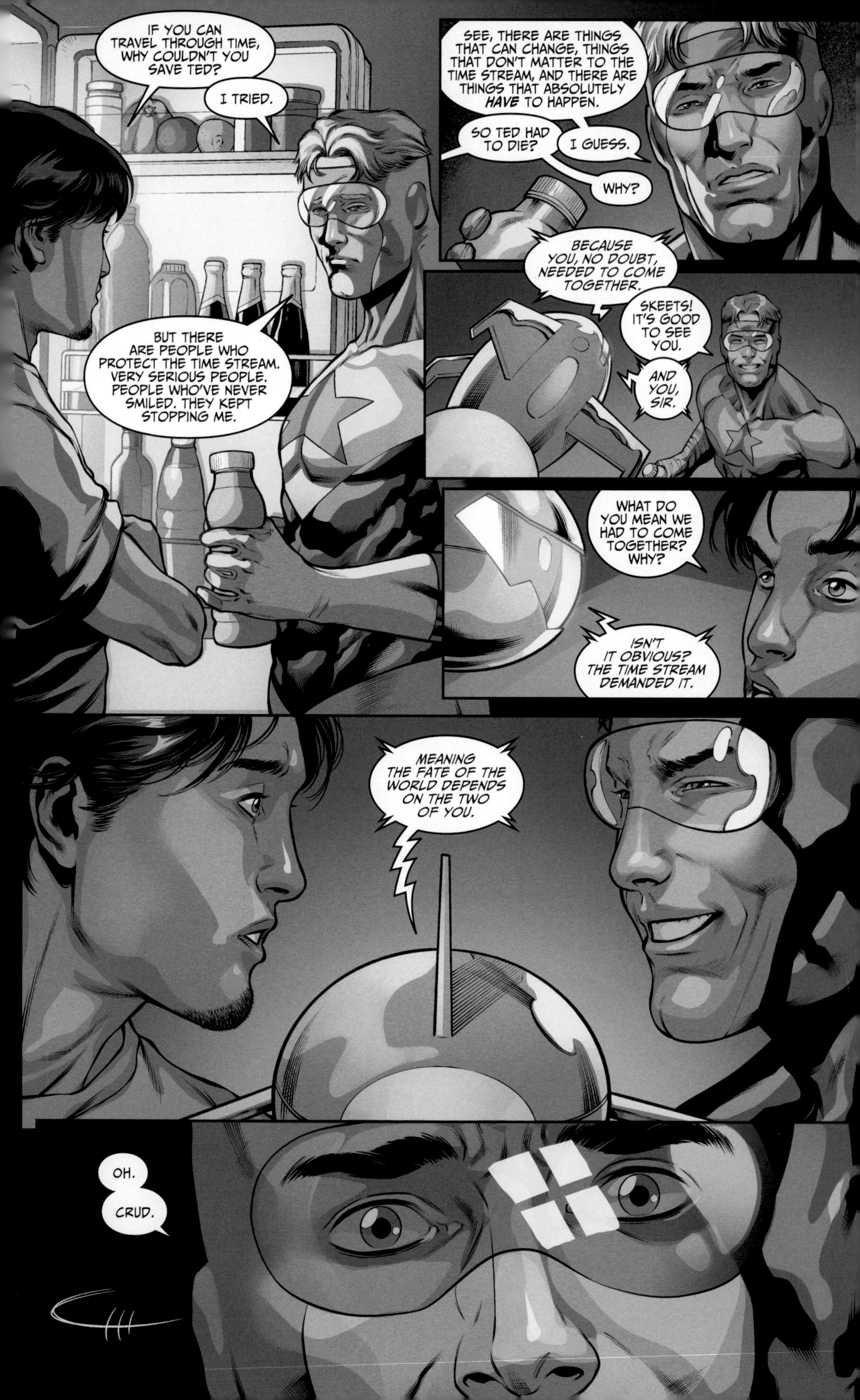

IF YOU CAN TRAVEL THROUGH TIME, WHY COULDN'T YOU SAVE TED?
I TRIED.
BUT THERE ARE PEOPLE WHO PROTECT THE TIME STREAM. VERY SERIOUS PEOPLE. PEOPLE WHO'VE NEVER SMILED. THEY KEPT STOPPING ME.
SEE, THERE ARE THINGS THAT CAN CHANGE, THINGS THAT DON'T MATTER TO THE TIME STREAM, AND THERE ARE THINGS THAT ABSOLUTELY HAVE TO HAPPEN.
SO TED HAD TO DIE?
I GUESS.
WHY?
BECAUSE YOU, NO DOUBT, NEEDED TO COME TOGETHER.
SKEETS! IT'S GOOD TO SEE YOU.
AND YOU, SIR.
WHAT DO YOU MEAN WE HAD TO COME TOGETHER? WHY?
ISN'T IT OBVIOUS? THE TIME STREAM DEMANDED IT.
MEANING THE FATE OF THE WORLD DEPENDS ON THE TWO OF YOU.
OH.
CRUD.

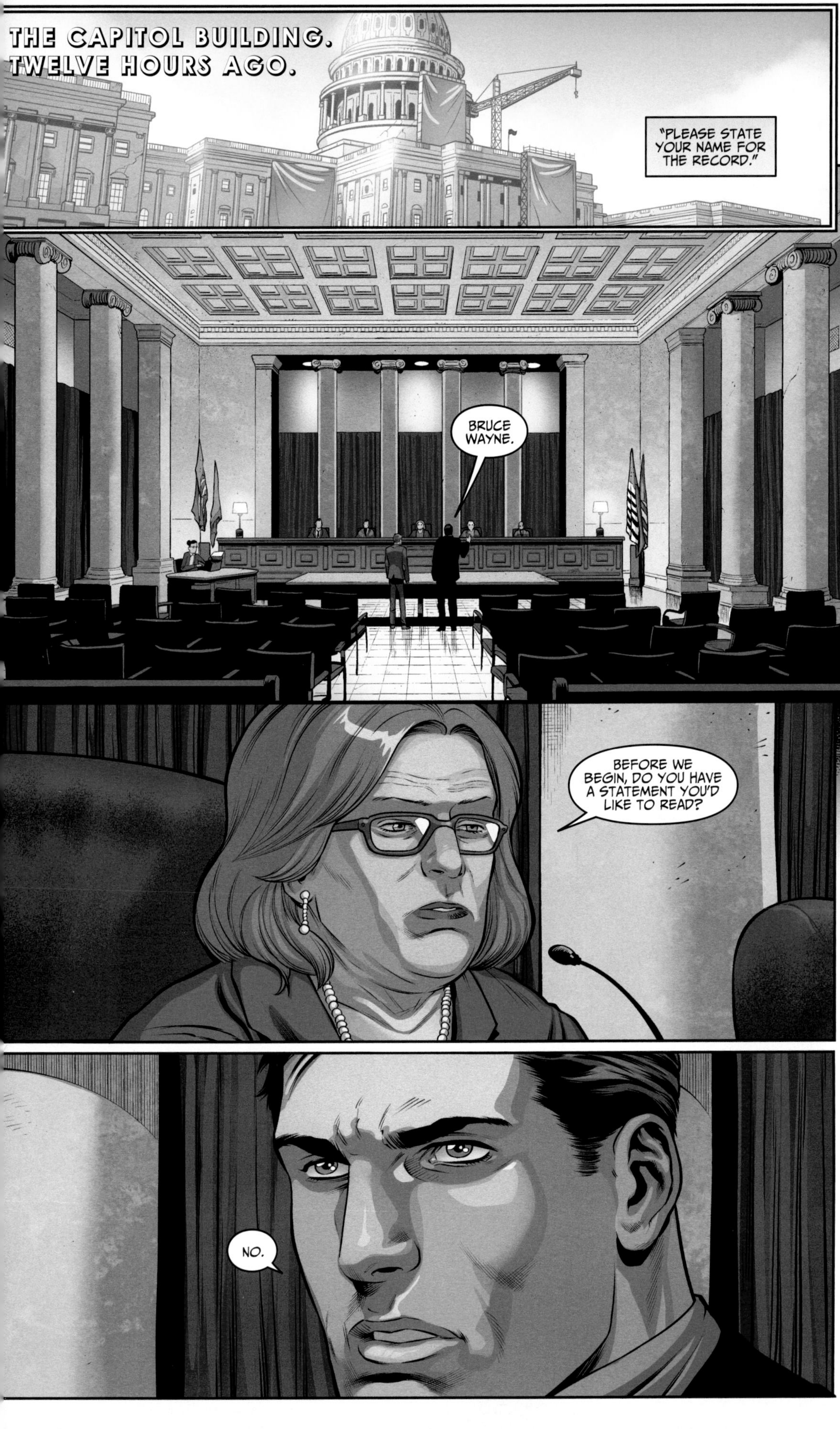
THE CAPITOL BUILDING.
TWELVE HOURS AGO.
"PLEASE STATE YOUR NAME FOR THE RECORD."
BRUCE WAYNE.
BEFORE WE BEGIN, DO YOU HAVE A STATEMENT YOU'D LIKE TO READ?
NO.

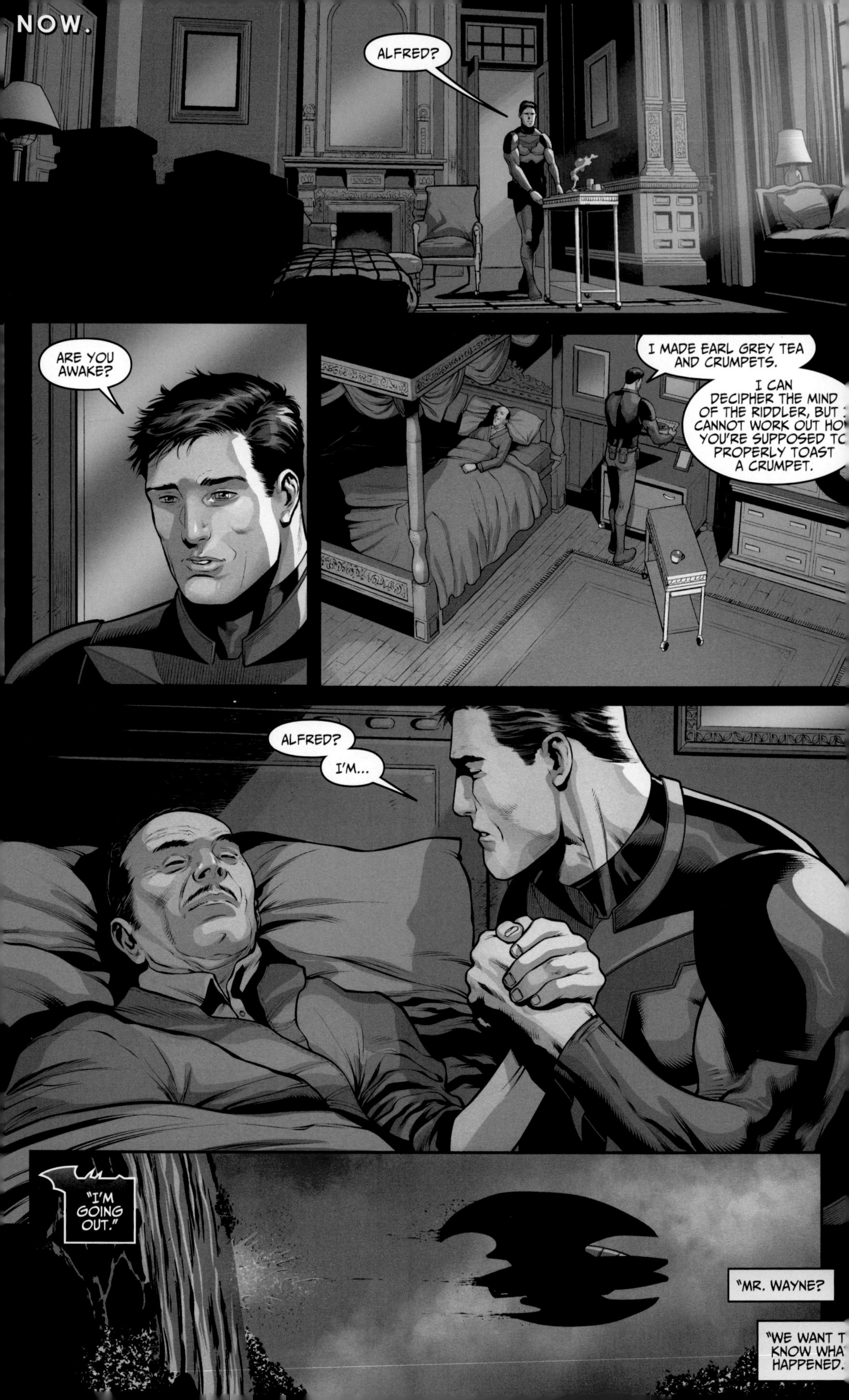
NOW.
ALFRED?
ARE YOU AWAKE?
I MADE EARL GREY TEA AND CRUMPETS.
I CAN DECIPHER THE MIND OF THE RIDDLER, BUT I CANNOT WORK OUT HOW YOU'RE SUPPOSED TO PROPERLY TOAST A CRUMPET.
ALFRED?
I'M...
"I'M GOING OUT."
"MR. WAYNE?
"WE WANT T KNOW WHA HAPPENED.

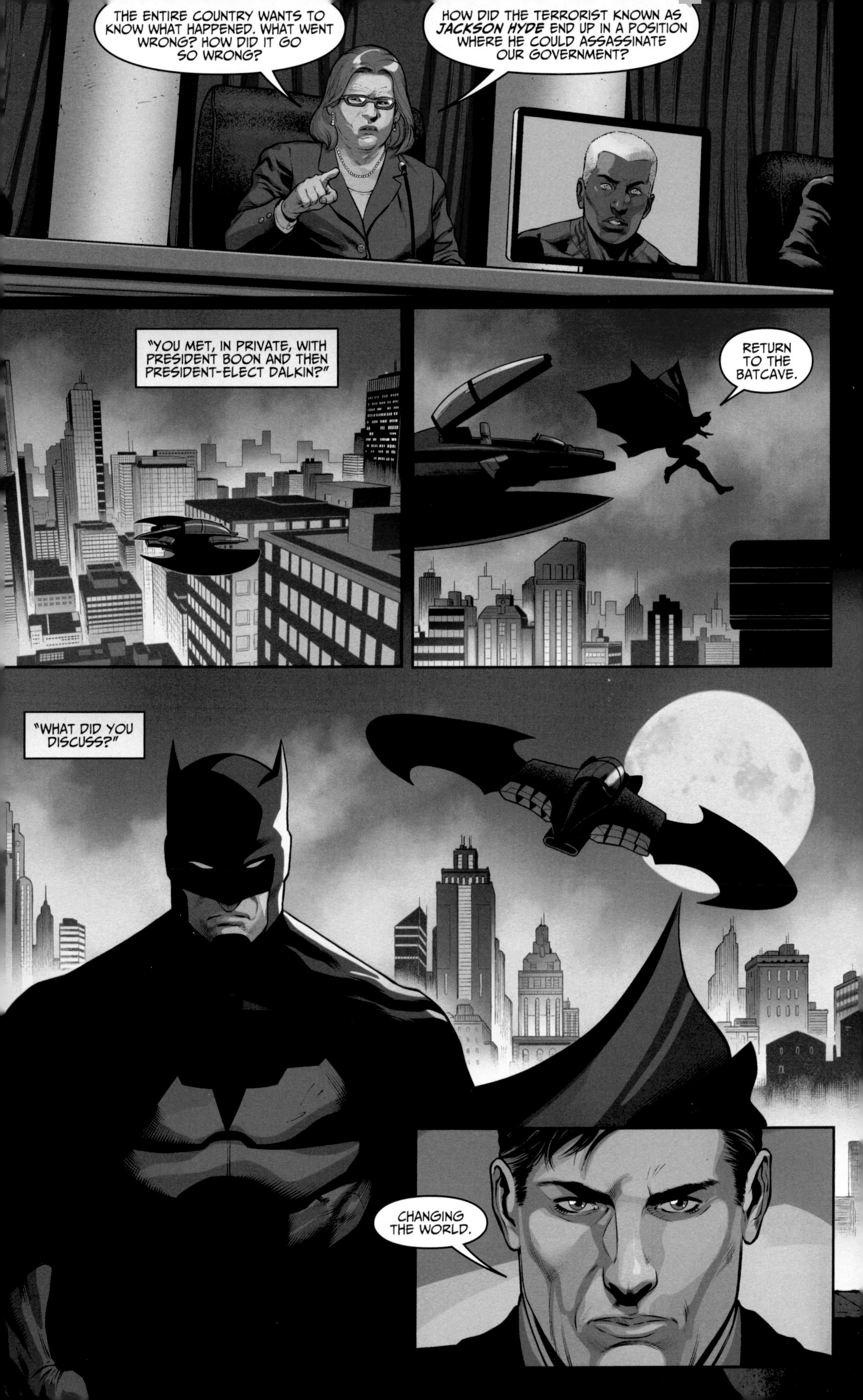
THE ENTIRE COUNTRY WANTS TO KNOW WHAT HAPPENED. WHAT WENT WRONG? HOW DID IT GO SO WRONG?
HOW DID THE TERRORIST KNOWN AS *JACKSON HYDE* END UP IN A POSITION WHERE HE COULD ASSASSINATE OUR GOVERNMENT?
"YOU MET, IN PRIVATE, WITH PRESIDENT BOON AND THEN PRESIDENT-ELECT DALKIN?"
RETURN TO THE BATCAVE.
"WHAT DID YOU DISCUSS?"
CHANGING THE WORLD.

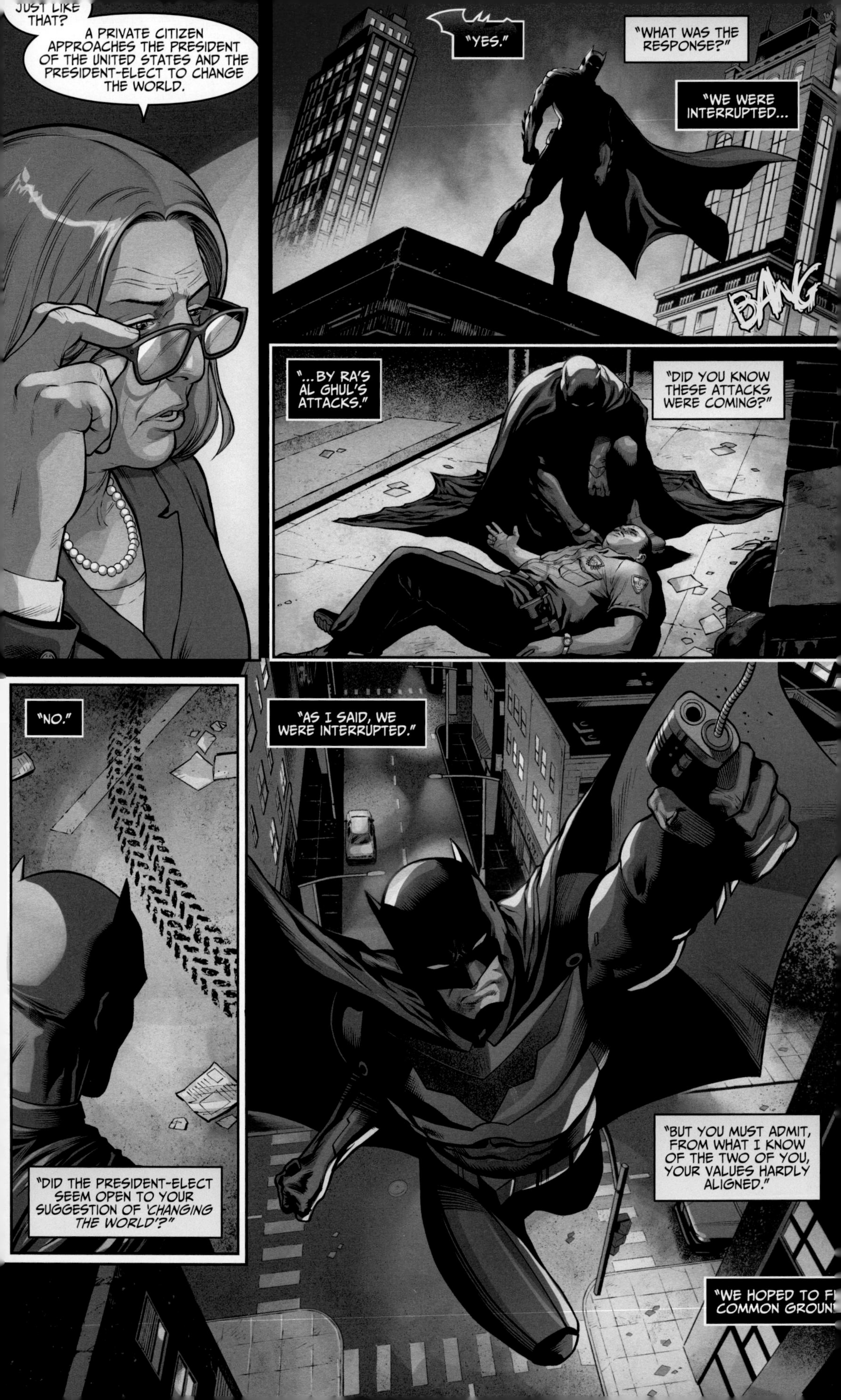
JUST LIKE THAT?
A PRIVATE CITIZEN APPROACHES THE PRESIDENT OF THE UNITED STATES AND THE PRESIDENT-ELECT TO CHANGE THE WORLD.
"YES."
"WHAT WAS THE RESPONSE?"
"WE WERE INTERRUPTED...
BANG
"...BY RA'S AL GHUL'S ATTACKS."
"DID YOU KNOW THESE ATTACKS WERE COMING?"
"NO."
"DID THE PRESIDENT-ELECT SEEM OPEN TO YOUR SUGGESTION OF 'CHANGING THE WORLD'?"
"AS I SAID, WE WERE INTERRUPTED."
"BUT YOU MUST ADMIT, FROM WHAT I KNOW OF THE TWO OF YOU, YOUR VALUES HARDLY ALIGNED."
"WE HOPED TO FI
COMMON GROUN

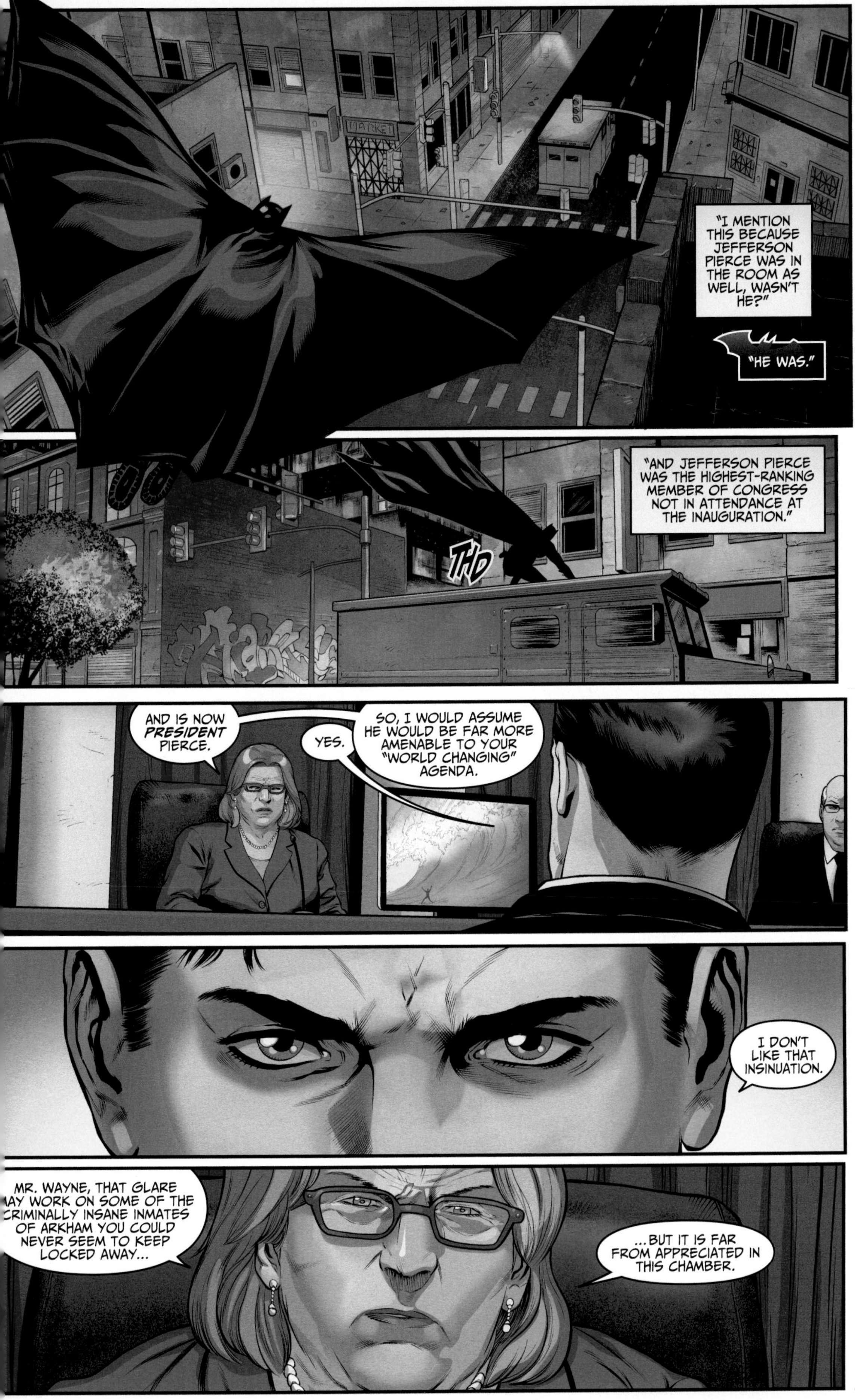
"I MENTION THIS BECAUSE JEFFERSON PIERCE WAS IN THE ROOM AS WELL, WASN'T HE?"
"HE WAS."
"AND JEFFERSON PIERCE WAS THE HIGHEST-RANKING MEMBER OF CONGRESS NOT IN ATTENDANCE AT THE INAUGURATION."
THD
AND IS NOW *PRESIDENT* PIERCE.
YES.
SO, I WOULD ASSUME HE WOULD BE FAR MORE AMENABLE TO YOUR "WORLD CHANGING" AGENDA.
I DON'T LIKE THAT INSINUATION.
MR. WAYNE, THAT GLARE AY WORK ON SOME OF THE CRIMINALLY INSANE INMATES OF ARKHAM YOU COULD NEVER SEEM TO KEEP LOCKED AWAY...
...BUT IT IS FAR FROM APPRECIATED IN THIS CHAMBER.

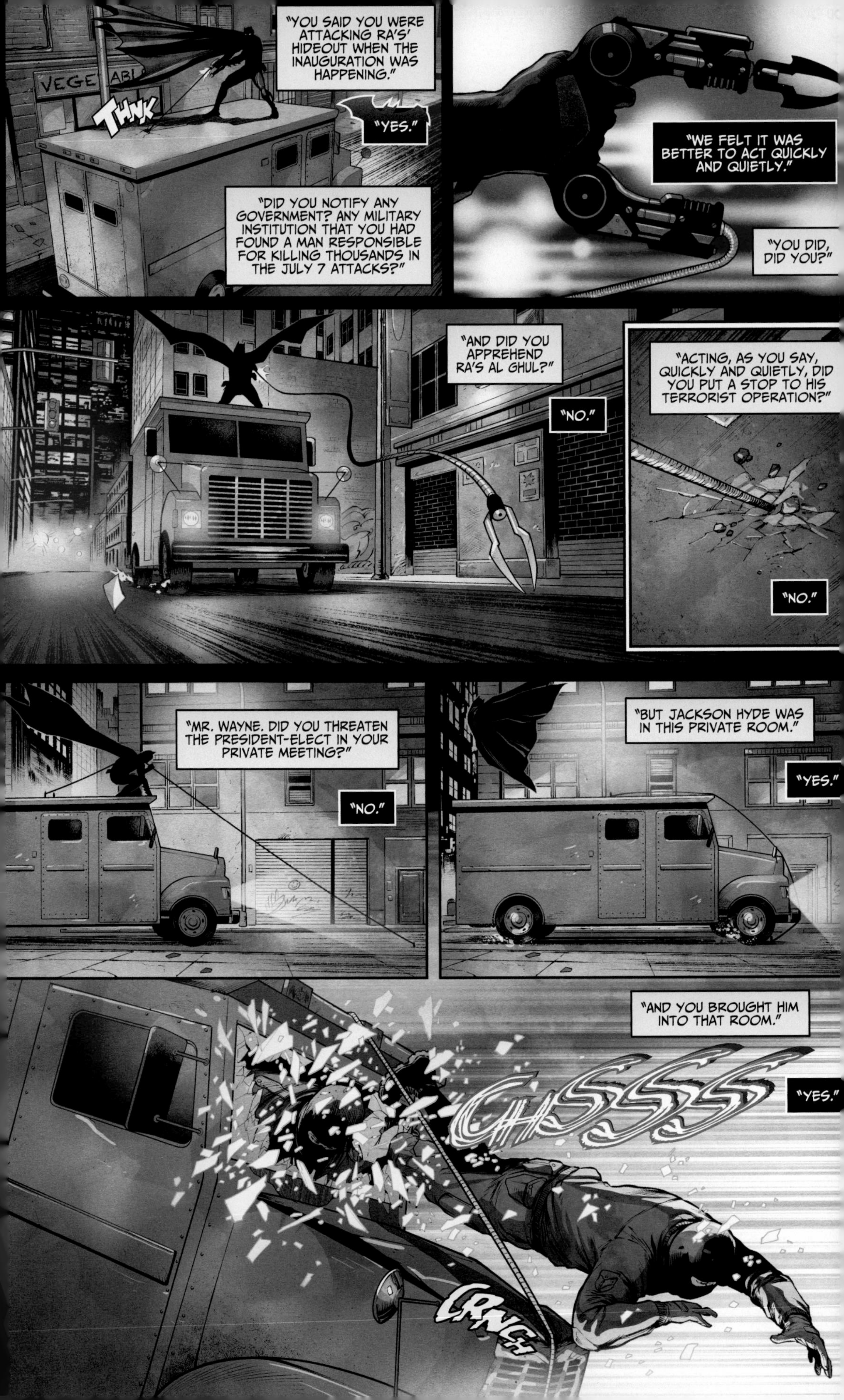
"YOU SAID YOU WERE ATTACKING RA'S' HIDEOUT WHEN THE INAUGURATION WAS HAPPENING."
VEGE
THNK
"YES."
"DID YOU NOTIFY ANY GOVERNMENT? ANY MILITARY INSTITUTION THAT YOU HAD FOUND A MAN RESPONSIBLE FOR KILLING THOUSANDS IN THE JULY 7 ATTACKS?"
"WE FELT IT WAS BETTER TO ACT QUICKLY AND QUIETLY."
"YOU DID, DID YOU?"
"AND DID YOU APPREHEND RA'S AL GHUL?"
"NO."
"ACTING, AS YOU SAY, QUICKLY AND QUIETLY, DID YOU PUT A STOP TO HIS TERRORIST OPERATION?"
"NO."
"MR. WAYNE. DID YOU THREATEN THE PRESIDENT-ELECT IN YOUR PRIVATE MEETING?"
"NO."
"BUT JACKSON HYDE WAS IN THIS PRIVATE ROOM."
"YES."
"AND YOU BROUGHT HIM INTO THAT ROOM."
CHSSSS
"YES."
CRNCH

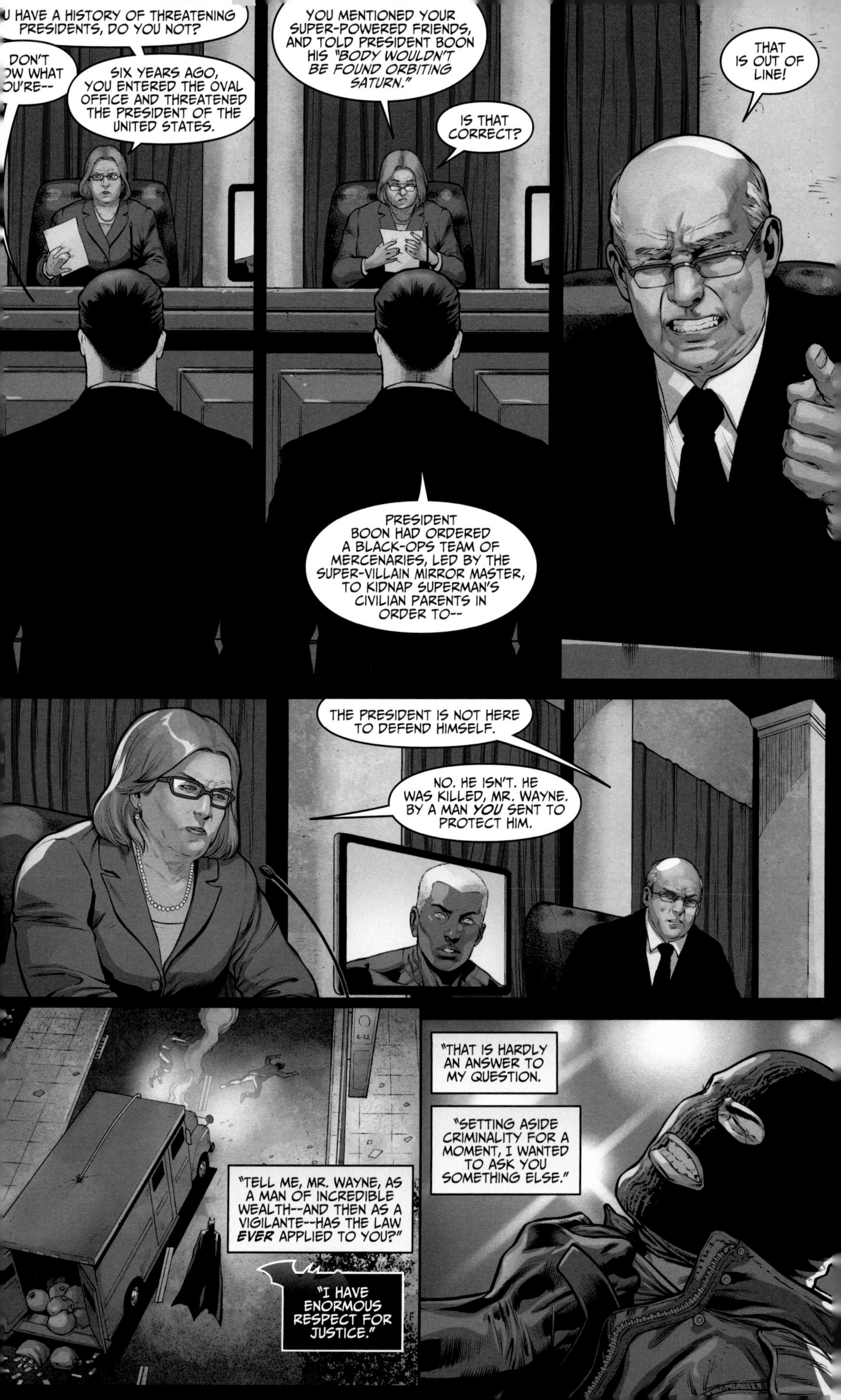

U HAVE A HISTORY OF THREATENING PRESIDENTS, DO YOU NOT?
DON'T OW WHAT OU'RE--
SIX YEARS AGO, YOU ENTERED THE OVAL OFFICE AND THREATENED THE PRESIDENT OF THE UNITED STATES.
YOU MENTIONED YOUR SUPER-POWERED FRIENDS, AND TOLD PRESIDENT BOON HIS "BODY WOULDN'T BE FOUND ORBITING SATURN."
IS THAT CORRECT?
PRESIDENT BOON HAD ORDERED A BLACK-OPS TEAM OF MERCENARIES, LED BY THE SUPER-VILLAIN MIRROR MASTER, TO KIDNAP SUPERMAN'S CIVILIAN PARENTS IN ORDER TO--
THAT IS OUT OF LINE!
THE PRESIDENT IS NOT HERE TO DEFEND HIMSELF.
NO. HE ISN'T. HE WAS KILLED, MR. WAYNE. BY A MAN YOU SENT TO PROTECT HIM.
"TELL ME, MR. WAYNE, AS A MAN OF INCREDIBLE WEALTH--AND THEN AS A VIGILANTE--HAS THE LAW EVER APPLIED TO YOU?"
"I HAVE ENORMOUS RESPECT FOR JUSTICE."
"THAT IS HARDLY AN ANSWER TO MY QUESTION.
"SETTING ASIDE CRIMINALITY FOR A MOMENT, I WANTED TO ASK YOU SOMETHING ELSE."

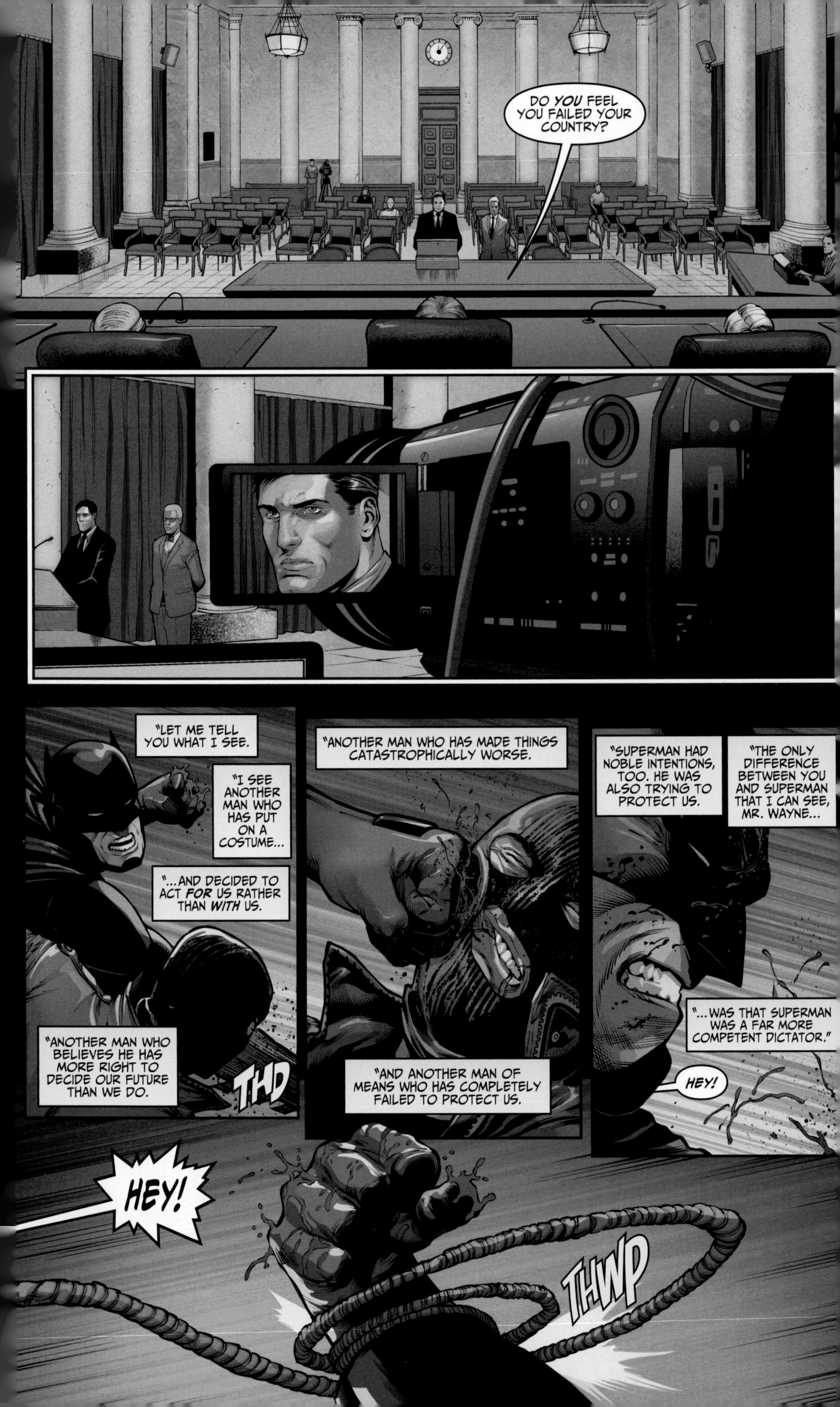

DO *YOU* FEEL YOU FAILED YOUR COUNTRY?
"LET ME TELL YOU WHAT I SEE.
"I SEE ANOTHER MAN WHO HAS PUT ON A COSTUME...
"...AND DECIDED TO ACT *FOR* US RATHER THAN *WITH* US.
"ANOTHER MAN WHO BELIEVES HE HAS MORE RIGHT TO DECIDE OUR FUTURE THAN WE DO.
THD
"ANOTHER MAN WHO HAS MADE THINGS CATASTROPHICALLY WORSE.
"AND ANOTHER MAN OF MEANS WHO HAS COMPLETELY FAILED TO PROTECT US.
"SUPERMAN HAD NOBLE INTENTIONS, TOO. HE WAS ALSO TRYING TO PROTECT US.
"THE ONLY DIFFERENCE BETWEEN YOU AND SUPERMAN THAT I CAN SEE, MR. WAYNE...
"...WAS THAT SUPERMAN WAS A FAR MORE COMPETENT DICTATOR."
HEY!
HEY!
THWP

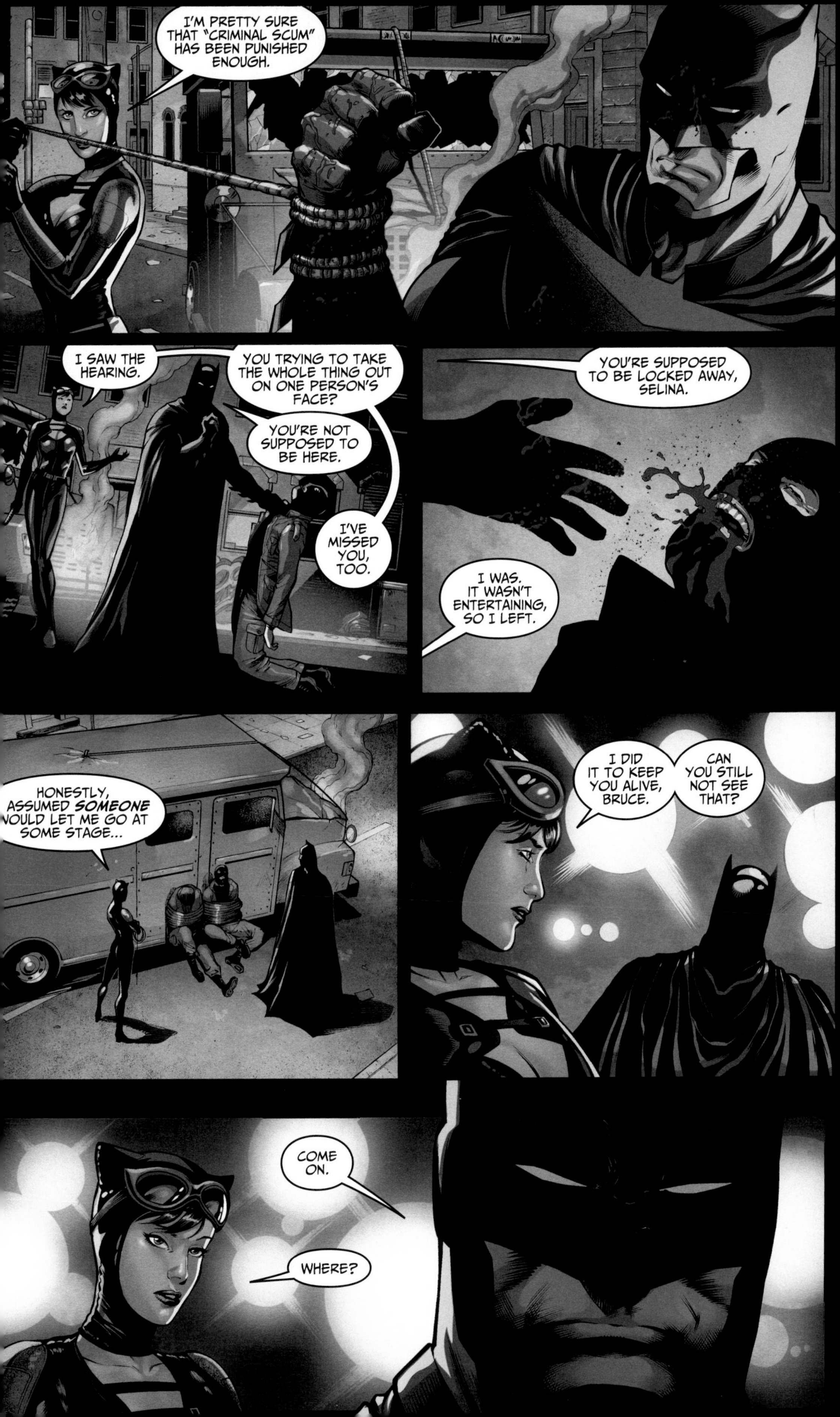
I'M PRETTY SURE THAT "CRIMINAL SCUM" HAS BEEN PUNISHED ENOUGH.
I SAW THE HEARING.
YOU TRYING TO TAKE THE WHOLE THING OUT ON ONE PERSON'S FACE?
YOU'RE NOT SUPPOSED TO BE HERE.
I'VE MISSED YOU, TOO.
YOU'RE SUPPOSED TO BE LOCKED AWAY, SELINA.
I WAS. IT WASN'T ENTERTAINING, SO I LEFT.
HONESTLY, ASSUMED *SOMEONE* WOULD LET ME GO AT SOME STAGE...
I DID IT TO KEEP YOU ALIVE, BRUCE.
CAN YOU STILL NOT SEE THAT?
COME ON.
WHERE?

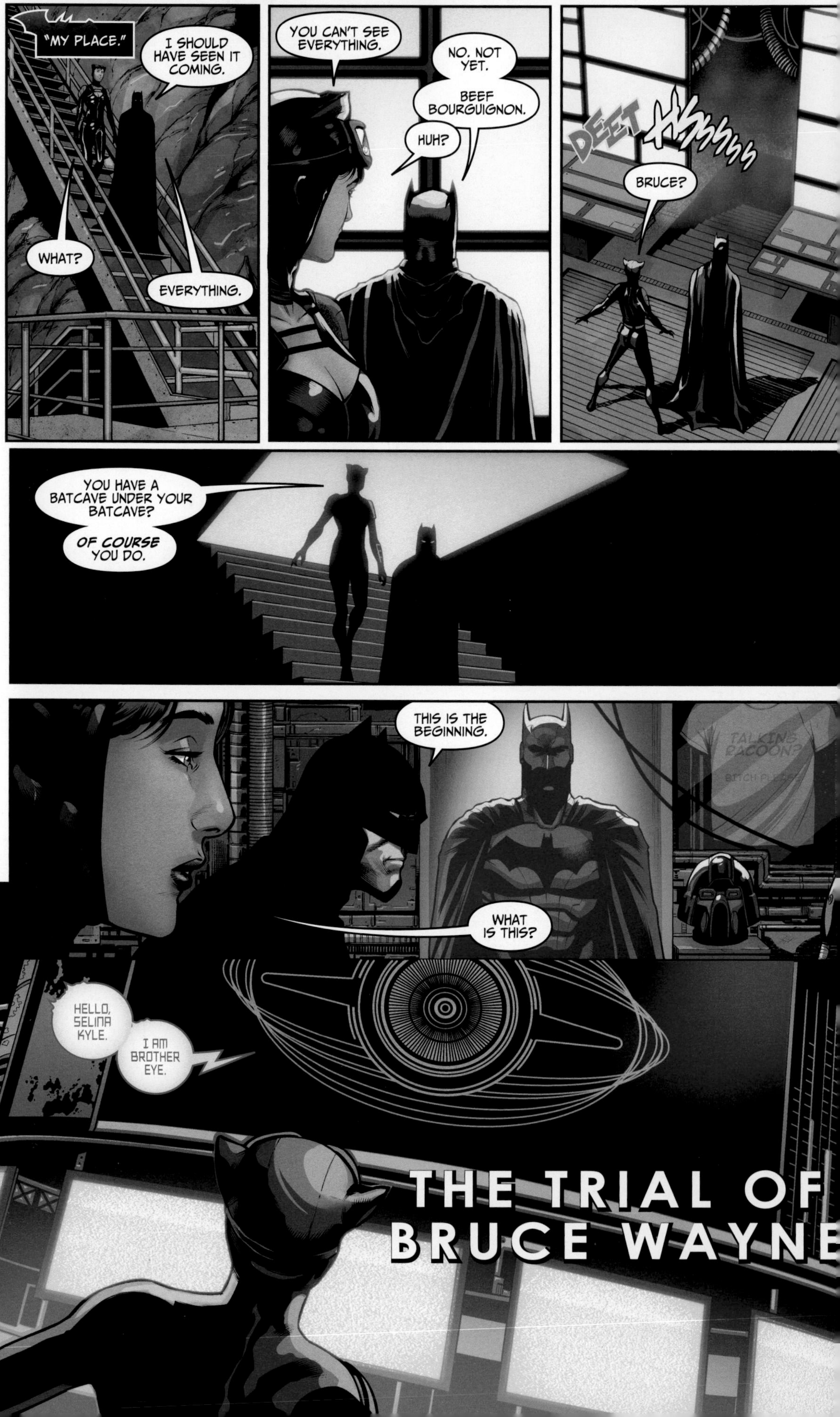
"MY PLACE."
I SHOULD HAVE SEEN IT COMING.
WHAT?
EVERYTHING.
YOU CAN'T SEE EVERYTHING.
NO. NOT YET.
BEEF BOURGUIGNON.
HUH?
DEET
HSSSSSS
BRUCE?
YOU HAVE A BATCAVE UNDER YOUR BATCAVE?
OF COURSE YOU DO.
THIS IS THE BEGINNING.
TALKING RACOON?
WHAT IS THIS?
HELLO, SELINA KYLE.
I AM BROTHER EYE.
THE TRIAL OF BRUCE WAYNE

Character designs by Bruno Redondo

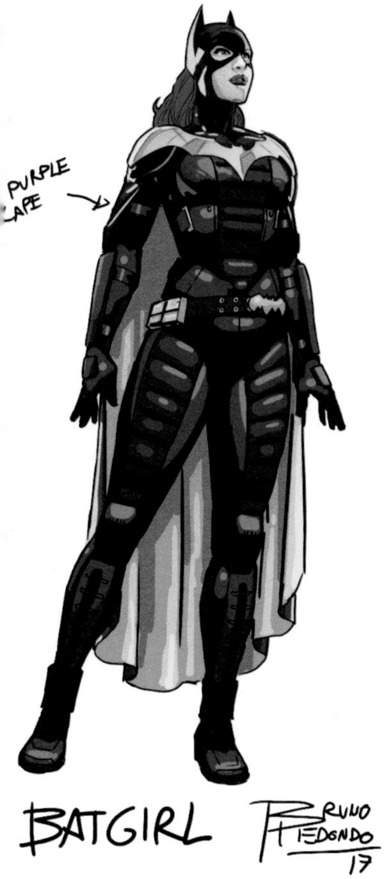

PURPLE CAPE
BATGIRL
BRUNO REDONDO 17

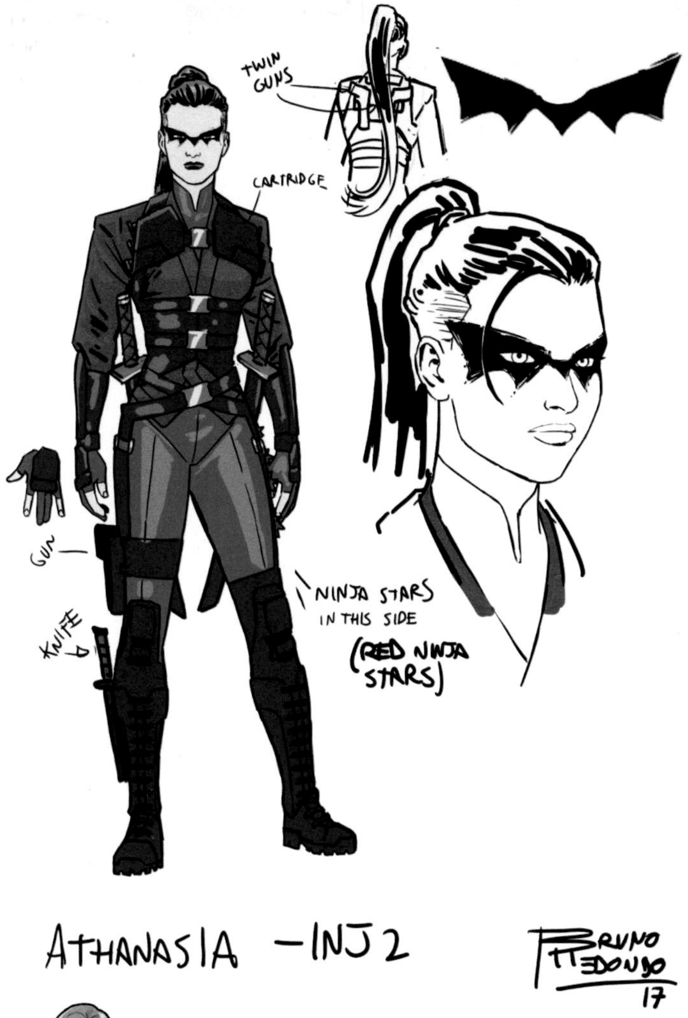

TWIN GUNS
CARTRIDGE
GUN
KNIFE
NINJA STARS IN THIS SIDE
(RED NINJA STARS)
ATHANASIA -INJ2
BRUNO REDONDO 17

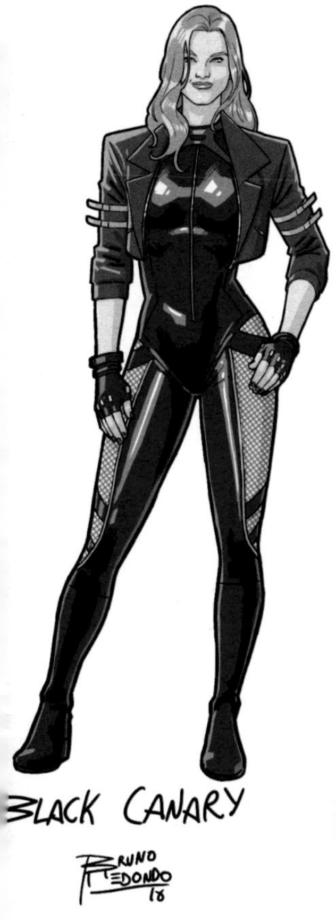

BLACK CANARY
BRUNO REDONDO 18

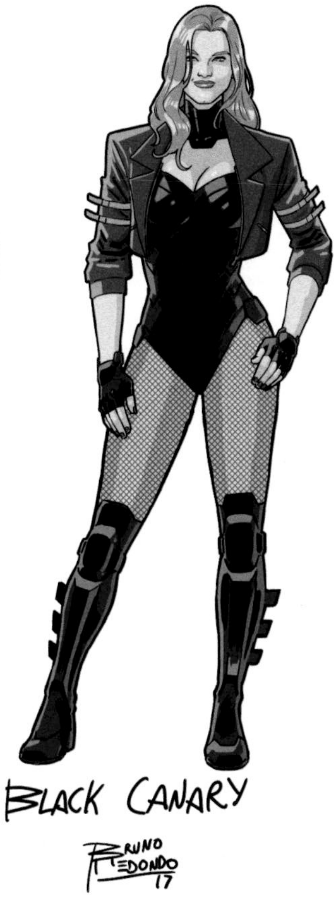

BLACK CANARY
BRUNO REDONDO 17

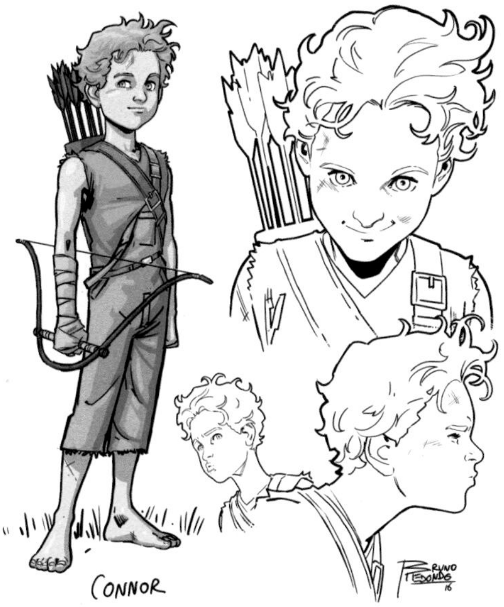

CONNOR
BRUNO REDONDO 16

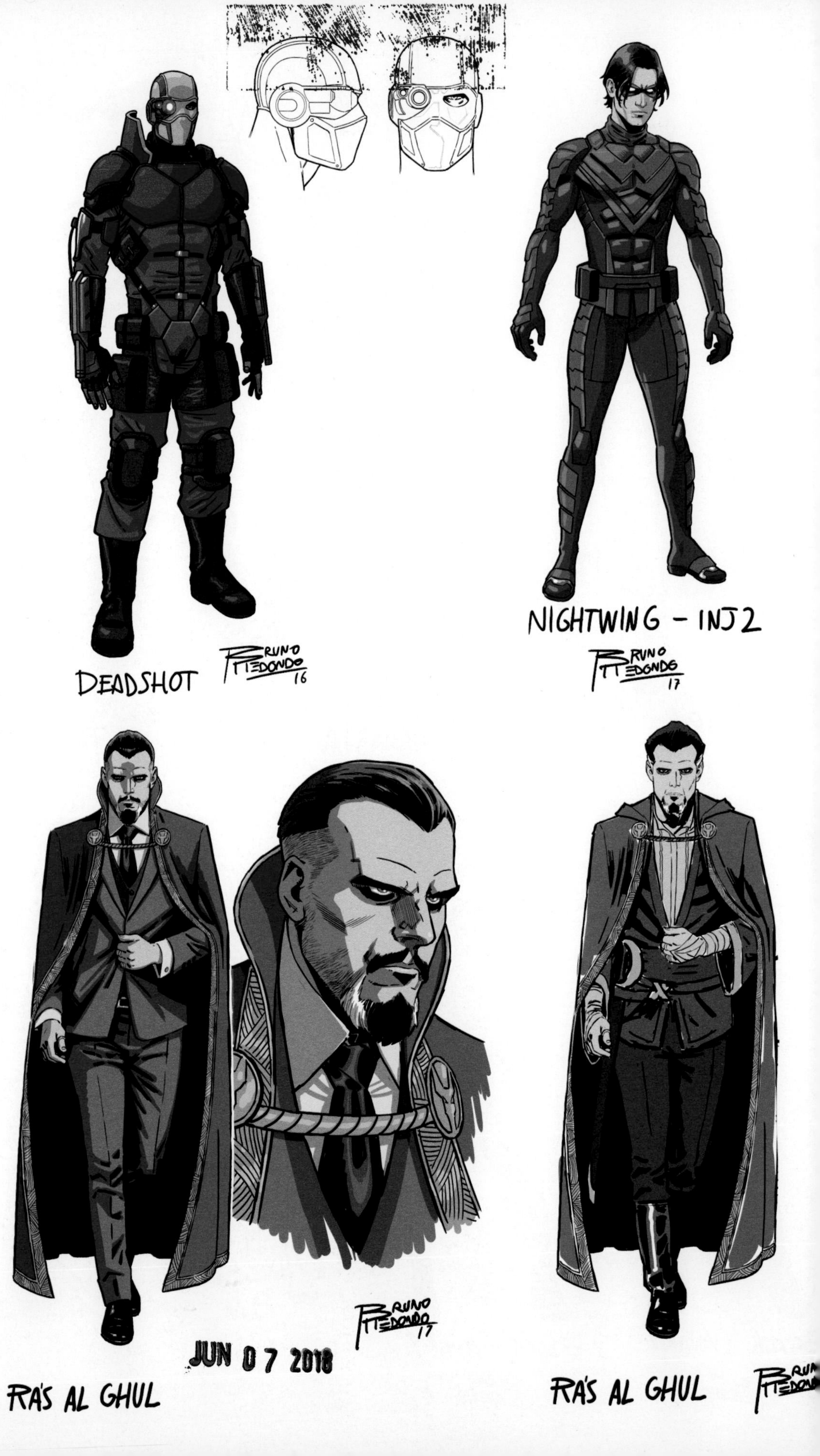
DEADSHOT
BRUNO REDONDO 16
NIGHTWING - INJ2
BRUNO REDONDO 17
BRUNO REDONDO 17
JUN 0 7 2018
RA'S AL GHUL
RA'S AL GHUL